Java Electronic Commerce Sourcebook

All the Software and Expert Advice You Need to Open Your Virtual Store

Java Electronic Commerce Sourcebook

All the Software and Expert Advice You Need to Open Your Virtual Store

Cary A. Jardin

WILEY COMPUTER PUBLISHING

John Wiley & Sons, Inc.
New York • Chichester • Weinheim • Brisbane • Singapore • Toronto

Executive Publisher: Katherine Schowalter
Editor: Tim Ryan
Assistant Editor: Pam Sobotka
Managing Editor: Carl Germann
Electronic Products, Associate Editor: Mike Green
Text Design & Composition: Benchmark Productions, Inc.

Library of Congress Cataloging-in-Publication Data:
Jardin, Cary A., 1974-
  Java electronic commerce sourcebook : all the software and expert
advice you need to open your virtual store / Cary A. Jardin.
    p.   cm.
  Includes index.
  ISBN 0-471-17611-7 (pkb./CD–ROM)
  1. Java (Computer program language)   2. World Wide Web
(Information retrieval system)   I. Title.
QA76.73.J38J357   1997
658.8'4--dc21
                                           96-49117
                                             CIP

ISBN: 0-471-17611-7
Printed in the United States of America
10 9 8 7 6 5 4 3 2 1

This book is dedicated to friends no longer with us, Helen Sock and Anthony Francis Xavier Jardin; friends just joining us, Tyler Barron born August 26,1996; and eternal friends, Norinne E. Jardin, Jim A. Jardin, and Bill A. Jardin.

—Cary A. Jardin

Contents

Part Three Secure Commerce With Java

Introduction

*J*ava Electronic Commerce Sourcebook was developed to guide all levels of Internet merchants, from novices to programmers, through the process of creating their own Web shop. How you will use this book depends on your Internet knowledge and experience level. *Java Electronic Commerce Sourcebook* is divided into three parts. If you are interested in setting up shop quickly, you will want to read Parts One and Two. For those of you that have programming knowledge and want to build your own application, you will want to review Part One and focus on Parts Two and Three. The following breaks down each of the three sections and their chapters. To better understand which chapters are meant for you, please read the following chapter outline before diving into *Java Electronic Commerce Sourcebook*.

Part One—Life on the World Wide Web

Part One includes introductory material and background information on the Internet. Part One introduces and explains significant Internet concepts and "Buzz Words" in a non-technical manner. Novices will find Part One crucial to their Internet experience, Internet users will learn the true definition of many Internet "Buzz Words," and programmers will review Internet fundamentals. It is imperative to understand Part One before moving on to Parts Two and Three. Part One is divided into the following three chapters.

Chapter 1, "Life on the World Wide Web," introduces you to the Internet, Internet history, and graphical examples of how the Internet works, giving you a strong foundation for the rest of Java Commerce. Use this chapter as a reference for client/server, IP, protocols or any other Internet technical issues.

Chapter 2, "Getting on the Net," provides you with information on how to obtain Internet access and your very own Web site. Issues such as dealing with an ISP, dial-up access, and dedicated connection are covered in this chapter.

Chapter 3, "Selling On The Web," discusses advertising and marketing on the Internet. You will learn how to create a commerce site that people will enjoy visiting time and time again, and learn the information you need to initially bring people to your site.

Part Two—Setting Up Shop

Part Two begins with hardware products and advances to example code for creating a Web site. These chapters contain the bulk issues for setting up your own Web shop. Novices will need a good understanding from Part One to fully utilize the concepts in Part Two. Programmers and non-programmers alike will find valuable information in this section. Part Two is divided into the following six chapters.

Chapter 4, "Tools of the Trade," provides information on Web server hardware and software, as well as an overview of what is involved in setting up a Web installation.

Chapter 5, "Order Forms," dives into the more technical concepts involved in setting up shop on the Web. Make sure you have a firm understanding of the fundamentals discussed earlier before reading this chapter. This chapter exposes you to the technologies available to create Web commerce solutions, and provides programmers with information to create applications.

Chapter 6, "Credit-Card Transactions," discusses the credit-card transaction process. Topics such as IC Verify, Merchant ID, and CardShield are covered.

Chapter 7, "CardShield—The Complete Commerce Solution," focuses on the new CardShield technology. Shielded Technologies' secure credit-card transaction service is fully detailed with explanations on how to use the technology.

Chapter 8, "Java Order Entry," presents information for merchants who wish to create a custom shop. Graphic design tools coupled with some examples comprise this chapter.

Chapter 9, "Database Front End with JDBC," provides an introduction to Java Data Base Connectivity. This chapter provides a general overview of JDBC, as well as an example commerce application using JDBC.

Part Three—Secure Commerce with Java

Part Three provides lots of Java code and Java tools for programmers. Except for Chapter 15, "Emerging Technologies," all the chapters in Part Three are designed for programmers. Part Three assumes that you are familiar with programming fundamentals and have some programming experience. Computer amateurs should concentrate on Parts One and Two to create their Web shop before moving into Part Three.

Chapter 10, "Java Commerce Tools," provides tools that furnish essential functionality for Web commerce development, specifically for Java-based Applet and CGI development.

Chapter 11, "Using the CardShield API" provides an insight into using the CardShield API for the creation of custom applications. This chapter provides an interface overview of the CardShield API—supplied functionality.

Chapter 12, "Single Page CGI" begins the trilogy of Java plug and play commerce solutions. Specifically, Chapter 12 provides ready to use single page CGI solutions. HTML and "feeder" Applets are supplied to aid the examples. JDBC, flat file, IC Verify, and CardShield API variations of the base CGI will be supplied.

Chapter 13, "Shopping Cart CGI" extends the single page CGI model into a multi-page shopping cart solution, including JDBC, flat file, IC Verify, and CardShield API variations of the base CGI will be supplied.

Chapter 14, "Applet Commerce Solutions" provides Applet-based commerce solutions relying on the CardShield, and JDBC technologies.

Chapter 15, "Emerging Technologies," discusses new Java technologies.

The World Wide Web

1

Life on the
World Wide Web

Chapter 1 is essential reading if you are new to the Internet; it is review material if you have already explored the Information Superhighway. Besides Internet history, you will learn how the Internet works. This chapter introduces you to IP addresses, TCP/IP, client/server, networks, and other technical issues. You will learn the names and meanings of many Internet buzz words, such as HTML, URL, GUI, browser, HTTP, CGI, and others.

Network for the World

Modern life depends heavily on certain essential networks, like water, electricity, television, and telephone. The Internet is well on its way to becoming the next network staple of modern life, and for good reason. The Internet is the Network for the World.

The World Wide Web is a function that relies on the Internet. In other words, the Web is an application that uses the Internet to transport data. The Web and the Internet are distinct yet dependent entities. For one reason or another, the two terms are used interchangeably. Seven times out of 10 when someone uses the word "Internet," he or she really means the "Web." The remainder of the time, "Internet" is used as a substitute for "e-mail." The term Internet is almost never used in its proper context.

What Is the Internet?

The **Internet,** simply put, is a whole bunch of computers connected together. Remember the telephone that you could construct out of two plastic cups and a string? Think of the cups on either end of the string as the World Wide Web browser, the string as the Internet. The browser relies on the Internet to supply information. The Internet is the network that supplies network applications with connection to other computers.

The Internet is called a "transport mechanism." The Internet transports digital information from point A to point B. Think of the cup phone, where on one end is Alice and on the other is Bob. If Alice wants to talk to Bob, she speaks into the cup. Just to make things interesting, let's add a third phone connected to another person named Cap. Now Alice has no way of talking to Cap directly; rather, she talks to Bob, who then talks to Cap. In Internet lingo, Alice had to make one "JUMP" to reach Cap. Figure 1.1 shows the route Alice must take to communicate with Cap. In this manner Bob "routes" Alice's information to Cap.

From the cup phone example, you should have a feel for what the Internet actually is, as well as for the relationship between the Internet and the Web. Here are some questions to ponder:

Figure 1.1 Bob routes Alice's information to Cap.

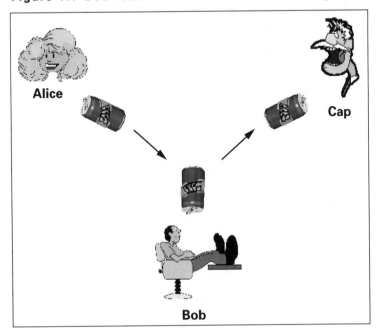

Alice

Cap

Bob

- If I say something into my phone, how does it reach the other side of the world?

- How does the Internet know to which cup to send my message?

- How do I get a cup?

In this chapter, these and many other questions will be answered. The goal of this chapter is to lay the structural groundwork for your newly found Internet literacy.

How the Internet Came to Be

All the hype currently surrounding the Internet makes it easy to think of the Internet as a new technology, when in fact, it has been around the military and academic and scientific research communities for more than 25 years. It is only recently that the masses—individual consumers—got connected. The cost associated with being on the Internet has dropped dramatically in the past couple of years, and will continue to do so for the foreseeable future. The cost per Internet connection has been the primary growth factor of the Internet. As that cost decreases, the accessibility of the Internet will become less of a luxury and more of a necessity. The Internet is not a new technology, just one that has gotten cheaper and more accessible.

People are equipped with multiple ways to communicate ideas and thoughts, but computers are not so fortunate. Computers have limited ways to communicate with other computers. The traditional way to transfer information from one computer to another is by using a disk or another form of "removable" media. The word "removable" is used because the media physically has to be removed from one computer and placed into another. When you need to take a file from your computer and copy it onto the computer down the hall, you do so by putting the file on a disk and then loading the file onto the second computer, thereby transporting the information from one computer to another. This approach is commonly called "sneaker net"—the sneakers on your feet are the transport media.

As functional as sneaker net is, it is limited by how fast you can run from one computer to another, or by the **bandwidth**. The bandwidth of the sneaker net is limited to your endurance and to how much your disk can hold. Sneaker net starts to break down when you need to transfer information between a ground-based computer and a machine strapped to a missile. This type of application is called a **real-time network**, which means that the computers cannot wait for your disk to arrive. In real-time applications, information is transported as it becomes available. It is this need for real-time communication between computers that spawned the birth of the Internet.

Pioneer Internet Efforts

By the early 1960s, computers had become an integral part of the U.S. government, and computer networks had become a crucial part of the U.S. military. As you can see in Figure 1.2, everything from missile systems to communication channels depended on large computer networks. The networks at that time worked very much like the cup phone discussed earlier.

If something happens to Bob, Alice has no way of talking to Cap. The problem with information needing to "jump" over certain parties to reach its destination is called **topology**. To the military topology posed a big problem, especially at the height of the Cold War in the 1960s. The military viewed its current network situation as a major point of vulnerability. For example, if a nuclear warhead had wiped out Bob, how could Alice tell Cap to fire another missile? See the problem?

To solve this problem, the National Physics Laboratory in England came up with a method known as **packet switching**. The information to be sent is broken into separate pieces, each containing the information needed to get to its destination. In this manner, each message follows a separate path but still ends up at the same place. This concept worked especially well to transport data from one side of the continent to the other. Figure 1.3 diagrams an Internet Protocol (IP) packet as it would be sent through the Internet.

Figure 1.2 Computer systems of the U.S. military.

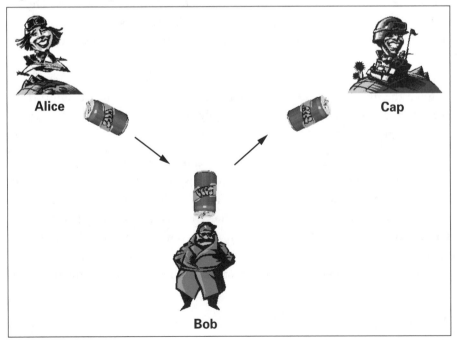

Figure 1.3 Internet Protocol packet definition.

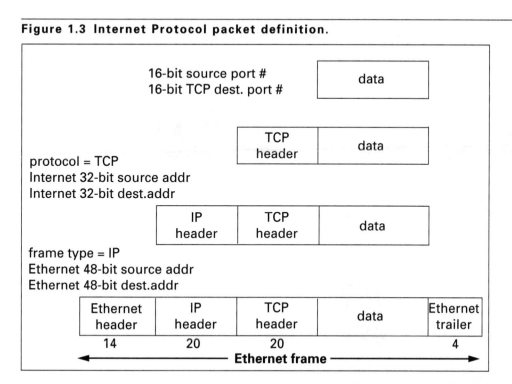

You might see where packet switching would come in handy for the military. Look at the existing phone network as a big wire, or transport media, and try to think of all the possible ways that a packet could get from Los Angeles to New York. The elegance of this packet routing might not be completely evident, so let's break it down. The problem starts when one computer wants to talk to another computer. Because computers work better with numbers than with text, let's call the computer on the left 198.102.105.0 and the computer on the right 198.102.105.1. These numbers, called Internet Protocol (IP) addresses, may look confusing, but they uniquely identify the computers (Figure 1.4).

Because each IP is unique, if each message sent contained the destination IP, the packet would arrive at the proper computer. Now, let's apply that concept to the cup phone, this time adding even more phones. Look what happens if we break one of the communication lines. Messages are still routed to the appropriate IP, even if multiple communication lines are broken. Figure 1.5 shows multiple network line failures, with no effect on the network's ability to deliver information.

Using the existing phone lines, computers could communicate even if only a handful of phone lines were still intact after a nuclear holocaust. Not the nicest scenario, but you can see how reliable communication becomes through the use of unique IP addresses!

Figure 1.4 Computer systems of the U.S. military, with unique computer names.

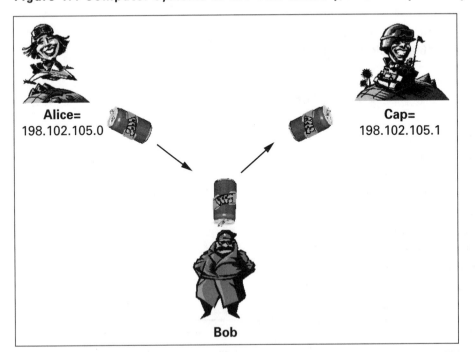

If you would like a precise historical account of the Internet, check out this Web site: http://www.discovery.com/DCO/doc/1012/world/technology/internet/inet1.1.html.

Figure 1.5 Multiple network line failures.

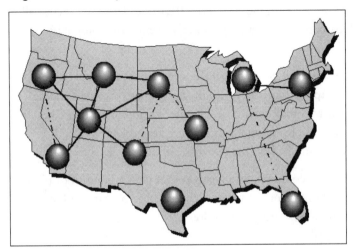

In the beginning, a few brave souls with a lot of money laid the groundwork for Web commerce. These companies provided primitive services to a Web clientele, usually making little or no profit. Some success stories exist, but for the most part, these commerce pioneers saw little financial success on the Web. The Web was not, and is not, a cheap advertising medium. Having "www" somewhere on your business card has its advantages, but to date, selling on the Web has not been cost-effective. New, Java-empowered Web commerce facilitators are changing the prospects for Web commerce. Figures 1.6 and 1.7 depict two Internet commerce pioneers' work.

The Web commerce pioneers could rarely justify Web development costs by their Web sales, but being first does have its advantages. Every company that publicized early on the Web had the potential to be mentioned in a CNN technology report. The Web was and still is a great advertising medium, on and off the Web. Web commerce pioneers had a value-added bonus to

Figure 1.6 The Netscape Navigator browser.

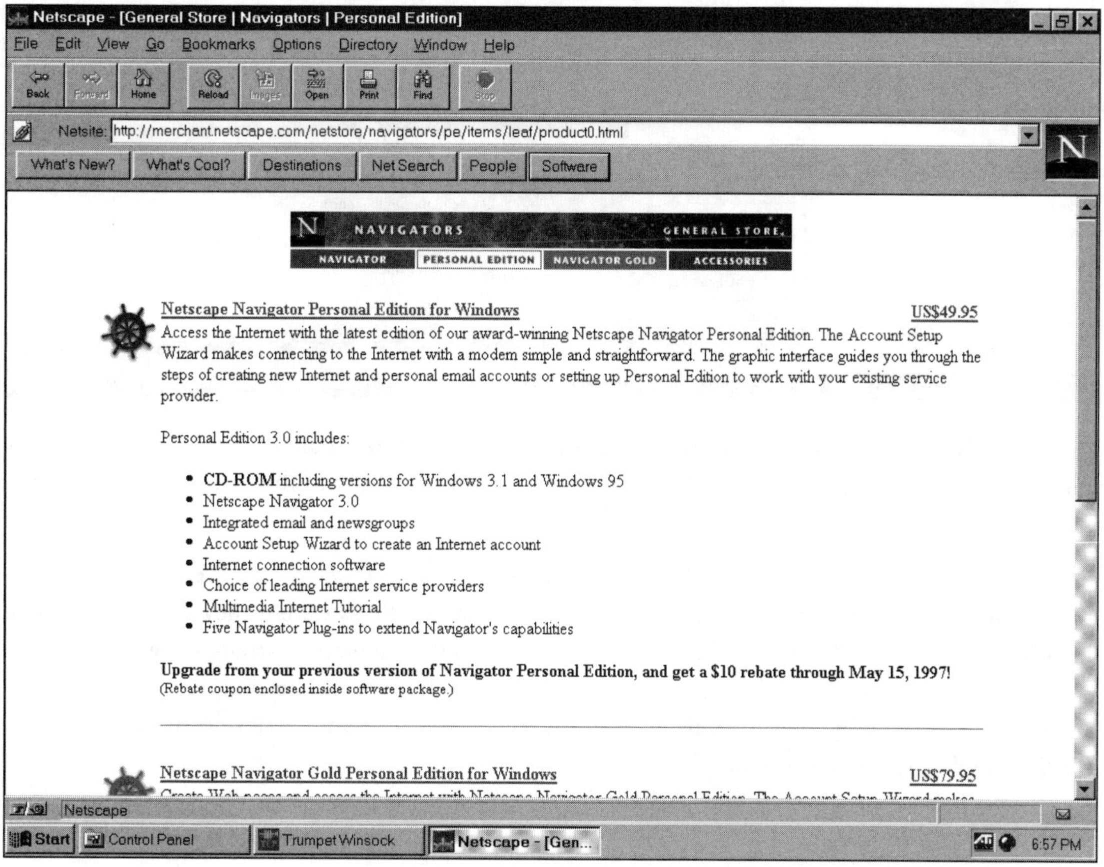

Figure 1.7 The Internet Shopping Network's opening screen.

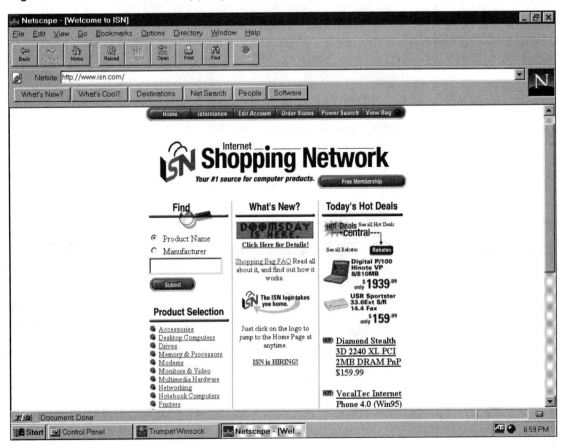

the Web advertising game. Non-commerce sites provide a billboard appeal, and commerce sites take the concept one step further: While viewers are looking at the billboard, why not let them buy something?

For Web commerce pioneers, the idea of selling and making money on the Web was a long-term goal. The cost of their early efforts could not be justified by sales, but they could be justified by advertising potential. Today, Web commerce is still consumed with the trade-show mentality: "Mine is bigger than yours." However, facilitating Web commerce has become so affordable that costs can be *justified* by sales. Getting Web traffic might not be as easy as it once was, but once traffic is built, profits can be made.

Figure 1.8 Growth of Internet users based on IP dispersement.

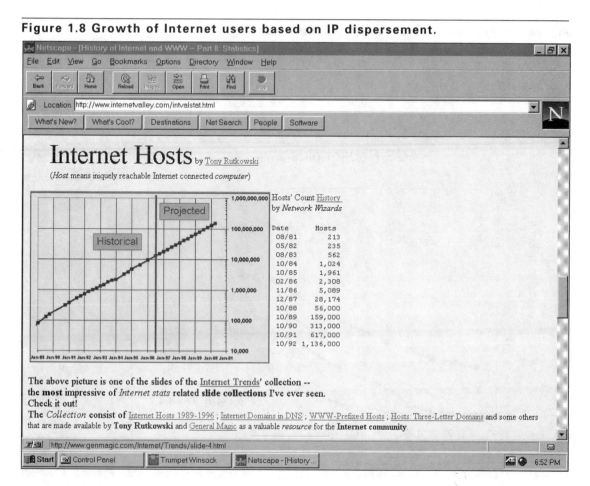

Connecting the World

You are now well on your way to getting connected. The phrase "getting connected" has found its way into everyday life. The Internet has become more than just a network—it is a new mindset.

What makes the Internet different is the number of computers connected to it, as well as its immense geographic span. The Internet wasn't always that way; it used to consist of a few big, ugly computers. What happened? It often seems as if the Internet appeared out of the clear blue sky and materialized as a massive technological explosion. In fact, it did (Figure 1.8).

In 1988, the Internet consisted of an estimated 200,000 users. Even the most conservative estimates show that there are now 30 million users. Internet growth is exponential, with the total number of users expected to reach 200 million by the year 2000. This growth rate is astonishing, especially when compared with the growth of other such other media as television, which has

Figure 1.9 Growth rates of recent technologies.

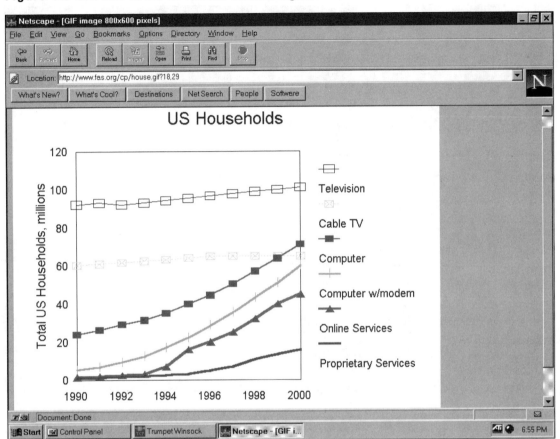

reached a plateau. Figure 1.9 plots the growth of radio, television, cable television, and Internet in number of households being connected.

The Internet has far exceeded the growth rate of television, without offering brain-dead viewing pleasure as does TV. Most Internet content requires a greater mental effort than flipping channels. Getting connected takes more effort than setting up a TV, and it usually costs more. Why is the Internet so popular given these "limitations"? More and more people are spending a decent chunk of change to "be on the Net," each of them looking for something different. This trend is reminiscent of the westward expansion of the United States, when settlers set out looking for gold, love, religion, or a different way of life. In many ways, the Internet is bringing this frontier spirit to a new generation.

The Internet is making its way into every home in the United States. It is estimated the Internet will be in 80 percent of households by the year 2010, which brings us to our next significant problem. We introduced the IP address as an unique way to identify a computer, and that it is. The problem now is that there is a limit to the number of possible unique addresses. IP addresses are made up of 32-bit numbers, which equates to 4,294,967,296 unique computer names. To give you an idea of the sure size of the Internet, all unique IPs are expected to be in use by the year 2002. To accommodate this problem, a new standard is in the making that would give the Internet the possibility of 3.402823 times 10 to the thirty-eighth power unique computer names. That equates to 5.839055 times 10 to the twenty-eighth power IPs for every woman, man, and child in the entire world.

Keep in mind that Internet devices will get smaller and cheaper. For example, wouldn't it be great to have an Internet device in your car that can keep track of your driving records, schedule maintenance, or even inform you of a great place to eat a couple miles ahead? This is not a sci-fi amenity; it will happen. The Internet will connect the world, not just in the sense of e-mail or Web sites. Rather, the Internet will provide a new era of the Information Age, one in which information will be where you want it, when you need it, and presented as if you never could have lived without it.

Internet Technologies

By this time you should be fairly confident that the Internet is a computer network. As we learned earlier in this chapter, a computer network comprises computers talking to one another. However, that two computers are connected does not imply that they are talking to each other. It is up to the applications to take advantage of the network resources that exist on the computer. This leads to the old chicken-and-egg problem. Did the Internet drive application development, or did the applications drive the expanse of the Internet?

> **TCP/IP** The applications that ride on top of the Internet network are responsible for transferring data from one computer to another. E-mail is a good example of an application that uses the facilities the Internet provides. To be more specific, e-mail programs use TCP/IP (Transmission Control Protocol / Internet Protocol) to communicate information from one computer to another.

TCP/IP is a protocol that governs how data is sent from one computer to another. It uses the IP address to route the information to the appropriate destination computer. In a sense, TCP/IP is the glue that bonds an application onto the Net.

For the most part, Internet applications that use TCP/IP can be broken down into two categories, clients and servers. Simply put, a client will ask the server for some sort of information. The server will respond by fulfilling the client's request for information. Let's take a second to apply the cup phone example. Let's use Alice, Bob, and Cap again, but now let's refer to each person by his or her

Figure 1.10 A Web browser gets information from the Internet and presents it to the end user.

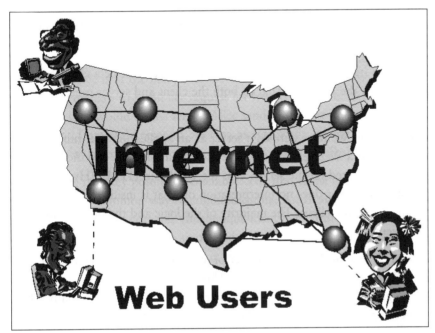

is "How do I apply this model to electronic commerce?" The whole point of Web commerce is to get order information from a customer. You need to understand how this Web model supports the concept of "form" information and how you may secure the customer's information over the Internet.

Securing Customer Information

The discussion of the first issue takes more time than the second, so let's cover the second issue right now. The Internet is designed to transmit raw information from point A to point B—the key here is *raw* data. The Internet makes no promises about the security of the information being transferred. That is, information that is being sent between the client and the server may be monitored by a third party, or a "packet sniffer." These devices are able to listen in on an Internet conversation, presenting a serious breach of security. The way to avoid this is to convert the *raw information* into a form that is known only by the two parties, the client and the server. Whereas Hyper Text Transfer Protocol (HTTP) is basic communication between browser and server, **Hyper Text Transfer Protocol Secure (HTTPS)** does the same thing as HTTP and ensures that the communication between the browser and the server is secure.

Information Processing via CGI and FORMS

Now that you know how secure information can be sent over the Internet, the problem of gathering and processing the information still exists. This problem does not have a nice, tidy solution. Rather, the solution takes two distinct paths. The first will be referred to as the CGI & FORM approach, and the second will be the Java Commerce approach.

In the beginning there was no way to create a data-entry device using Hyper Text Markup Language (HTML). HTML version 2.0 introduced the concept of forms and fixed this problem by including input devices such as text edit fields, radio buttons, and others. Once the data had been collected, it was up to a **Common Gateway Interface (CGI)** to process the data. The CGI takes the form's information and generates as output an HTML page. On the outside, it seems simple enough; on the inside, programming a CGI is quite a challenge for a programmer and may very well be impossible for a normal HTML artist.

The primary fault with the CGI & FORM approach is that it is a major pain. Things that seem simple end up requiring weeks of programming and a lot of thought and effort, not to mention the hassle of testing and debugging a service provider's host machine. In layman's terms, "normal" Web server software is relatively cheap; "secure" server software is considerably more expensive.

The Java Commerce approach eliminates all of the CGI & FORM problems. Granted, you do still have to program, unless you use CardShield, in which case you simply embed a commerce applet into your HTML document. Java lets you create secure commerce solutions without having to worry about any implied HTML constraints or the limitations of Web server software. Java is definitely the complete choice for secure electronic commerce.

Java: Making It All Happen

On the dawn of the initial release of Java, if you found an animation on a Web site you would probably send a mass e-mail to all your friends, telling them about your new discovery. Pre-Java, for the most part, Web pages were a lifeless medium for displaying text and graphics. Java gave Web authors a tool to facilitate Web-based animation. As time passed, Java animation turned into animated, interactive applications. Application developers began using Java to create powerful cross-platform applications that could be easily distributed to the world via the Web. Clearly, the Java trend will continue and will provide dynamic, full-featured, and most of all, entertaining Web content. Java-based Web content is paving the way for the mass market acceptance of the Web and the Internet.

Universal Compatibility

Java technology goes far beyond the confines of what is now considered Web technology. Java frees the technologically challenged from having to know anything about computers. Just as the current Web browser provides the means to view data without any knowledge of the machine it came from, Java provides the mechanism for executing applications without any knowledge of the machine they are being run on. This concept really hits home when you compare how people currently buy software and how people currently rent movies. Go into any software store, eavesdrop discreetly, and you will hear the sales staff ask the potential buyers three common questions: "What type of computer do you have?", "How fast is your computer?", and "How much RAM do you have?" All these questions are valid and necessary to sell software that is appropriate for a buyer's computer. However, a good majority of consumers get lost after the first question, making computers, in general, out of reach for a sizable portion of the population.

Renting a movie, on the other hand, is fairly simple; the consumer only has to select the movie to view. Java provides the means to take software, and computers in general, to a level of simplicity equal to that of renting a movie. All that potential users have to contend with is selecting the application to use. The Web, in this analogy, is a limitless movie rental store, open 24 hours a day, that rents movies for free.

Economical Commerce Solutions

The Internet is not an inherently secure media for the exchange of volatile information. To facilitate secure communication over the Internet, both the client and server applications must take an active role in securing the "line." In the days of CGI-based commerce solutions, the process of securing the communication line usually equated to expensive proprietary solutions. Commerce developers were forced to make assumptions of client software capabilities, as well as to be bound to a specific group of costly server applications. Java allows developers to recapture the freedom lost with proprietary solutions and so inevitably lower the cost of secure commerce solution.

Java technology has brought with it the idea of homogeneous, intelligent network clients. This concept doesn't hold much merit if you look at Java only as a way to facilitate animation on the Web. The concept starts forming when the Web is viewed as a global software distribution mechanism. In that case, the Web is used to distribute Java-based applications. In this model, developers are given the opportunity to create commonly accessible network applications.

As for secure Web commerce, Java provides the means to develop commonly accessible, secure, and cost-effective solutions. By opening up the playing field that the secure commerce solution provides, the cost of secure commerce development will continue to drop and the relative ease of development will continue to increase.

Summary

This chapter introduced the Internet and specific Web commerce issues. The remaining chapters in Part I will introduce some common Web and commerce issues that you might already know. Use this chapter as a reference for client/server, IP, protocols, or any other Internet technical issues. All the technologies used in the Internet can be broken down into concepts found in this chapter. It is crucial that you maintain a firm grasp of ground-level Internet technologies used to develop any Internet application, including Web commerce.

2

Getting on the Net

This chapter is devoted to taking the guesswork out of setting up shop on the Internet. Topics such as "dial-up" access, "dedicated" connection, and a whole slew of techie jargon will be clarified and explained. At the end of this chapter, you will have a clear understanding of what is required to set up a secure Web shop. You can get there from here, and this chapter will show you how.

Net Access

You have to start somewhere, so let's start with getting your single computer up on the Internet—you want to gain "Net access." **Net access** means that a computer has ready access to the Internet. Out of the box, most computers do not have Net access; special hardware is needed, and Net access requires an account at a local **Internet Service Provider (ISP)**. The hardware isn't the hard part. In most cases, the hardware is a modem, and modems are inexpensive relative to other computer hardware. The difficulty comes when the computer has to start talking to an ISP.

An Internet Service Provider is a company with dedicated Internet access and many modems for users to dial into. Having modem banks to allow users to connect to the Internet is not a prerequisite for an ISP. Rather, ISPs provide an Internet connection that can come in many different forms. Let's take a closer look at what exactly an ISP is.

The Internet has been previously defined as a bank of connected computers. The Internet is formed by each computer's connection to one or more computers, forming a network "topology." Topology is a concept from a branch of mathematics called **Graph Theory**, which is concerned with how dots are connected to each other by a line. Each of the dots is called a **node**, and each line is called a **connection**. With that information, let's map out the Internet.

Figure 2.1 shows how computers are connected on the Internet; it also shows where your ISP is connected to the Internet. On the far left of the figure is your computer, and somehow you need to get to your ISP. Once you get there, you then have access to the entire Internet. The ISP is called your entry point to the Internet, or your "On-ramp to the Information Superhighway." Getting a connection to your ISP can take two routes: "dial-up" or "dedicated" access.

If you were the first on your block with Internet access, ISDN, or a computer, for that matter, here is an opportunity to give yourself a firm pat on the back. Your hard-earned dollars have fueled the way for the advance of technology. Think of it like this: "I paid more for it so others could get it cheaper." That is exactly what your early embrace of technology does.

Haven't you noticed that if you want the newest products, you have to pay top dollar for them? Early adopters pay the initial development costs for the product. Once the development costs are met, the manufacturer can afford to lower the price because the risk of losing their shirt is gone.

Figure 2.1 Just as a home user has an ISP, so does an ISP.

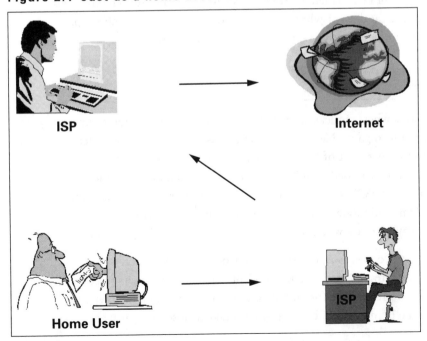

ISP   **Internet**

Home User   **ISP**

The current Internet population is paying far more than others will in two or three years. Similarly, as the cost of an Internet connection drops, the population of the Internet grows. Figure 2.2 shows the relationship between the Internet population and the average cost of connection.

This price per connection is an order of magnitude higher for facilitators of Web commerce. It's not just the home user who has to pay an arm and a leg to be on the Web; companies that wish to offer their services on the Web are bound by the same price factors as non-commercial users, plus some other inherent expenses.

Everyone who is connected to the Internet has to pay an ISP in some form or another. Traditionally, companies that facilitated Web commerce could not get away with a dial-up account. In fact, most companies to date that have a commerce page do have some sort of dedicated connection, which is usually denoted as the general term "ISP and transport cost." Once the connection is set up, the company has to create its commerce site—herein lies the major battle for Web commerce. The ISP and transport costs are not cheap; add the cost of a Web development team, and you have a major expenditure. The initial capital outlay has to be weighed against the benefits and profits to be found on the Web. This analysis alone has kept a majority of large and small business off the Web.

Before you get discouraged about your potential adventure in Web commerce, look at some of the historical problematic points. The first problem is the cost of doing business on the Web,

Figure 2.2 As the Internet population grows, connection costs shrink.

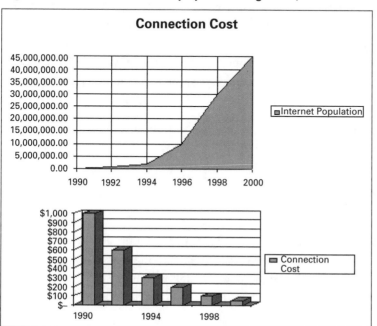

which has decreased, and will continue to decrease. For now, just concentrate on this saying: "It will get cheaper; that is just the nature of technology."

The second problem, one even more basic than cost, is availability. Web commerce is a relatively new thing, and unfortunately the press coverage about nonsecure commerce solutions scared many potential buyers away. This problem has been solved; Java- and non-Java-based commerce solutions have grown into stable and widely adopted standards. However, the bad press about the risk of Web commerce still lingers. This will undoubtedly erode with time; to the new generation of Web users it should be as foreign as a 9600bps modem.

Dial-up Access

Dial-up access is probably the most common mechanism for getting on the Internet. It entails having a modem or **Integrated Services Digital Network (ISDN)** connection that, through software, you connect and disconnect from your ISP. That is, hardware that is on your computer initiates a call to a similar piece of hardware at your ISP. Once the call goes through, the software, on both your computer and your ISP, starts setting up a **Point-to-Point Protocol (PPP)**. PPP is really what its name implies; it sets up a way for data to be transported between you and your ISP. Once the PPP has set up your "transport layers," you are on the Net.

The line from your computer to your ISP is dotted in Figure 2.3 because the dial-up connection is not a constant connection to the Internet. With a dial-up connection, the connection between you and your ISP exists once you initiate the call; when your call is finished, you break the connection and terminate the call. This type of connecting and disconnecting usually meets most Internet users' needs. When you want to get online you fire up your modem. When you are done, you terminate the call. However, if you plan to have your own Web site you will need a dedicated line between your Web page and the Internet because the connection to the Internet must exist at all times.

Most ISPs provide hosting facilities, enabling you to set up a Web shop with only a dial-up connection. This is an option that allows you to dial up and access your site when you want, but the physical HTML pages reside on the ISP's computer. You can think of this as renting a space on the Internet.

Dial-up Hardware

Let's say you want to set up a Web shop, a Web page on which you sell a product or service. The first goal is to find a reasonable ISP that can host your Web site. We will discuss how to choose a good ISP later, but for now let's just say you've found one. The ISP will first ask you what kind of connection hardware you have Currently, there are two answers to this question: either **modem** or ISDN.

Figure 2.3 Dial-up access is shown as a dotted line because it is not a constant connection to an ISP.

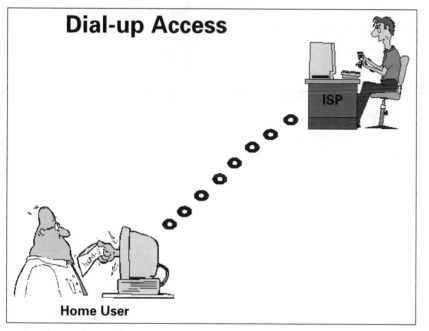

Modems, the traditional connection device, range in speed from 2400 bits per second (bps) to 28,800bps. Most modems purchased now are in the 14,400bps to 28,800bps range. Although modems are slower than ISDN, you can use a normal phone line, with some provisions from the phone company, and a modem to connect. ISDN, on the other hand, requires a special phone line and different hardware, but ISDN transfers data two to five times faster than normal modems. Figure 2.4 shows the progression of dial-up hardware connection speeds through the years. The graph shows an increase in connection speeds within the last three years. This is primarily due to the introduction of ISDN technology to home users.

Once you have your connection hardware figured out, the next step is to tell your ISP that you want it to host your Web site. On one of your ISP's computers, you are allocated a certain amount of personal disk space. Your ISP will set it up so that you can use your drive space to install your own Web site via your dial-up hardware. HTML files can be added to or modified in your rented space by using FTP (File Transfer Protocol) software from your computer.

The only drawback is that most service providers do not use secure Web software. For most individuals trying to set up a Web shop this means that they cannot take credit-card orders unless they use an application such as CardShield by Shielded Technologies. Dial-up access provides a cost-effective means to set up shop on the Web. Dial-up users may be hindered by

Figure 2.4 The progress of dial-up hardware connection speeds.

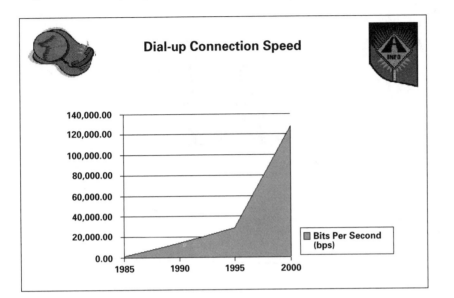

not having total creative freedom, but they get what they pay for. Users who want unique, individual, and not off-the-shelf solutions usually have the funds to support a dedicated connection. However, with Java, 90 percent of Web commerce applications can be facilitated using dial-up access.

Dedicated Access

In Figure 2.3, the dotted line was used to show your computer's connection to your ISP. In Figure 2.5, the ISP had a solid connection elsewhere, due to the hierarchy of ISPs, which means that your ISP has its own ISP, thereby forming a "dedicated" connection to another ISP. All the ISP connections together form the Internet. By getting your own dedicated connection to your ISP, you now have a constant connection to the Internet, making you an ISP.

ISPs provide access to the Internet by offering dial-up facilities. In this book, we will not go into how you can set up your own ISP business—just understand that it is a possibility.

By having a dedicated Internet connection, you have much more control over your Web site. Dedicated access allows you to handle secure transactions, authorize credit cards, and do anything else your heart desires. The catch is, it is expensive, and you have a lot of options from which to choose.

Figure 2.5 Dedicated access is shown as a solid line because it is a constant connection to an ISP.

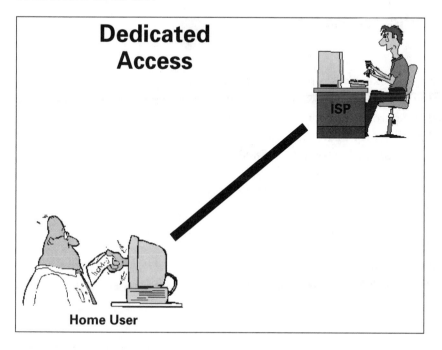

Connection Types

Figure 2.6 shows the current contenders in the dedicated access arena. However, before we get into each of the different connection options, let's clarify what we mean by a dedication connection. Say you have a dial-up Internet access account, but you never terminate the call. That is, you call up an ISP and then never disconnect. You will have a really big phone bill, but what you just created is a dedicated connection using dial-up hardware. The big phone bill is called the **transport cost**, which represents the cost to transmit the data from your computer to your ISP. Once the data is at the ISP, the ISP will charge you to route your data into the Internet, much like a toll road. This cost is called, appropriately enough, **Internet Service Charge**.

With that covered, let's get into some of the alternatives available within dedicated access. Each option will be presented with an approximate breakout of each of its inherent costs. Please note that these fees may, and probably will, vary from one geographic region to another. The information given may appear somewhat technical, but we will discuss it in detail later in the book.

Figure 2.6 The different types of dedicated connections have different speeds.

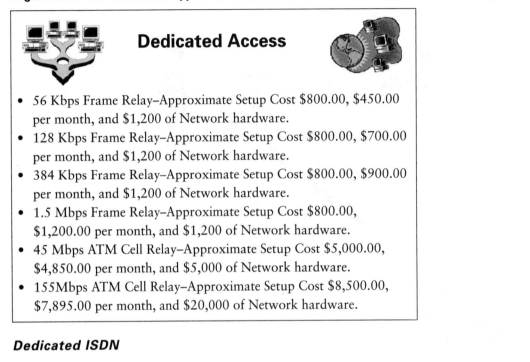

Dedicated Access

- 56 Kbps Frame Relay–Approximate Setup Cost $800.00, $450.00 per month, and $1,200 of Network hardware.
- 128 Kbps Frame Relay–Approximate Setup Cost $800.00, $700.00 per month, and $1,200 of Network hardware.
- 384 Kbps Frame Relay–Approximate Setup Cost $800.00, $900.00 per month, and $1,200 of Network hardware.
- 1.5 Mbps Frame Relay–Approximate Setup Cost $800.00, $1,200.00 per month, and $1,200 of Network hardware.
- 45 Mbps ATM Cell Relay–Approximate Setup Cost $5,000.00, $4,850.00 per month, and $5,000 of Network hardware.
- 155Mbps ATM Cell Relay–Approximate Setup Cost $8,500.00, $7,895.00 per month, and $20,000 of Network hardware.

Dedicated ISDN

Dedicated ISDN

Max speed: 128kbps

Hardware cost: $400 to $2000, depending on whether you are connecting a network or a single computer

Setup cost: $200 to $500, depending on ISDN availability

Monthly transport cost: $600 and up, depending on local or long distance charges

Monthly ISP cost: $200 to $300

ISDN is usually thought of as a dial-up solution, but it was originally used as a dedicated connection. ISDN uses the same copper twisted-pair cable as regular phone lines, and, in general, ISDN connections can be moved more cost-effectively, but it isn't as fast as other dedicated solutions. ISDN, as a dedicated solution, might be cheaper than other solutions. The main key is whether speed is an issue.

Frame Relay

Frame Relay

Max speed: 1.544Mbps (T1)

Hardware cost: $2000

Setup cost: $1000 to $2000, depending on the provider

Monthly transport cost: $200 to $800, depending on the provider and connection speed

Monthly ISP cost: $400 to $1500, depending on the provider and connection speed

Frame relay is probably the most commonly used high-speed dedicated connection. The frame relay supports speeds from 56Kbps to 1.544Mbps. It gets a little tricky here because for speeds of 128Kbps and higher, all the hardware and physical transport media are the same. Getting a 128Kbps frame relay moving at 1.544Mbps is as simple as making a couple of phone calls. Comparing this to dedicated ISDN, 128Kbps frame relay is usually less expensive per month. Startup costs are more for a frame relay, but whereas ISDN maxes out at 128Kbps, frame relay allows your connection to grow with your Web site.

High-Speed Connections

High-Speed Connections

Minimum speed: 1.544Mbps (T1)

Maximum speed: 45Mbps (T3)

Hardware cost: $16,000 to $32,000

Setup cost: Based on tariffs and availability

Monthly transport cost: $4000+

Monthly ISP cost: Anywhere from free to $3000 based on the phone companies' Internet structures

We will discuss connections faster than T1 only to inform you that they do exist. Currently, the pricing is up in the air as we wait for the phone and cable television companies to battle it out. The phone and cable companies are in an equal position to provide this service. It might seem a little odd to think of cable companies as Internet providers, but they have the ability to provide high-speed dedicated services to every home. In fact, in some areas of the United States, cable companies already have the infrastructure in place to provide T3 speeds to home users. Someday T3 connections will be as common as a 28.8 modem, but for now T3 connections are fast, they cost a lot of money, and they can rarely be justified for small installations.

All of these dedicated connection types serve the purpose of having continuous access to the Internet. If you need your own dedicated access line, a good ISP can direct you to the path that best fits your needs. Finding the right ISP is crucial.

Selecting the Right ISP

A good ISP can make all the difference in the world, not just during your setup stage, but throughout your use of your Web site; an ISP's skill can contain the amount of downtime that your site experiences. That's right, downtime. ISPs are vulnerable to the same computer failures as the rest of us. The difference is that a good ISP can quickly and efficiently handle any problems that may occur.

One of the biggest mistakes people make in selecting an ISP is to look exclusively at the total cost. In many cases, the less costly ISPs might not have the resources to handle your needs. Let's take a close look at some common ISP issues.

Node Degree

Node degree refers to the number of connections the ISP has to the Internet. For example, let's take a look at a couple of different ISP configurations. The first is a very dangerous scenario, one in which the ISP's node degree is 1.

An ISP with a node degree of 1 forces your service to rely on one single connection to the Internet. If that connection goes down, your Web site is no longer visible to the Internet. Some ISPs will say, "We have only one connection to the Internet, but it is really fast." The truth is that connections do go down, and you want to be with an ISP that does not rely on a single point of failure.

Bandwidth Requirements

Another scenario concerns **bandwidth** requirements—the connection speed. Say your ISP has one T1 (1.544Mbps) connection to the Internet, and you have a T1 connecting your computer to the ISP. See a problem? If you were the only customer that the ISP had, this would not be a problem, but usually ISPs have several, if not several hundred, customers.

Your Web site will have to compete with other customers' sites, resulting in your not realizing the full potential of your T1. This problem is called "overallocation of bandwidth," and it occurs when ISPs offer their service to more people than they can handle.

The Questions to Ask

The following are some useful questions that you can ask of potential ISPs. Keep in mind that if the ISP can't answer these questions, you probably don't want that vendor in the first place.

Network Topology

Who are you connected to, and what is the speed of a connection? When an ISP answers this question, draw a little graph like the one shown in Figure 2.7 so that later you can compare each ISP's topology.

Network Utilization

How many simultaneous dial-up and dedicated connections do you support? Write down each class of connection and the number of connections for each. This will give you a semi-accurate idea of how much bandwidth the ISP has allocated. This is a very important question, for it directly affects the performance of your dedicated connection. For example, if you have a T1 that can handle 1.5Mbps, but your ISP has allocated all but 500Kbps of its bandwidth, you might as well get a cheaper connection. You will never get the full utilization of the T1.

Figure 2.7 Example graph of ISP connectivity.

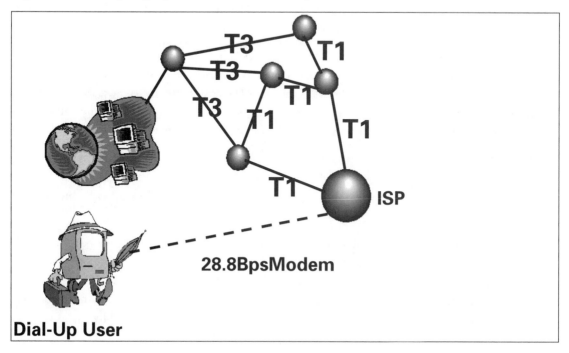

The last question really isn't a question; it has to do with the general "vibe" you get from the ISP. You want an ISP you can work with, one that is easily accessible and makes you feel comfortable asking questions. You need to feel that your ISP is knowledgeable and is there to serve your needs.

ISPs are crucial to the existence of your Web site. Whether you have a dial-up or dedicated connection, a good ISP can very easily justify a slightly inflated price tag. In fact, for many Web "shop-keeps" their ISP is their resident Internet guru, who is always available to answer questions. The bottom line is this: Choose an ISP that you feel comfortable with, one that you can work with.

Additional ISP Information

Policies and cost structures differ from ISP to ISP. For example, some ISPs do not charge a startup fee if you sign a extended service contract. Also, some ISPs do not provide CGI support for dial-up users. Issues such as these should be discussed when you examine potential ISPs.

For Web merchants who wish to take the CGI approach to commerce, the ability to upload and execute CGI applications is a must. However, not all ISPs provide CGI access to their users. They use such excuses as "It violates system security" or "It protects us from potential virus attacks"; both of these claims are debatably incorrect. The fact of the matter still remains: If you need CGI support make sure you can get it.

Another issue is pricing structure and billing. Most ISPs bill on a per-month basis, but what "per month" means can vary. Some ISPs bill a single flat rate for use of their facilities; others charge per hour of use, with so many hours being free. The cost common to most ISPs is the setup cost. This fee may vary, and in some cases it may be waived. Be sure to get, in writing, a statement of monthly costs as well as setup costs before choosing your ISP.

The ISP business appeared out of nowhere. It attracted people from a number of different disciplines, some looking to provide a needed service, others just looking for a quick dollar. The ones that really know what they are doing are like gold, and they can help you with almost every aspect of your site development.

Others can make your life miserable—your site may not be stable and you may have to do all your own support and trouble-shooting. This is not intended to scare you, or to say that small ISP companies are better than large ISP companies. Rather, keep in mind that not all ISPs are created equal. Some might be cheaper but offer less support; others might cost a little more but have a trained staff to answer questions. The bottom line is to choose your ISP carefully.

Leveling the Playing Field

The concept of a "virtual storefront" is very important to the Web commerce model, not so much for large corporations, but rather for smaller, less-known companies. For large companies, selling on the Web is just another distribution channel for their product. For smaller companies, the Web provides the means to create a virtual presence that has the potential to compete with larger corporate competition. In this manner, the Web can level the commercial playing field, allowing smaller companies to compete in the global marketplace.

The idea of leveling the commercial playing field is not a new one; in fact, it began with the first wave of major Web growth. Its basis is that large and small companies alike rely on their Web presence alone to attract customers on the Web. In this manner, the Web levels the playing field by allowing large and small companies to play for the same consumer dollar. To many, the Web offers a great equalizer effect. Companies that could not compete in the global market before can now do so. Formerly unknown companies are springing up to offer competitive products in market places formerly unreachable. The Web offers enough opportunities for entrepreneurs to make the fact that Wild Wild West and the World Wide Web both were coined as WWW no coincidence.

Bare Bones Commerce Essentials

All Internet commerce solutions require certain fundamental elements. For example, to accept credit card transactions, you need some way of authorizing the transaction. All commerce solutions deal with the transferring and processing of sensitive financial information, and so the transmission of such information needs to be handled appropriately.

Back in the days before Java commerce, Internet commerce solutions had to rely on secure Web server software to transmit the information a user entered in a form to a waiting CGI application. Sun and some other vendors provided methods for Java applets to communicate with a server, giving the programmer the ability to create custom commerce applets. Nonprogrammers took advantage of Java-based solutions such as CardShield to create commerce solutions. However, programmers and nonprogrammers alike still required certain key elements to create a Java commerce solution.

CardShield

Probably the most cost-effective and simple commerce solution is CardShield. It provides all you need to create a Java commerce solution, but it does require your own Web page. Simply put, CardShield is an applet that you can plug into your Web page to facilitate most of your commerce needs (Figure 2.8).

Figure 2.8 Shielded Technologies' Web page offers some helpful advice at www.shielded.com.

Because CardShield does not require any server-based software to run in order to process order information, you do not need a dedicated Internet connection. The only thing you do need is a spot on the Web. This usually means that you have an area dedicated to your needs on your ISP's server. You will be required to enter a line of HTML into your Web shop page, and CardShield will handle the rest. If you already have an existing page and all you need is a commerce solution, use CardShield and you will be ready to take orders in less than a half an hour.

Although CardShield is a really powerful commerce solution, it is by no means a cure-all. Some commerce solutions need to tie into real-time databases or provide some other type of custom features. For these cases, custom applications will need to be built. Based on the particular need, the development might require a fairly complicated solution. For this reason, most custom commerce solutions require a dedicated Internet connection so that client applets can access a common server to process the collected information. Keep in mind that a dedicated connection also requires a dedicated computer to act as the server for the HTML pages and commerce information.

Custom commerce solutions provide a lot of flexibility but are usually fairly expensive. The CardShield solution offers an inexpensive, nontechnical commerce solution. Both fulfill commerce needs, so you'll need to determine which solution best fits your requirements. We will discuss and give examples of both solutions in Chapter 3. For now, get an idea of what your commerce need will entail.

Getting Connected on a Budget

Before Java came on the scene, Internet commerce was not for anyone with a small budget. With the advent of products such as CardShield, Internet commerce became affordable. Figure 2.9 lists CardShield's limitations.

Don't assume that CardShield is a cure for every company's commerce needs; more or less, it provides an off-the-shelf solution. What Java has done for Internet commerce is distance it from expensive, secure Web server software packages and time-intensive CGI programming. Custom applications still require dedicated connections, but now Java provides the mechanisms to cut costs substantially for Internet commerce. This cost reduction takes two paths, each of which has its own associated cost break:

- The CardShield method

- The custom Java solution

The CardShield Solution

CardShield offers two options to handle electronic commerce. The first is the CardShield applet.

The applet is designed in a Wizard fashion; it will ask you a series of questions about your company and what you want to sell. After you have completed the questionnaire, you will be given instructions on how to place your new secure commerce applet in your Web page. That's it—no programming, just a few plain-English questions to answer. If CardShield can fill your commerce needs, you probably don't need to do any programming. If your needs fall out of the bounds of CardShield's capabilities, Shielded supplies a CardShield **Application Programming Interface (API)** that you can use to make your own commerce applet. The API provides all the methods you need to process credit-card transactions securely.

Custom Solutions

When your commerce needs fall outside the bounds of the CardShield solution, you are probably looking at spending more money. Sun and other manufacturers provide methods to transmit secure information over the Internet. Crafting your own secure commerce solution will require

Figure 2.9 CardShield is inexpensive, but it does have its limitations.

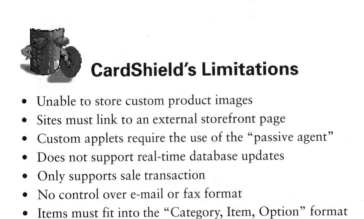

CardShield's Limitations

- Unable to store custom product images
- Sites must link to an external storefront page
- Custom applets require the use of the "passive agent"
- Does not support real-time database updates
- Only supports sale transaction
- No control over e-mail or fax format
- Items must fit into the "Category, Item, Option" format
- Provided applet provides no means for customization

development or use of client and server applications. Although custom-built applications might cost more, they do offer ultimate freedom—and a way of making your commerce solution stand out from the crowd.

Custom solutions are just that, custom. You have total control of your commerce solution, but be warned. Almost all custom solutions require a dedicated connection to host your commerce server application. This will be the application that the individual commerce applets contact to process the transaction. If your needs take you down this route, contact your local ISP and discuss your options.

By far, the most inexpensive Internet commerce solution is CardShield. CardShield does not require a dedicated connection; in fact, it is designed to run just fine with a normal dial-up account. What you are losing for the price is individuality because all CardShield commerce applets look the same. However, this often works in your favor because when people see the CardShield applet, as shown in Figure 2.10, they know that "this is where I place my order."

The CardShield and straight Java development methods of commerce both have their pros and cons. We will discuss this option in more detail in Chapter 3, where we will also provide example commerce solutions that may help. At this point glance at what you are looking for in a commerce solution, and get an idea of what option best fits your needs.

Figure 2.10 The CardShield Applet Wizard.

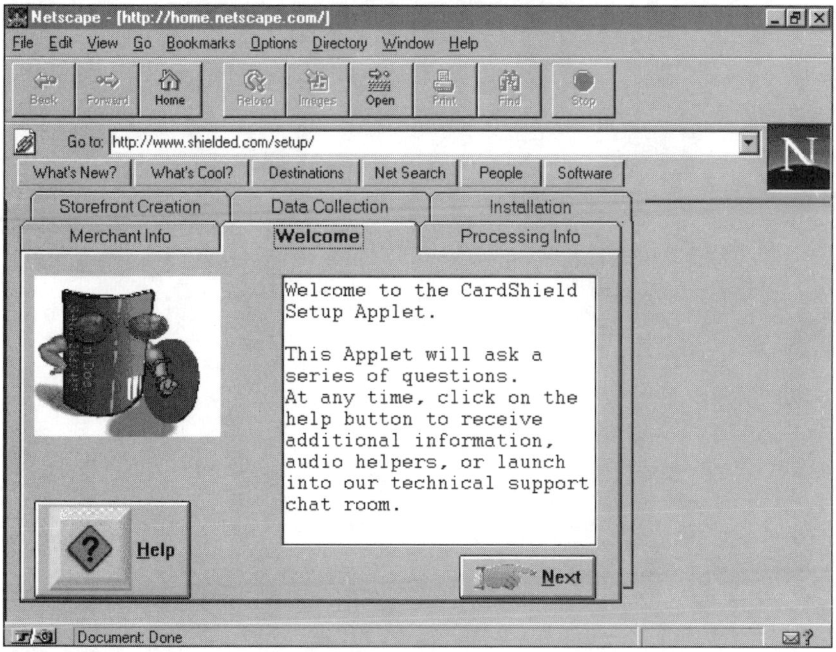

Summary

In this chapter, we discussed some specific commerce issues: dedicated or dial-up access, finding a good ISP, and custom-built applications versus CardShield. This might be the first time you have been exposed to these issues. If so, you might need to take some time and make sure you are comfortable with the content of this chapter. Once you are comfortable with the material in this chapter, you will be well on your way to creating your own Internet commerce solution.

This chapter has set down the beginnings of a virtual road map to your Internet commerce solution. The next chapter will provide you with information on how to create a successful selling machine on the Internet.

3

Selling on
the Web

S elling of any type is an art. Successfully selling a product takes knowing your
clientele and knowing the demand for your product. Selling on the Web is no different. The Web market is not necessarily a tough sale—you just need to know
how to target your audience properly, and, above all, you have to have a draw.
Getting people to come to your site is crucial. People must want to pull up your
Web site, and once you have them there, you can make the sale. This chapter gives
you a guideline to what works, what doesn't, and how to give your Web site the
"Web Savvy" it needs to draw a crowd.

Prospective Buyers

The Web offers a way to target a broad range of markets directly, but these markets are limited to the Web population. Although the Internet might seem like a
huge marketing arena, you really need to take a look at who is on the Web. As
Figure 3.1 illustrates, the Web population now, and in the future, conforms to the
three stages of the technology bell curve: the early adopter stage, the mass market
stage, and the phase-out stage.

Figure 3.1 Technology bell curve.

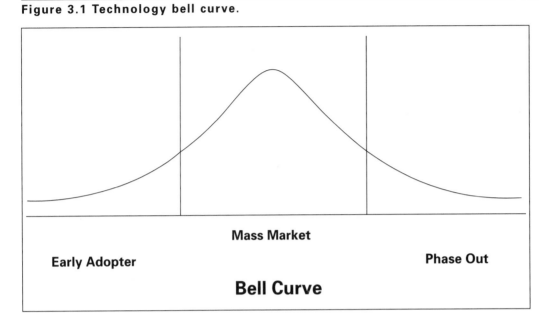

Mass Market

Early Adopter

Phase Out

Bell Curve

Early Adopters

When technology is first released, the typical purchaser is the person next door, the one who always has to have the newest and most innovative products. To these early adopters, their desire to possess the new technology overcomes any reluctance they may have to pay its relatively high price. Early adopters get the technology off the ground and launch it into the mass market.

Like it or not, the Internet is still very much in the hands of the early adopter. Computer buffs, techno-jockeys, students, and people with supplemental income are a large part of the total current Web population. Add to them the users who have Internet access at work and make playing on the Web look like a productive part of the office place.

Mass Market

It is easy to say that the Internet is going to grow. Based on current growth rates, the Internet will become as common as cable TV within the next 10 years. However, these growth rates fail to accommodate for the difficulty factor associated with the Internet. Anyone who has set up a PC to connect to an Internet Service Provider (ISP) would agree that the process has a long way to go before it will be considered easy.

Remember your feeling of accomplishment when you first connected to the Internet and were able to use your Web browser? It was a good feeling—you had achieved a not-so-easy feat; you "got connected." Getting connected sounds easy, but,in fact, it does take a decent amount of technical knowledge to set up a connection to the Internet. After you got connected, you may even have said that your grandmother could not have done that, but your grandmother probably did not set up her own TV or VCR either. This statement describes the barrier to the development of the mass market for the Internet: The Internet must be easier to set up than a VCR and must offer more than TV to break into the mass market.

The Internet is on the verge of breaking into the mass market, but before that can happen, it has to become more accessible and offer more entertainment appeal. Advertisers are beginning to leverage the knowledge they gained from television ads and apply it to Web content. Web commerce applications are following, and shall continue to follow, by providing entertaining, value-added, and nonobtrusive means for buying and selling products (see Figures 3.2, 3.3, and 3.4).

Home Internet access has by no means reached its peak. Look at the technology life cycle in Figure 3.1 and notice where the line gets almost vertical right before the big hump. Right now, the Internet is reaching the end of the early adopter phase and is just starting to reach the mass market. Take a look around; products from yogurt to TV stations now have some sort of hook to

Figure 3.2 The ID4 home page.

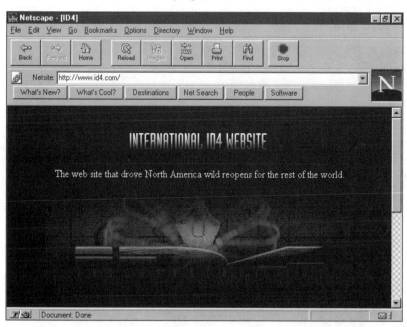

Figure 3.3 The Chain Reaction Web site.

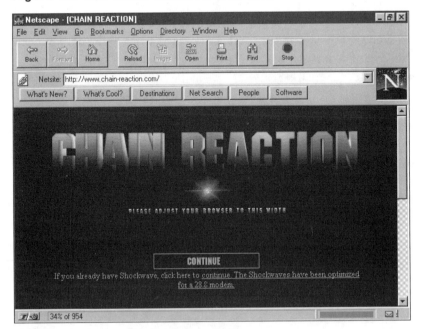

Figure 3.4 MTV Online's Web site.

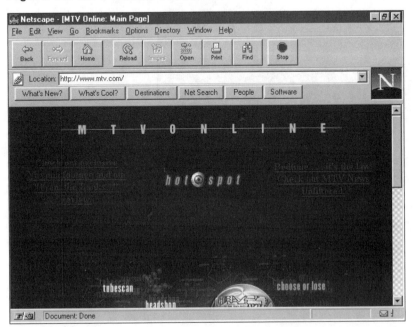

the Internet. In fact, a popular yogurt in the United States now provides an e-mail address for its customer service department.

Some new developments on the technology wave will bring the Internet into its golden age, the mass market. Internet will become more available in a very short time. New devices that plug into a TV and provide Internet access via a telephone or cable connection will get the masses "up on the Net." Only recently have WebTV devices brought mass market appeal to the Web. Companies such as Philips, Magnavox, Mitsubishi, and Sun are leading this push to bring the Web to the masses. It is now up to Web content providers to bring the masses to the Web.

Until recently, getting "up on the Net" has been a difficult and costly adventure. In fact, terms like "up on the Net" have actually added to the confusion and frustration of getting Internet access. To many, the concept behind the buzz phrase "on the Net" was something magical. A lot of people believed, and still do believe, that getting "up on the Net" would give them a new, enlightened experience.

Beside the small population of Internet users who actually know what they are doing, there is a large population of users who struggled for weeks, if not months, to connect their computers to the Internet, with the hope that it would provide something special. For many, what they found was the World Wide Web, a static thing that could display pages of text. By no means does the Web have the appeal of television. The Internet has not entered the mass market stage of its product life cycle yet for two reasons: the difficulty involved in getting access and the static nature of the Internet's content.

The Internet is the textbook example of a market in transition. The Internet is still in the late phase of early adoption, but not quite yet to the point of mass market. Our original question was "What is the Internet market population?" The answer is computer users, office workers, graphic artists, and some home users. If you think about it, this list really encompasses a large number of people, especially the office worker group, which will become the "catalyst agent" that launches the Internet into the mass market. It will be their demand for home Internet access that will bring Internet into the mainstream.

Targeting a product on the Internet can be a tricky task. Take some time to analyze your target audience, keeping in mind the current and future Internet populations. This will provide you with a good picture of your target audience. Take Yahoo! for example. Yahoo! creates widescope Web content without losing the underlying substance of the Web site (see Figure 3.5).

Figure 3.5 Yahoo! presents Web content that appeals to the general Web audience.

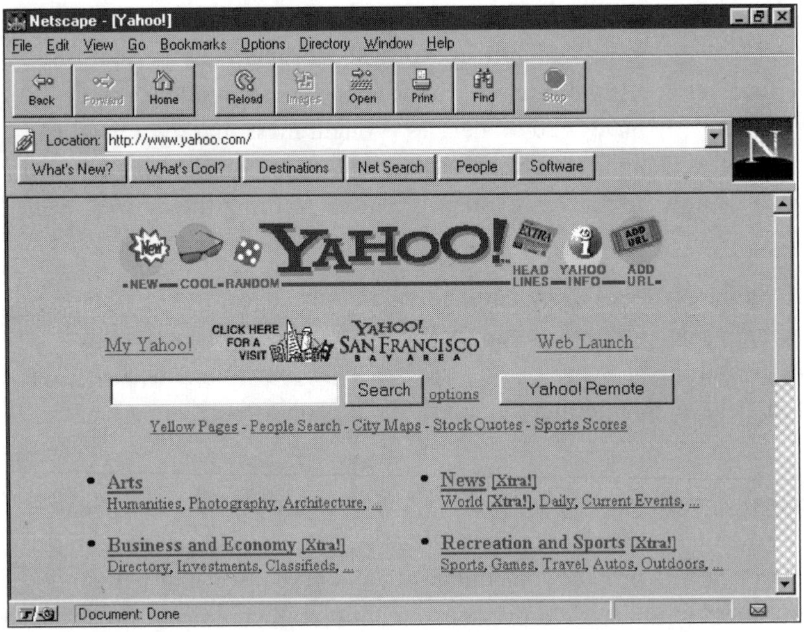

Learning by Example

Commerce on the Internet is really in its infancy. Secure credit-card transactions have been available only in the last couple of years. The majority of Web sites sell goods by using their trusty customer service telephone number. Internet commerce up until the Java revolution has been clumsy at best, but it still provided an effective model on which to base the next generation of Internet commerce using Java.

The summer of 1995 saw an explosion of secure Web commerce solutions. Installations began popping up, offering online commerce to Web patrons. The first sites were merely order forms that customers had to enter, where they sometimes even had to calculate their own totals. These simple electronic order forms really had no appeal to the Web population. The first-generation commerce solutions made two big mistakes: They asked online customers too many questions and they asked them to join some sort of club (see Figure 3.6).

The typical Internet user knows the value of information and is usually immediately turned off by too many questions. Asking for valid order information is considered reasonable, but asking too many questions is not. For example, Figure 3.7 illustrates a site that only asks vital order information.

Figure 3.6 Internet Shopping Network (www.isn.com) used to require customers to join a club before they could purchase products.

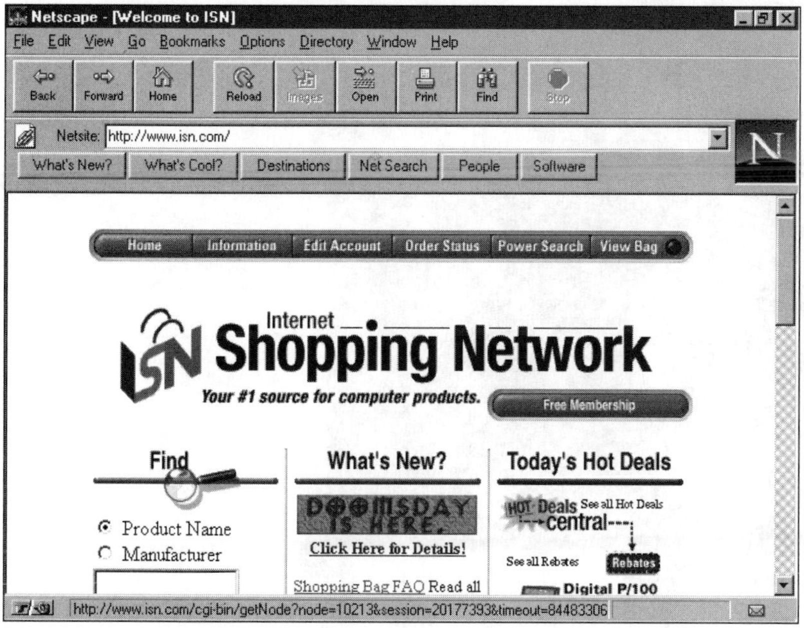

If the early pioneers of Web commerce have passed on any wisdom to the next generation, it is that simplicity is everything. People do not want to wait for two or three minutes just to view your company's logo. The initial fix to this problem was to provide two sets of pages, one with innovative graphics and the other with plain text (see Figure 3.8).

This was a good try, but most people on the Web were not satisfied with either of these options. Keep in mind that the Web needs the appeal of television, not the appeal of newspapers. The Web population wants to see colorful, well organized graphics that don't take a year to view. Graphics that stand out, make an impact, and possibly move are the key. Dimension X is one company that is creating provocative Web sites for such clients as Intel. Figure 3.9 shows their own Web page.

The primary factor in closing a sale on the Web is simplicity. Commerce has to be transparent to the customer, in the sense that they are aware of their expenditures, but they aren't worried about the security of the data. Customers also do not want to divulge any more information than is necessary to fill out the order form.

Figure 3.7 The Jake Dog site (www.jakedog.com) uses a plain but effective order form.

Figure 3.8 BellSouth offers its entire site in text-only view (yellowpages.bellsouth.com).

Figure 3.9 Dimension X has been a key player in providing a new wave of active Web content through the use of Java animation (www.dimensionx.com).

A lot of companies have made the mistake of putting an "About Our Security" button on their order form. This essentially sets up a red flag for newcomers to Web commerce, and it annoys the knowledgeable. When you use your credit card, you know the risks associated with its use, but you don't really want the sales representative to say, "Are you sure you don't want to use cash?" Shielded Technologies, Inc., guarantees the security of a transaction using CardShield. In the early days of the Internet, commerce security was an issue, but Java solutions have eliminated that problem.

Virtual Shopping Cart

Recently, HTML- and CGI-based commerce solutions have introduced the concept of a virtual shopping cart (see Figure 3.10).

The shopping cart model gives the customer a logical ordering mechanism. Customers select items for purchase as they are displayed, which are then retained for a later "checkout." In this manner, customers do not have to write item numbers and prices as they browse so that they can fill out an order form later (see Figure 3.11). The shopping cart is a fairly complicated task to

**Figure 3.10 Crutchfield online offers a shopping cart interface
(www.crutchfield.com)**

implement using traditional HTML- and CGI-based commerce; however, Java makes this task much easier. The shopping cart model provides an intuitive, easy-to-use, and informative user interface that should be the standard for successful Web commerce solutions.

The Web population looks for value-added benefit from ordering on the Web. Customers must have a reason to buy an item on your site rather than down the street, and the Web transaction has to be just as easy.

Traditionally, Internet commerce wasn't as easy as a trip to a local vendor. The major problem was with the currency. Java commerce solutions have changed this. Now Web commerce solutions are as easy as opening a wallet—and more secure than traditional credit card transactions.

Java commerce solutions provide the means to put Internet commerce into the hands of those who previously could not afford the expense. Java solutions have the potential to take Internet commerce to a new level by providing user-friendly and secure ways for people to spend money. Every user on the Web has the potential to spend money; they just need to be given the means to do so.

Figure 3.11 Tower Hobbies requires users to keep track of product numbers (www.towerhobbies.com).

A Successful Web Commerce Model

The World Wide Web is not a simple advertising medium. Consider a billboard, whose content looks the same to all viewing it. A billboard ad is intended to be seen by all, and the actual number of viewers can be judged based solely on the billboard's location. In some ways, the Web is like big billboards, but it is capable of much more.

The similarities and marketing potential of billboards and Web sites are separate, but similar. A billboard is a simple form of advertising; the billboard speaks to you. On the Web, the sites that look like interactive billboards seem to get the most traffic (see Figure 3.12), and if you haven't already figured it out, Web traffic is what sells.

Gravity Boards, a San Diego–based skateboard manufacturer, has a great example of a Web billboard. Granted, not all products are visible and showy, but all products can be displayed obviously. Successful Web commerce sites need to have a television appeal. For example, the G board interface (see Figure 3.13) comes out and grabs you, like a billboard that came to life.

Figure 3.12 www.windows95.com billboards.

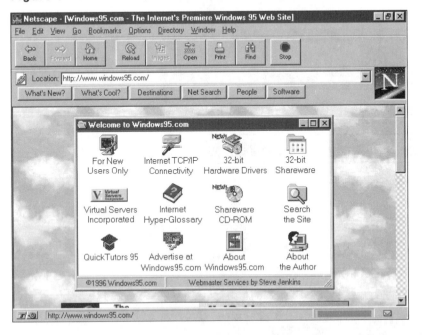

Figure 3.13 G board Web site (www.gravityboard.com).

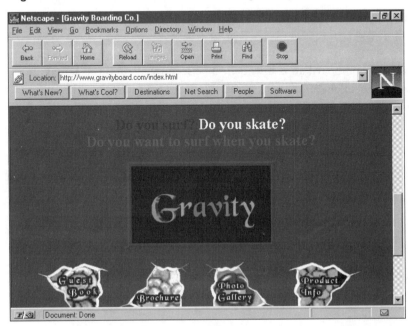

This type of point-and-shoot interface is the key to a successful Web commerce model. The site needs to be simple and catchy, and it must provide the customer with an easy, fast, and special means for obtaining the product.

Billboards look the same to every viewer, and so should a Web site. Regardless of connection speed or physical platform characteristics, a Web site should look the same to all. Figures 3.14, 3.15, and 3.16 show the the G board site on Mac, PC, and SGI equipment, respectively.

They all look basically the same. This is not always possible because some Web browsers do not have graphics capabilities. In this case, you need to consider your target audience and try to please as many people as possible.

Optimizing Your Graphics

In creating a high-intensity graphic Web site, it is very easy to forget the need for speed. It is a myth that high-intensity graphics require fast Internet connections, but it is true that high-intensity graphics require more optimization.

With the advances in image compression, large images no longer require large physical sizes. Here is a great example of an optimized Java commerce site. The order entry applet uses a "background loader" to download needed images while the user is busy doing something else. This is

Figure 3.14 G board Web site on a Mac.

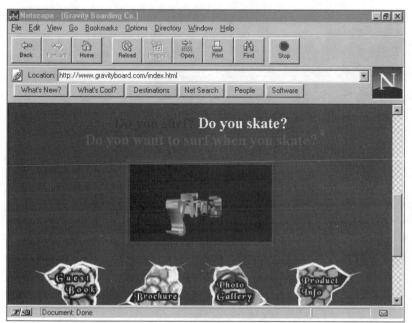

Figure 3.15 G board Web site on a PC.

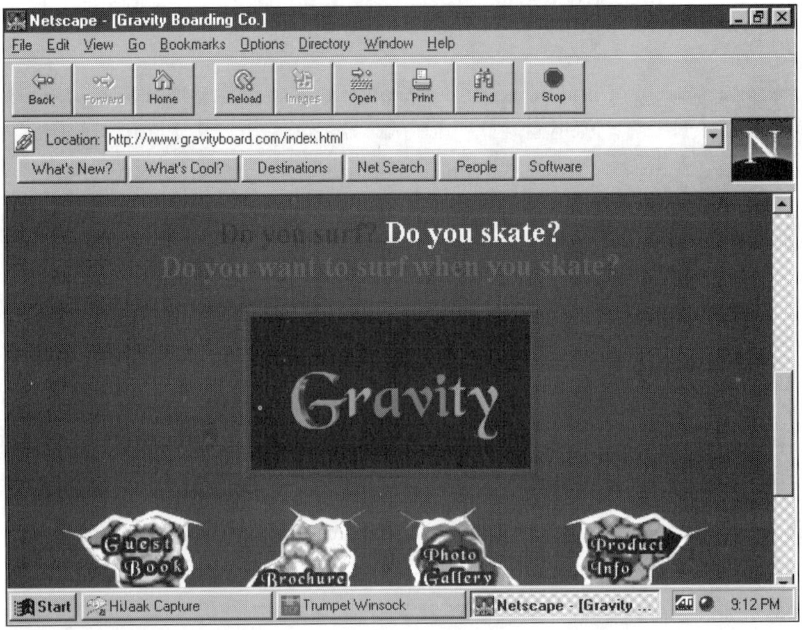

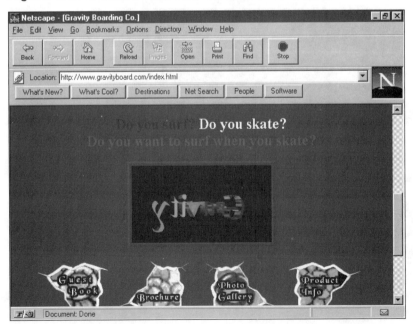

Figure 3.16 G board Web site on an SGI workstation.

an excellent way to avoid penalizing users with slower connections. Not all your customers will be connecting using a dedicated, high-speed Internet connection. Thus, your site should accommodate all connection speeds. This is usually done by catering to the lowest common denominator. Customers with faster connections will not mind the speedy viewing pleasure, and customers with slower connections will appreciate not having to wait too long before your site appears.

Here are some tips for building a commercial Web site.

Keep your site as unobtrusive as possible. People coming to your site should feel welcome to buy something or just to browse your product or service. You want to make your site as appealing as possible, without trying to force feed a potential customer. If you create a site that people want to visit, you will sell.

The static use of good, clean, and well-optimized graphics or animation is vital. Your site should have a television appeal, and you want to sell to your customer during the commercial break.

Keep It Simple Stupid (KISS) should be your battle cry. If a Web novice can get onto your site and order your product, you have a hit.

Last, try to make Web customers feel as if they are getting some sort of value-added bonus by buying on the Web. If people think they are getting a great deal or something extra, word of mouth will launch your Web site into the stratosphere.

These words of advice will guide you in the creation of a successful Web commerce site. Keep to the Web site fundamentals, and you will be beating customers off with a stick.

Advertising Your Web Site

Unfortunately, some really great Web sites go unnoticed because no one knows to go there. The "hit count" of a Web site is once again very much like a billboard. Billboards in the center of town will be viewed more often than a billboard five miles from nowhere, and the same holds for Web sites. Web sites do have one advantage over billboards. A good billboard might get two looks from the same individual, whereas a Web site has the potential to keep customers coming back for more. *WebSavvy* is a term used to describe the quality of a Web site that makes people return time and time again.

A common mistake in Internet commerce is to assume that customers will find your site simply because your product is good. Just as customers probably cannot find you because your company is listed in a generic telephone directory, customers may not find you simply because you have a page on the Web. Advertising gets customers to your site, and once you have them there, you can make the sale.

Banner Ads

On the Web, there are a number of ways to advertise your site, some more expensive than others, and some more effective than others. You have probably seen **banner ads** on the majority of the popular sites on the Web (see Figure 3.17).

Banner ads recently have become a way for companies to advertise on the Web. These banner ads provide a Web billboard to attract attention to your site. They are an effective way of obtaining Web traffic, but they are not cheap. Here are some ball park figures for you to mull over. Figures 3.18 and 3.19 were taken directly from Netscape's and Yahoo!'s Web pages. For updated pricing and accurate information visit their Web sites:

```
URL: http://home.netscape.com/ads/ad_rate_card.html
URL: web.yahoo.com/derek/yahoo/adindex/rate.html
```

Figure 3.17 Netscape Search banner advertisement.

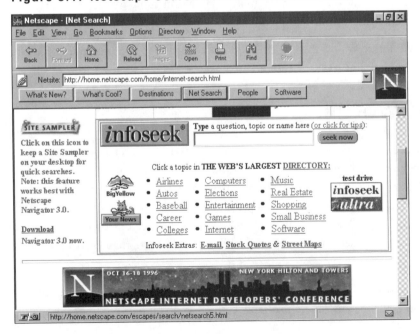

Figure 3.18 Cost of Netscape banner advertising.

NETSCAPE BANNER ADVERTISING PROGRAMS AND RATE CARD

Millions of Internet users begin each cyber-journey with a visit to our site and by using Navigator, continue to return over and over.

For advertisers in this new media environment, advertising at Netscape is simple, the value unquestionable: Netscape is the premier foundation buy. It provides:

- The broadest coverage of the Internet

- A way to affect brand opinions and reach experienced users as well as tap into the flood of new users

- A way to deliver brand messages quickly and concisely

- The best way to fulfill interactive marketing objectives and link promotions to entire sales messages

As the central resource, Netscape provides advertisers with the flexibility to reach the audience in mass or within a targeted and segmented context. The audience includes heavy users and core developers who come to explore the latest happenings available from Netscape and its community. What's more, Netscape introduces thousands of "newbies" to the Web every day.

Although some consider the Internet to be an uncharted territory, with unknown values and uncertain benefits, Netscape provides advertisers with solutions to the need for market coverage and a means of reaching consumers who are engaged on the Internet now. There is no better place to reach the Internet market.

All Banner Advertising Programs include a banner linked directly to the advertiser's Web site. All are offered on a monthly basis. In each program, banners ROTATE once at least every ten minutes.

The following details will guide you through the evaluation and purchase process. Select the information you need and get answers to your questions.

For additional information, please see Frequently Asked Questions.

Figure 3.18 Cost of Netscape banner advertising. (Continued)

	PLATINUM	GOLD	SILVER	TOTAL COVERAGE	BANNER ADVERTISING ON DESTINATIONS	FIXED PAGES
Net[†] Cost per Month	$20,400	$17,000	$12,750	$46,000	$8,500	$12,750
Guaranteed Impressions/ Month	1,000,000	750,000	500,000	2,250,000	500,000	Call
Net[†] Cost per Thousand (CPM)	$20.40 (Through 10/96)	$22.66	$25.50	$20.40	$17 (Through 10/96)	Call
Pages in Rotation	6	5	5	16	8	
Page Placement	Net Search DisplayText ca Assistance DisplayText ca DisplayText ca	Net Search What's New? DisplayText ca DisplayText ca Yellow Pages	Net Search What's Cool? DisplayText ca DisplayText ca People	All pages Platinum Gold, and Silver programs	DisplayText ca General News DisplayText ca Finance Marketplace Sports Travel Entertainment	DisplayText ca FishCam

To request more information, please complete the inquiry form. Netscape also provides advertising on its international Web Sites. For information, please contact one of our International Advertising Managers.

[†]'Net' assumes an agency discount applies. Agencies must be recognized by the SRDS.

BANNER AD SUBMISSION PROCESS

Materials are due to Netscape no later than seven days prior to the banner advertisement start date and must adhere to the technical specifications. Banner advertising start dates occur on the first day of each month and Wednesday of each week. If a start date coincides with a weekend or holiday, it will occur on the prior business day.

Figure 3.18 (Continued)

I. Contact Netscape's Advertising Representative for availability.

II. No later than seven days prior to the banner advertisement start date, send the following materials:

- Mail the signed contract and insertion order to your Advertising Representative.

- GIF—e-mail as attachment to admgr@netscape.com. Please, no compression.

- URL, following the syntax 'http://server.domain.com/file.type', in the same email attachment as GIF image.

III. Any late submissions will be held until the following Wednesday and you will be notified.

TERMS OF PAYMENT

I. Sponsors will be invoiced by the first day of the contract period.

II. Payment is due net 30 days from the date of invoice receipt.

III. Insertion orders must accompany the banner advertising contract.

IV. A signed contract must be delivered seven days before publication date.

V. Reservations will not be held without a signed contract.

VI. Proof sheets are handled by contacting your Advertising Representative.

TECHNICAL SPECIFICATIONS FOR NETSCAPE ADVERTISING

FILE FORMATS

Image File Format	GIF only
Image Dimensions	468 pixels wide by 60 pixels deep
Image File Size	72 dpi maximum at actual size; 10 Kb maximum file size
Interlacing Mode	Please specify
MAP Files	Not accepted

Figure 3.18 Cost of Netscape banner advertising. (Continued)

Animated Banner Ads	GIF89 only. Must be accompanied by a non-animated GIF to be considered. Loop must stop after 4 seconds.

FILE NAMING CONVENTIONS

U.S.	'mycompany_myprogram_ad.gif' (example: netscape_gold_ad.gif)
Japanese	'mycompany_ja_ad.gif' (example: netscape_ja_ad.gif)
French	'mycompany_fr_ad.gif' (example: netscape_fr_ad.gif)
German	'mycompany_de_ad.gif' (example: netscape_de_ad.gif)

DEFINITIONS

Clicks—Every time a visitor clicks on your banner, it is counted as a "click." This measurement method lets you judge the response to any ad that you are running.

Click Ratio—A ratio that indicates the success of an advertiser in attracting visitors to click on their ad. For example, if during 1 million impressions there are 20,000 clicks on your banner, your click ratio is 2%.

Impressions—The number of times a banner image is downloaded to a page being viewed by a visitor. This is the standard way of determining exposure for an advertisement on the Web.

Hits—The term "hits" is used by Webmasters to describe the relative horsepower that their site can successfully handle. It has no relevance to an advertiser.

Portal Page—When a banner ad is clicked on, the visitor is linked to this page which is the advertiser's Web site or special Web page. Portal pages are often created specifically to work with the banner ad.

Figure 3.19 Cost of Yahoo! advertising. (Continued)

Yahoo! Advertising Rate Card

Yahoo! offers flexible online advertising options designed to promote your Web site to a large targeted audience. Net rates are based on choice of programming, banner positioning, and monthly page views. Each banner advertisement links directly to an advertiser's Web site or co-branded promotion package. Options include:

- **Run of Yahoo!**—Banners are scheduled across pages within the Yahoo! directory, on the search page and presented with general search results.

- **Interactive Promotions**—Use customized promotions integrating sweepstakes or contests to launch Web sites, events, products and services. Capture invaluable demographic, brand, and product preference information. Yahoo! takes care of coordinating the design, hosting, and administration of all promotions. Want huge exposure? Be on the Yahoo Front Page. Want to target a promotion? Run it in a Yahoo! category.

- **Run of Category**—Banners can be scheduled through specific categories (e.g., Entertainment) and with search results originating within the categories, to provide targeted audience by interest area.

- **Fixed Category Pages**—Banners can be placed on specific pages within categories in the Yahoo! directory for highly targeted advertising.

- **Search Words**—Banners can be presented with the search results for specific words to directly target special interests.

Page Views (per month)	Run of Yahoo!	Run of Category	Fixed Category Pages
	(Monthly Net Rate per Thousand Page Views)		
500,000+	$20.00	$20.00	$30.00
250,000+	n/a	$30.00	$40.00
100,000+	n/a	$40.00	$45.00
Up to 100,000	n/a	n/a	$50.00

Figure 3.19 Cost of Yahoo! advertising. (Continued)

Search Words (all rates are net)		Advertiser Usage Reports	
Active	$1,000/month	Online Daily Reports	$200/month
Highly Active	$1,500/month	Weekly Reports	No Charge
Super Active	$3,000/month	Monthly Audited I/PRO	fee waived at $5,000+/month advertisers

Promotions (all rates are net)	
Front Page	$50,000/two weeks
Category	$25,000/month/1 million page views

General Guidelines

See: Advertiser Information Index.

New advertiser runs start on the 1st or 15th of a month.

Banners and insertion orders must be delivered at least seven (7) days prior to the start of an insertion term.

Banners must be submitted as image files in GIF format, 460 pixels wide 55 pixels high, under 8KB size.

Advertiser must provide a URL and thirty (30) character alternative text line for each banner. Banner changes during the insertion term must be delivered at least three (3) business days prior to change.

Advertising is subject to Yahoo!'s Standard Terms & Conditions.

Rates are net and subject to change at any time.

Available Advertising Spots

The following standard advertising spots may be purchased, subject to availability. Yahoo! reserves the right to make changes at any time.

Figure 3.19 (Continued)

Advertising Categories	Monthly Page Views Per Spot	Net Rate Per Spot	Available Spots
* RUN OF YAHOO!	*	*	*
* Run of Yahoo! Pages	*1,000,000	*$20,000	*5
* Search Options Page	*1,000,000	*$20,000	*2
* General Search Results	*1,000,000	*$20,000	*10
* RUN OF CATEGORY	*	*	*
* Arts	*500,000	*$10,000	*2
*	*250,000	*$7,500	*2
* Business & Economy	*1,000,000	*$20,000	*6
* Computers & Internet	*1,000,000	*$20,000	*4
*	*500,000	*$10,000	*6
* Education	*500,000	*$10,000	*1
*	*250,000	*$75,000	*2
* Entertainment	*1,000,000	*$20,000	*8
*	*500,000	*$10,000	*4
* Government, Science & Social Science	*500,000	*$10,000	*3
*	*250,000	*$7,500	*2
* Health	*500,000	*$10,000	*1
*	*250,000	*$7,500	*2
* News	*500,000	*$10,000	*3
* Recreation	*1,000,000	*$20,000	*2

Figure 3.19 Cost of Yahoo! advertising. (Continued)

Advertising Categories	Monthly Page Views Per Spot	Net Rate Per Spot	Available Spots
*	*500,000	*$10,000	*4
* Reference	*250,000	*$7,500	*3
* Regional	*1,000,000	*$20,000	*3
*	*250,000	*$7,500	*2
* Reuters News	*1,000,000	*$20,000	*3
*	*500,000	*$10,000	*4
* Society & Culture	*500,000	*$10,000	*2
* Sports Scoreboard	*Call	*	*Call
* Weather	*Call	*	*Call
* Quotes	*Call	*	*Call
* FIXED CATEGORY PAGES	*	*	*
* 5,000 different pages available	*Call	*	*Call
* Search Words	*Call	*	*Call

advertise@yahoo.com

Copyright © 1994-95 Yahoo

How Banner Ads Work

Banner ads can be found on most major Web sites. The idea behind them is simple—and very similar to the billboard principle. Just as a billboard along a heavily traveled road will be seen by all passing that way, banner ads work the same way. Banner ads can be purchased from highly popular sites. While Web patrons visit that site they get the opportunity to view the banner ad. In a sense, banner ads can be viewed as renting real estate on a Web page.

The pricing structure varies from site to site, with the basic underlying premise that you get what you pay for. Some sites sell advertising on a per-view basis; others have a bulk rate. For example, most search engines offers"Context Sensitive" banner ads. That is, if a user does a search for something related to the banner ad, that ad is displayed. Services such as these usually charge on a hits-per-month basis.

Careful selection of potential banner ad placement is crucial. Cruise the Web and try to put yourself into the mind of your potential customer to determine the most effective use of your advertising dollars. Once you have chosen the site, information about banner add placement is usually readily accessible.

Pointers

Web sites commonly have "pointers" to other associated Web sites. For example, a number of skateboard sites on the Web place free pointer adds to the G board site as shown in Figure 3.20. This means of obtaining Web traffic might not attract the most visits, but it is cheap and effectively draws your target audience.

The G board's site is once again a great example of this phenomenon. Through the beauty of a good Web profile engine, a piece of software that can give some useful information about Web traffic, we are able to see these phenomena in action. The sites shown in Figures 3.21, 3.22, and 3.23 all have pointers to the G board site.

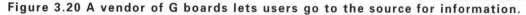

Figure 3.20 A vendor of G boards lets users go to the source for information.

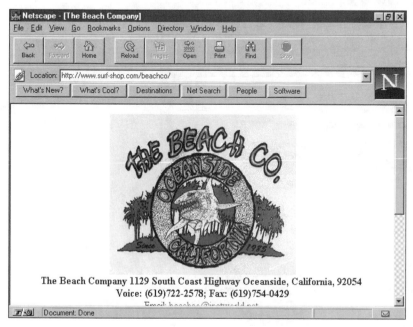

Figure 3.21 The Surf-Shop site.

Figure 3.22 The Oceansnow site.

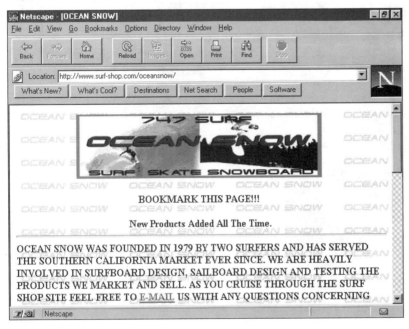

Figure 3.23 The Rancho site.

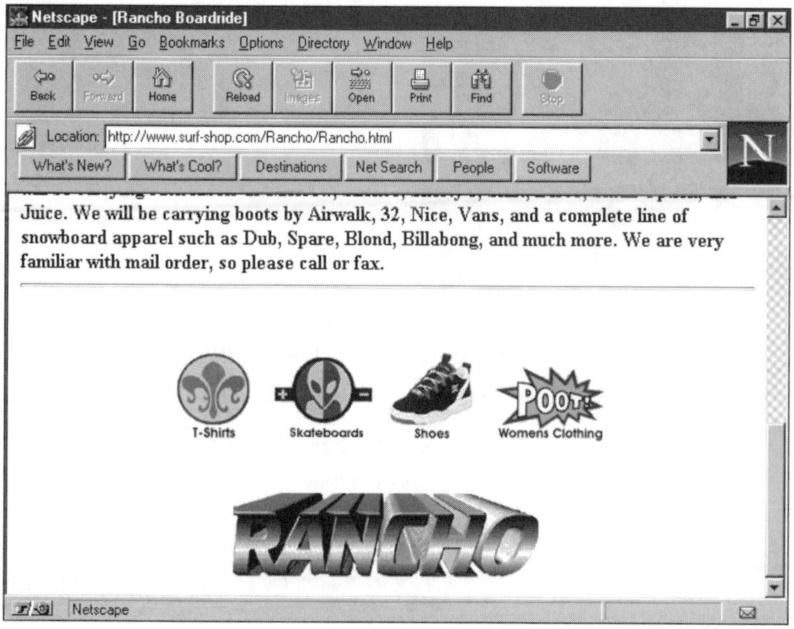

In a one-month time frame, G boards received 10,000 hits from these sites. Of those hits, 1,000 resulted in a sale. During another month, a banner ad was placed in one of the sites mentioned, and 100,000 hits were received from these sites. Of those hits, 5,000 resulted in a sale. The figures show that strategically placing pointers to your Web site can be just as effective, if not more effective, as high-priced banner ads.

Pointer ads usually cost far less than banner ads, but they do provide two different forms of marketing. Banner ads act as a great broadcasting medium, reaching a large population of unfiltered Web viewers. Pointer ads, on the other hand, do a pretty good job at filtering Web traffic to your actual target audience. The effectiveness of each approach depends on your actual product. Vertical markets do relatively well using pointer ads, while broad markets may benefit from banner ads. Either way, in order for your commerce site to be effective, you need Web traffic.

Summary

The Web is going to get easier, cheaper, faster, and bigger at a rate not yet fathomable. As a Web commerce developer, you will have a bigger, more diverse clientele from which to draw.

Figure 3.24 The virtual storefront.

Nevertheless, the question for commerce facilitators should be broken into two distinct decisions: when to hit the market and how to facilitate a commerce solution.

When is the opportune time to enter the Web market is entirely based on the market set you wish to hit. In this chapter, the concept of waiting for the mass market was introduced. However, the current Internet market might be composed of the ideal target audience for your product. Or, if your product needs the adoption by the mass market, now might be the perfect time to start ramping up. In either case, knowledge of your product is crucial, and the information presented in this chapter aids in the decision.

The following chapters will provide all the information needed to fully appreciate and act on the question of "how do I do this?". Included in this information will be examples from a variety of different-sized companies to aid you in your decision. Creating a successful, cost-effective Web commerce site is by no means rocket science. Rather, it involves knowing the marketplace, the product(s) to sell, and the media to sell through. Figure 3.24 depicts the next wave of commerce, a virtual store. With the information in this chapter, you are now armed with the knowledge of what to do.

Selling products on the Web may not be as easy as you would think. The actual sale is not the hard part; getting people to your site is. In this chapter, you were exposed not only to the composition of the Web population, but also to the key factors needed to bring that population to your site. From your standpoint getting people to your site may very well be your easiest task. Once they have been there, giving them a reason to come back is the hard part. This chapter gave you some advice on how to create a commerce site that people will enjoy visiting time and time again. It also gave you the information you need to bring people to your site initially. Follow this advice and you will have a lean, mean selling machine.

Part

2

Setting Up Shop

Tools of the Trade

Every profession has its own set of tools. Part of the process in learning a new trade, is knowing what tools to use and how to use them. This chapter presents an overview of what is involved in setting up a Web installation, including an overview of Web hardware and software, the tools of the Web trade.

As discussed in Chapter 2, setting up a Web shop can take one of two distinct paths:

1. Use "off the shelf" solutions with an inexpensive dial-up account

2. Set up your own Web installation with a dedicated connection

Setting up your own Web installation is orders of magnitude harder than facilitating commerce with a dial-up account. However, some solutions do require a dedicated connection. After completing this surmountable task, the Web site developer will be rewarded with the four T's of the Web:

1. Tips—Helpful words of wisdom from the voice of experience

2. Tricks—Quirky knowledge gained only through experience

3. Tools—Software, hardware, and contact information to be stored for later use

4. Talent—Tangible, dollar value–equated knowledge

Web Servers

In the industry, the term "Web server" holds an ambiguous meaning. The software that serves up Web data to a hungry browser is called a "Web server," and a dedicated computer whose entire role in life is to fulfill Web browser requests is also called a "Web server." You might think that these two terms go hand in hand: You to have the Web server software running on a Web server machine. However, it is completely legal to load a Web server application on a normal desktop computer. Then why do you denote a specific type of computer as a Web server? The answer to this question lies in the architecture of the Web server software.

In Chapter 2, the concept of client/server applications was introduced to the extent of providing a "30,000-foot view" of the system architecture. From a "30,000-foot view" level, the concepts driving client/server architecture can be viewed only as little black dots connected by smoke and mirrors.

For the purpose of this discussion, the client can be synonymous with a Web browser. The browser is the user interface of the Web, and to many the browser is an icon of the Web. A Web

Figure 4.1 Client/server technology.

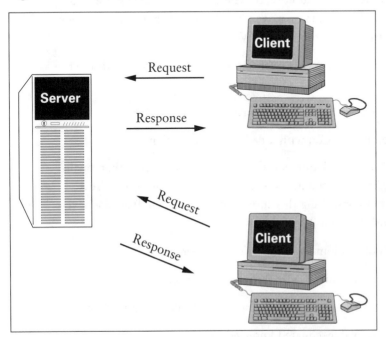

browser's entire purpose in life is to allow users to "surf" the Web. That is, the browser goes from one Web server to another requesting information local to the server.

The individual servers are responsible for retrieving the Web page for each browser's request. The key point here is *each browser's request*. That is, a Web server is responsible for fulfilling the needs of multiple browsers simultaneously. The need for a Web server to concurrently process multiple browsers' requests is the single requirement putting Web server hardware and software in a different class from the typical desktop computer and application.

A few years ago there was a big flurry in the computer world, more precisely the PC world, about **multitasking,** the computer's ability to do more than one thing at a time. This was not a new concept to individuals outside of the PC world, but to PC users it held the promise of sluggish machines.

In the context of a Web server, a multitasking computer would be able to fulfill the needs of more than one browser at a time. This feat of science might not instantly surprise you because it is an inherently intuitive idea, but it is not as simple as it might seem. For example, your computer might contain a Pentium processor, or CPU. This CPU and all other CPUs can execute only one instruction at a time, which might lead to the conclusion that computers with these types of CPUs are not capable of multitasking. This would be true if all applications did nothing but crunch numbers. Most applications rely on other computer resources, such as a keyboard, hard drive, or display, all of which are separate entities from the machine's CPU (see Figure 4.2).

Putting this in context of a Web server application, when the server software receives a request from the browser it will process the request and fetch a file from the hard drive. In a non-multitasking computer, the computer must wait until the hard drive has fetched the needed file. A multitasking computer would be able to use the time, which would have been spent waiting for the hard drive to return, to process other browser requests.

Figure 4.2 Resource management of an operating system.

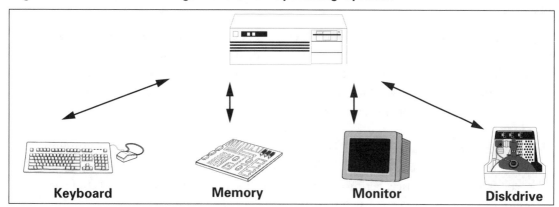

| Keyboard | Memory | Monitor | Diskdrive |

Choosing the right tool for the job is sometimes more difficult than the job itself. Web server applications are not like regular desktop applications. Running a Web server on a machine optimized for desktop applications is like using a knife to eat peas—it can be done, but by no means is it the most efficient mechanism. Selecting the right hardware and software for a Web server may look like a formidable task. If you take some time to analyze the client/server architecture of a Web server, as well as the demands bestowed on the server, you will be able to diagnose problematic points correctly and find an appropriate workaround.

Hardware

Today's desktop computers are optimized for general computing needs. When computers are dedicated to a certain task they can be optimized to perform just that task. In the case of a dedicated Web server, the following can be assumed:

1. There is little or no need for optimized graphics display.

2. The CPU will be used to fulfill small, multiple, and simultaneous operations.

3. Disk access must be as fast as possible.

4. The amount of memory needed will depend on the number of consecutive users.

The CPU processor types available to fulfill a Web server needs come in two types, fast single processors and slower multiple processors. A combination of the two is optimal, but it is fairly expensive. In recent months the cost of entry-level multiple processor systems has dropped dramatically. Within reason, two processors are better than one. A single, high-speed processor might be able to push through individual calculations faster, but multiple processors can do simultaneous calculations. A good example of this is the difference between a 200mhz Pentium Pro and a Dual 120mhz Pentium machine. The Pentium Pro almost doubles the price of the dual Pentium and is substantially slower. If you can afford it, multiple processors are definitely the solution of choice for Web server platforms.

The drive space and RAM required for a Web server depend on the size and workload of the Web server. Web server applications need quick hard drives and a substantial amount of RAM, both of which are necessary and neither of which can be in excess. Just to give some sort of ground-zero requirement, drive space should be over 1 gig, and memory should be greater than or equal to 32 meg. More of either or both can never hurt.

Web Server Solutions

A number of vendors have jumped on the bandwagon to provide turnkey Web server solutions. These computers vary in price, performance, and fault-tolerance levels. Here is a list of some of the solutions available. For complete information, contact the vendor directly.

Figure 4.3 SGI's WebFORCE CHALLENGE Server is very fast and a pinnacle of performance.

Vendor: Silicon Graphics

Product: WebFORCE CHALLENGE Servers

Contact: www.sgi.com

Price: Base price $20,000 ± 5000

Features: SGI prides itself on producing robust, scalable products, and the WebFORCE is no exception. The WebFORCE is a UNIX-flavored machine that is based on the MIPS RISC CPU. Low end models contain four symmetric processors. Without getting into too much detail, this machine is fast and for all-out Web server performance, it is viewed as a pinnacle of performance.

Operating System: This solution is not cheap. It is a great system, but it does require UNIX knowledge. Later in this chapter, a discussion of UNIX-based machines will go into this further.

Suggested Use: For a high-traffic, graphic-intensive site or for a Web provider, this will provide a stable and scalable solution. However, it is overkill for a small Web installation.

Web server hardware has a definite range of capabilities. In most cases, you get what you pay for, but that is not to say that the most expensive tool is the one you should use. To the contrary, you should use the tool that best fits your current and future needs. The tool that you choose should be able to grow with your needs and provide you with a stable mechanism for the delivery of your Web site.

Software

The current Web server software market is exploding. Some server software is cheaper than others, some provides more features, some does special little things, and others just try to fit what everyone else has done into one big Web server. Needles to say, choosing Web server software can be a not-so-easy task. Before you dive head first into the pool of Web server confusion, keep in mind the operating system's role in the execution of the Web server application. Although you might be bound to a specific operating system, they are not all created equal. When sorting through vendor-provided benchmarks, comparing one server's performance to another server's performance on a different operating system is not like comparing apples to apples.

Figure 4.4 The SPARC and Netra computers from Sun Microelectronics provide performance, stability, and competitive prices.

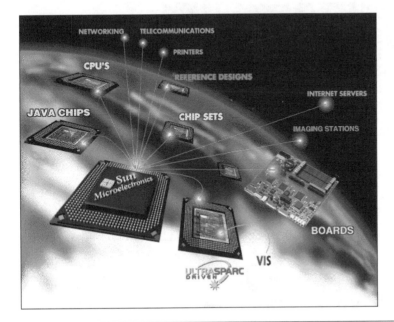

Vendor: Sun Microelectronics

Product: SPARC Family and Netra

Contact: www.sun.com

Price: Base price $6000 ± 2000

Features: Sun has been making robust, stable solutions for many years. The SPARC family of computers has become the staple of large Web sites. They provide performance, stability, and competitive prices. The new Netra family of machines provides a level of ease not matched in the SPARC family, at a lower cost.

Operating System: The SPARC and Netra computers are UNIX based; however, the Netra adds a Web type of interface for administering the system.

Suggested Use: A large population of Web sites uses SPARC machines. They are best suited for an enterprise's primary Web server. At the low range, they meet the high end NT-based servers.

Figure 4.5 DecAlpha computers provide a low-cost, high-performance solution to Intel-based computers.

Vendor: Digital Equipment Corp.

Product: DecAlpha Family

Contact: www.dec.com

Price: Base price $6000 ± 1000

Features: DecAlpha computers are most commonly used as NT boxes. They provide a low-cost, high-performance solution to Intel-based computers. These machines are not binary compatible to Intel machines. Thus, most off-the-shelf windows/NT software will not run on them.

Operating System: Flavors of UNIX or NT can be used on the DecAlpha computers.

Suggested Use: The DecAlpha family provide more scalable solutions than Intel-based machines. If you need more performance or high-end features not available in Intel-based machines, but still want to use NT, DecAlpha is for you.

Vendor: IBM, Compaq

Product: Variety of Intel-based systems

Contact: www.intel.com

Price: Base price $1500 ± 1500

Features: Intel Pentium family of products provide a low-cost solution. In recent months, memory and CPU price drops have made fairly powerful machines available for under $2000.

Operating System: Flavors of UNIX or NT

Suggested Use: Pentium-based solutions are adequate for most Web installations. Dual Pentium solutions can be had for under $2000 and can provide a more than adequate solution for a small to midsized Web site.

A Word on Operating Systems

As discussed earlier, Web server software is not like regular desktop applications. Web server applications require quite a bit from the operating system. The operating system is responsible for the safe execution of the server process, as well as each process associated to its client browser. The operating system is also responsible for balancing the utilization of the CPU, memory, hard disk, and network resources.

For this reason, the operating system chosen for your Web server should be able to provide these services to your Web server applications. Without getting into a long and sometimes heated discussion of NT versus UNIX, just keep in mind that both operating systems have their associated pros and cons. One thing for certain is that the internal mechanism on which a Web server application will rely varies dramatically between these two systems. Comparing performance of different Web servers residing on different operating systems is, at best, comparing apples to oranges.

Secure Transactions

Chapter 2 discussed the concept of a protocol. That is a standard method for two applications to communicate. HTTP stands for HyperText Transport Protocol; similarly, HTTPS stands for HyperText Transport Protocol Secure. The difference is that HTTPS servers support a mechanism for securely transmitting information entered into a Web page, as well as giving Java applets the ability to transmit and receive secured information using tools provided by Sun. Another major difference is that HTTPS server applications cost substantially more than regular HTTP servers (see Figure 4.6).

Traditionally all Web commerce solutions required an HTTPS server, and for the most part they still do. The CardShield solution uses its own patented security mechanism and requires only an HTTP server. Also, custom-built Java commerce solutions utilizing Sun's SSL, Secure Socket Layer, use their own embedded security and similarly do not require an HTTPS server. Java commerce solutions allow you to utilize a less expensive, unsecured Web server, but if you must have a server that supports HTTPS, the same server will also support HTTP. HTTPS is, simply put, an added bonus to an HTTP server.

Figure 4.6 HTTP versus HTTPS.

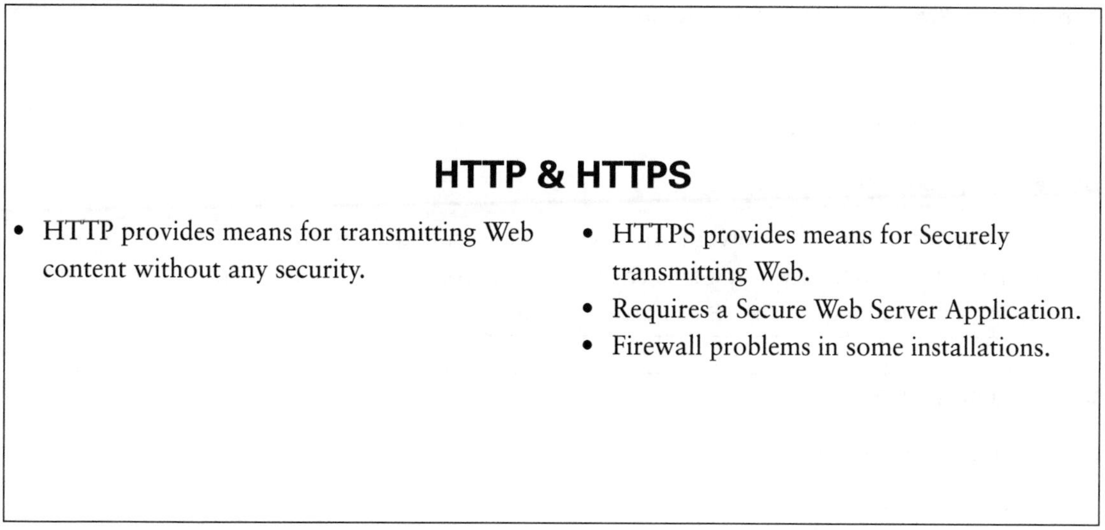

HTTP & HTTPS

- HTTP provides means for transmitting Web content without any security.

- HTTPS provides means for Securely transmitting Web.
- Requires a Secure Web Server Application.
- Firewall problems in some installations.

Web Server Software Packages

Vendor: Netscape

Product: FastTrack Server

Secure Product: Yes

Contact: http://home.netscape.com/comprod/server_central/index2.html

Price: $295

Platforms: SGI, NT, DEC, HP

Operating Systems: All major operating systems supported

Features: Netscape servers hold a whopping amount of the Web server market. It provides a stable, full-featured solution at a competitive price.

Vendor: Microsoft

Product: Microsoft Internet Information Server

Secure Product: Yes

Contact: http://www.microsoft.com/inforserv/

Price: Free with NT Server 4.0

Platforms: All available NT platforms

Operating Systems: NT

Features: Internet Information Server (IIS) provides all functionality needed in a Web server application. Installation is a breeze, but it falls short on some needed server-based options. If you are running NT and need a quick fix, IIS is a great solution.

Vendor: O'Reilly Software

Product: Web Site Professional

Secure Product: Yes

Contact: http://web site.ora.com

Price: $495

Platforms: Intel Family Architecture

Operating Systems: Windows 95 and NT

Features: Web Site offers a lot of cutting-edge features, as well as great performance. The only drawback is its limited platform base.

Vendor: NCSA

Product: HTTPd

Secure Product: No

Contact: http://hoohoo.ncsa.uiuc.edu

Price: Free

Platforms: All major platforms

Operating Systems: Mac, NT, UNIX

Features: HTTPd is a thrilling Web server. It is small, fast, and powerful; however, it does not support security.

Figure 4.7 Jeeves, Dynamically Extendible Web Server.

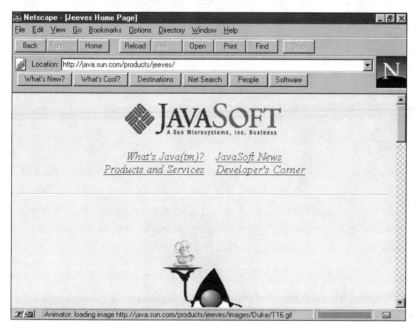

Vendor: JavaSoft

Product: Jeeves (Name might change when released)

Contact: http://www.javasoft.com/jeeves

Price: Not available

Platforms: All Java-ready platforms

Operating Systems: All Java-ready operating systems

Features: Jeeves is a Web server written in Java that breathes new life into the aging Web server technology. Jeeves, like JavaOS, is dynamically extensible. For example, if you wanted to write a CGI script to authorize credit-card transactions, with Jeeves you could write that CGI and then "merge" your functionality into the base functionality of the Web server. Jeeves is an emerging technology not yet available.

Setting Up a Site

Setting up a new Web installation means starting from ground zero. Where ground zero is actually depends on the specific installation. Regardless, three fundamental elements are required for any Web site:

1. Connection to the Internet

2. A computer with a Web server application loaded and running

3. A single, or series of, HTML page(s)

Where you are will determine your starting point. If you have a Net connection and a machine running a Web server, you're more than 80 percent done. For those starting with nothing, be assured that it is not as difficult as you might think. Take one step at a time, with the first step being the key and fundamental element of an operating Web site—a connection to the outside world, a connection to the Internet.

Getting on the Net

The process of getting a dedicated Internet connection has come a long way in a very short time. Beginners used to learn along with the so-called experts. The technology has improved, and the demand has become more common. The process can be broken down into two sections:

1. Physical network connection

2. TCP/IP connection

Going back to the good old days of this technology, these two needs would require the expertise of two entirely separate companies. The phone company would supply a connection from point A to point B, where point B supplied your TCP/IP connection. At point B, an ISP would be responsible for the Internet part of the process. The ISP would use the cable supplied by the phone company to set up a TCP/IP network with your Web site. Recently, the phone companies started jumping on the bandwagon and providing both the physical connection and the ISP. Regardless, it is usually a good bet to begin this entire process with a phone call to your phone company. A good 70 to 80 percent of the time it can provide you with more information than you will know what to do with.

Physical Network Connection

The whole idea of having a Web site is to allow people from various locations to access information on your Web server. If your Web server isn't connected to anything, this may pose a problem. A "physical network connection" is a fancy way of saying "a wire cable going from your Web site to your ISP." Much as other copper wires carry electricity to your home, a network cable is responsible for carrying information from your Web site to your ISP's and from your ISP out onto the Internet. Because in most cases the length of cable required to go from your computer to your ISP is greater than a mile, it is not feasible for you simply to run the cable yourself. Thus, we need the telephone company.

Telephone companies have miles upon miles of cables ready and available for you to use, but for a fee, of course. It is completely correct to think of your relationship with the telephone company as a rental agency. You are renting a cable from it, and because it makes money from the rental, let it worry about the logistics of getting the cable to connect you to your ISP. The phone company has been doing just that for years.

TCP/IP Connection

The TCP/IP connection is what is referred to as the "Transport Layer" because it does just that—it transports information across your Physical Network Connection. The transport layer will use the physical network connection to transmit information between you and your ISP. TCP/IP is the standard way to facilitate this sort of communication, which revolves around the concept that there is a need to send and receive information from one computer, with an IP address, to

Figure 4.8 Transport layer utilizes the physical network connection.

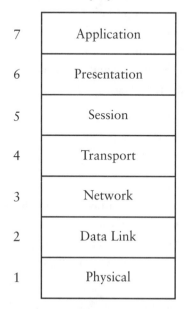

OSI 7-layer model

another, with an IP address. The trick is setting your Web server up with an IP address. This process can be broken into three steps:

1. Obtain the needed hardware to utilize the physical network connection to send and receive TCP/IP information.

2. Obtain an IP address from your ISP.

3. Configure the operating system to utilize the supplied IP address to communicate to the Internet.

The first two items depend on the ISP. Your ISP will recommend the hardware you will need to communicate with its network; similarly, it will issue you an IP address or a series of addresses. Along with your IP address, you will be given a "domain." A **domain** is a unique way of naming your company, for example, "your company.com" where "your company" is replaced with the name of your company. Your ISP will ask you for your domain name, at which time you will need to choose a domain name that has not yet been used on the Internet. To aid you in your selection you may use a program called Telnet to access an online directory of all domain names in use. To do so, use the Telnet application to connect to *internic.net*. Once connected, type "who-is-your company.com"; if it returns to you saying "no entry found," you have your new domain name.

After your ISP issues you a domain and a set of associated IP addresses, you will need to configure your Web server to use this new IP to provide its services to the Internet. This is done by modifying the operating system's network configuration to include the TCP/IP protocol and the supplied IP address. The process for installing an IP address in a Web server varies from operating system to operating system. Consult the documentation provided with your operating system or ask your ISP. Chances are the ISP has done exactly what you are doing many times before.

As a general point to mention, ISPs make their money by providing you with Internet access. It is in their best interest to help you, as much as possible, facilitate your need to get your Web server on the Net. Use your ISP as a resource to aid you in your task.

Installing a New Web Server

As stated earlier, sometimes the hardest part of a task is trying to find the right tool. Once you have selected the Web server hardware and software, all that is left is to pour yourself a big cup of Java, kick up your feet, grab your keyboard, and start going at it. Compared to the amount of time that you spent trying to figure out what to get, the process of configuring and installing your Web server will seem insignificant.

Once all the cables are plugged in and you have a working TCP/IP network connected to your service provider, the first step is to set up your Web server with its assigned IP address. Figure 4.9

Figure 4.9 NT TCP/IP setup screen.

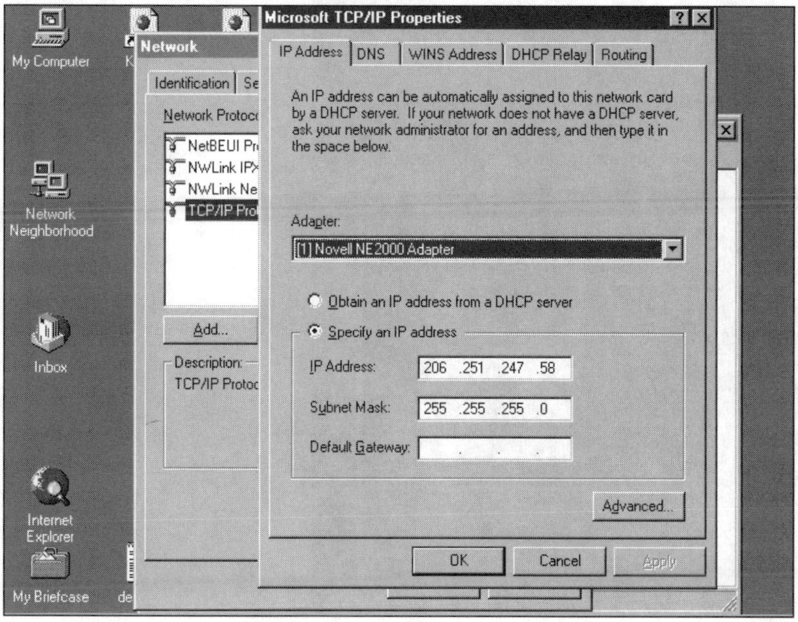

shows where to enter the TCP/IP-specific information, all of which will be supplied by your ISP. The process of setting up a UNIX computer with the TCP/IP-specific information consists of modifying certain text configuration files. For further information, refer to your documentation.

Once you believe everything is all set up, test your newly created Internet connection by issuing the command "ping internic.net". This will verify that everything from the Internet's point of view is working. Ping will send a small amount of data to internic.net, which internic.net will send right back to your connection, or in net jargon "back to your IP." The response to your ping command should look similar to Figure 4.10.

When you have received a satisfactory response from your "ping" test, it is time to install the Web server software. Most of the name-brand Web server software comes with a well-documented Web setup guide. Follow the instructions and you should be just fine, but before you begin installation make sure your have thought about the following:

1. Where to put the Web Server software?

2. Where to put the HTML, graphic, and Java files that will make up your Web site?

3. Is there plenty of space on the drive to contain the Web site?

Figure 4.10 Ping response.

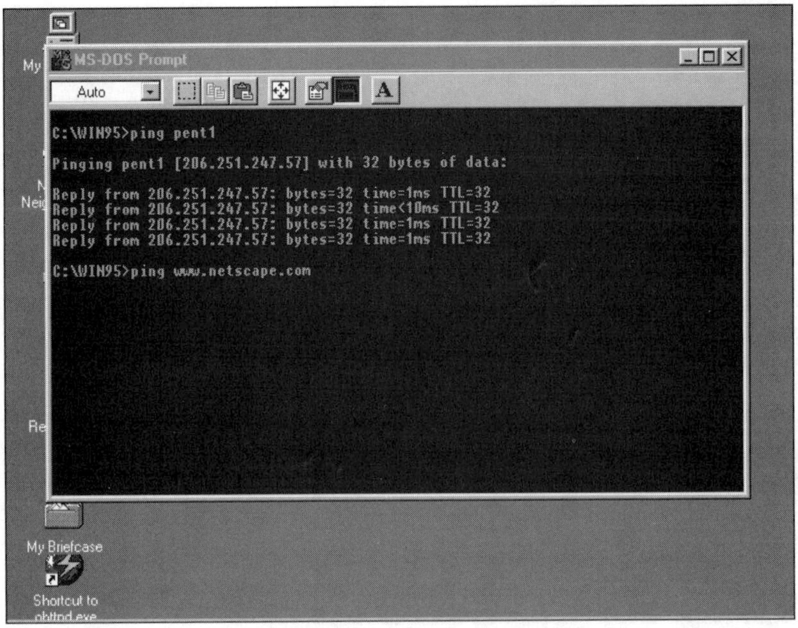

All Web server software will provide a mechanism to administer the Web server. For some, this means another application that must be used to set different characteristics of the Web server. Other servers, such as Netscape, will use a Web browser to access the server's configuration. That is, you will use your browser to do administration things to the Web server software. The only reason this is mentioned is that it sometimes throws people who may not be used to using a browser in that way.

When you have completed the installation of your Web server software, step back and tell your boss you need some sort of bonus, for you have completed what is by no means a trivial task. Be assured that the next installation you will set up will not be half as difficult. Regardless, if you ever intend to install another Web installation, you have this one working and have earned the right for your colleagues to call you the "Webmaster."

Creating Your Web Site

Now that you have a connection to the Internet, and a Web server to deploy your message to the World, the only thing left is to create your message. When you enter your browser to go to, say, www.xprime.com, this URL gets mapped to a specific HTML file on a computer named WWW in the domain XPRIME.COM. So, now that you have a ready and willing Web server, all that you need to do is replace that file with your own. For example, Microsoft Internet Information Server (IIS) by default setting will fetch "index.html" in the "webroot" directory. "Index.html" is called the entry point of your Web server, due to the fact that it is the default document for the system. When someone enters into their browser your Web server's computer name and domain, "yourcomputername.yourdomain.com", they will receive this index file.

The entry point for your site is now the starting point for your new Web site. The next chapter will discuss some tools to create HTML pages, as well as entire Webs sites. For now, be content with the fact that you achieved your initial goal: You have a working and connected Web server. So, go ask for a raise.

Summary

This chapter has taken you from ground zero, wherever that may have been, to having a functional Web server. The next step is to begin to create your Web site. This chapter provided some information on Web server hardware and software, as well as an overview of what is involved in setting up a Web installation. A general note to this chapter is that if someone is going to make money from your need to create a Web installation, be sure to utilize that person to the fullest potential. The telephone company and your ISP do this for a living, and they are usually more than willing to aid you in any way possible. However, there is one thing that you need to do yourself, and that is create your Web commerce site. The goal of the next few chapters is to make the process of creating this site as painless as possible.

Creating CGI and
Applet Order Forms

Within the pages of this chapter you will be exposed to a variety of different tools and resources for the development of custom commerce solutions. The goal of this chapter is to provide some useful information for the development of commerce order forms. Commerce Web sites are composed of a number of different pieces; this chapter focuses on the development of the piece that makes money, the order form. A complete set of examples is presented in Chapters 12 and 13 and is included on the accompanying CD. The goal of this chapter, for programmers and nonprogrammers alike, is to provide the fuel for future custom development. The content does lean toward the technical, but it offers some valuable information for nonprogrammers as well.

Data Input on the Web

HTML and the Web provide a uniform cross-platform delivery agent for information. Web browsers will present HTML content in a uniform manner regardless of the platform. Traditionally, HTML content was composed of different media objects embedded into text. As time passed, HTML began taking its cross-platform delivery powers into the realm of cross-platform data acquisition.

Beginning with HTML V2.0, the concept of HTML forms started to emerge. The initial constructions provided a mechanism with which to acquire data from HTML embedded widgets, such as radio buttons, text edit fields, and list boxes. Much as with regular HTML code, the browser would read in the HTML document and place these input widgets on the document, as it would for a graphic. However, the browser would be responsible for the delivery of this form information back to the Web server. When the Web server obtained this information, it would execute a CGI program to handle the information. This process might seem like a good, pleasant, and useful way of fulfilling the need to do something with the information obtained from the Web page, when, in fact, it turns into a horrid mess as the complexity of the input grows. Later in this chapter, the uses, pitfalls, and improvements of CGI technology will be discussed in more detail.

When Java first came on the scene, not all that long ago, its primary use was animation—so much so that many compared it to another technology, emerging at the same time, that could produce equally amazing animation. For a time, Macromedia Director's ShockWave and animated GIF files were compared with Java. Eventually Java began to stand out as a full-blown development environment capable of far more than any rival competition.

Yes, animation was a big thing on the Web—it had never been seen before, and it produced mass hysteria in the Web community. As Java found its way into more and more full-featured applications, more people began to take Java seriously. Users received Java as a full-featured development tool that provides answers to many of the problems ailing the Web. Later in this chapter, we will explore Java as a full-featured tool for data acquisition on the Web, and we will discuss linking Java data acquisition with the power of JDBC.

Java and CGI will continue to offer variations of data acquisition on the Web. Each provides its own unique solutions for data acquisition. However, in the field of electronic commerce on the Web, Java provides a secure, powerful, and simplified solution that has no match. Java gives electronic commerce off-the-shelf solutions that have revolutionized, and will continue to revolutionize, Web commerce.

CGI Data Acquisition—Post Processing

To fully understand the concept behind CGI applications, you must understand the nature of the interaction between a browser and a Web server, which can be broken down into three distinct phases of client/server communication:

1. The browser requests a resource, in the form of a URL, from the Web server.

2. The Web server fetches the resource and ships the contents back down to the browser.

3. The browser receives the requested resource and then terminates the connection.

The problem with this method might not be apparent, primarily because this interaction works just fine for static resources, such as images or text files. The problems start with the introduction of CGI applications producing dynamic content.

Take, for instance, the case of a simple order-entry HTML page. The HTML page containing all the code necessary for the browser to display the form is a static file. That is, the file doesn't just get up and change its content; it is a lifeless collection of bytes, lounging on your hard drive somewhere. When the Web server gets a request for that file, all it has to do is fetch it and send it back down the line.

Now, take a second to think about what happens after the user inputs the information on the HTML form and presses the "Submit" button. As we just specified in the guidelines for browser and server interaction, the browser will ask the server for a resource, which just happens to be an application, and the server will respond by providing that resource to the server. This method works well for static files because they can be fetched and "regurgitated." When the server is asked to display a CGI application, the server is responsible for executing that CGI application and returning the results. In the case of the order-entry form, the CGI will be given the information and will produce the appropriate HTML output.

The CGI will receive the information from the browser, only after the user is done entering the information. The CGI must post-process the information that came from the user because it cannot process information while it is being inputted. This becomes a problem when, say, one field that a user is expected to fill out depends on another field. As in Figure 5.1, the HTML form has a drop-down list of states and another of zip codes. We can predict that a user may enter a state that does not correspond to the selected zip code. In that case, the CGI would have to inform the user of the error after the mistake had been made, instead of limiting the user's selection of zip codes based on the state selection. This limitation revolves around the browser/server interaction and the nature of CGI applications. The post-processing limitation might not seem significant now, but later, when the problem is expanded in the section "Keeping the State," the problem can be properly viewed as the monster it truly is.

CGIs—Mysteries Unleashed

If you think CGI applications are a fancy name for a fancy thing, they're not. A CGI application takes information in from the browser and produces HTML coded output. Once again, the only difference between a CGI and a regular application is its ability to take information from the Web server and produce HTML formatted output. To really appreciate the simplicity behind CGI applications, you need to think in terms of command-line applications. **Command-line applications** are applications that are executed from the operating system's command line and that produce text

Figure 5.1 HTML State and Zip code selection list.

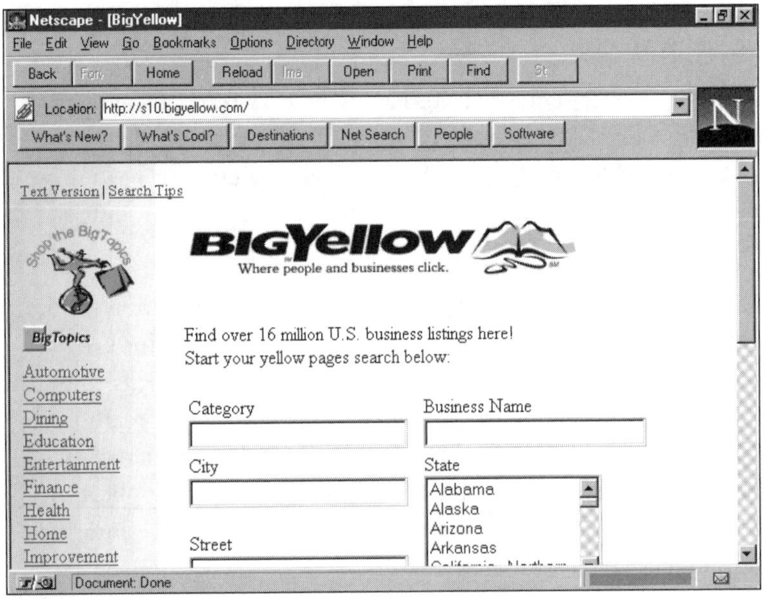

output to the screen. In DOS, this would be the equivalent of the "dir" command; in UNIX, the "ls" command. Both "dir" and "ls" could be executed from a command line to produce textual output on the screen. Different variations could be achieved by adding flags to the command, such as "dir /p" or "ls -u".

CGI applications are identical to console applications—not just from the programming standpoint, but also from the output and input standpoint. When the Web server executes the CGI application, it will do so by executing, internally, the CGI from a command line. The server will pass the arguments (that is, the HTML form information) to the CGI by means of command-line flags. The server will issue the complete command line, including all HTML form information, from an internal command prompt. By creating an internal command line, it has the ability to redirect the CGI's output from the screen to the browser that issued the request. (See Figure 5.2.)

CGI applications are, for all intents and purposes, command-line applications. There is no elaborate mechanism in place for the Web server to feed information to the CGI and to get responses. The device is identical to your executing the CGI from a command line. Although this mechanism provides a simple tool for one program communicating with another, it definitely has its shortcomings:

Figure 5.2 How a Web server executes a CGI.

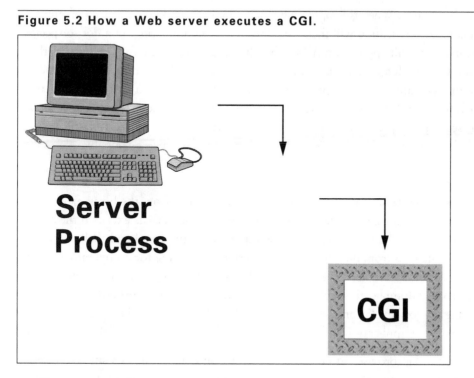

- Slow response time

- Use of relatively large amounts of memory and CPU resources

- Inability to keep state information

Slow Response Time

"Slow response time" refers to the time it takes from the moment when the Web server gets the request from the browser to when the Web server fulfills the request and sends it to the browser. In a CGI situation, the server must do the following to fulfill the browser's request:

1. The Web server must create a new command line shell from which to execute the CGI. In the Windows world, this action is equivalent to creating a new DOS window.

2. Once the command shell is created, the Web server will execute the CGI command and wait for an appropriate response.

Memory and CPU Resources

If it doesn't seem like that big a deal, try to look at it from the point of view of memory and CPU resources. For the Web server to create a command shell, it needs to execute an application that is a part of the operating system. When this operating system application, known as a command interpreter, is running, the application will then issue the CGI execution string. In a not so specific version, the Web server will call application A, which will then call application B. Herein lies the major problem with CGI: Both applications A and B require their own amount of memory and their own amount of CPU time. For CGI applications that don't get a lot of use, these two factors do not create a significant problem. The problem arises when the CGI is expected to service a constant flow of browser requests per second. In such cases, the Web server will need to fulfill the requests as quickly as possible, and with as few CPU and memory resources as possible.

Keeping the State

Earlier, when the process by which a CGI application fulfills a request from the browser was explained, the back-end cleanup steps were left out. After the Web server has executed the command shell from which the CGI application is to be executed, both the command shell and the CGI applications are unloaded from memory. This is a very normal thing for an operating system to do. Once the application is complete, there is no need to keep that application in memory. However, in the case of CGI applications, this seemingly normal and logical procedure adds multiple layers of complexity to the CGI program. The reason for this might not be apparent, so let's look at a fairly normal CGI application.

A Web user uses his or her browser to purchase something on the Web from a site that offers a shopping cart for the user's convenience. The user puts an item in the shopping cart and goes to the next page. From a CGI standpoint, the item that the user wishes to place into the shopping cart is fed to the CGI. How is the CGI going to keep track of the user's shopping cart if the CGI is expected to send the user to a new HTML page and then terminate? The CGI cannot maintain a variable, in memory, holding the contents of a specific user's shopping cart. Rather, the CGI must store that information in a file that contains all of the user's information. This might seem like a simple task, but now start thinking about all the "What ifs?".

- What if the user presses the browser's Back button? The shopping cart file must be able to delete the last item entered.

- What if the user enters items into the shopping cart but never checks out? The file will need a time-out period to allow deletion of nonactive users.

- What if there is more than one user on the system at a time? The CGI must be able to create unique user identifications.

What we are describing is a state machine. A **state machine** is a concept in discrete mathematics that can be summed up by this statement: "You are here and with some input, you will go there." The positions at which the machine can rest at are **states**; they are positions at which the machine can be placed based on the input. A shopping cart CGI begins with an empty cart state. When an item is added, the state will go from the empty state to the one-item state. If an item is removed, it will go back to the empty state. The CGI is responsible for keeping the specific state information for each user currently on the system. Figure 5.3 shows a small set of states that can be visited with a CGI shopping cart application.

In a state machine, the number of states that need to be accounted for is proportional to the size of the application. CGI applications not only need to keep track of the state the machine is currently in, it also needs to keep track of all machines for all users—and all of this needs to be done simultaneously. The solution to this problem is usually a library that the CGI uses to store state and user information in a file that can be read and updated to maintain the machine. Figure 5.4 is a JavaDoc-generated document describing such a library; this file can be found on your CD-ROM.

```
package CommerceUtils;

import java.io.IOException;
```

Figure 5.3 CGI shopping cart state machine.

Figure 5.4 User state diagram.

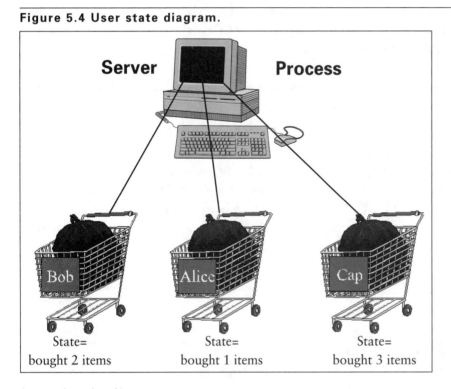

```
import java.io.File;
import java.util.Random;


//inifile.java

/**
 * The <tt>usermanager</tt> provides the ability to keep track of a
 * user as they make their way through a series of connected
 * Web pages.  In specific, the <tt>usermanager</tt> provides the
 * means to facilitate a "Shopping Cart" Commerce interface.
 *
 * The system revolves around two distinct sets of data, static and
 * statefull.  The Static set remains constant regardless of state.
 * State information contains information local to the current Web page.
 * If the user decides to "go back" to a previous page, the information will
 * reflect this jump.
 *
 * @version 1.0
 * @author Cary A. Jardin
 */
```

```java
public class usermanager extends Object{
    private static String Static_Header    =    "STATIC";
    private static String BaseHeader        =    "STATE";
    private static int     BaseState        =    345;
    private static int     NameLength       =    8;

    private String    BasePath             =    ".\\";
    private String    StateExtension       =    ".usr";
    private boolean   CopyPrevState        =    true;
    private inifile   StateStorage         =    null;
    private Random    filegenerator        =    new Random();
    private boolean   OkState              =    false;

    /**
     * NextState provides the next state identifier
     */
    public   int      NextState            =    0;

    /**
     * The User property contains the unique UserID
     */
    public   String   User                 =    "";


    //Constructors

    /**
     * The constructor will load the state specified by "State"
     * for "UserID".  On success the state information will be
     * available, and NextState will be incremented to the next
     * state.
     *
     * If the object is unable to be created properly, all methods
     * will return an error.
     *
     * The CpyLast flag can be set to copy the information from the
     * last state the NextState.
     *
     * @param UserID           The user ID, if value is null a new User will
     *                         be initiated.
     * @param State            The state's information to load.
     * @param basepath         The base path of where the User files are to be stored.
     *                         Assumed to contain a trailing a "\".
     * @param stateextension   The extension to append onto the User files.
     * @param CpyLast          Copy all of the information stored in the past state,
     *                         into the NextState. Used if one state retains a memory
```

```
 *                           of prior state.
 * @exception IOException    Will be thrown for two reasons, each of which will
 *                           contain the following message, "Invalid State", or
 *                           "Invalid UserId"
 */
public usermanager(String UserID, String State,
                   String basepath, String stateextension,
                   boolean CpyLast) throws IOException
{
    super();
    initstate(UserID,State,basepath,stateextension,CpyLast);
}



/**
 * The constructor will load the state specified by "State"
 * for "UserID".  On success the state information will be
 * available, and NextState will be incremented to the next
 * state. This constructor assumes that default values for the following
 * will be used, basepath, stateextension, CpyLast.
 *
 *
 * @param UserID            The user ID, if value is null a new User will
 *                          be initiated.
 * @exception IOException   Will be thrown for two reasons, each of which will
 *                          contain the following message, "Invalid State", or
 *                          "Invalid UserId"
 */
public usermanager(String UserID, String State) throws IOException{

    super();
    initstate(UserID,State,BasePath,StateExtension,CopyPrevState);
}

/**
 * This constructor will init a new User, and load the beginning state. Further
 * default value for the following will be used, basepath, stateextension,
 * CpyLast.
 *
 * @exception IOException   Will be thrown for two reasons, each of which will
 *                          contain the following message, "Invalid State", or
 *                          "Invalid UserId"
 */
public usermanager() throws IOException{

    super();
```

```
        initstate(null,null,BasePath,StateExtension,CopyPrevState);
}


/**
 * Retrieves the passed state property's value.
 *
 * @param property       The property's value to retrieve.
 * @param DefaultValue   If the property does not exist, this value will be returned.
 * @return               Returns either the property's value, or DefaultValue on error.
 */
public String GetStateProperty(String property, String defaultvalue){
    if(!OkState)
        return defaultvalue;
    else
        return StateStorage.GetProperty(BaseHeader + NextState , property, defaultvalue);
}


/**
 * Adds a property and a value to current state.
 *
 * @param property       The property's name to add.
 * @param Value          The passed property's value.
 * @return               Returns false if the property already exists.
 */
public boolean AddStateProperty(String property, String value){
    if(!OkState)
        return false;
    else
        return StateStorage.AddProperty(BaseHeader +NextState ,property, value);
}



/**
 * Modifies a property's value in the current state.
 *
 * @param property       The property's name to be modified.
 * @param Value          The passed property's value.
 * @return               Returns false if the property does not exist
 */
public boolean ModifyStateProperty(String property, String value){
    if(!OkState)
        return false;
    else
        return StateStorage.ModifyProperty(BaseHeader +NextState ,property, value);
}
```

```
/**
 * Checks the existence of a state property.
 *
 * @param PropertyName    The property to check.
 * @return                Returns true if the property exist.
 */
public boolean StatePropertyExists(String property){
    if(!OkState)
        return false;
    else
        return StateStorage.PropertyExits(BaseHeader + NextState , property);
}


/**
 * Deletes the passed state property.
 *
 * @param PropertyName    The property name to delete.
 * @return                Returns false if the property does not exist.
 */
public boolean DeleteStateProperty(String property){
    if(!OkState)
        return false;
    else
        return StateStorage.DeleteProperty(BaseHeader +NextState ,property);
}


/**
 * Retrieves the passed static property's value.
 *
 * @param property        The property's value to retrieve.
 * @param DefaultValue    If the property does not exist, this value will be returned.
 * @return                Returns either the property's value, or DefaultValue on error.
 */
public String GetStaticProperty(String property, String defaultvalue){
    if(!OkState)
        return "";
    else
        return StateStorage.GetProperty(Static_Header , property, defaultvalue);
}


/**
 * Adds a property and a value to the static information.
 *
 * @param property        The property's name to add.
 * @param Value           The passed property's value.
 * @return                Returns false if the property already exists.
```

```java
    */
public boolean AddStaticProperty(String property, String value){
        if(!OkState)
          return false;
      else
          return StateStorage.AddProperty(Static_Header,property, value);
}

/**
  * Modifies a property's value in the static set.
  *
  * @param property        The property's name to be modified.
  * @param Value           The passed property's value.
  * @return                Returns false if the property does not exist
  */
public boolean ModifyStaticProperty(String property, String value){
    if(!OkState)
        return false;
    else
        return StateStorage.ModifyProperty(Static_Header ,property, value);
}

/**
  * Checks the existence of a static property.
  *
  * @param PropertyName    The property to check.
  * @return                Returns true if the property exists.
  */
public boolean StaticPropertyExists(String property){
    if(!OkState)
        return false;
    else
        return StateStorage.PropertyExits(Static_Header , property);
}

/**
  * Deletes the passed static property.
  *
  * @param PropertyName    The property name to delete.
  * @return                Returns false if the property does not exist.
  */
public boolean DeleteStaticProperty(String property){
    if(!OkState)
        return false;
    else
        return StateStorage.DeleteProperty(Static_Header ,property);
```

```
    }

    /**
     * Saves the state information to the user's file.
     *
     * @return              Returns true if the file is successfully saved.
     */
    public boolean SaveState(){
          if(!OkState)
              return false;
        else
            return StateStorage.SaveToFile();
    }

    private void initstate(String UserID, String State,
                    String basepath, String stateextension,
                    boolean CpyLast) throws IOException
          {

            String Filename = "";

            BasePath        =     basepath;
            StateExtension  =     stateextension;
            CopyPrevState   =     CpyLast;

            //check for the file
            if(UserID == null){
                CopyPrevState   = false;
                NextState       = BaseState;
                Filename        = GenFileNewName();
                StateStorage = new inifile(GenFileNewName());
            }
            else{

                User = UserID;

                if(!FileExists(UserID)){
                    throw(new IOException("Invalid UserId"));
                }

                StateStorage = new inifile(BasePath + UserID + StateExtension);

                //load the state;

                if(!StateStorage.SectionExits(State)){
                    throw(new IOException("Invalid State"));
                }
```

```
            try{
                NextState = new Integer(State).intValue() + 1;
            }
            catch(Exception e){
                throw(new IOException("Invalid State"));
            }

            //delete it if it exists
            StateStorage.DeleteSection(BaseHeader+NextState);

            if(CopyPrevState)
                StateStorage.CopySection(BaseHeader + (NextState - 1),BaseHeader +
NextState);
            else
                StateStorage.NewSection(BaseHeader + NextState);
        }

        OkState = true;
    }

    private boolean FileExists(String tryme){

        File trymefile = null;

        try{
            trymefile = new File(BasePath + tryme + StateExtension);
        }
        catch(Exception e){
            //If their is a problem, don't use that file
            return true;
        }

        return trymefile.exists();
    }

    private String GenFileNewName(){

        String  temp    = "";
        String  good    = "";
        File    tryme   = null;

        for(;;){
            //generate a random id
            temp = "" + Math.abs(filegenerator.nextInt());

            User = temp;
            //see if that id exists
```

```
        try{
            if(temp.length() > NameLength)
                good = BasePath + temp.substring(0,NameLength-1) + StateExtension;
            else
                good = BasePath + temp + StateExtension;
            tryme = new File(good);
        }
        catch(Exception e){
        }

        if(!tryme.exists())
            break;
    }

    return good;
    }


}
```

The supplied user manager class provides a simplified way of creating complicated CGI applications. Nevertheless, writing CGI applications is by no means easy. Not only do you have to deal with the maintenance of the state machine, you also have to deal with added states that are associated with post-processing the HTML form information. The more you think about CGI, the more bewildered you will become. It works exceptionally well for small applications, but for large applications, it proves to be very demanding from both the programming and computer resource viewpoints.

Improvements to CGI

In the industry, it is well known, and documented, that CGI applications could not produce the type of performance needed for busy CGI-based Web sites. To meet this need, a number of different vendors have come up with alternative solutions to the problem. As with most new technologies, the powers at play in the development of the technology are jockeying to make their solution a standard. At this time, there is no widely accepted replacement for CGI applications. The following contains some brief information about each of the separate solutions, including where to find more information.

FastCGI

Product: FastCGI

Contact: http://www.fastcgi.com

Features: FastCGI provides the same language-independent qualities of CGI, but it incorporates a new set of features, allowing it to function in even the most intensive applications.

ILU Requester

Product: ILU Requester

Contact: http://www.digicool/releases/WD-ILU-Requestor.html

Features: ILU Requester provides an object-oriented model for distributed server-based objects. Objects can dynamically extend the Web server's capabilities to meet your specific CGI needs. Although very much like Jeeves, Sun's Java-based Web server, it does not limit itself to a specific development language. This method offers a clean, elegant, and fast solution to CGI.

Netscape Server API

Product: NSAPI (Netscape Server API)

Contact: http://home.netscape.com/misc/developer/conference/proceedings/s5/sld003.html

Internet Server API

Product: ISAPI (Internet Server API)

Contact: http://nt.bnt.com

SAPI Spyglass Server Application Development Interface

Product: SAPI Spyglass Server Application Development Interface

Contact: http://www.spyglass.com

Apache API

Product: Apache API

Contact: http://www.apache.org

Features: NSAPI, ISAPI, SAPI, and Apache API are all essentially server-side plug-ins. CGI applications are created to merge with the specific server. They all have similar characteristics; however, each requires its own specific interface—and that is why there are so many of them.

Java—The Distributed Solution

If you step back and take a look at what CGI actually is, you will find that it is a textbook model of centralized computing. This approach matches that used in the days of mainframe applications, when the "dumb" client machines were not responsible for execution of the application in use. The mainframe was the central point of processing power; it was responsible for the proper execution of each of the client applications.

The term "dumb" was used to describe the client machines, for they are, in fact, called "dumb terminals." They were used as an interface mechanism with users. In many ways, a Web browser is a dumb terminal: It acts solely as an interface between the information stored, various Web servers, and the end user. Along the same lines, CGI applications perform an identical role to stored mainframe applications. This model of centralized computing offers the ability to span cross-platform display mechanisms, but it does have some limitations. The Java revolution, much like the PC revolution, has brought intelligence to the client platforms. It has taken centralized CGI applications and moved them into distributed, client-based solutions. Figure 5.5 shows many to one mapping of clients to a central server.

Figure 5.5 Distributed processing model.

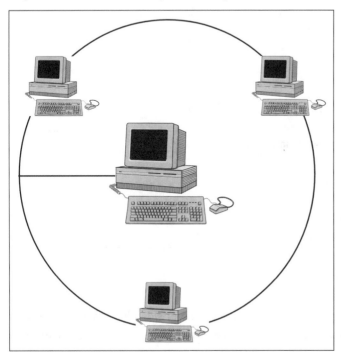

As previously discussed, the majority of the problems with implementing a CGI commerce application are caused by the post-processing nature of CGI. The Java-based alternative to CGI provides solutions that are considerably less complicated and, for the most part, more intuitive. The problems faced when creating a CGI solution are specific to the nature of CGI; on the other hand, Java solutions are framed in a more familiar context for most programmers. Java solutions are not constrained by the post-processing mechanism of CGI; they therefore can provide a more interactive experience.

Take the example that was used to illustrate the post-processing mechanism of CGI—a state and Zip code selection list. In CGI, users could initially select an invalid combination of state and Zip code. The user would not be informed of the problem until he or she had submitted the HTML form. Java is an intelligent client, which means it has the ability to provide instant feedback. Using the same example of the state and Zip code selection list, with Java the user would not be allowed to make an invalid entry. The client can dynamically make decisions, such as to limit the user's selection of Zip codes based on the state selected. This might sound like a small problem, but keep in mind it is always more effective to prevent a problem than to fix it after it has happened.

Ubiquitous Database Clients with JDBC

Java clients can provide a vast audience with a common interface, one that can be used for a full variety of self-contained applications. For business and commerce solutions, having an interface that can't collect information is almost as useless as a modem without a phone. Herein lies the need and purpose of JDBC, Java Data Base Connectivity. JDBC gives Java applications the ability to communicate with a variety of databases. Java empowered with JDBC cannot only collect information into a central repository, but can act as a dynamic distribution agent of centralized data. Java, coupled with JDBC, provides database client solutions that span platform boundaries to do everything, exist everywhere, and be accessible all the time.

CGI Script Form Solutions

By now, you should have a pretty good idea of the shortcomings of HTML- and CGI-based data acquisition. Issues such as speed and complexity of programming should ring a bell. The CGI and HTML approaches definitely present some problems with large applications, but for small, single-form processing, CGI isn't all that bad. In fact, for many small needs, writing a Java applet could be viewed as overkill. CGI solutions have been around for quite some time and will continue to exist to provide small-scale Web commerce solutions.

CGI Authoring Tools

For small applications, CGI applications have to verify the information in the form and do some minimal processing of the acquired information. In these cases, tools called CGI generators can be used to give nonprogrammers the ability to create simple CGI "scripts." These script generators, as they are called, make CGI applications accessible to nonprogrammers. Script generators can provide simple data acquisition forms or the basis for more complicated commerce solutions. Either way, these tools provide enough usefulness and functionality to check out. The following is a list of CGI authoring tools.

> **S c r i p t s** Notice the use of "scripts" after CGI? Many people in the industry refer to CGI applications as scripts to eliminate the anxiety associated with programming. Scripts are programs that are written in a script language, such as Perl, UNIX Shell, and DOS batch-file programming.

CyberTerp

Product: CyberTerp

Contact: http://www.hyperact.com/

Features: CyberTerp provides a full-featured mechanism for creating CGI applications.

CGI Script Libraries

One of the best ways to program is to leverage what someone else has done, then try to mold it to fit your specific needs. CGI scripts are no exception to this rule. The number of CGI libraries available on the Web is amazing. Almost anything you can think of has been done before, and it is now ready for you to use. Knowing what is out there, and how to get it, will be an invaluable approach to creating a CGI solution. The following is a list of CGI script libraries and where they can be found.

Web Developer's Virtual Library: CGI

Library: Web Developer's Virtual Library: CGI

Contact: http://www.charm.net/~web/Vlib/Providers/CGI.html

Features: The WDVL is a major Web developer resource, bridging the spectrum between W3C and Yahoo! by providing local content and thousands of links to CGI resources.

Figure 5.6 Screen shot from WebGenie.

CGI*Star

Product: CGI*Star

Contact: http://www.webgenie.com/

Features: CGI*Star provides a straightforward means of creating powerful CGI form processors. WebGenie offers a test platform for your generated CGIs. Figure 5.6 is the WebGenie home page.

INTRCOM's Interactive CGI Library

Library: INTRCOM's Interactive CGI Library

Contact: http://www.intrcom.com/manuals/forms.html

Features: INTRCOM provides a number of form processors and other interactive utilities to enhance your WWW pages.

Programming Your Own CGI Application

Unfortunately, programming is a fact of life in the world of CGI applications, but that does not have to be a bad thing. CGI programming is seen by many as a great entry point for non-programmers to begin developing applications. If you have programming knowledge, you will find that CGI application development is very rewarding and relatively simple. Just keep in mind that you can write CGI applications in almost any language in which you feel comfortable; you are not bound to use languages like Perl. For nonprogrammers, CGI applications are a great place to begin. For programmers and nonprogrammers alike, a great book to help develop your CGI skills is John Deep's *Developing CGI Applications with Perl*, published by John Wiley & Sons.

> **Java CGI** Using Java to program CGI is becoming more and more popular. Java provides a wealth of useful functionality, not to mention its cross-platform nature, to the CGI developer.

Applet Solutions

Applets are full-fledged, full-featured applications that just happen to access the Internet. The days of applets being seen as merely tools for Web-based animation is gone. Java and applets have come to be known as an effective tool for all sorts of application development. For the purpose of Web commerce, the best use of applets is to provide secure, interactive, and simple interfaces in which to allow the user a secure purchasing mechanism.

CGI applications are capable of providing Web users with sufficient means to facilitate commerce. The point is not as simple as saying that one method can do what the other can't. One technology just works better than the other. CGI applications are completely capable of facilitating commerce; however the way in which it is done differs from what the users understand. CGI solutions do not provide the level of instant gratification that Java provides. CGI users might have to work their way through a number of different HTML pages to complete the order. This is especially poor, considering the current speed limitations of the current Internet user.

Applets give the user instant gratification by presenting information in a more interactive manner. Instead of making users take it upon themselves to complete a series of Web pages for a single order, applets provide a quick, interactive, and all-in-one interface. "Quick" is really the key word here, for if users spend longer than one or two minutes to purchase a product, they are no longer making an impulse buy. This might not seem like a selling point for an applet-based commerce solution, but the fact remains: When people want to buy something, especially people on the Internet, they do not want it to be an all-day process. As shown in Figure 5.7 with the CardShield applet, applets provide commerce solutions that are quick, easy, and secure.

Security. Beyond anything, the single biggest concern regarding the Web commerce solution is security. Whether this is a valid concern, or just a topic that the media can use as filler, is debatable. Either way, security is in the minds of all Web users, and it needs to be addressed. Applets and CGI both offer the same basic security measures, and without looking at RCS (Random Class Security) by Shielded Technologies, Inc., they are equal. When you throw RCS on the scale, the balance definitely starts to lean toward Java as the more secure. Shielded Technologies guaranties the security of any transaction that uses RCS; no similar guarantee exists for any CGI-based security method.

Figure 5.7 CardShield applet.

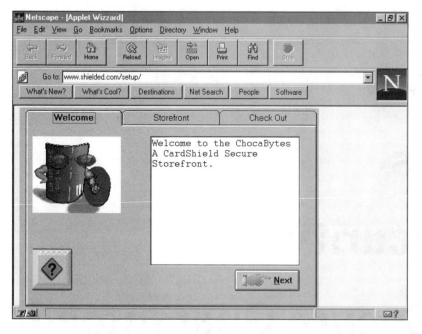

Creating Applet Solutions

Sun did a very sneaky thing when it named Java—it doesn't even sound like a programming language. C and C++ are known as hard-core programming languages, and for most people, they conjure the idea that only rocket scientists can use them. Java is a close relative to C++, but don't let that throw you. People who are comfortable with C++ will have no problem picking up Java. Individuals who know other languages will find Java to be very straightforward, and possibly even less foreign than C++. For everyone else, computer people and non-computer people alike, they don't have to learn Java to have their own commerce applet. Chapter 7 will explain how to set up and use CardShield by Shielded Technologies, which requires no programming and only basic computer knowledge to create your own commerce applet. Figure 5.8 shows Shielded's security guarantee which applies to all commerce applications written with the CardShield API.

Visual Tools

Programmers and nonprogrammers are seeing the ease of visual programming tools. **Visual programming** refers to a point-and-click approach to creating applications, to the extent that simple applications can be created without ever using the keyboard. There are a number of visual tools on the market; Visual Café by Symantec stands out as particularly good. Visual tools give pro-

Figure 5.8 Shielded Technologies Guarantee.

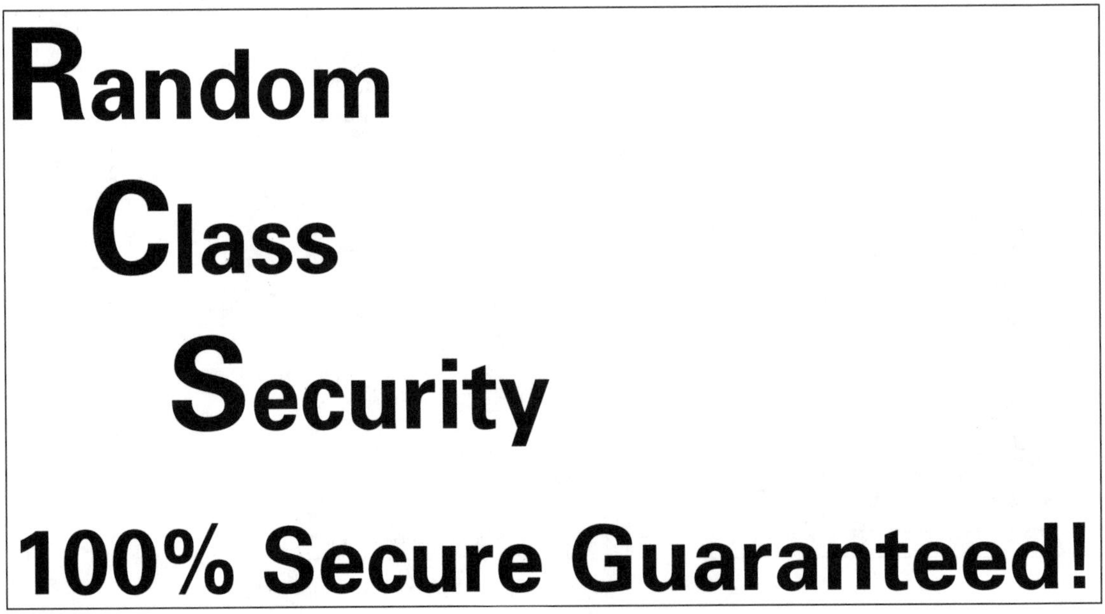

Random

Class

Security

100% Secure Guaranteed!

grammers the ability to create applications rapidly, and nonprogrammers are amazed at what they can do. In either case, visual development tools are the logical choice for nonprogrammers and programmers alike. *Symantec Visual Café Sourcebook* (to be published by Wiley in Spring 1997) provides the means to take full advantage of visual programming. Figure 5.9 shows an example of the Visual Café IDE (Integrated Development Environment).

Summary

Many people are beginning to see the scope of the Java revolution: It not only affects the Web, it affects the whole computing world. Using Java as remote database clients might seem completely logical and effective; however, the technology is new enough that this is still a cutting-edge vision. Java and JDBC provide all the tools necessary to facilitate secure Web commerce, and to provide a level of security that has no equal. This chapter exposed you to the technologies available to create Web commerce solutions. In general, custom commerce solutions require a decent amount of programming.

The goal of this chapter was to provide some insight into creating commerce solutions from scratch, including where to find and how to use help resources. If you do not think of yourself as

Figure 5.9 Visual Café.

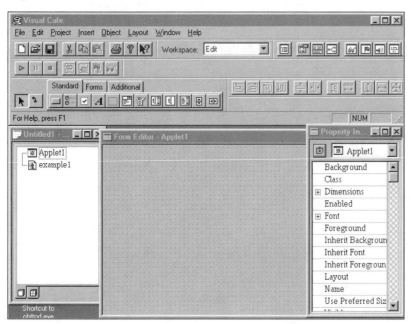

a programmer, you are not alone—neither does half of the Microsoft development staff. Seriously, do not let the fact that a custom solution requires programming stop you. Rather, take a stab at it. This chapter gave you some example resources to aid in development, and Chapters 12 and 13 are teeming with prefab examples, ready for you to explore. The best way to learn how to program is by example.

6

Credit-Card Transactions

This chapter discusses the credit-card transaction process and gives you the information you need to choose the right solution. Topics such as IC Verify, Merchant ID, and CardShield are covered.

Handling Credit Cards

Imagine yourself walking aimlessly, trying to find something to eat; however, you have no cash, only a credit card. If you have ever been in this situation, you know that the first thing you look for, when searching for a potential restaurant, is the obvious signs that the merchant accepts credit cards. The first sign would undoubtedly be the sign outside the store telling the world "plastic accepted here." If you fail to see any obvious signs outside, you might get desperate enough to venture into the establishment to look for the icon of credit-card sales, the little box that the merchant uses to swipe your card. In this scenario alone, you are exposed to two icons of credit-card sales. Whenever you see either of these icons, you are assured that that merchant is a secure facility for the processing of credit transactions.

On the Web, there is no such icon. And there is no standard processing mechanism, such as the card swipe machine. On the Internet, each facilitator of Web commerce is solely responsible for the secure processing of its clients' credit transactions. As a facilitator of Web commerce, you have a responsibility to your customers to provide a secure mechanism for processing their orders. Figure 6.1 shows a mechanism commonly used to reassure customers that the Web merchant is taking pains to secure their order.

The media—and companies trying to sell secure solutions—have depicted the Web as a big, bad, nasty place, a place teeming with people waiting to steal you blind with fraudulent credit-card charges. Whether this is a valid concern or just another "cold fusion" media hype still remains to be seen. As a facilitator of Web commerce, you must provide the most secure facility possible for your clients. Although there is no standard, off-the-shelf mechanism for doing so, certain fundamental elements must be present in all commerce sites:

1. A secure mechanism for the transport of order information

2. An application for processing order information

3. A merchant ID

4. A method for credit-card authorization

Figure 6.1 Web commerce pages often contain an "About Our Security" link.

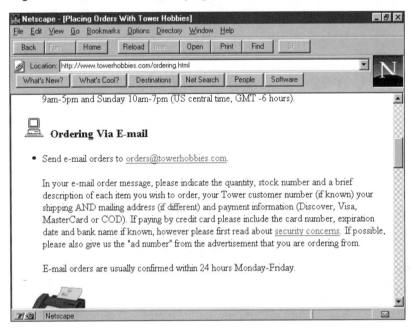

Secure Transport

Chapter 2 discussed some of the methods, such as HTTPS, for the secure transport of volatile information. If your commerce solution involves CGI-based form processing, you have limited options for a secure transport method. CGI commerce solutions are bound to using HTTPS for their secure transport needs. HTTPS relies on the client and server's ability to securely transport the HTML form information. For applet-based commerce, the choice of a secure transport mechanism isn't as cut-and-dried.

Applets are fully capable applications, and so can handle secure communication in their own way. With applets, you can write your own secure transport mechanism; however, it takes a decent amount of programming. The more viable option is Sun's Java-based security package, which provides a prefab mechanism to communicate with a server, using the same security package. This method would require both a custom client and a custom server to be written for your application.

A plethora of companies are trying to provide secure commerce mechanisms, including VeriFone and Microsoft, with its BackOffice merchant services. HTTPS provides an adequate level of security for Web commerce, as does Sun's SSL and Shielded Technologies' RCS. The choice of a secure transport mechanism depends greatly on how deeply you want to go into the bowels of Web commerce. To give you a little more direction, Chapter 12 will provide some examples for both CGI and Applet commerce solutions.

Processing Credit Cards

Once the order information has made it safely to the waiting hands of either your CGI or your applet, you have to do something with the information. One useful thing is to process the credit-card information, not just for the obvious reason of getting paid but also to verify that the user has entered a valid credit-card number. This real-time verification process is not 100 percent necessary. Web solutions can provide real-time processing or post-processing of credit-card transactions. Figure 6.2 illustrates this fundamental architectural difference.

Batch Processing

It is fully legal for your Web commerce solution to pool all of your orders together to be processed on a regular basis. This type of processing is called **batch processing**. Think about a store that, instead of processing your credit card at the time of the sale, writes down your information and processes all of the credit cards at the end of the day. In terms of a Web commerce solution, this means that instead of processing the transaction at the time it is entered, all the

Figure 6.2 Batch and real-time processing.

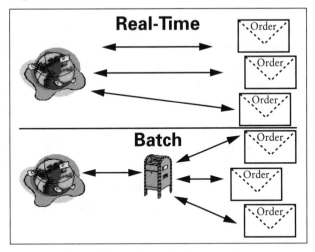

orders are simply put into a file to be processed at a later time. The major issues for this method are the following:

- The inability to inform the user of input errors

- The inability to inform the customer immediately if the card is accepted or declined

- Longer order processing time

For some people, the inability to quickly and accurately inform the user of an error isn't that big a deal; for others, it is unacceptable. Say you are Joe/Jane user, who came to a Web site to purchase a pair of shoes. Joe/Jane user uses the provided interface to order a great new pair of sneakers. However, a 9 was transposed for a 6 on the credit-card number input field. With post-processing, Joe/Jane would have to be contacted to clarify the error. For the most part, consumers assume that they would be prompted if they entered an invalid entry. In all fairness, this is not that big a concern. It primarily revolves around the image you want to instill in your customers.

Along the lines of the input error issue, the second issue is not being able to inform the users immediately of a problem with their credit card. This issue is a little bit more embarrassing: It is one thing to inform a user that the input is invalid, but it is another to say that his or her credit is no good. From the standpoint of a Web commerce provider, it really makes no difference. If the card cannot hold a charge, then there is no money to be had. From the users' point of view, an interface that lets them either cancel their order or simply use another card, without having to talk to an actual person, is a definite plus. The alternative to this method would put the user into the situation of having to explain to a customer service representative why their card is no good.

Probably the most detrimental side effect to batch processing is giving the user the impression that the order is not handled immediately. Web clientele want the value-added feeling that by placing their order on the Internet, it is of higher priority than another order placed by fax, or telephone. Call it technological supremacy, but Web users feel that the Web should offer the most advanced high-tech mechanisms possible, and part of that is online, rapid order entry. It is completely possible to give your users the impression that their order is processed in real time, but if they find out it is not, they might not purchase from your Web site in the future.

On the plus side, you can create a batch processing commerce solution at a fraction of a real-time solution's cost. The big reason for the cost break is that batch-processing solutions do not require your own dedicated Internet access, and you are free to use off-the-shelf credit-card transaction devices. Batch processing also requires less programming, for it does not require a lot of verification and authorization procedures. Batch processing provides an effective solution for companies that have a limited number of transactions per day. In creating your own Web commerce site, it is important to keep this solution in mind as a low budget, simplistic alternative to real-time processing solutions.

Real-time Processing

For many people using credit cards has become a way of life. Most people have a certain script associated with credit-card purchasing. When using a credit card at a place of business, the usual routine is to give your card to an employee, who then processes the transaction. If the employee wrote down your credit-card number on a piece of paper, you probably would be a little leery. The more you use your credit card, the more conditioned you become to expect the transaction processing to take place at the time of the sale. When users make a purchase on the Internet, they expect the Web commerce application to play by the same rules of credit-card conduct to which they are accustomed. The set of problems that faced batch processing are the strengths of real-time processing:

- The ability to inform the user of input errors

- Real-time order confirmation

- Faster order processing time

Users make errors; that is just common knowledge. In creating a user interface, it is usually common practice to notify the user as soon as possible about any detectable error. Doing so eliminates the need for "damage control" procedures and streamlines the back-end processing of data. In the case of Web commerce, immediately notifying a user of invalid input not only does away with a back-office support staff for handling the errors, but also condenses the processing of the order information. Users have come to expect real-time feedback, especially when it comes to Web applications—anything else would be less than average.

Users would prefer to be informed electronically if there is a problem with their card. In the batch-processing model, the user would have to be contacted personally if the card was invalid. With the ability of real-time order processing comes the ability to give real-time feedback, and with that comes the ability to accept or decline the card at the time the order is entered. The importance of this feature of real-time processing should not be underestimated. The ability to accept or decline the transaction while the users can still be reached eliminates the need for you to deal with anything but valid and paid orders. If a card is invalid, the user must either cancel the order or use a different card. In either case you will not be bothered with any order unless it is a valid, legitimate, and paid order.

Real-time processing not only gives the user the sense that the order is processed faster, it actually can be processed faster and more cheaply. Large-volume sites will see this benefit more than small-volume sites. Small-volume sites might not need the ability to tie directly to a back-office, accounting, or order-entry application. Rather, they can process the orders equally fast if the orders sit in a file until they get home from their day job. Large volume sites can eliminate the need for the input of redundant data and expedite the order more quickly than an order that requires manual intervention. For both small- and large-volume sites, it never hurts to make it look as if you know what you are doing.

Merchant ID

When you are issued a credit card, you are given a credit-card number. Without being obvious, this number is used to identify the account with which the credit card is associated. On the other side of the rainbow, each merchant that has the ability to accept your credit card must have a merchant ID. This merchant ID is associated with the merchant's bank account. In a typical transaction, the customer will give his or her credit-card number to the merchant. The merchant will then use a device to submit the credit-card number and his or her merchant ID to a card authorization service. With the information given to the authorization service, it will then proceed to debit the account associated with your credit card and credit it to the account associated with the merchant's merchant ID. In essence, if you want to accept credit cards, you must obtain a merchant ID.

Just as credit-card numbers are used for spending, merchant IDs are used for taking money. That is, a merchant ID is the mechanism by which the merchant gets paid. The money from the credit card gets debited from the customer's account and is credited to the merchant's account.

How long this process takes depends on whether the merchant ID is obtained through the merchant's bank or if it is obtained through a third party. In some cases, the money is credited to the merchant's account at the time of the sale; others have a holding policy. The companies that issue merchant ID are the merchant's entry point to facilitating electronic sales. Though their facilities the merchant will get paid; in this way these companies are the merchant's key to the most common form of electronic fund transfers, credit-card sales.

Merchant IDs can be obtained from a number of different sources. Because the merchant ID is essentially a link between the merchant's bank account and the customer's credit card, the best place to start is your bank. Most banks can issue merchant IDs and get you established. If you are starting from scratch and need both a merchant ID and a merchant account, Wells Fargo Online provides a wide range of Internet service for home banking and for merchants. Here is a list of some useful Web resources for obtaining all of your banking and credit-card needs:

- www.wellsfargo.com

- www.rontek.com

- www.verifone.com

It is usually good practice to rely on the expertise of a banking institution, at least when it comes to getting a merchant ID. Most banks will have a packet with all the information you will need, waiting and ready to ship to you. It is worth noting that banks are not the only source for obtaining a merchant ID; there are, in fact, companies that specialize in getting merchants up and ready to accept credit cards as a source of payment. The best source to find these companies is in your local yellow pages. Whether you end up getting your merchant ID from your bank or from your phone book, here is the essential information you will need:

- Credit-card type—Specifies the type of authorization service you will use

- Terminal type—Specifies the type of mechanism you will use to authorize the transaction

- Merchant number—May go by a number of different names, all of which are essentially a merchant ID

- Terminal ID—Specifies your particular location

- Primary and secondary access phone numbers—These will be needed to call up and process a transaction

Method for Credit-Card Authorization

Both post- and real-time processing methods need some way of processing the transaction with a credit-card fulfillment service. For non-Internet merchants, the card swipe machine is the tool of choice for this task. For Web commerce merchants, the mechanism used to process the credit card varies based on the specifics of the commerce solution. For example, if your Web commerce solution takes on the batch-processing method, you may wish to simply hand enter the daily orders into a card swipe terminal. For real-time solutions, the process of authorizing the credit card must be automated to let an application facilitate the authorization without any human intervention. The following is a list of all the possible authorization mechanisms. They each provide a unique set of characteristics to blend seamlessly into your commerce solution.

- Card swipe terminal

- CardShield

- IC Verify

Card Swipe Terminal

Card swipe devices are probably the most common form of authorization device for non-Web-based commerce merchants. These devices are based on some sort of user input, either swiping a card through a magnetic reader or manually entering the credit-card number and expiration date. Due to this minor drawback, this method of authorization is unable to facilitate real-time processing solutions. That is not to say that these devices are not useful—quite the contrary. For solutions that can work with user intervention, card swipe terminals provide an inexpensive, compact, and relatively simple mechanism for authorizing credit-card transactions. If you wish to pursue this solution further, contact the same source that you used to obtain your merchant ID. Your bank or credit-card fulfillment house usually has specials on these devices.

CardShield

Compared to all the other credit-card authorization mechanisms, CardShield (see Figure 6.3) is the new kid on the block. What CardShield provides is a two-tier, Java-based commerce solution. For those who do not wish to do any sort of programming, CardShield provides a mechanism for an off-the-shelf commerce solution, which will be discussed in Chapter 7. CardShield also provides a Java-based API for the processing of credit-card information. Both the API and the storefront applet are geared for real-time processing only. However, CardShield does not require dedicated access for either the API or storefront applet. Essentially CardShield is a service; as a service provider, Shielded Technologies will try to make it as appealing as possible for you to use its service. The ability to facilitate Web commerce with a dedicated Internet connection, and with-

Figure 6.3 CardShield from Shielded Technologies, Inc.

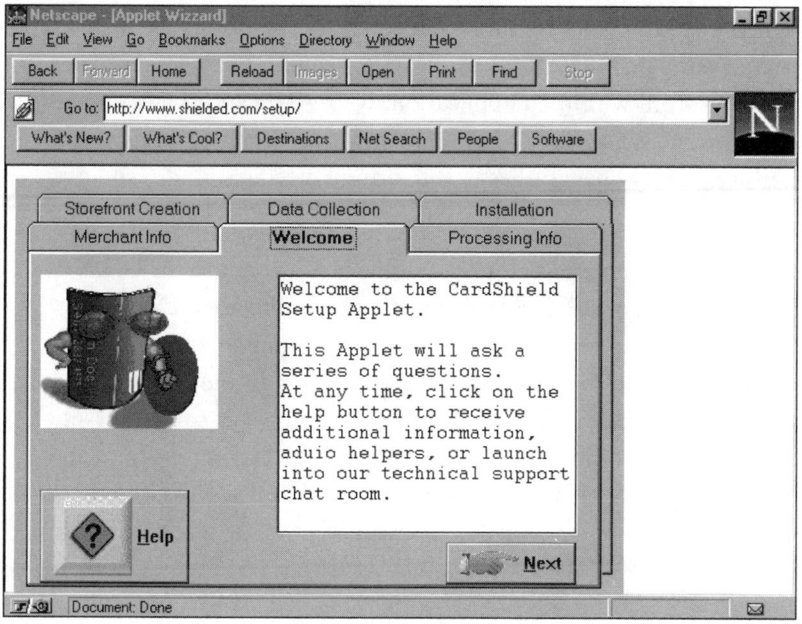

out having to write a line of code, is definitely a selling point. Shielded Technologies offers the following value-added benefits of using its service:

- A secure environment for the transmission of credit-card information over the Internet

- The ability to create a Java storefront without any programming knowledge

- Real-time processing of credit-card transactions, without a dedicated Internet connection

- E-mail notification of orders to Web merchant

- Fax notification of orders to Web merchant

- Access to daily transaction logs

- Full one-month history report mailed with each month's invoice

Shielded Technologies offers a wide variety of solutions to the problems ailing Web commerce. From the quick and dirty solution to the million-dollar neon and animation storefront, CardShield offers a benefit that might appear to be free—the mechanism to access the service is free, but the service itself is not. CardShield is the conduit to the service.

IC Verify

If the card swipe terminal is the standard processing mechanism for non-Web commerce merchants, then IC Verify (see Figure 6.4) is the standard for Web commerce solutions. IC Verify is an application from, appropriately enough, IC Verify that allows a clean and simple mechanism to perform credit-card authorization from within an application. IC Verify also provides a user interface form that manually processes credit-card information, which allows it to be used for batch processing solutions; however, its real benefit lies in the form of a request and response type interface for applications.

IC Verify provides an application that perpetually runs on a machine, a demon for UNIX users, that looks for the existence of request files inside a predetermined directory. Once the application sees a request file, it responds by reading and processing the contents of this file. When the application has handled the request in the in file, it then creates an out file. Through this mechanism, CGI or other applications have the ability to process the credit-card transaction quickly. IC Verify is a complete and highly functional product, but it does lack ease of use and ease of setup. To help IC Verify with this problem, the following section will discuss how to set up an IC Verify installation. Once it is set up, it works like a dream. Getting it ready is the hard part.

Figure 6.4 IC Verify.

If you have access to a dedicated connection, IC Verify and CardShield offer relatively equal solution. If you have access to a dedicated connection, CardShield provides e-mail, fax, and settlement file facilities while IC Verify simply processes transactions. Chapter 10 provides an "icverify" Java wrapper to harness the power of this tool. Also, Chapters 12 through 14 will present IC Verify as a alternative to CardShield in all examples.

Setting Up IC Verify

IC Verify supplies a really elegant solution, but it is a little behind the times. Currently, the only version of the IC Verify software shipping is DOS-based. IC Verify is planning to release new Windows NT, Windows API, and UNIX-based solutions shortly; for now, Henry Ford's motto applies—"You can have any color as long as it is black." IC Verify offers almost the exact same service as CardShield; however, it does require a dedicated connection. Chapter 10 supplies the tools to access IC Verify's functionality easily.

Setting Up the Merchant Information

IC Verify is considered an industry standard, and as such, most sources for credit-card fulfillment services, like Wells Fargo, will provide cheat sheets. Telling your fulfillment services that you will be using IC Verify not only makes life simpler during installation, it also ensures that everything is properly set up on their side. It is generally a good idea to have all of the provided information at hand while you are installing the software.

The first step in the install is to execute the "install" application provided on the distribution disk (see Figure 6.5). This will put all needed files into their appropriate locations and scan for all available modems. IC Verify can use more than one modem to process orders; thus, during the installation process it will search for all available modems on all available COM ports. If you are installing a plain-Jane DOS machine, this will not be a problem. Windows NT controls access to COM ports and in doing so will post an error message when the install application tries to access an invalid COM port (see Figure 6.6). This is not a big hangup; simply ignore the message.

Once the installer has completed its task, it is time to set up IC Verify to include your specific merchant information. After the installer is finished, it will execute the "ICSETUP" application to give you a mechanism to enter your merchant information. In most cases, this process should be a fairly straightforward task, due primarily to the IC Verify specific setup information provided by your fulfillment service. The only slightly frustrating thing is that you have to fax a provided form to ICVERIFY to receive a confirmation number required to complete the installation (see Figure 6.7).

Figure 6.5 Directory of IC Verify distribution disk.

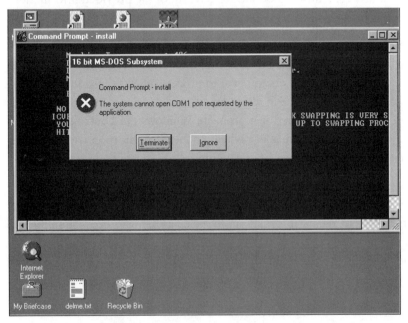

Figure 6.6 NT COM port error.

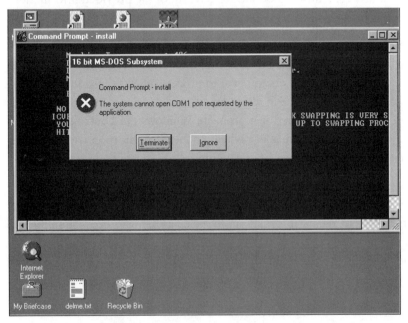

Figure 6.7 IC Verify requires a validation key to complete the installation.

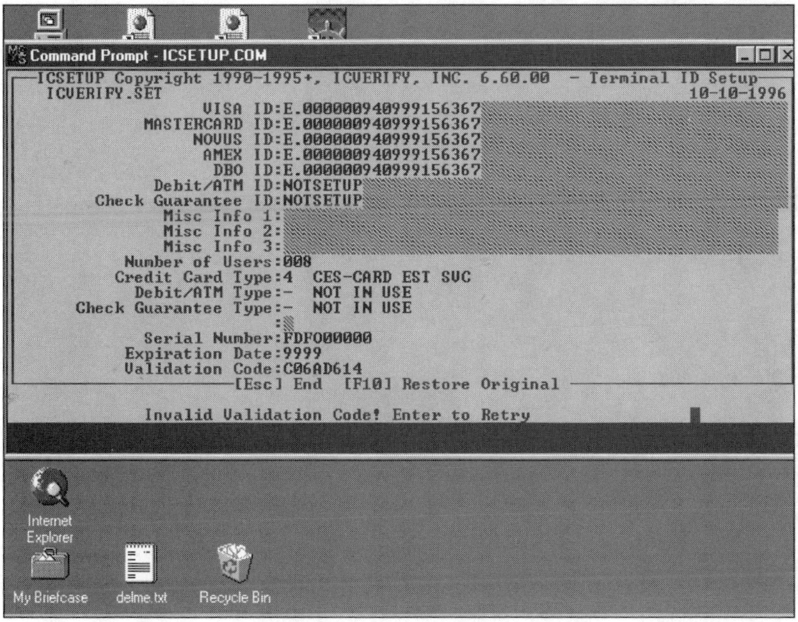

When everything seems to be going well, the next step is to create or modify your application to create IC Verify input files and to read input files. The process by which your application will go about authorizing a transaction is the following:

1. Create an IC Verify batch input file.

2. Execute IC Verify with the proper command-line options.

3. Read in the generated output file.

Create an IC Verify Batch Input File

The IC Verify input and output files are both in plain-text, comma-delimited format. The fields of the input are specified in Appendix I and J of the IC Verify documentation. For most instances, a large majority of the fields provided will be set to null. Figure 6.8 shows a sample input file containing 10 different transaction requests.

As you can see, there is nothing special about these files. The only tricky part comes in naming the input and output files. In most Web applications of IC Verify, you are not guaranteed that only one user will try to purchase something at any one time. That is, two people could try to

Figure 6.8 Sample IC Verify batch input file.

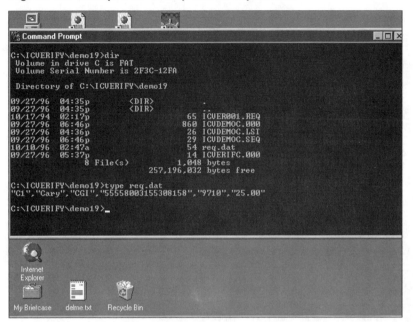

purchase something at the same time. To handle this circumstance, your application needs to be able to create input and output file names dynamically. The following Java class provides ready access to create and manage IC Verify ready input files.

```java
package CommerceUtils;
//request.java

/**
 * <tt>request<\tt> is a storage and serialization device
 * for IC Verify request files. Input is assumed to be in
 * the proper, valid format.
 *
 * Only sale transactions are supported.  Not a lot of call
 * for on-line return desk.
 *
 * NOTE : Expiration date should be stored in YYMM format
 *
 * @version 1.0
 * @author Cary A. Jardin
 */
public class request extends Object{
```

```
    private static String SaleToken = "C1";

    private String Clerk          =    "";
    private String Comment        =    "";
    private String CardNumber     =    "";
    private String Expiration     =    ""; //in YYMM format
    private String Amount         =    "";
    private String ZipCode        =    ""; //Optional
    private String Address        =    ""; //Optional
    private String Merchant       =    ""; //Optional
//Constructors

    /**
     * The constructor acts as a loading device for the internal
     * request storage.
     *
     *
     * @param clerk        Clerk field
     * @param comment      Comment field
     * @param cardnumber   The Credit Card to process
     * @param expiration   The Credit Card's expiration date in YYMM form
     * @param amount       The amount of the sale in ##.## form
     * @param zip          The zipcode of the customer, optional can be ""
     * @param address      The address of the customer, optional can be ""
     */
    public request(String clerk, String comment, String cardnumber,
        String expiration, String amount, String zip, String address){
super();
        Clerk         =         clerk;
        Comment       =         comment;
        CardNumber    =         cardnumber;
        Expiration    =         expiration;
        Amount        =         amount;
        ZipCode       =         zip;
        Address       =         address;
}

    /**
     * The constructor acts as a loading device for the internal
     * request storage.
     *
     *
     * @param clerk        Clerk field
     * @param comment      Comment field
     * @param cardnumber   The Credit Card to process
     * @param expiration   The Credit Card's expiration date in YYMM form
```

```
 * @param amount        The amount of the sale in ##.## form
 */
public request(String clerk, String comment, String cardnumber,
    String expiration, String amount){

    super();
    Clerk        =        clerk;
    Comment      =        comment;
    CardNumber   =        cardnumber;
    Expiration   =        expiration;
    Amount       =        amount;
    ZipCode      =        " ";
    Address      =        " ";
}



/**
 * The constructor acts as a loading device for the internal
 * request storage.
 *
 * NOTE: This constructor is ONLY used for locations that have
 * a single installation of IC Verify for multiple companies.
 *
 * @param IgnoreME      Really! Ignore the var
 * @param merchant      The merchant .set file to use
 * @param comment       Comment field
 * @param cardnumber    The Credit Card to process
 * @param expiration    The Credit Card's expiration date in YYMM form
 * @param amount        The amount of the sale in ##.## form
 * @param zip           The zip code of the customer, optional can be ""
 * @param address       The address of the customer, optional can be ""
 */
public request(boolean IgnoreME, String merchant, String comment, String cardnumber,
    String expiration, String amount, String zip, String address){

    super();
    Clerk        =        "";
    Comment      =        comment;
    CardNumber   =        cardnumber;
    Expiration   =        expiration;
    Amount       =        amount;
    ZipCode      =        zip;
    Address      =        address;
    Merchant     =        merchant;
}
```

```
/**
 * Serializes the fields into a comma delimited format.
 *
 * @returns     Returns the stored fields in a comma delimited format.
 *
 */
public String Serialize(){
    String out = "";

    out = "\""+SaleToken+"\",";

    if(Merchant != "")
        out += "\"~"+Merchant+"~\",";
    else
        out += "\""+Clerk+"\",";

    out += "\""+Comment+"\",";
    out += "\""+CardNumber+"\",";
    out += "\""+Expiration+"\",";

    if((ZipCode != "") || (Address != ""))
        out += "\""+Amount+"\",";
    else{
        out += "\""+Amount+"\"";
        return out;
    }

    if(Address != "")
        out += "\""+ZipCode+"\",";
    else{
        out += "\""+ZipCode+"\"";
        return out;
    }

    out += "\""+Address+"\"";
    return out;
}

}
```

Command Line Execution of IC Verify

ICVERIFY command-line execution allows an application to launch a credit-card processing engine of sorts. All of the supported command-line options can be found in Appendix K of the IC Verify documentation. The particular interesting options for Web commerce are the /B and /D flags. The /B flag provides the ability to specify the input and output batch-processing files. The

/D flag works very well for testing purposes, for it simulates dialing and does not actually process any requests. Through the use of these flags, your application can handle all of its credit-card needs. The following command-line parameter will process the requests in the file called "in.txt" and spit out the results in the "out.txt" file: ICVERIFY /B in.txt out.txt.

Reading the Generated Output File

The IC Verify output file is very similar to the input file, with a few field changes to accommodate the needed error strings, which can all be found in Appendix D of the IC Verify documentation provided. Just as the input file didn't hold any hidden secrets, neither does the output file. Figure 6.9 shows a sample output file containing 10 different transaction responses.

The output file falls prone to the same problem that the input file has when two requests are issued during the same time. The process in your application to handle the output file must not only be able to create a unique filename, it is also responsible for the deletion of the input file. Deleting the input file, after it has been used, performs the necessary "garbage collection" to keep unused files deleted and gives the input filename creation mechanism the ability to choose an unused filename quickly. The following Java class provides ready access to manage IC Verify formatted output files.

Figure 6.9 Sample IC Verify batch output file.

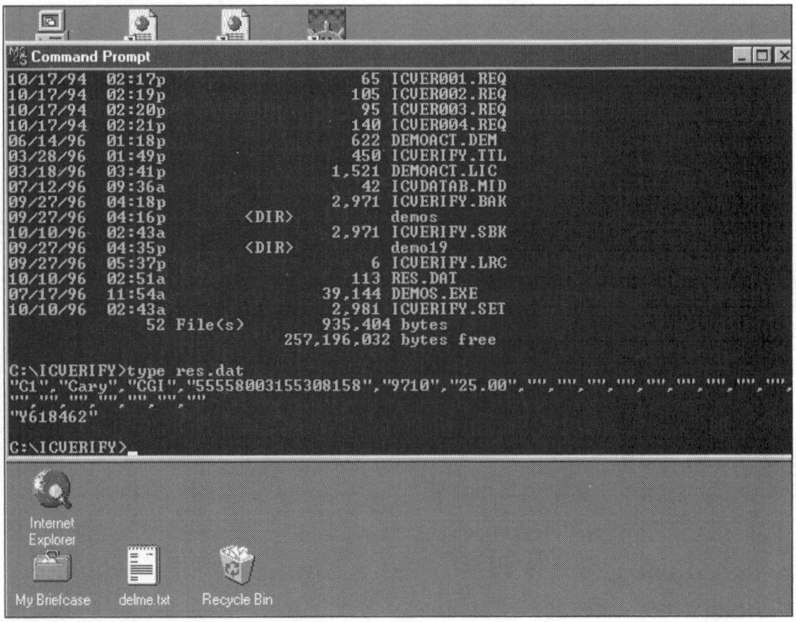

```
package CommerceUtils;

import java.util.StringTokenizer;

//response.java

/**
 * <tt>response<\tt> is a storage and loading device
 * for IC Verify response files. Input is assumed to be in
 * the proper, valid format.
 *
 * Only sale transactions are supported.  Not a lot of call
 * for on-line return desks.
 *
 * NOTE : Evaluated Response should be set to format type B
 *
 * @version 1.0
 * @author Cary A. Jardin
 */
public class response extends Object{

        /**
         * Approved will be true if the transaction was approved.
         */
        public boolean Approved        = false;

        /**
         * If the transaction was approved ApprovalCode will hold the
         * six digit approval code, else the value will be "".
         */
        public String  ApprovalCode    = "";

        /**
         * If the transaction was approved ReferenceNumber will hold the
         * eight digit Reference code, else the value will be "".
         */
        public String  ReferenceNumber = "";

        /**
         * If the transaction was denied ErrorCode will hold the
         * error code. Also if there is a problem with the constructor's
         * input, ErrorCode will be "BADFRM"
         */
        public String  ErrorCode       = "";
```

```
/**
 * The CardNumber of the transaction
 *
 */
public String  CreditCardNum    = "";

/**
 * The constructor will take the supplied Echo, and strings and
 * parse them into the appropriate public vars.
 *
 * @param Echo          Echo of the initial request.
 * @param Response      The response line, in comma delimited.
 *
 */
public response(String Echo,String Response){

    super();
    LoadCardNumber(Echo);
    ProcessResponse(Response);
}

private void ProcessResponse(String Authorization){

    //Char 0 is a '"', Char 1 is 'Y' for approved, 'N' for declined
    //String should be in the format "YAAAAAARRRRRRRR", or "YAAAAAA"
    if(Authorization.charAt(1) == 'Y'){// good
        try{
            Approved = true;
            ApprovalCode     = Authorization.substring(2,8);
            if(Authorization.length() > 10) //check to see if the Refnum is appended
                ReferenceNumber = Authorization.substring(8,16);
            else
                ReferenceNumber = "";
        }
        catch(Exception e){
            Approved = false;
            ErrorCode = "BADFRM";
        }
    }
    else{
        try{
            Approved = false;
            ErrorCode     = Authorization.substring(2,Authorization.length()-1);
        }
        catch(Exception e){
            Approved = false;
```

```
                    ErrorCode = "BADFRM";
            }
        }

    }

    private void LoadCardNumber(String Echo_Line){

        StringTokenizer parser = new StringTokenizer(Echo_Line,",",false);

        // Skip Sale Command;
        parser.nextToken();

        //Skip the Clerk
        parser.nextToken();

        //Skip the Comment
        parser.nextToken();

        //Load the Card Number and forget the rest
        CreditCardNum = StripField(parser.nextToken());
    }

    private String StripField(String StripME){

        String out = "";

        for(int i = 0;i < (StripME.length() - 1);++i)
            if(StripME.charAt(i) != '"')
                out += StripME.charAt(i);

        return out;
    }

}
```

Summary

The mechanism and facilities to process credit-card transactions are not by themselves difficult or confusing. With a few phone calls and lots of patience, you can begin processing credit cards without even breaking a sweat. The problem comes when you try to make an existing technology mold around your needs. Some existing technologies are better suited to different solutions.

This chapter gave you the information you need to choose the right solution for your business. If your needs lead you to a CardShield solution, Chapter 7 will discuss in detail how to set up a

CardShield merchant and how to create your own CardShield storefront applet. If your needs take you down the path of a custom solution, this chapter gave you the knowledge to set up your own credit-card transaction processing application. You were also shown some sample Java code to interface with an IC Verify system. This source code will be used in a Chapter 12 example to create a complete commerce CGI application to process HTML-based order information.

Setting up a merchant account and all the associated processing elements might be the most time-intensive element of Web commerce. It takes time to set up all the needed accounts and to get all the right numbers. Although you might be in a mad rush to get your commerce site operational, it will be worth your while to take some time and properly set up your means of credit-card processing. If the system is properly set up, it will work like a dream. If there is a problem with the setup, you will play the "It's not my fault, it is your fault" game with your fulfillment services. Plan your steps carefully, and make sure that everything is functioning properly, for the credit-card processing module of your commerce solution is what processes the money. Without it, you don't get paid.

CardShield
The Complete
Commerce Solution

This chapter focuses on the new CardShield technology and takes a hard look at what is involved in getting online with CardShield. If you want to set up shop quickly on a low budget, this chapter is for you.

CardShield—The Service

Throughout the previous chapters, mentions of CardShield have found their way into almost every discussion. From the discussion of dedicated Internet access versus dial-up access to batch versus real-time processing, CardShield seems to offer a wide variety of solution alternatives. See Figure 7.1. By now you're probably curious about CardShield—just what is it?

CardShield is a service provided by Shielded Technologies, Inc. A service is useless unless customers have access to that service, and the same holds for CardShield. CardShield provides all of the mechanisms necessary, for free, that are needed to create a Web commerce solution. Web commerce developers, though, tend to take one of two possible directions when it comes to providing Web commerce solutions:

- Quick and dirty solutions

- Custom solutions

Figure 7.1 Shielded Technologies, Inc., Web site (www.shielded.com).

Quick and dirty solutions are meant to provide a fast and simple tool for creating a Web commerce solution. These solutions might not be as fancy as a custom-built solution, but they get the job done. To fulfill this need, Shielded Technologies created the CardShield storefront Wizard. No programming necessary, minimal knowledge of computers, knowledge of the products to sell, and about a half an hour to kill are all that you need to create your very own Java storefront that is ready for business. The CardShield storefront Wizard puts the ability to create a Web commerce solution in the hands of an entirely new audience. Traditionally, Web commerce required some sort of programming, but the CardShield setup Wizard can produce a ready-to-install commerce solution. A complete guide on how to use the CardShield storefront Wizard will be provided later in this chapter, along with a list containing all the information you will need to complete the Wizard.

Although the CardShield setup Wizard provides the means to create a ready-for-business storefront, it by no means is capable of fulfilling the commerce needs of *all* companies. Some companies sell products that do not fit into the tidy packages that the setup Wizard requires. Other companies might simply want to create their own store, with their own look and feel. For these reasons, Shielded Technologies freely distributes its class library API for credit-card processing. For custom solutions, using the CardShield API inherits the same benefits as the prefab

CardShield storefront Wizard, with the added bonus of being able to decorate your own store. Chapter 11 will discuss the CardShield API in depth.

It Is Free, for a Price

CardShield is possibly a revolutionary new Web commerce solution, but there is no such thing as a free lunch. Everyone has to make money in some way, even nonprofit organizations. The CardShield software included on the CD-ROM is free to everyone. Shielded Technologies makes its money on the use of the service. The key element in the last sentence is "use of." CardShield is a transaction-based service—if you don't use the service one month you don't pay for anything. The cost of doing business with CardShield is very straightforward and contains only two different elements:.

- One-time startup fee

- Per-transaction cost

Startup Fee

On the accounting and processing end of CardShield, a number of tasks need to be completed to allow a customer to use the system. For the most part, these tasks are centered around getting a customer ready to process a credit-card transaction— the entire purpose of the service. The startup fee is a one-time charge of $110, which covers the costs associated with all administrative and setup tasks. This fee is billed on the completion of the Java merchant setup applet, and it must be paid within 30 days or the merchant will be deleted from the system. Later in this chapter, the Java merchant setup applet will be illustrated.

Per-transaction Fee

One of the nice things about paying to use the CardShield service is that if you don't use it, you don't pay. The CardShield per-transaction cost is broken down into three usage levels. Regardless of the usage level, Shielded Technologies charges $.20 for each fax, which applies to only to those customers who choose to be notified of an order via fax. The following is a breakdown of the per-transaction costs and their associated usage levels. Keep in mind that these prices do not include the additional $.20 charge for fax customers.

- $.60 per transaction for usage of 1 to 100 transaction(s) per month

- $.50 per transaction for usage of 100 to 200 transactions per month

- $.40 per transaction for usage of 200 and more transactions per month

Monthly Statement

With use of the CardShield service comes the delivery of the associated good and bad news. The bad news is that you owe Shielded Technologies money for your transactions in that month. The good news is that you will receive a report each month On the months you don't use the CardShield service, you will not receive a statement. The following is a list of information included in the monthly usage report for each transaction:

- Date and time of the transaction

- All client information entered

- Credit-card number and expiration date

- Authorization code

- IP address of client

- Total time taken to complete order

Registering with the Service

On the Shielded Technologies' Web page, you will find the option to set up a new account. This option is your entry point into the CardShield service. From this option will appear the storefront Wizard applet, ready to take all of your vital merchant information. The process of completing the Wizard is broken into three sections. The first two are mandatory for all merchants wishing to use the CardShield service. The last option needs to be completed only by merchants choosing to use the CardShield-generated storefront applet. The sections of the install appear in this order:

1. Billing information setup

2. Credit-card transaction processing setup

3. Storefront Wizard

Setting Up Your Billing Information

The CardShield setup applet is the gatekeeper between you and the CardShield service. It not only acts as the initial installation facility, it also is used to change any of your merchant or store information. The setup applet begins by asking if you would like sound clips to accompany your installations, as well as a checklist of items you will need (see Figure 7.2). No, this is not elevator

Figure 7.2 You can select audio clips to accompany your installation.

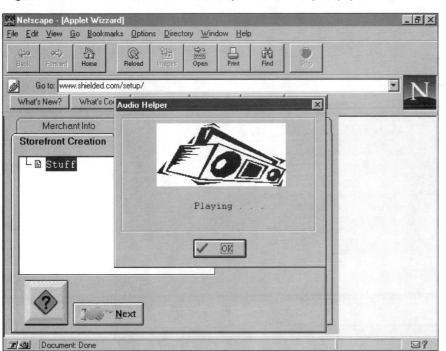

music to help you remain calm during the installation. Rather, the sound clips offer a step-by-step verbal explanation and/or clarification of what the current setup screen is asking for. Help is accessible at any point of the installation process, containing all the same material as is in the audio clips. However, the audio information is a more general aid, rather than a specific explanation. The audio clips are helpful, but they take a long time to load.

Once you have decided for or against audio, you are presented a screen containing all the steps the applet will perform. Also, at the bottom of the screen is an option to select if you already have an existing account. If you select this option, you will be prompted for a customer number and password. This will then lead you to another screen where you can select the part of the setup to which you want to jump. New members must follow the setup sequentially, but existing users can select their area of interest. Both new and existing members can select "OK" to continue with the setup.

The first item on the setup list (see Figure 7.3) is the billing information, and it is the first step in the setup of a new member. The billing information portion of the applet is broken into a merchant

Figure 7.3 Main setup applet selection list.

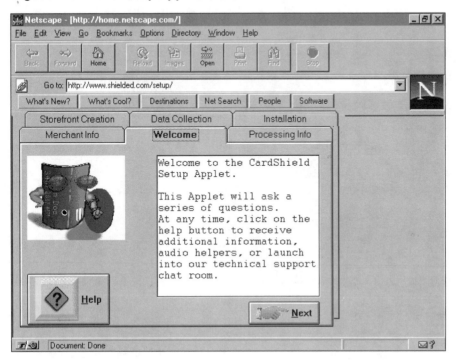

information section and a service option section. The merchant information section will ask for some generic information about the new merchant—name, address, fax, and so on. The service option screen will allow you to set up the type of order notification you would like. Selecting the fax option will ask you for your fax number, the e-mail option will ask for an address, and the daily transaction file will explain how to go about getting the transaction file.

Once the service options have been set, CardShield will issue a user name and prompt you for a password. These two items will be needed to allow for modifications in the setup applet, as well as provide the necessary ftp login information to retrieve the daily transaction report. For obvious reasons, these two items should be kept safe and available; however, if either are lost, a call to CardShield customer service will rectify the problem.

After the service options have been selected, the applet will return to the initial step list screen to show the completion of the first step by a check on the list. The next step is to set up the merchant processing information (see Figure 7.4). For any reason, you can choose to exit the setup procedure at this time. When you return, simply select the next option on the selection list, and you will be on your way.

Figure 7.4 Merchant information setup.

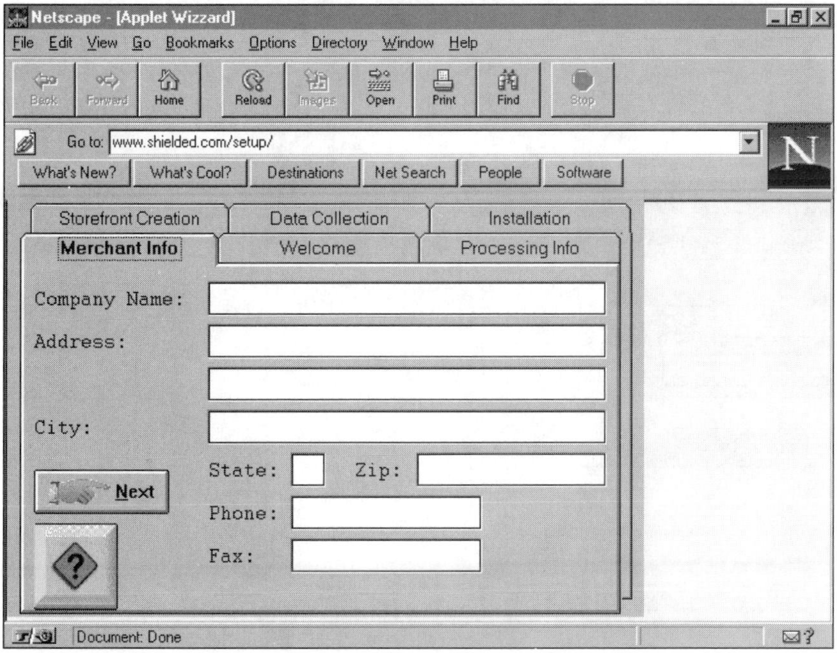

Setting Up Your Processing Information

The processing information CardShield requires is by no means intuitive unless you are familiar with all the credit-card processing networks. The processing of credit-card transactions is not a standard thing. More than 10 major networks process transactions, each of which requires its own set of information. To handle this problem, the CardShield setup applet will ask initially for the network you will be using. All subsequent screens will reflect the needs of the chosen network. The information required for the complete setup of the CardShield processing setup is identical to the information needed to set-up an IC Verify application; therefore, it is a good idea to ask your bank for an IC Verify-specific information sheet.

After the completion of the credit-card processing information (see Figure 7.5), the setup applet will ask you to confirm your user name and password to authorize the completion of the merchant setup information (see Figure 7.6). This confirmation will authorize the initial CardShield setup charge to be billed. The newly created merchant account is ready for testing once the setup charge is authorized; however, accounts will not be able to process a transaction for 24 hours. Existing members are not asked to confirm their user names and passwords; rather, they are returned to the main setup step list.

Figure 7.5 Processing information setup.

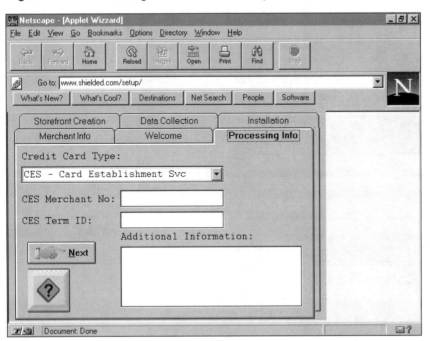

Setting Up Your New Java Storefront

In a conventional storefront, the process of setting up the items for sale usually means placing the items at their appropriate locations. Items of the same type go in one area, another type another area, until all items, and their associated "support" items, are in the right spot. For CardShield, users who want to take advantage of the CardShield storefront, the process of setting up shop on the Web is very similar to that of a normal store.

The CardShield storefront functions in two parts. The first part is a setup applet in which items can be added, modified, or deleted. The second part of the loop is the part the customer will see, the storefront. The setup applet is responsible for "stocking" the storefront, to the extent that the setup applet can even label an item in the store as out of stock. The look, feel, and the features found in the CardShield storefront will be discussed later in this chapter. For now, the focus will be on getting the store ready for business.

Item Management

In a regular store, placing items in their appropriate location might entail picking up the item and placing it into position. In the CardShield storefront, this process is streamlined into an expanding

Figure 7.6 Final confirmation to create a new merchant.

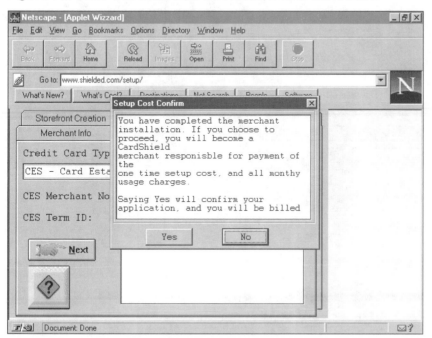

outline tree located in the Item Manager. This expanding outline tool is very similar to a file and directory tree, in that directories can contain files or other directories. Exploring the contents disk is as simple as expanding a directory to see the contained files. The Item Manager (see Figure 7.7) uses the same principle to explore the contents of a store, except directories are categories, files are items, and it uses a new element called options.

Categories, like directories, exist solely to provide some sort of logical division of items. To add a new category select the spot at which to add the category, and click the Category button at the bottom of the page. Categories can be deleted by selecting the category to delete and then pressing the Delete key, and categories can be modified by double-clicking on the specific category. Warning: when you delete a category, you also delete all the items contained in that category (see Figure 7.8).

Adding, editing, and deleting an item are almost identical to the processes for doing the same for a category, except for two differences. The first difference is that categories can't contain items or other categories, but items may contain only their associated options. The second is that each item will contain more information than was associated with a category. Each item is a unit of sale, that is, items are what the customer will purchase. Items must contain all the pertinent information about that item, like the price to charge. (See Figure 7.9.)

Figure 7.7 The Item Manager inside the storefront setup.

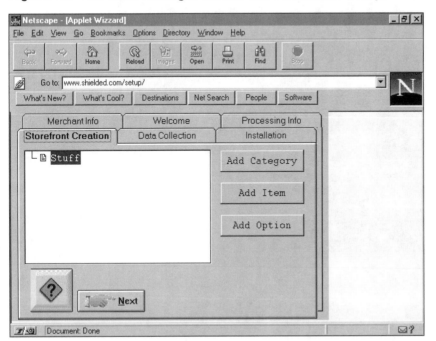

Sometimes, options can be added to an item at an additional cost (see Figure 7.10). For example, a used car salesman might try to push a number of different options to accompany a used car, like tires. Items can contain options (see Figure 7.11), and each option will have its own associated cost, which will be added to the cost of the initial item.

The CardShield Item Manager provides a fast and simple mechanism for creating and maintaining the CardShield storefront. Categories contain either other categories or items, and items can contain options, and options are just options. Once you have mastered this concept, you will find that using the Item Manager will become inherently simple and intuitive.

Custom Input

From the merchant's perspective, two vital pieces of information are needed to fulfill the order: what the customer wants to order and how to get it to the customer. The first part is taken care of with the Item Manager. The second issue is handled by the custom input section of the setup applet. CardShield has a generic set of information that is required, such as name, address, telephone, and so on. Through the custom input editor (see Figure 7.12), custom information may be added to obtain information from the customer above and beyond the generic CardShield set of information. This information will accompany the e-mail or fax

Figure 7.8 Category, item, and option hierarchy.

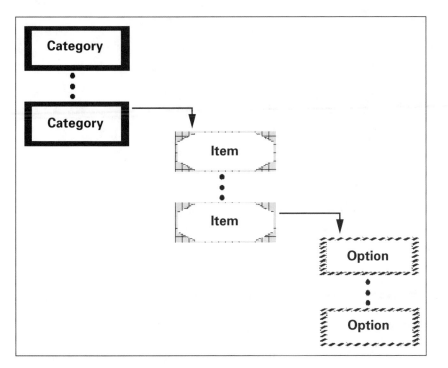

order notification, and it will appear in the daily transaction file. To add or delete a field, select the field and click either the Add or Delete button. The data fields contained in CardShield cannot be deleted, for they are an integral part of the customer wallet feature, which will be discussed later in the chapter.

Installing the Storefront

Once the setup applet has been completed, the storefront is ready for business (that is, except for the small fact of not being able to accept credit cards for 24 hours after the setup was completed). The last screen in the setup applet, the one right before thank-you and good bye, gives instructions on how to place the newly created store into an HTML page. The placement is really more of a link. You must link one of your pages to the new storefront applet page. That is, in HTML terms, you need to set an *href* to the URL provided. For example, say that you have an existing page that describes your product. Inside the document you would want to insert the following line:

```
<A href="PROVIDED URL"> ORDER NOW! <\A>
```

Figure 7.9 Category add, edit screen.

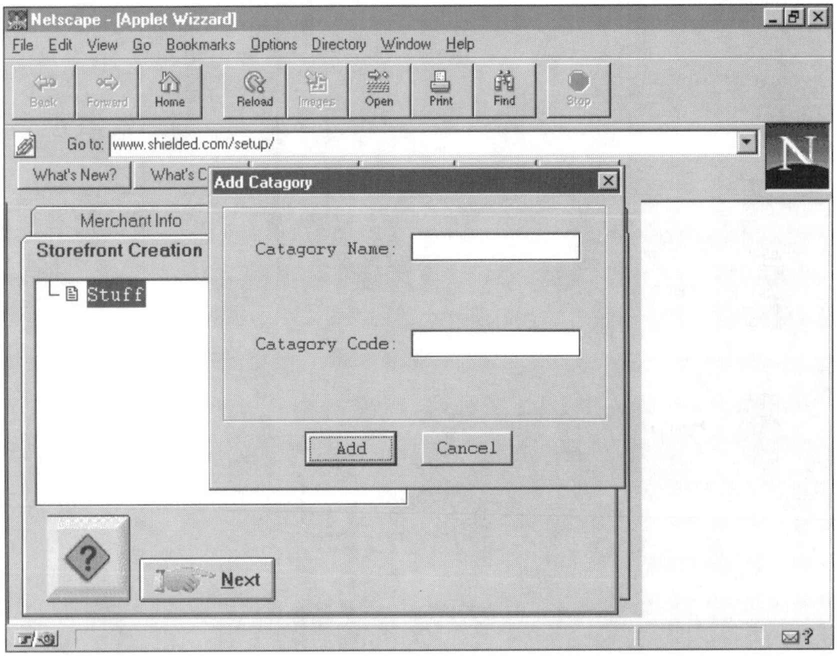

This example is the simplest way to add CardShield to a Web site. Shielded Technologies' Web site offers an entire library of HTML storefront presentation examples at http://www.shielded.com/examples/. Peruse the HTML presentation library for an example that fits your needs.

Using CardShield

Shielded Technologies' primary goal for CardShield is to provide a secure, standard, inexpensive, and painless method of facilitating Internet credit-card transactions. All applications that are written using the CardShield API class libraries, including the CardShield storefront, inherit all the benefits of using the CardShield service. Of the four goals set forth by Shielded Technologies for CardShield, three have been accomplished. Secure transport of volatile credit-card information over the Internet was its first goal, and that has been achieved. Developing painless and inexpensive methods for creating Web commerce solutions were also achieved. The final goal was to present a standard mechanism for Web-based commerce, which might be a little ambitious but nevertheless possible. CardShield provides developers with the tools needed to facilitate Internet commerce, as well as the security and ease of use demanded by the Web user.

Figure 7.10 Item add, edit screen.

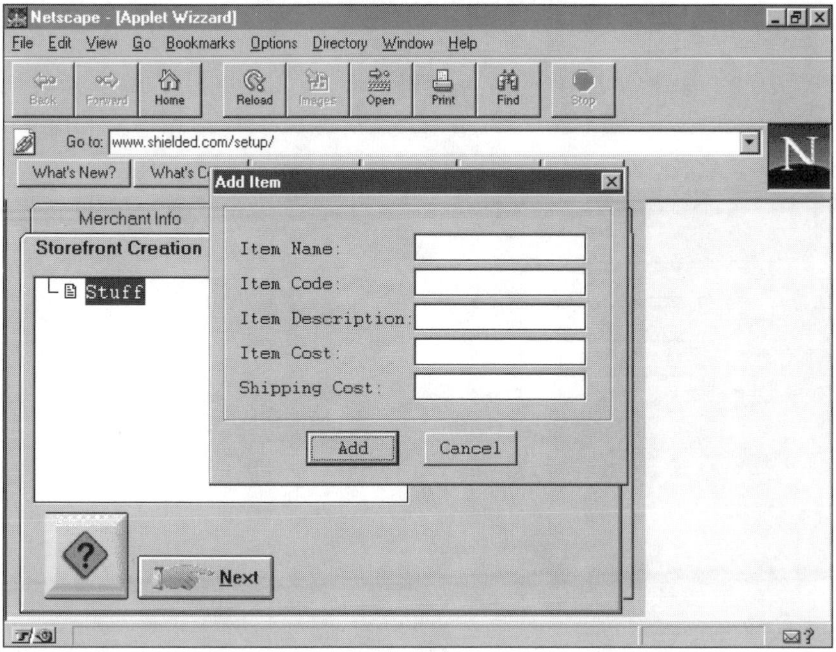

The Shield Will Protect

CardShield uses Shielded Technologies' patented security mechanism, RCS, which stands for Random Class Security. Without our going too deeply into the details of RCS (which is exactly what Shielded wants), RCS is a method of security that is not bounded to one fixed security algorithm such as RSA or PGP. RCS uses a constantly changing set of security algorithms to secure communication. Shielded Technologies is so sure of RCS's ability to transport volatile information securely over the Net that it guarantees the transport. Shielded Technologies will pay for any monetary damages that are a direct result of a breakdown of RCS.

Storefront Features

The CardShield storefront makes Web commerce available to a population of merchants formerly excluded from Web commerce. The features of the storefront, from the merchant's perspective, have been exposed in this chapter. However, if the customers aren't happy, they won't buy. The Shielded Wallet is a feature that has streamlined order entry for customers using both custom

Figure 7.11 Option add, edit screen.

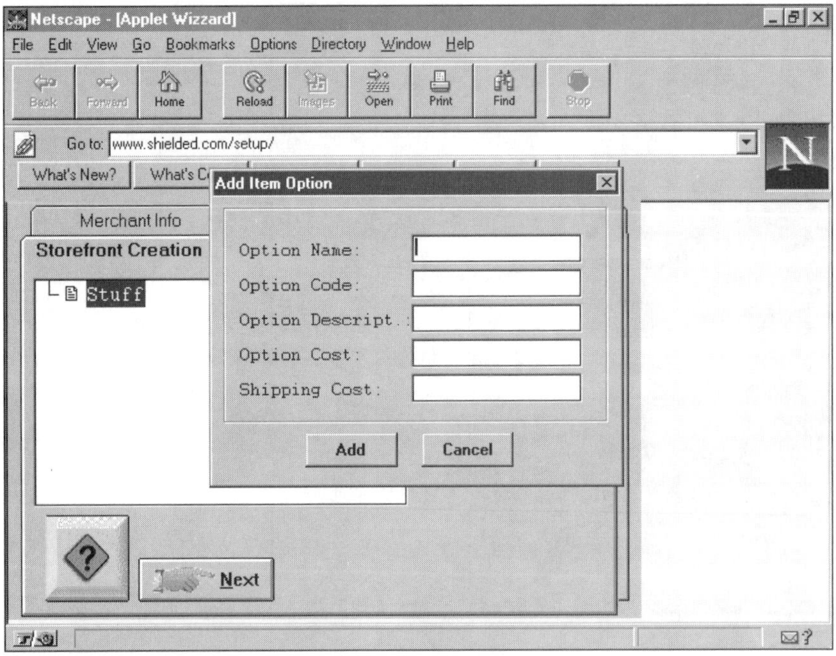

applications and the CardShield storefront. The other feature of the CardShield storefront that is worth mentioning is its rapid item selection.

The item selection tree offers users rapid access to the desired product. Once the user has found the item, he or she can place selected items in the shopping cart for later purchasing. The combination of a shopping cart and rapidly accessible item selection is teamed with a key word item search to offer the users a very rapid means of purchasing (see Figure 7.13).

Summary

Web commerce solutions can come in many different forms. Regardless of their form, they must all fulfill a common purpose. The primary point of selling things on the Web is to provide the

Figure 7.12 Custom input field add, edit screen.

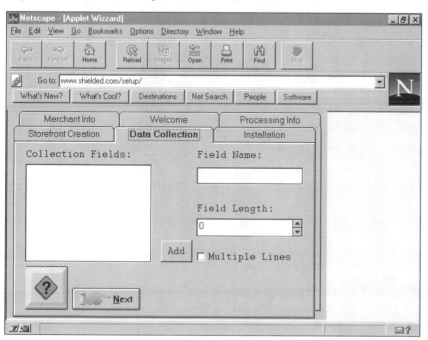

means for a customer to purchase a product. We might assume that this is a fairly straightforward task. All Web commerce solutions must provide a common set of features for the customer, primarily an order-entry mechanism and a payment mechanism. This need and use of common Web based functionality constitute the battle cry for CardShield.

CardShield offers something for almost every merchant doing business on the Web. For small companies, CardShield is their one-stop shopping experience for a Web commerce solution. For midsized companies, CardShield offers the ability to do business on the Web in a more cost-effective and streamlined manner. Large companies utilize CardShield to compensate for lack of time or lack of resources. Whatever the case, CardShield offers a large variety of features to suit most any need. This chapter covered some of the formalities of CardShield and provided a hard look at what is involved in getting online with CardShield. Chapter 11 will explore custom

Figure 7.13 Rapid item selection with the selection tree.

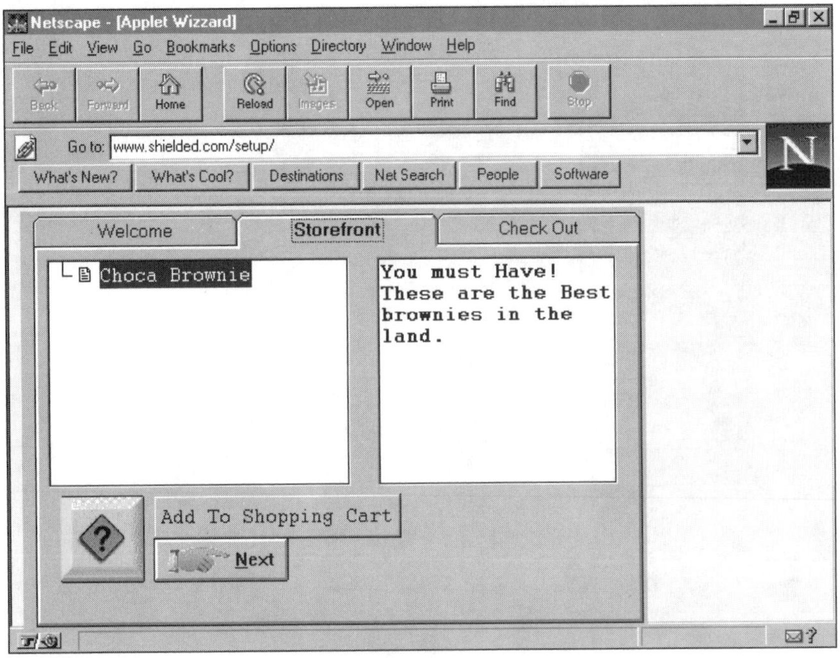

applications using CardShield. If you began this chapter with a vague understanding of CardShield, you are ending it with a good understanding of what CardShield is and how to use it.

Java Order Entry

For the more technical reader, this chapter presents information for merchants who want to create a custom shop. Explanations and examples of HTML, applets and applications, are explored.

Applets and Applications

Many people are not familiar with the concept that Java applications are not necessarily applets. If you take a look at the general Web population, you will find that Java knowledge can be broken into three distinct categories, fitting a bell curve model, small, large, and small. The first group is slightly behind the technology curve and believes that Java is simply a rollover from the big coffee house craze. The middle, and possibly the largest, group is made up of the individuals who know Java from applets on the Web. Finally, the last and smallest group is the Java developers. Of the three groups noted, only the last and smallest group has any concept of a non-Web application written in Java, and for good reason. Applets by far are the most visible ambassadors of Java; however, they debatably are not the most useful. Java applets and applications alike both have their own intended fields of use; they are, in a way, the same tool but each with a different specialty.

HTML and Applets

Probably, the best way to think of applets are as applications that can live only inside a Web browser. In a normal operating system environment, applications are launched by entering a command or clicking with a mouse. The application is launched by your operating system for you to use, until the program terminates or the machine is turned off. This concept becomes important when you look at how applets are launched and how they are executed.

Normal applications are launched from the operating system, and applets are launched by the browser. Getting a little deeper, the command to execute an applet is embedded inside an HTML document. That is, the Applet is embedded inside the browser. With normal applications, the operating system is responsible for the execution of the application. In the case of an applet, the browser is responsible for the execution, termination, display, and all other runtime characteristics. The following HTML document launches a "HelloJava" applet that will be created later in this chapter.

```
<HTML>
<HEAD>
<TITLE> A simple program </TITLE>
</HEAD>
<BODY>

<APPLET CODE="hello.class" WIDTH=283 HEIGHT=190></APPLET>

</BODY>

</HTML>
```

Take a look at the above document, and notice how the applet is being called from within the document. Also, notice that the *WIDTH* and *HEIGHT* are specified. Applets live within an HTML document, and in doing so they are controlled by the browser. The height and width are just some of the aspects of the applet over which the browser has control In the field of Java-based Web commerce, and in particular order-entry applications, the browser's having control of an applet is not such a good thing. Later, this chapter will discuss some of the problems that face applets in a browser's world, as well as some security issues imposed on an applet by the browser that hinder some needed functionality.

Hello Java!

Not all code written in Java is an applet. If this were true, Java would have been created specifically for that purpose. To the contrary, applets are merely a type of program that can be written in Java. The Java code that follows was generated by Symantec Café's application Wizard to say

"HELLO JAVA!", and it is fairly uncomplicated. Notice the use of the word applet in the line *public class hello extends Applet*? This single line of code gives this Java code all of the attributes associated with a Java applet. Later in the chapter, when the different types of Java applications are discussed, you will be able to see the striking similarities, but for now study the code. For Java programmers there might not be much to study. If you are coming from a C/C++ background or learning Java as a first language, there is no better way to learn than through example.

```
/*
    This class is a basic extension of the Applet class.  It would generally
    be used as the main class with a Java browser or the AppletViewer.  But
    an instance can be added to a subclass of Container.  To use this applet
    with a browser or the AppletViewer, create an html file with the
    following code:

    <HTML>
    <HEAD>
    <TITLE> hello </TITLE>
    </HEAD>
    <BODY>

    <APPLET CODE="hello.class" WIDTH=283 HEIGHT=190></APPLET>

    </BODY>

    </HTML>

    You can add controls to hello with Cafe Studio.
    (Menus can be added only to subclasses of Frame.)
 */

import java.awt.*;
import java.applet.*;

public class hello extends Applet {

    public void init() {

        super.init();

        //{{INIT_CONTROLS
        setLayout(null);
        resize(283,190);
        label1=new Label("HELLO JAVA!", Label.CENTER);
        add(label1);
```

```
        label1.reshape(68,75,147,15);
        //}}
    }

    public boolean handleEvent(Event event) {
        return super.handleEvent(event);
    }

    //{{DECLARE_CONTROLS
    Label label1;
    //}}
}
```

Java Applications—Not Applets

Java is a full-functioned programming language, and as stated before, applets are not its primary focus. Just to give you an idea of Java's capabilities, the next version of WordPerfect will be written in Java, and the next major version of Windows 95 will have Java support built into the operating system. When an application is compiled with Java, it is formed into a class file. A class file

Figure 8.1 Hello Java! Applet.

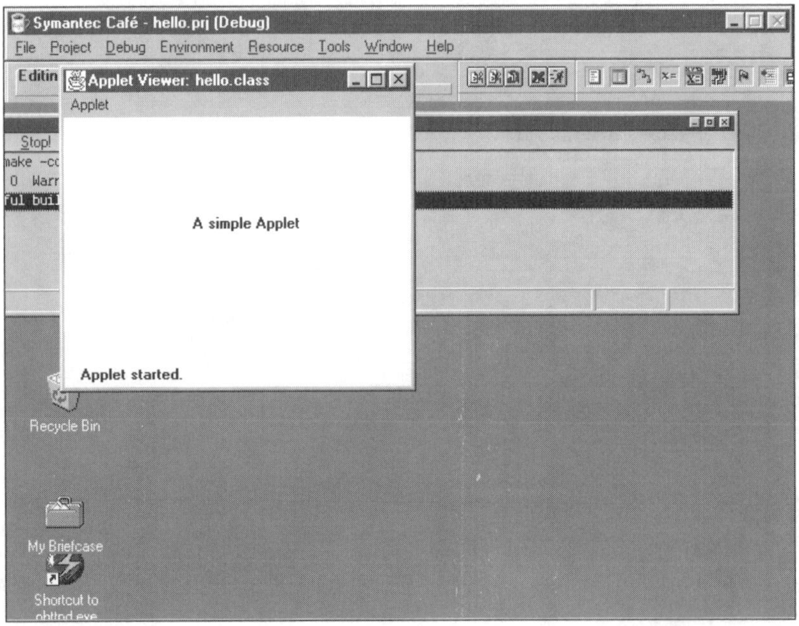

is directly analogous to a normal executable file, to the extent that for some Sun computers, class files are the normal executable files. Without getting into a long discussion about Java and the Java Virtual Machine (JVM), programs written in Java can do anything that programs written in C/C++ can do. Applets are just a type of application with limitations that normal Java applications, or stand-alone applications, are subject to. Stand-alone Java applications are full-featured, fully capable applications.

Command-Line Applications

Command-line applications are not graphic-oriented. *dir* and *ls* are both command-line applications, and so are CGI applications. These applications revolve around input coming in, standard in, and information going out, standard out. If Java's sole intent was to produce applets, such applications would render themselves impossible. But Java can do more than just applets; Java can create console applications. All of the cross-platform and developer creature comforts that Java contains can be used, and are being used, to provide powerful command-line applications and CGIs.

As seen in the "Hello Java!" applet, a single line of code made the application into an applet. The following is a console application generated by Symantec Café's application Wizard to say "HELLO JAVA!". Notice the size difference. Console applications are inherently less complicated, largely because they are not graphic-oriented. Notice as well how the application is executed ,as displayed in Figure 8.2. Chapter 12 will give some example CGIs written in Java, which utilizes the same model of Java code to create a CGI application.

```java
import java.awt.*;
import java.io.IOException;

public class hello {

    public static void main(String args[]) {
        System.out.println("HELLO JAVA!");
        System.out.println("");
        System.out.println("(press Enter to exit)");
        try {
            System.in.read();
        } catch (IOException e) {
            return;
        }
    }
}
```

Figure 8.2 Hello Java! Console Application.

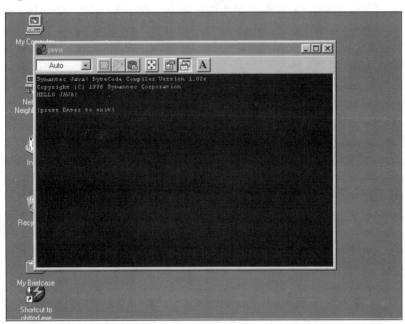

It's a GUI, Just Not an Applet

One of the reasons for denoting an applet as a subset of the Java language is due to its limitations. An applet has to live within the bounds of its parents' browser, so it has to abide by the browser's rules. Later in this chapter, the topic of an applet's security restrictions will be addressed. For now, the following will give you an idea of what we mean by restrictions:

- No ready access to the local machine's disk drives

- May communicate only with the machine in which the executable resides

- No means to have a menu bar inside the main applet window

There are more. Applets are constrained in a number of ways which stand-alone applications are not, but they do have their associated benefits. Stand-alone applications offer functionality that cannot be found in an applet, but stand-alone applications need to be downloaded and then launched. The moral of the story: Just because Applets are capable of only a set amount of functionality does not mean that Java, as a development language, is bound by the same constraints. The solution can be done in Java, though it may not in an applet.

The application that follows is an example of a Java stand-alone Windows application generated by Symantec Café's application Wizard. This form of Java application is directly mappable to the functionality in an applet, but without any constraints. The actual size might seem a little large; however, this application is doing much more. Notice that toward the middle the line "public static void main(String args[]) {", which is identical to the above console application. Stand-alone applications are the same as console applications except they create a frame, which can be equated to creating a window. Rummage through this code, for it provides a great model on which to base further development.

```java
/*
    This class is an extension of the Frame class for use as the
    main window of an application.

    You can add controls or menus to hello with Cafe Studio.
 */

import java.awt.*;

public class hello extends Frame {

    public hello() {

        super("HELLO JAVA!");

        //{{INIT_MENUS
        MenuBar mb = new MenuBar();
        fileMenu = new Menu("&File");
        fileMenu.add(new MenuItem("&New"));
        fileMenu.add(new MenuItem("&Open..."));
        fileMenu.add(new MenuItem("&Save"));
        fileMenu.add(new MenuItem("Save &As..."));
        fileMenu.addSeparator();
        fileMenu.add(new MenuItem("E&xit"));
        mb.add(fileMenu);
        editMenu = new Menu("&Edit");
        editMenu.add(new MenuItem("&Undo"));
        editMenu.addSeparator();
        editMenu.add(new MenuItem("Cu&t"));
        editMenu.add(new MenuItem("&Copy"));
        editMenu.add(new MenuItem("&Paste"));
        mb.add(editMenu);
        helpMenu = new Menu("&Help");
        helpMenu.add(new MenuItem("&About..."));
        mb.add(helpMenu);
```

```
    setMenuBar(mb);
    //}}

    //{{INIT_CONTROLS
    setLayout(null);
    addNotify();
    resize(insets().left + insets().right + 352, insets().top + insets().bottom + 254);
    //}}

    show();
}

public synchronized void show() {
    move(50, 50);
    super.show();
}

public boolean handleEvent(Event event) {

    if (event.id == Event.WINDOW_DESTROY) {
        hide();            // hide the Frame
        dispose();         // tell windowing system to free resources
        System.exit(0); // exit
        return true;
    }
    return super.handleEvent(event);
}

public boolean action(Event event, Object arg) {
    if (event.target instanceof MenuItem) {
        String label = (String) arg;
        if (label.equalsIgnoreCase("&About...")) {
            selectedAbout();
            return true;
        } else if (label.equalsIgnoreCase("E&xit")) {
            selectedExit();
            return true;
        } else if (label.equalsIgnoreCase("&Open...")) {
            selectedOpen();
            return true;
        }
    }
    return super.action(event, arg);
}

public static void main(String args[]) {
```

```
        new hello();
    }

    //{{DECLARE_MENUS
    Menu fileMenu;
    Menu editMenu;
    Menu helpMenu;
    //}}

    //{{DECLARE_CONTROLS
    //}}

    public void selectedOpen() {
        (new FileDialog(this, "Open...")).show();
    }
    public void selectedExit() {
        QuitBox theQuitBox;
        theQuitBox = new QuitBox(this);
        theQuitBox.show();
    }
    public void selectedAbout() {
        AboutBox theAboutBox;
        theAboutBox = new AboutBox(this);
        theAboutBox.show();
    }
}


/*
    This class is a basic extension of the Dialog class.  It can be used
    by subclasses of Frame.  To use it, create a reference to the class,
    then instantiate an object of the class (pass 'this' in the constructor),
    and call the show() method.

    example:

    AboutBox theAboutBox;
    theAboutBox = new AboutBox(this);
    theAboutBox.show();

    You can add controls to AboutBox with Cafe Studio.
    (Menus can be added only to subclasses of Frame.)
 */

class AboutBox extends Dialog {
```

```
public AboutBox(Frame parent) {

        super(parent, "About", true);
    setResizable(false);

    //{{INIT_CONTROLS
    setLayout(null);
    addNotify();
    resize(insets().left + insets().right + 292, insets().top + insets().bottom + 79);
    label1=new Label("Simple Java SDI Application");
    add(label1);
    label1.reshape(insets().left + 12,insets().top + 18,174,16);
    OKButton=new Button("OK");
    add(OKButton);
    OKButton.reshape(insets().left + 204,insets().top + 12,72,26);
    //}}
}

public synchronized void show() {
    Rectangle bounds = getParent().bounds();
    Rectangle abounds = bounds();

    move(bounds.x + (bounds.width - abounds.width)/ 2,
         bounds.y + (bounds.height - abounds.height)/2);

    super.show();
}

public synchronized void wakeUp() {
    notify();
}

public boolean handleEvent(Event event) {
    if (event.id == Event.ACTION_EVENT && event.target == OKButton) {
            clickedOKButton();
            return true;
    }
    else

    if (event.id == Event.WINDOW_DESTROY) {
        hide();
        return true;
    }
    return super.handleEvent(event);
}
```

```
    //{{DECLARE_CONTROLS
    Label label1;
    Button OKButton;
    //}}

    public void clickedOKButton() {
        handleEvent(new Event(this, Event.WINDOW_DESTROY, null));
    }
}

/*

    This class is a basic extension of the Dialog class.  It can be used
    by subclasses of Frame.  To use it, create a reference to the class,
    then instantiate an object of the class (pass 'this' in the constructor),
    and call the show() method.

    example:

    QuitBox theQuitBox;
    theQuitBox = new QuitBox(this);
    theQuitBox.show();

    You can add controls, but not menus, to QuitBox with Cafe Studio.
    (Menus can be added only to subclasses of Frame.)
 */

class QuitBox extends Dialog {

    public QuitBox(Frame parent) {

            super(parent, "Quit Application?", true);
        setResizable(false);

        //{{INIT_CONTROLS
        setLayout(null);
        addNotify();
        resize(insets().left + insets().right + 261, insets().top + insets().bottom + 72);
        yesButton=new Button("Yes");
        add(yesButton);
        yesButton.reshape(insets().left + 68,insets().top + 10,46,23);
        noButton=new Button("No");
        add(noButton);
        noButton.reshape(insets().left + 135,insets().top + 10,47,23);
        //}}
    }
```

```java
public synchronized void show() {
    Rectangle bounds = getParent().bounds();
    Rectangle abounds = bounds();

    move(bounds.x + (bounds.width - abounds.width)/ 2,
         bounds.y + (bounds.height - abounds.height)/2);

    super.show();
}

public synchronized void wakeUp() {
    notify();
}

public boolean handleEvent(Event event) {
    if (event.id == Event.ACTION_EVENT && event.target == noButton) {
            clickedNoButton();
            return true;
    }
    else
    if (event.id == Event.ACTION_EVENT && event.target == yesButton) {
            clickedYesButton();
            return true;
    }
    else

    if (event.id == Event.WINDOW_DESTROY) {
        hide();
        return true;
    }
    return super.handleEvent(event);
}

//{{DECLARE_CONTROLS
Button yesButton;
Button noButton;
//}}

public void clickedYesButton() {
    System.exit(0);
}
public void clickedNoButton() {
    handleEvent(new Event(this, Event.WINDOW_DESTROY, null));
}
}
```

Figure 8.3 Sample Java stand-alone GUI.

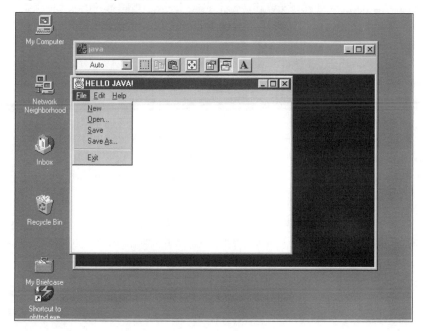

Collecting the Information

By now, you should be able to recognize three different types of Java applications, all of which can be used to collect information, of some sorts, back to a central repository. The use of console applications to collect HTML form-based information was covered in Chapter 6, in the form of CGI applications. The other two forms of Java applications are applets and stand-alone applications. These two forms are are similar enough that further discussions on how to collection GUIs will simply refer to applet creation.

Abstract Windows Toolkit

Applet users input screens, or collection devices, are essentially a whole bunch of data and text fields that the users can use to enter information. When you start talking about facilitating this using Java, keep in mind the supplied Java facilities to accomplish such a task. The Abstract Windows Toolkit (AWT) is the set of window development tools Specifically, the AWT is a set of GUI devices such as radio buttons, check boxes, text edit fields, other widgets, and standard dialogs.

The portability of Java comes from interpreters that implement and provide services to the JVM. A section of these services is dedicated to providing a standard set of GUI building blocks, which are implemented on the local platform. This set of GUI building blocks is the AWT. All graphic-based Java applications must use the AWT to produce any type of GUI. Seeing how almost everything that is needed to facilitate a user input screen is found in the AWT, functioning properly is a pretty big concern.

Cross-Platform, Cross-Browser Problems

Ask any Java programmer what the biggest problem is with Java, and he or she will tell you the AWT. Without getting into all the known bugs, note that cross-platform and cross-browser support of the AWT varies. However, before you start getting the wrong idea of the AWT, it isn't all that bad. As long as you are aware that anomalies exist, you can facilitate, for the most part, quick and dirty countermeasures.

The AWT is available to any Java application on any Java-ready platform. This might not sound like such a big thing, but the opposite of this statement is that Java applications have all AWT services and facilities built in to themselves. The difference between these two statements has to do with conformity. If the application contains all needed AWT functionality, you could assume that the application would be able to present its GUI no matter what the platform. With the AWT existing on the local machine, the application is at the mercy of the local platform's implementation to display correctly. That alone wouldn't be such a bad thing if all implementations of the AWT ensured standard display characteristics, but they don't.

It is true that Java code will execute on any Java-enabled platform; so does the AWT. However, in the case of the AWT, it runs, but it appears different from platform to platform and from browser to browser. It is possible, and highly regular, to counteract most of these differences; doing so gets a little complicated, but it can be done. The bottom line is that you should not count on your Java-based GUI to look exactly the same on all platforms and on all browsers.

GUI Creation with Symantec's Café

Anyone who has ever had the displeasure of hand-coding a GUI will preach about resource editors. For those of you who have never had to hand-code a GUI, or have no idea what "hand-coding" means, consider yourself lucky. Back in the days before resource editors, the programmer was responsible for declaring, calculating position, and in general maintaining all of the widgets' properties. Resource editors save the programmer from the time-intensive task of laying out and manipulating a GUI. The benefit of such a tool became evident after programmers had a chance to see a resource editor in work and then look at what its code generated. The following code listing is the hello applet before Symantec's Café resource editor made it into a GUI order-entry screen.

```
import java.awt.*;
import java.applet.*;

public class Hello extends Applet {

    public void init() {

        super.init();

        //{{INIT_CONTROLS
        setLayout(null);
        resize(230,190);
        label1=new Label("Before");
        add(label1);
        label1.reshape(61,73,98,15);
        //}}
    }

    public boolean handleEvent(Event event) {
        return super.handleEvent(event);
    }
```

Figure 8.4 Blank applet.

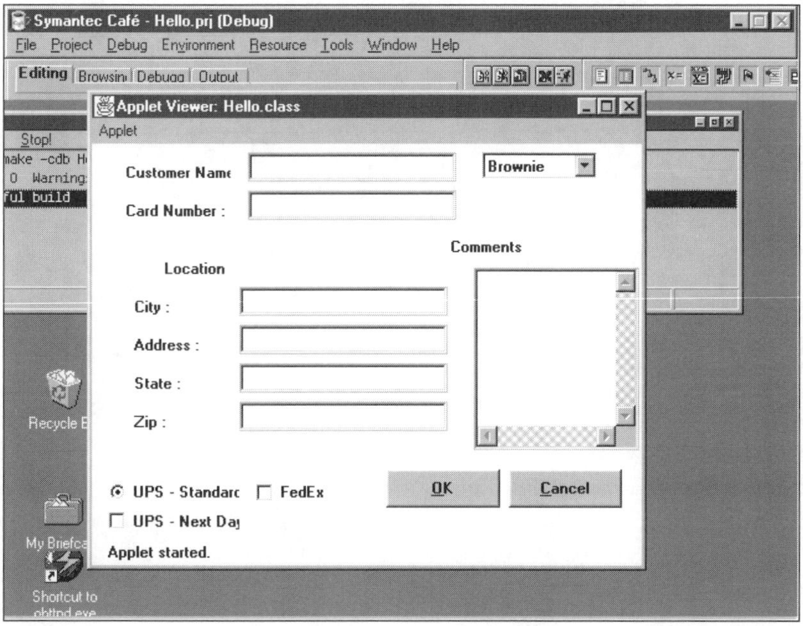

```
//{{DECLARE_CONTROLS
Label label1;
//}}
```

}

The Café resource editor is a WYSIWYG GUI builder. It provides a base set of widgets from which to create your GUI from. To newcomers of GUI development, the idea of graphically laying out a screen might seem as matter of fact as milk and cookies. However, resource editors are a luxury not to be taken for granted. With Symantec's integrated development environment, resource editor, and application Wizard, developers are able to focus on the application-specific code, rather than on other tedious mechanical tasks. The following code listing is the hello applet after Symantec's Café resource editor made it into a GUI order-entry screen. Notice in the large body of code all the declarations for widgets. This applet was created without writing any code, and all that is shown was generated.

```
import java.awt.*;
import java.applet.*;

public class Hello extends Applet {

    public void init() {

        super.init();

        //{{INIT_CONTROLS
        setLayout(null);
        resize(443,309);
        RegionPanel=new Panel();
        RegionPanel.setLayout(null);
        add(RegionPanel);
        RegionPanel.reshape(7,90,294,150);
        group1= new CheckboxGroup();
        CityEdit=new TextField(16);
        RegionPanel.add(CityEdit);
        CityEdit.reshape(112,22,168,23);
        label1=new Label("Location", Label.CENTER);
        label1.setFont(new Font("Dialog",Font.BOLD,12));
        RegionPanel.add(label1);
        label1.reshape(14,0,112,15);
        label2=new Label("City :");
        RegionPanel.add(label2);
        label2.reshape(14,30,70,15);
        AddressEdit=new TextField(16);
```

```
RegionPanel.add(AddressEdit);
AddressEdit.reshape(112,52,168,23);
label3=new Label("Address :");
RegionPanel.add(label3);
label3.reshape(14,60,70,15);
StateEdit=new TextField(16);
RegionPanel.add(StateEdit);
StateEdit.reshape(112,82,168,23);
label4=new Label("State :");
RegionPanel.add(label4);
label4.reshape(14,90,70,15);
ZipEdit=new TextField(16);
RegionPanel.add(ZipEdit);
ZipEdit.reshape(112,112,168,23);
label5=new Label("Zip :");
RegionPanel.add(label5);
label5.reshape(14,120,70,15);
CityEdit1=new TextField(16);
add(CityEdit1);
CityEdit1.reshape(126,7,168,23);
label6=new Label("Customer Name :");
add(label6);
label6.reshape(14,15,98,15);
CityEdit2=new TextField(16);
add(CityEdit2);
CityEdit2.reshape(126,37,168,23);
label7=new Label("Card Number :");
add(label7);
label7.reshape(14,45,98,15);
ItemSelect= new Choice();
add(ItemSelect);
ItemSelect.reshape(315,7,112,75);
ItemSelect.addItem("Brownie");
ItemSelect.addItem("G Board");
ItemSelect.addItem("More Stuff");
UPSS=new Checkbox("UPS - Standard",group1, true);
add(UPSS);
UPSS.reshape(14,262,105,23);
UPSS1=new Checkbox("UPS - Next Day");
add(UPSS1);
UPSS1.reshape(14,285,105,22);
FedEx=new Checkbox("FedEx");
add(FedEx);
FedEx.reshape(133,262,105,23);
edit1=new TextArea(7,13);
add(edit1);
```

```
        edit1.reshape(308,97,133,143);
        label8=new Label("Comments : ");
        add(label8);
        label8.reshape(276,73,70,15);
        OKBtn=new Button("&OK");
        add(OKBtn);
        OKBtn.reshape(238,255,91,30);
        CancelBtn=new Button("&Cancel");
        add(CancelBtn);
        CancelBtn.reshape(336,255,91,30);
        //}}
    }

    public boolean handleEvent(Event event) {
        return super.handleEvent(event);
    }

    //{{DECLARE_CONTROLS
    Panel RegionPanel;
    CheckboxGroup group1;
    TextField CityEdit;
    Label label1;
    Label label2;
    TextField AddressEdit;
    Label label3;
    TextField StateEdit;
    Label label4;
    TextField ZipEdit;
    Label label5;
    TextField CityEdit1;
    Label label6;
    TextField CityEdit2;
    Label label7;
    Choice ItemSelect;
    Checkbox UPSS;
    Checkbox UPSS1;
    Checkbox FedEx;
    TextArea edit1;
    Label label8;
    Button OKBtn;
    Button CancelBtn;
    //}}

}
```

Figure 8.5 Symantec's Café Generated GUI.

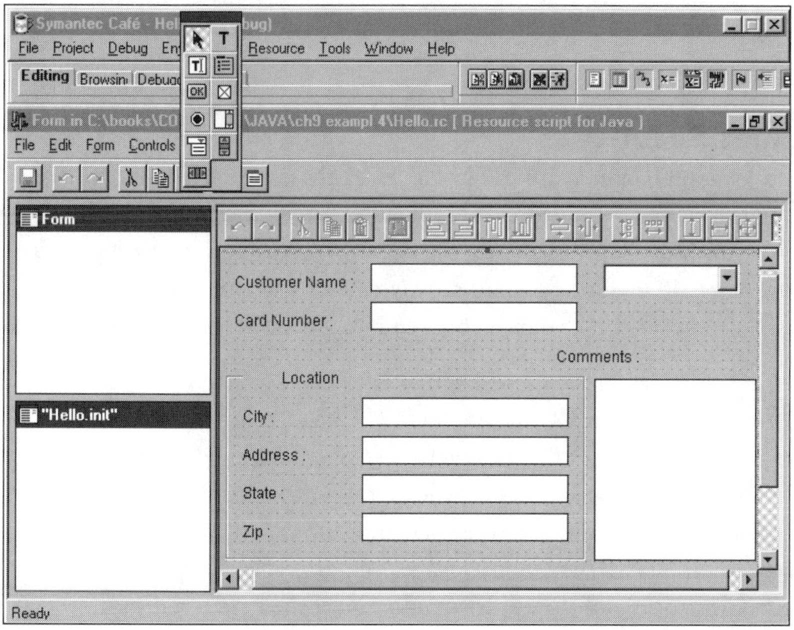

Automatic GUI Creation with Symantec's Visual Café

Visual programming is a relatively new technology. The basic premise behind it is to hide as much code from the developer as possible. This might seem like a drastic step, but in essence it allows for the pure development of "glue" code. That is, it allows the developer to focus on writing the code that is specific to the application. Just as the above resource editor created the GUI for an applet, Visual Café does the same thing but makes it even simpler. For nonprogrammers, this still might sound like rocket science, but in fact visual programming is much simpler than writing straight code. If you are interested in Visual Café, look for my new book, *Symantec Visual Cafe Sourcebook*, coming Summer 1997 from Wiley.

Storing the Data

Creating a GUI for users to enter information is only half the battle. The other half is getting the collected information back to a central repository. Once again, this might seem like a relatively simple task—just open up a file or a database and shovel the information into it. The problem with both of these approaches lies in the limitations of an applet. In specific, applets may talk only to the computer that holds the class files. Possibly even more crippling is an applet's inability to write to server-based files. For these reasons, it is not uncommon for people to believe that applet-based data collection is not possible, which couldn't be farther from the truth, for it *can* be done. You just have to get a little creative.

Getting Around Applet Security

As stated before, stand-alone Java applications are not hindered by the same security restrictions as applets. This fact gives us one obvious workaround to applet security—use a stand-alone application. However, for one reason or another, the primary reason for using Java to facilitate data collection is to take advantage of an applet's rapid deployment characteristics. So, you are back to trying to find a feasible solution, which can be broken into two different categories: server and CGI based solutions.

The CGI approach is a hybrid of Java and CGI technology. The basic principle revolves around an applet's ability to jump the browser to a new URL. That is, an applet has the ability to send the browser, which is displaying the applet, to a new location on the Web. A data collection applet, can load the URL with the information from the user, and ships it off to the waiting CGI For example, a site might contain an HTML order-entry page, and an applet facilitating the same thing. In this case, both the HTML form and the applet would report their information to the same CGI. Using Java in this way eliminates all of the associated problems with HTML forms and gains all of the associated applet intelligence. Chapter 12 contains an applet-to-CGI solution for further examination.

The server-based approach dedicates a server application to carry out all of the taska applets aren't supposed to do. An applet can communicate to its origin computer and no one else. Further, it can't write to a file on a server; it can only read. To eliminate this problem, servers can be constructed to perform the "naughty" actions of an applet such as writing to a file or fetching information from another server. Such a server is contained in Chapter 14. The other solution that falls under the server category is connecting to a JDBC server. Using JDBC in this manner is covered extensively in Chapter 9.

Both workarounds require a decent amount of programming, but never fear. help is near. Chapter 12, to be exact. Java-based data collection offers users the convenience of an intelligent agent, all the while surveying the crucial task of getting the information back for processing. Chapter 14 gives examples of each type of solution to help you as you create your own applet data collection device.

Summary

There is more to Java than just applets. Java is a full-featured development language that can accommodate everything from CGI applications to stand-alone GUI applications to applets. Notice how applet is handled as a special case of a Java application— for good reason. As you learned in this chapter, applets have certain characteristics that hinder Web-based data collection, but there are workarounds. One such workaround is a JDBC solution that will be discussed in Chapter 9. This chapter exposed you to what applets are and what Java is. It exposed you to some helpful tools for creating GUI input devices, and it pointed you to Chapter 12 for all your hard-core example needs. Most of all, this chapter should leave you with the feeling that Java can do it all—you just have to be creative.

9

Database Front
End with JDBC

The intent of this chapter is to provide factual JDBC information, including how JDBC impacts electronic commerce. JDBC offers the means to tie Web commerce solutions to back office database facilities The example in this chapter is used only as a demonstration device, and it should be used as such. Chapters 12 through 14 present real-world JDBC commerce examples. The focus of this chapter is on providing background information; real world examples are left for future chapters.

JDBC

Java Data Base Connectivity (JDBC), without restating the intent hidden in the name, connects Java to a database. For those coming from the Microsoft world, the term ODBC might ring a bell. ODBC is the mechanism by which Windows-based applications can gain access to a database, without worries of database-specific issues. That is, before ODBC (Object Data Base Connectivity) was introduced, applications that wished to access database information would have to talk directly to the database vendor's interface. These interfaces usually vary from one vendor to another, making it almost impossible for an application to access more than a couple of database sources. ODBC and JDBC provide a standard mechanism through which applications can obtain information from a database without having to worry about any vendor-specific issues.

That ODBC and JDBC sound alike, and act alike, is no coincidence for they are based on the same standard. X/Open SQL CLI (Call Level Interface) is an industry standard for SQL (Standard Query Language)-level client support. One of the inherited benefits of creating an open standard, besides the obvious freedom from specific issues, is the ability to leverage existing technology. In the case of JDBC, the open standard of ODBC was in place and contained a decent amount of vendor support. JDBC was able to leverage this technology to provide instant access to a substantial pool of database vendors' support. This by no means implies that JDBC technology is dependent on ODBC; rather, JDBC uses ODBC to provide a short-term fix. A number of vendors have signed on to create their own JDBC drivers, which will effectively eliminate JDBC's use of ODBC. The following is a list of database vendors signed on to support JDBC; further information can be found at http://splash.javasoft.com/jdbc/.

- Borland International

- Bulletproof

- Cyber SQL

- DataRamp

- Dharma Systems

- Gupta

- IBM's Database 2 (DB2)

- Imaginary (mSQL)

- Informix Software

- Intersoft

- Intersolv

- Object Design

- Open Horizon

- OpenLink Software

- Oracle Corporation

- Persistence Software

- Presence Information Design

- PRO-C

- RogueWave Software

- Recital

- SAS Institute

- SCO

- Sybase

- Symantec

- Thunderstone

- Visigenic Software

- WebLogic

- XDB Systems

Java-Provided Tools

To provide access to JDBC, Java created an add-on library to the Java Development Kit (JDK) that will be shipped as standard equipment in the next major revision of the JDK. This new library, java.sql, gives Java applications the needed tools to issue SQL statements, retrieve data sets, and do other important database type things. More specific information can be found at http://splash.javasoft.com/jdbc/. Brian Jepson's *Java Database Programming*, published by John Wiley & Sons, provides more in-depth information about this technology. The use and level of detail of JDBC for this book is to provide commerce solutions with the ability to utilize a database. Later in this chapter, an example of such a commerce solution is presented.

Drivers

Let's go back to the discussion of what JDBC is and how it fits in with java.sql. The plain and simple truth is that JDBC, in particular java.sql, is a wrapper around a set of standard database vendor support libraries. That is, even though java.sql supplies the access to JDBC, you will still need either a driver for each database you choose to access or a driver to access ODBC.

Types of JDBC drivers can be broken into four distinct categories. In comparison to ODBC, JDBC drivers can be quite a bit more complicated. ODBC assumes that all of its drivers will be native to the ODBC platform; however, Java cannot make such assumptions. The result: JDBC drivers can be natively implemented or can exist completely in Java, or in combinations of these two options. Each solution provides its own set of characteristics; for example, Java code is portable but slower than native code, and native code is faster but not portable.

The following is a list of JDBC driver types:

- JDBC to ODBC bridges

- Native Internet-ready driver with a Java wrapper

- Native driver with a Java wrapper

- All Java solution

JDBC to ODBC bridge drivers suffer from the same ailment as all the solutions that access native code, and that ailment is native code. The use of native code hinders the usability and portability of a Java solution. JDBC to ODBC bridge drivers provide java.sql a DLL, as well as the DLL's Java wrapper, to access the facilities of ODBC. Allowing JDBC to access ODBC facilities gives JDBC access to the large pool of ODBC database vendors' drivers. JDBC to ODBC bridges allow JDBC the ability to access all accessible ODBC databases.

Internet-ready and non-Internet-ready native JDBC drivers refer to the ability of a native JDBC driver to access a database server over the Internet. This means that Internet-ready drivers must specify a fully qualified domain and server (database.domain.com), thus giving the driver the ability to access remote database resources. Non-Internet drivers require the database server to be on the same machine as the calling Java applications. These solutions can be viewed as the first attempt to port existing drivers to a Java implementation; however, they are still hindered by the use of native code.

From the discussion of the prior JDBC driver solutions, it may become clear that the use of native code in a JDBC driver it not such a good thing. You may also infer that the logical solution to the use of native code is to implement the driver entirely in Java, which by chance is the last classification of JDBC drivers. All Java-native JDBC drivers relieve all the associated problems with native code. All Java drivers give applets ready availability to utilize JDBC, a feat close to impossible with native drivers.

JDBC is a new technology, and as such it will undergo some growing pains. Currently, JDBC drivers are available primarily from third-party vendors. Database vendors will probably begin shipping JDBC drivers alongside ODBC drivers, but at present JDBC drivers are not readily available. The following is a list of JDBC driver manufacturers, including the type of driver they produce:

- JavaSoft's JDBC-ODBC Bridge

- WebLogic's jdbcKona, an Internet-ready native driver with support for Oracle, Sybase, MS SQL Server

- WebLogic's jdbcKonaT3, an all Java driver that relies on an ODBC server and supports all ODBC-supported databases

- Visigenic's VisiChannel, an all Java driver that relies on an ODBC server and supports all ODBC supported databases

- DataRamp's Client for Java, an all Java driver that relies on an ODBC server and supports all ODBC supported databases

- Borland's InterClient, an all Java client that requires no native support and supports access to Borland's Interbase server 4.0

- Imaginary's mSQL-JDBC driver, an all Java client that requires no native support and supports access to Microsoft's SQL server

- Intersolv's DataDirect, an Internet-ready native driver with support for Oracle and Sybase

- OpenLink's JDBC Drivers, a set of Java drivers that rely on a native server to communicate with one of the supported databases (Oracle, Informix, Sybase, MS SQL Server, CA-Ingres, Progress, Unify, and Postgress95)

- Intersoft's Essentia-JDBC, a Java driver that relies on a native server to communicate with the single supported database, Intersoft's Essentia

- SCO's SQL-Retriever, a set of Java drivers that rely on a native server to communicate with one of the supported databases (Informix, Oracle, Ingres, Sybase, and Interbase)

- SAS's SHARE*NET driver, an all Java client that requires no native support and supports access to SAS, and via SAS/ACCESS, Oracle, Informix, Ingres, and ADABAS

Further information and an up-to-date list can be found at http://splash.javasoft.com/jdbc/jdbc .drivers.html.

Using JDBC

As mentioned earlier, to utilize the facilities found in java.sql, a JDBC driver must be obtained to communicate with the database server. The acquisition of an appropriate JDBC driver is mandatory for the proper execution of java.sql; the selection of the JDBC driver is key. Not all drivers are created equal, and likewise not all drivers cost the same. Selecting a driver to suit your needs is crucial. For example, some driver solutions may not be used by applets. Each JDBC driver supplies its own unique set of characteristics and should be assessed carefully before using. For the purpose of demonstrating the use of JDBC, a commonly used driver, WebLogic's jdbcKona product, was chosen that demonstrates the typical use of JDBC technology.

WebLogic's JDBC Support

WebLogic offers two sets of drivers, a Java and a native implementation. The native driver, jdbcKona, utilizes a DLL from which the JDBC driver accesses the database information. This method has its shortcomings, but it benefits from the pure speed of native code. It should be noted that the jdbcKona product is not readily accessible from within an applet. Using jdbcKona, accessing JDBC from within an applet would require a special "Applets JDBC Server" to be created, which is exactly what WebLogic did to create its Java-based JDBC driver.

WebLogic's Java-based JDBC driver (jdbcKonaT3) comes in the flavor of a three-tiered solution. What a three-tiered solution entails is a client, middleware, and a server. In the case of a WebLogic's JDBC implementation, the client would be the JDBC client, the middleware would be jdbcKonaT3, and the server would be the database server. What the jdbcKonaT3 provides is a system comprising a JDBC driver, a server, and native database accessing routines that allow all Java applications to connect to a database server. Further information can be found on WebLogic's Web page, http://www.weblogic.com.

Example JDBC Client

By the nature of database application, each is unique. Some applications may query for an order, and others for customer information. Providing a detailed and all-encompassing example JDBC client is an insurmountable task. Figure 9.1 displays a primitive data entry screen allowing users to enter customer information. Following the figure is a complete source listing for this application.

```
/*
   A basic extension of the java.awt.Frame class
*/

import java.awt.*;
```

Figure 9.1 JDBC Order Entry Application.

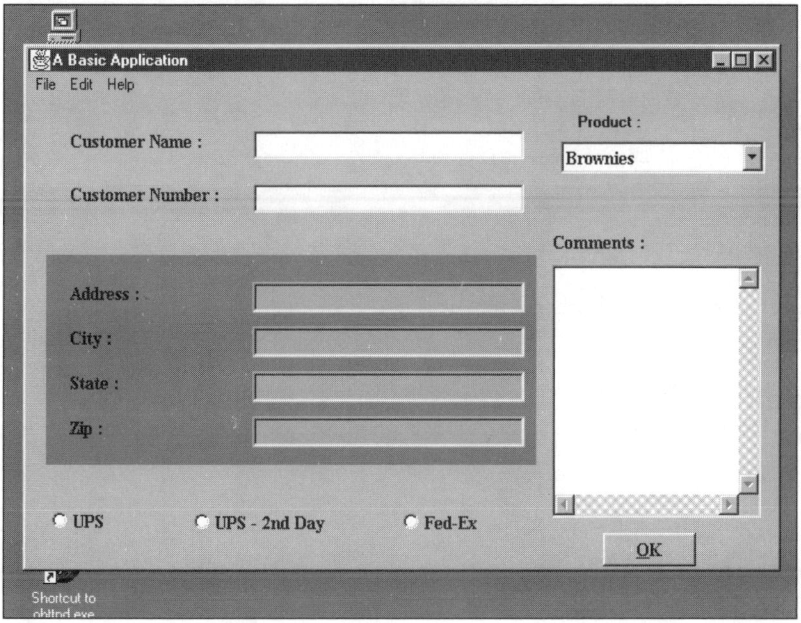

```
import java.sql.*;
import weblogic.db.jdbc.*;
import java.util.Properties;

public class JDBCAGENT extends Frame {
        void OkBtn_Clicked(Event event) {

          try{

                //Setup the database login properties
                Properties props = new java.util.Properties();
                props.put("user",      "JDBCAGENT");
                props.put("password",  "BLAHBLAH");
                props.put("server",    "DUALBEAST");

                //Get the JDBC class, and initialize the driver with the login properties.
                Class.forName("weblogic.jdbc.dblib.Driver");
                java.sql.Connection conn =
java.sql.DriverManager.getConnection("jdbc:weblogic:mssqlserver", props);


                //Create the SQL insert statment
```

```
            String insert = "insert into NEWORDER(NAME,NUMBER,ADDRESS) values "+
                "('"+
                CustName.getText()+"', '"+
                CustNum.getText()+"', '"+
                Address.getText()+"')";

        //Open a stament constext
        Statement stmt1 = conn.createStatement();

        //execute the insert
        stmt1.execute(insert);

        //Close the statement and the connection
        stmt1.close();
        conn.close();

    }catch(Exception e)//Generic handeler
    {
        OUTPUT.setText("NO GOOD - " + e.getMessage());
        return;
    }
            (new QuitDialog(this,"", false)).show();
    }

    void Open_Action(Event event) {
            OpenFileDialog.show();
    }

    void About_Action(Event event) {
            (new AboutDialog(this, "About...", false)).show();
    }

    void Exit_Action(Event event) {
            (new QuitDialog(this, "Quit the Application?", false)).show();
    }

    public JDBCAGENT() {

            //{{INIT_CONTROLS
            setLayout(null);
            addNotify();
            resize(insets().left + insets().right + 605,insets().top + insets().bottom +
385);
            setBackground(new Color(12632256));
            OpenFileDialog = new java.awt.FileDialog(this, "Open",FileDialog.LOAD);
            label1 = new java.awt.Label("Customer Name :");
```

```
label1.reshape(insets().left + 21,insets().top + 25,141,17);
label1.setFont(new Font("TimesRoman", Font.BOLD, 14));
add(label1);
CustName = new java.awt.TextField();
CustName.reshape(insets().left + 183,insets().top + 25,219,24);
CustName.setFont(new Font("TimesRoman", Font.PLAIN, 14));
add(CustName);
label2 = new java.awt.Label("Customer Number :");
label2.reshape(insets().left + 21,insets().top + 67,141,17);
label2.setFont(new Font("TimesRoman", Font.BOLD, 14));
add(label2);
CustNum = new java.awt.TextField();
CustNum.reshape(insets().left + 183,insets().top + 67,219,24);
CustNum.setFont(new Font("TimesRoman", Font.PLAIN, 14));
add(CustNum);
Products = new java.awt.Choice();
Products.addItem("Brownies");
Products.addItem("G -Boards");
Products.addItem("More Stuff ...");
add(Products);
Products.reshape(insets().left + 429,insets().top + 25,165,70);
Products.setFont(new Font("TimesRoman", Font.BOLD, 14));
textArea1 = new java.awt.TextArea();
textArea1.reshape(insets().left + 423,insets().top + 130,171,199);
add(textArea1);
label3 = new java.awt.Label("Comments :");
label3.reshape(insets().left + 411,insets().top + 102,93,21);
label3.setFont(new Font("TimesRoman", Font.BOLD, 14));
label3.setForeground(new Color(0));
add(label3);
panel1 = new java.awt.Panel();
panel1.setLayout(null);
panel1.reshape(insets().left + 15,insets().top + 123,396,164);
panel1.setBackground(new Color(8421504));
add(panel1);
label4 = new java.awt.Label("Address :");
label4.reshape(6,21,141,17);
label4.setFont(new Font("TimesRoman", Font.BOLD, 14));
panel1.add(label4);
Address = new java.awt.TextField();
Address.reshape(168,21,219,24);
Address.setFont(new Font("TimesRoman", Font.PLAIN, 14));
panel1.add(Address);
label5 = new java.awt.Label("City :");
label5.reshape(6,56,141,17);
label5.setFont(new Font("TimesRoman", Font.BOLD, 14));
```

```
panel1.add(label5);
City = new java.awt.TextField();
City.reshape(168,56,219,24);
City.setFont(new Font("TimesRoman", Font.PLAIN, 14));
panel1.add(City);
label6 = new java.awt.Label("State :");
label6.reshape(6,91,141,17);
label6.setFont(new Font("TimesRoman", Font.BOLD, 14));
panel1.add(label6);
State = new java.awt.TextField();
State.reshape(168,91,219,24);
State.setFont(new Font("TimesRoman", Font.PLAIN, 14));
panel1.add(State);
label7 = new java.awt.Label("Zip :");
label7.reshape(6,126,141,17);
label7.setFont(new Font("TimesRoman", Font.BOLD, 14));
panel1.add(label7);
Zip = new java.awt.TextField();
Zip.reshape(168,126,219,24);
Zip.setFont(new Font("TimesRoman", Font.PLAIN, 14));
panel1.add(Zip);
Group1 = new CheckboxGroup();
UPS = new java.awt.Checkbox("UPS", Group1, false);
UPS.reshape(insets().left + 19,insets().top + 311,100,40);
UPS.setFont(new Font("TimesRoman", Font.BOLD, 14));
add(UPS);
TwoDay = new java.awt.Checkbox("UPS - 2nd Day", Group1, false);
TwoDay.reshape(insets().left + 135,insets().top + 312,117,40);
TwoDay.setFont(new Font("TimesRoman", Font.BOLD, 14));
add(TwoDay);
FedEx = new java.awt.Checkbox("Fed-Ex", Group1, false);
FedEx.reshape(insets().left + 303,insets().top + 312,100,40);
FedEx.setFont(new Font("TimesRoman", Font.BOLD, 14));
add(FedEx);
OkBtn = new java.awt.Button("&OK");
OkBtn.reshape(insets().left + 465,insets().top + 340,75,26);
OkBtn.setFont(new Font("TimesRoman", Font.BOLD, 14));
add(OkBtn);
OUTPUT = new java.awt.Label("");
OUTPUT.reshape(insets().left + 81,insets().top + 347,351,31);
add(OUTPUT);
setTitle("A Basic Application");
//}}

//{{INIT_MENUS
mainMenuBar = new java.awt.MenuBar();
```

```
            menu1 = new java.awt.Menu("File");
            menu1.add("Open...");
            menu1.add("Save");
            menu1.add("Save As...");
            menu1.addSeparator();
            menu1.add("Exit");
            mainMenuBar.add(menu1);

            menu2 = new java.awt.Menu("Edit");
            menu2.add("Cut");
            menu2.add("Copy");
            menu2.add("Paste");
            mainMenuBar.add(menu2);

            menu3 = new java.awt.Menu("Help");
            menu3.add("About");
            mainMenuBar.add(menu3);
            setMenuBar(mainMenuBar);
            //}}
    }

    public JDBCAGENT(String title) {
        this();
        setTitle(title);
    }

public synchronized void show() {
    move(50, 50);
    super.show();
}

    public boolean handleEvent(Event event) {
    if (event.id == Event.WINDOW_DESTROY) {
    hide();            // hide the Frame
        dispose();
        System.exit(0);
        return true;
    }
            if (event.target == OkBtn && event.id == Event.ACTION_EVENT) {
                    OkBtn_Clicked(event);
            }
            return super.handleEvent(event);
    }

    public boolean action(Event event, Object arg) {
            if (event.target instanceof MenuItem) {
```

```
                    String label = (String) arg;
                    if (label.equalsIgnoreCase("Open...")) {
                            Open_Action(event);
                            return true;
                    } else
                    if (label.equalsIgnoreCase("About")) {
                            About_Action(event);
                            return true;
                    } else
        if (label.equalsIgnoreCase("Exit")) {
            Exit_Action(event);
            return true;
        }
            }
            return super.action(event, arg);
    }

    static public void main(String args[]) {
        (new JDBCAGENT()).show();
    }

    //{{DECLARE_CONTROLS
    java.awt.FileDialog OpenFileDialog;
    java.awt.Label label1;
    java.awt.TextField CustName;
    java.awt.Label label2;
    java.awt.TextField CustNum;
    java.awt.Choice Products;
    java.awt.TextArea textArea1;
    java.awt.Label label3;
    java.awt.Panel panel1;
    java.awt.Label label4;
    java.awt.TextField Address;
    java.awt.Label label5;
    java.awt.TextField City;
    java.awt.Label label6;
    java.awt.TextField State;
    java.awt.Label label7;
    java.awt.TextField Zip;
    java.awt.Checkbox UPS;
    CheckboxGroup Group1;
    java.awt.Checkbox TwoDay;
    java.awt.Checkbox FedEx;
    java.awt.Button OkBtn;
    java.awt.Label OUTPUT;
    //}}
```

```
//{{DECLARE_MENUS
java.awt.MenuBar mainMenuBar;
java.awt.Menu menu1;
java.awt.Menu menu2;
java.awt.Menu menu3;
//}}
}
```

The bulk of the application is GUI and overhead. The two points of JDBC specific code are contained to the initial importing or needed libraries and the code to handle the Okbtn click event. The importing of the JDBC libraries is contained to an import of java.sql.* and java.util.

Properties. Further, to use WebLogic's provided tools weblogic.db.jdbc.* must be imported. All together, these required libraries equates to three lines of code that will accompany all of your JDBC enabled Java applications.

```
import java.sql.*;
import weblogic.db.jdbc.*;
import java.util.Properties;
```

java.sql is the Sun-provided JDBC libraries. Older versions of the JDK do not contain these files, but they can be easily obtained from http://splash.javasoft.com/jdbc/jdbc.drivers.html or on the book's accompanying CD-ROM. java.sql is for all intents and purposes the programmer's interface to JDBC facilities, and as such it needs to be "imported" into a calling application.

weblogic.db.jdbc is an add-on to java.sql and provides some extra functionality; however, it is not free. DbKona is the proper name for this library, and it is sold as a JDBC utility and can be found at http://www.weblogic.com.

The last line is simply the Java-provided property facility. Properties provides the ability to store name value pairs in a self-contained unit. With JDBC, these properties are used for passing database login parameters.

The location where the actual JDBC work gets done is contained in the code that handles "what to do when the OK button gets clicked." The actual JDBC code of this application can be broken into four sections: setting up the database login parameters, connecting to the database, issuing the SQL statement, and closing the connection. These sections are denoted in the following code slice, and the slice is contained with a *try-catch* block to handle a generic exception. *SQLException*, *SQLWarning*, and *DataTruncation* are the thrown exceptions for java.sql, but the generic exception was handled to simplify the code.

```
try{

            //Setup the database login properties
            //These properites are used to login into the
                //database.
            Properties props = new java.util.Properties();

                //loads the database user name into the property list
            props.put("user",        "JDBCAGENT");

                //loads the database user's password into the property list
            props.put("password",   "BLAHBLAH");

                //loads the database's server name into the property list
            props.put("server",      "DUALBEAST");

            //Get the JDBC class, and initialize the driver with the login
                //properties.
            Class.forName("weblogic.jdbc.dblib.Driver");

                //Create the "Connection" object.  A connection is used as the
                //primary conduit for database communication. SQL staments
              //are created and exectued through the use of the Connection
                //object.
            java.sql.Connection conn =
java.sql.DriverManager.getConnection("jdbc:weblogic:mssqlserver", props);


            //Create the SQL insert statement. This is the actual
             //SQL string to be exectued.
             String insert = "insert into NEWORDER(NAME,NUMBER,ADDRESS) values "+
                 "('"+
                    //load the customer name into the SQL stament
                CustName.getText()+"', '"+

                    //load the customer number into the SQL stament
                CustNum.getText()+"', '"+

                    //load the customer's address into the SQL stament
                Address.getText()+"')";

        //Create the Stament object from which to execute
          // the "insert" SQL statement.
        Statement stmt1 = conn.createStatement();

        //execute the insert statement
```

```
        stmt1.execute(insert);

        //Close the statement and the connection
        stmt1.close();
        conn.close();

    //Generic handeler. More specific Exceptions can be caught,
    // but for this purpose this works fine.
    }catch(Exception e){

        OUTPUT.setText("NO GOOD - " + e.getMessage());
        return;
    }
```

Besides doing all of the routine setup and shutdown, the code to create and execute a SQL statement amounts to three lines. This demo application merely executes an insert to collect the acquired information. A complete commerce solution would require a substantially larger amount of SQL statements, and Chapter 12 will demonstrate a complete CGI commerce solution for additional help.

Summary

Accessing databases is never, and has never been, an open-and-shut task. JDBC offers a clean and precise solution to the problem, but by no means should it be considered a small and relatively simple tool. Adequately covering all the ins and outs of JDBC requires an entirely separate book. This chapter provides a general overview and an example of a commerce application using JDBC. Further examples of JDBC are included in Chapter 12; for now you should have a basic understanding of what JDBC is and some of the issues that surround it.

JDBC is a beast; java.sql provides shielding from a lot of the ugliness, but in general the underlying code of the JDBC is immense. If you are not comfortable with the JDBC concept, you are not alone—90 percent of Windows programmers try to stay as far away from ODBC as possible. It's not that 90 percent of Windows programmers don't use ODBC; they do. However, they just use tools that hide the ugliness. Java.sql is a small and intuitive interface that provides ready access to JDBC facilities, but nevertheless it can take some getting used to.

3

Secure Commerce With Java

Chapter 10

Java Commerce Tools

It has been said before that the Web lives in dog years. That is, life in the Web community moves orders of magnitude faster than in most other computer fields. What in another industry might take six or seven months to develop, Web developers are forced to achieve in a month. What makes this feat possible is the reliance on and leveraging of existing technology. Using off-the-shelf tools is vital to compete in the rapid development cycle of the Web. That is not to say that you should try to make a square block fit in a round hole; rather, if you know someone else has already gone through the trouble of inventing the wheel, why do it again? For this reason, this chapter provides some nice, tidy, ready-to-use tools that furnish essential functionality for Web commerce development. In specific, the tools provided are geared for Java-based CGI development. The following is a list of the supplied tools:

- CGI library

- Configuration file device

- Order storage facility

- User and state storage

- File string replacement facility

- IC Verify request file device

- IC Verify response file device

- IC Verify credit-card processing device

Each of these tools will be presented in turn. However, the discussion of how to use these tools will be left for Chapter 12. For now, each tool's discussion will be limited to an explanation and its intended usage.

Standard CGI Library

If you are familiar with writing CGI applications, you will be very much at home with the concept of a CGI application library. For those who are new to CGI development, a good CGI library eliminates the sometimes tedious task of CGI development. For example, a CGI must process certain environment variables to access the information sent from the HTML form and then parse the information into a useful form. A CGI library will take care of the CGI-specific tasks and allow you to focus on creating your application.

The following Java CGI library provides a mechanism for obtaining the information sent from an HTML form, along with some other useful features. However, you should be aware of a couple of things before you begin using the library. The first pertains only if you are trying to develop CGI applications to run on a Mac. Sorry, but the Macintosh does not support the mechanism for a standard CGI application; in particular, the Mac does not work with a concept of environment variables. If you must develop CGIs on a Mac, consult your Web server software for its special flavor of CGI.

The second issue is, once again, a platform issue. Java does not provide a clean mechanism for accessing environment variables. Programmers are forced to go outside Java, issue a shell command, and then process the results. This becomes a platform problem when you look at how to execute a new shell. That is, think of the Java program having to execute a command from the command prompt. To do so, the application must execute a new shell. In Windows 95 this command is "command.com /C". Window NT's command is "cmd.exe /C" where the "/C" tells the shell to terminate after it is finished. In order for the CGI library to function correctly, the proper shell execution string must be set. This is achieved by modifying the following line of code:

```
public String GetEnvString = "command.com /C set";
```

This value must be changed unless you are running under Windows 95, in which case you are already good to go. If this value is not set properly, the CGI library will fail and prove itself useless.

The CGI library is given to provide a strong, tested tool for the development of your CGI application. The CD-ROM that accompanies this book has a complete source listing as well as a JavaDoc-created API reference. Chapters 12 and 13 will use this library extensively to create the CGI application examples.

Standard CGI Library Interface

```
Class CommerceUtils.cgilib
```

```
java.lang.Object
   |
   +----CommerceUtils.cgilib
```

```
public class cgilib
extends Object
```

The cgilib provides ready access to Environment, and from information through the use of Env and FormVars properties. NOTE:GetEnvString must either be hardcoded, or passed on construct. This String is used to get a list of Enviroment paramters from the OS. i.e. set in DOS & UNIX. If you experience trouble with this class, verify that GetEnvString is set properly.

Variables

```
GetEnvString
   public String GetEnvString
```

GetEnvString must be set to the proper shell command to obtain the OS's environment variables. Win95 is set as default, for NT replace "command.com" with "cmd.exe". This variable must be set properly for this class to perform correctly.

```
Env
   public Properties Env
```

Env contains all current system environment variables. Look into java.util.Properties to access values.

```
FormVars
   public Properties FormVars
```

FormVars contains all fields returned from the HTML form. Look into java.util.Properties to access values.

Constructors

```
cgilib
   public cgilib()
```

Constructing cgilib without any parameters will force the use of the default GetEnvString. The constructor will go out to the environment, round up all Environment vars, and process them appropriately. Gets and Posts are supported.

cgilib
  public cgilib(String GetEnvCmd)

Constructing cgilib with the GetEnvCmd parameter will override the use of the default GetEnvString with the passed value. The constructor will go out to the environment, round up all Environment vars, and process them appropriately. Gets and Posts are supported.

Parameters:
GetEnvCmd - Overrides the default GetEnvString.

Methods

PrintHeader
  public void PrintHeader()

Outputs the proper CGI context header. Must be called before outputting result HTML page.

Redirect
  public void Redirect(String GotoURL)

Redirects the browser to goto the passed URL.

Parameters:
GotoURL - The URL to send the browser to.

HtmlTop
  public void HtmlTop(String Title)

Outputs the HTML header info, such as the title. After this call the page can be filled with the appropriate content vie System.out.println.

Parameters:
Title - The title of the HTML page.

HtmlBot
  public void HtmlBot()

Outputs the closing HTML tags.

MethGet
  public boolean MethGet()

Checks to see if the form was submitted to the CGI by a "GET" method.

Returns:
Returns true if the form used a "GET"

MethPost
`public boolean MethPost()`

Checks to see if the form was submitted to the CGI by a "POST" method.

Returns:
Returns true if the form used a "POST"

MyBaseUrl
`public String MyBaseUrl()`

Retrieves the CGI's base URL.

Returns:
Returns the base URL of the CGI.

MyFullUrl
`public String MyFullUrl()`

Retrieves the CGI's FULL URL, including all form information.

Returns:
Returns the FULL URL of the CGI.

MyURL
`public String MyURL()`

Retrieves the CGI's base URL.

Returns:
Returns the base URL of the CGI.

CgiError
`public void CgiError(String Title,`
`                     String Message)`

Outputs a Basic CGI Error page with the passed title and message.

Parameters:
Title - The Title of the error page.

Message - The Message in the error page.

PrintVariables
 public String PrintVariables()

Returns a formatted list of the form fields.

Returns:
Returns a line delimited list of form fields.

PrintEnv
  public String PrintEnv()

Returns a formatted list of the environment variables.

Returns:
Returns a line delimited list of environment variables.

Standard CGI Library Code Listing

A soft copy of the following code listing can be found on the CD-ROM that accompanies this book.

```java
package CommerceUtils;

import java.io.IOException;
import java.util.Enumeration;
import java.util.Properties;

//cgilib.java

/**
 * The <tt>cgilib</tt> provides ready access to Environment,
 * and from information through the use of <tt>Env</tt> and
 * <tt>FormVars</tt> properties.
 *
 * NOTE:<tt>GetEnvString</tt> must either be hardcoded, or passed on
 * construct.  This String is used to get a list of Enviroment
 * paramters from the OS.  i.e. <tt>set</tt> in DOS & UNIX.
 * If you experience  trouble with this class, verify that <tt>GetEnvString</tt>
 * is set properly.
 *
 * @version 1.10
 * @author Cary A. Jardin
 */

public class cgilib extends Object{
```

```
//Variable declaration

/**
 * <tt>GetEnvString<\tt> must be set to the proper shell command to obtain
 * the OS's environment variables.  Win95 is set as default, for NT
 * replace "command.com" with "cmd.exe".  This variable must be set
 * properly for this class to perform correctly.
 */

public String GetEnvString = "command.com /C set";

/**
 * <tt>Env<\tt> contains all current system environment variables.
 * Look into <tt>java.util.Properties<\tt> to access values.
 */
public Properties Env = new java.util.Properties();

/**
 * <tt>FormVars<\tt> contains all fields returned from the HTML form.
 * Look into <tt>java.util.Properties<\tt> to access values.
 */
public Properties FormVars = new java.util.Properties();

private int LastRead = 0;


//Constructors

/**
 * Constructing <tt>cgilib<\tt> without any parameters will force the use of the
 * default <tt>GetEnvString<\tt>. The constructor will go out to the environment,
 * round up all Environment vars, and process them appropriately. Gets and Posts
 * are supported.
 */
public cgilib(){
    super();
    if(getenv()){
        if(Env.getProperty("QUERY_STRING") != null){
            getQueryString();
            return;
        }
        getPostString();
    }
}

/**
 * Constructing <tt>cgilib<\tt> with the <tt>GetEnvCmd<\tt> parameter will override the
use of the
```

```
   * default <tt>GetEnvString<\tt> with the passed value. The constructor will go out to
   * the environment,
   * round up all Environment vars, and process them appropriately. Gets and Posts
   * are supported.
   * @param GetEnvCmd    Overrides the default <tt>GetEnvString<\tt>.
   */
public cgilib(String GetEnvCmd){
    super();
    GetEnvString = GetEnvCmd;
    if(getenv()){
        if(Env.getProperty("QUERY_STRING") != null){
            getQueryString();
            return;
        }
        getPostString();
    }
}

/**
 * Outputs the proper CGI context header. Must be called before outputting
 * result HTML page.
 */
public void PrintHeader(){
    System.out.println("Content-type: text/html\n");
}

/**
 * Redirects the browser to goto the passed URL.
 * @param GotoURL    The URL to send the browser to.
 */
public void Redirect(String GotoURL){
    System.out.println("Status: 302 Redirected");
    System.out.println("Content-type: text/html");
    System.out.println("Location: "+GotoURL);
    System.out.println("<HTML><HEAD>");
    System.out.println("<TITLE>Client Redirected</TITLE>");
    System.out.println("</HEAD><BODY>");
    System.out.println("The CGI script has redirected your browser to"+
    "<A HREF="+GotoURL+">this location</A>.");
    System.out.println("</BODY></HTML>");
}

/**
 * Outputs the HTML header info, such as the title.
 * After this call the page can be filled with the
 * appropriate content via <tt>System.out.println<\tt>.
 *
```

```
 * @param Title    The title of the HTML page.
 */
public void HtmlTop(String Title){
    System.out.println("<html>\n<head>\n<title>"
    +Title+"</title>\n</head>\n<body>\n");
}

/**
 * Outputs the closing HTML tags.
 */
public void HtmlBot(){
    System.out.println("</body>\n</html>\n");
    }

/**
 * Checks to see if the form was submitted to the CGI by a "GET"
 * method.
 * @return Returns true if the form used a "GET"
 */
public boolean MethGet(){
    if(Env.getProperty("REQUEST_METHOD") == null)
        return false;
    return (Env.getProperty("REQUEST_METHOD") == "GET");
}

/**
 * Checks to see if the form was submitted to the CGI by a "POST"
 * method.
 * @return Returns true if the form used a "POST"
 */
public boolean MethPost(){
    if(Env.getProperty("REQUEST_METHOD") == null)
        return false;
    return (Env.getProperty("REQUEST_METHOD") == "POST");
}

/**
 * Retrieves the CGI's base URL.
 * @return Returns the base URL of the CGI.
 */
public String MyBaseUrl(){

    String Port = "";

    if(Env.getProperty("SERVER_NAME") == null)
        return "";

    if(Env.getProperty("SERVER_PORT") != "80")
```

```
            Port = ":"+Env.getProperty("SERVER_PORT");


return("http://"+Env.getProperty("SERVER_NAME")+Port+"/"+Env.getProperty("SCRIPT_NAME"));
    }


    /**
     * Retrieves the CGI's FULL URL, including all form information.
     * @return Returns the FULL URL of the CGI.
     */
    public String MyFullUrl(){

        String Port = "";
        String QueryString = "";

        if(Env.getProperty("SERVER_NAME") == null)
            return "";

        if(Env.getProperty("SERVER_PORT") != "80")
            Port = ":"+Env.getProperty("SERVER_PORT");

        if(Env.getProperty("QUERY_STRING") != "")
            QueryString = Env.getProperty("QUERY_STRING");


        return("http://"+Env.getProperty("SERVER_NAME")+Port+"/"+
        Env.getProperty("SCRIPT_NAME")+"/"+Env.getProperty("PATH_INFO")+"/"+QueryString);
    }

    /**
     * Retrieves the CGI's base URL.
     * @return Returns the base URL of the CGI.
     */
    public String MyURL(){
        return MyBaseUrl();
    }

    /**
     * Outputs a Basic CGI Error page with the passed title and message.
     * @param Title      The Title of the error page.
     * @param Message    The Message in the error page.
     */
    public void CgiError(String Title, String Message) {

        PrintHeader();
        HtmlTop(Title);
```

```java
        System.out.println(Message);
        HtmlBot();
}

/**
 * Returns a formatted list of the form fields.
 * @return Returns a line delimited list of form fields.
 */
public String PrintVariables() {

    String output = "";

    try{
            Enumeration e = FormVars.propertyNames();

            for(String s ;e.hasMoreElements();){
                s = (String)e.nextElement();
                output += s + " = "+FormVars.getProperty(s)+"<br>";
            }
    }
    catch(Exception e){
        output +="FORM ERROR : NO ELEMENT";
    }

    return output;
}

/**
 * Returns a formatted list of the environment variables.
 * @return Returns a line delimited list of environment variables.
 */
public String PrintEnv(){

    String output = "";

    try{
            Enumeration e = Env.propertyNames();

            for(String s ;e.hasMoreElements();){
                s = (String)e.nextElement();
                output += s + " = "+Env.getProperty(s)+"<br>";
            }
    }
    catch(Exception e){
        output +="ENV ERROR : NO ELEMENT";
    }
```

```
            return output;
    }

    private boolean getenv(){

        try{
            Runtime r = Runtime.getRuntime();
            Process P = r.exec(GetEnvString);
            Env.load(P.getInputStream());
        }
        catch(Exception e){
            return false;
        }
        return true;
    }

    private String NextToken(String in){

        int start = LastRead;

        for(;LastRead < in.length();++LastRead)
            if((in.charAt(LastRead) == '=')||(in.charAt(LastRead) == '&'))
                break;

        if(start == (LastRead++ - 1))
            return "";
        else
            return in.substring(start,LastRead - 1);

    }

    private void getQueryString(){
        String parseme = Env.getProperty("QUERY_STRING");
        String token   = "";
        String field   = "";

        for(;;){
            field = NextToken(parseme);
            token = NextToken(parseme);
            FormVars.put(field,token);
            if(LastRead >= parseme.length())
                break;
        }
    }

    private void getPostString(){

        String input     = null;
```

```
        String token    = "";
        String field    = "";

        try{
            Integer tmp      = new Integer(Env.getProperty("CONTENT_LENGTH"));
            int size         = tmp.intValue();
            byte inbytes[]  = new byte[size];
            for(int i = 0;i < size;)
                i += System.in.read(inbytes,i,size-1);
            input = new String(inbytes,0);
        }
        catch(Exception e){
        }
        for(;;){
            field = NextToken(input);
            token = NextToken(input);
            FormVars.put(field,token);
            if(LastRead >= input.length())
                break;
        }
    }
}
```

Standard CGI Library Usage

The use of the CGI library is fairly straightforward. At the beginning of the CGI application, the *cgilib* should be created to give you instant access to all environment and form information. Creating *cgilib* would resemble the following code snippet.

```
public static void main(String args[]) {
        cgilib CGIinfo = new cgilib();
            .
            .
            .
            .
}
```

The library contains two constructors. The first, which is shown above, does not require any parameters; the second lets you pass in the environment string. Below is a simple CGI application that will regurgitate the passed-in form information in a nice, neat Web page. Notice the use of the environment parameter in the *cgilib* constructor.

```
import CommerceUtils.*;

public class cgi {
    public static void main(String args[]) {
        cgilib CGIinfo = new cgilib("cmd.exe /C ");
```

```
        CGIinfo.PrintHeader();
        CGIinfo.HtmlTop("TEST");
        CGIinfo.PrintVariables();
        CGIinfo.HtmlBot();
    }
}
```

As you can see, the *cgilib* allows you to construct CGI applications quickly without having to worry about tedious, code-intensive, CGI-specific tasks. Take some time to get familiar with the library, for it offers great features and you need to know they exist before you can use them. The following is the HTML and Web page output of the above CGI application launched from the following HTML form.

**Fig1 FORM

**Fig2 HTML output

**Fig3 Web output

Configuration and Storage Devices

Just as the CGI library provided an effective mechanism for dealing with common CGI-specific tasks, the following libraries provide some useful functionality for the storage and retrieval of information. By no means are these libraries specific to CGI applications. To the contrary, the provided libraries are general-purpose libraries, which just happen to have a logical use in CGI applications. These libraries consist of the following devices:

- Configuration file
- Order storage
- User state storage

Configuration File—INI file

The goal of the configuration file utility is to supply a clean and simple utility for retrieving and storing application information. For example, an application might want to store a set of user-defined characteristics that could be restored the next time the user uses the application. *inifile* provides this functionality through the use of a configuration file. Information can be stored, as well as retrieved from the configuration file, with a single line of code. There is, however, a catch: Applet security does not allow for the writing of files. Thus, for applets the library is bound to only retrieving application information. *inifile's* configuration file format is as follows:

```
[section 1]
value1=Value
   .
   .
   .

[section 2]
value1=Value
   .
   .
   .
```

Information is stored by providing three pieces of information: the section, the property, and the value. Likewise, information is retrieved by providing the section and the property's name.

Configuration File Interface

```
Class CommerceUtils.inifile
```

```
java.lang.Object
   |
   +----CommerceUtils.inifile
```

```
public class inifile
extends Object
```

The inifile provides a configuration file utility. Applets are not allowed to modify the config file. This is obtained by the use of the two constructors. Values are stored in the following format:

```
[Section]
#Comment
Property = Value
```

Variables

```
Curren_Section
   public String Curren_Section
```

Setting Current_Section makes all references local to that section until otherwise specified.

Constructors

```
inifile
   public inifile(String filename)
```

The passed file name is used to read in the local file. This file name will be used in subsequent calls to save the files. A relative or absolute path are accepted. If the file does not exist, the object will not contain any elements. NOTE: Do not use this constructor if using an Applet.

Parameters:
filename - The absolute or relative file path.

inifile
  public inifile(InputStream fileinput)

The input parameter is used only to initialize the object. Subsequent calls to save the file, will fail. NOTE: Use this constructor if using an Applet.

Parameters:
fileinput - Input stream of the config file.

Methods

NewSection
  public boolean NewSection(String SectionName)

Creates a new section with the specified name.

[SectionName]

Parameters:
SectionName - The section name to be added.

Returns:
Returns false if the section already exists. Otherwise true.

CopySection
  **public boolean CopySection(String From,
                              String To)**

Copies all the elements from one section, to another

[From]

~

~

[To]

~
~

Parameters:
From - The section to copy.
To - The section to copy to.

Returns:
Fails if either the "To" section already exists, or the "From" section doesn't exist.

DeleteSection
  public boolean DeleteSection(String SectionName)

Deletes the specified section.

Parameters:
SectionName - The section name to be deleted.

Returns:
Returns false if the section doesn't already exists.

AddProperty
  **public boolean AddProperty(String SectionName,
                              String PropertyName,
                              String Value)**

Adds a property and a value to the specified section. If the section doesn't exist, it will be created. On success the passed section will become the Current_Section.

[SectionName]
PropertyName=Value

Parameters:
SectionName - The section name into which the property is to be added.
PropertyName - The property name.
Value - The passed property's value.

Returns:
Returns false if property already exists.

AddProperty
  **public boolean AddProperty(String PropertyName,
                              String Value)**

Adds a property and a value to Current_Section.

```
[Current_Section]
PropertyName=Value
```

Parameters:
PropertyName - The property name.
Value - The passed property's value.

Returns:
Returns false if either the property already exists or if Current_Section is not set.

ModifyProperty
   public boolean ModifyProperty(String SectionName,
                                 String PropertyName,
                                 String Value)

Modifies the passed property's value. On success the passed section will become the Current_Section.

```
[SectionName]
PropertyName=Value
```

Parameters:
SectionName - The section name in which the property is contained.
PropertyName - The property name.
Value - The passed property's value.

Returns:
Returns false if the property does not exists.

ModifyProperty
   public boolean ModifyProperty(String PropertyName,
                                 String Value)

Modifies the passed property's value.

```
[Curren_Section]
PropertyName=Value
```

Parameters:
PropertyName - The property name.
Value - The passed property's value.

Returns:
Returns false if either the property does not exists, or if Current_Section is not set .

DeleteProperty
  public boolean DeleteProperty(String SectionName,
                                      String PropertyName)

Deletes the passed property. On success the passed section will become the Current_Section.

[SectionName]
XXPropertyNameXX

Parameters:
SectionName - The section name in which the property is contained.
PropertyName - The property name to delete.

Returns:
Returns false if the property does not exists.

DeleteProperty
  public boolean DeleteProperty(String PropertyName)

Deletes the passed property.

[Curren_Section]
XXPropertyNameXX

Parameters:
PropertyName - The property name to delete.

Returns:
Returns false if either the property does not exist, or if Current_Section is not set .

GetProperty
  public String GetProperty(String SectionName,
                            String PropertyName,
                            String DefaultValue)

Retrieves the passed property. On success the passed section will become the Current_Section.

[SectionName]

PropertyName=returned value

Parameters:
SectionName - The section name in which the property is contained.
PropertyName - The property's value to retrieve.
DefaultValue - If the property does not exist, this value will be returned.

Returns:
Returns either the property's value, or DefaultValue on error.

GetProperty
  public String GetProperty(String PropertyName,
                            String DefaultValue)

Retrieves the passed property.

[Current_Section]
PropertyName=returned value

Parameters:
PropertyName - The property's value to retrieve.
DefaultValue - If the property does not exist, this value will be returned.

Returns:
Returns either the property's value, or DefaultValue on error.

PropertyExits
  public boolean PropertyExits(String SectionName,
                               String PropertyName)

Checks the existence of a property.

[SectionName]
? PropertyName=value

Parameters:
SectionName - The section name in which the property is contained.
PropertyName - The property to check.

Returns:
Returns true if the property exists.

PropertyExits
  public boolean PropertyExits(String PropertyName)

Checks the existence of a property.

[Curren_Section]
? PropertyName=value

Parameters:
PropertyName - The property to check.

Returns:
Returns true if the property exists.

SectionExits
  public boolean SectionExits(String SectionName)

Checks the existence of a section.

?[SectionName]

Parameters:
SectionName - The section to check.

Returns:
Returns true if the property exists.

SaveToFile
  public boolean SaveToFile()

Saves the configuration to file name passed on construct. If the file already exists it will
be overridden. This function will fail if the InputStream constructor was used.

Returns:
Returns true if the file is successfully saved.

Configuration File Code Listing

```
package CommerceUtils;

import java.io.InputStream;
import java.io.OutputStream;
```

```
import java.io.FileOutputStream;
import java.io.FileInputStream;
import java.util.Hashtable;
import java.util.Properties;
import java.util.Enumeration;
import java.io.StreamTokenizer;


//inifile.java

/**
 * The <tt>inifile</tt> provides a configuration file utility. Applets are
 * not allowed to modify the config file.  This is obtained by the use of
 * the two constructors.
 *
 * Values are stored in the following format:
 * <br>
 * <br>
 * [Section]<br>
 * #Comment<br>
 * Property = Value<br>
 *
 *
 * @version 1.12
 * @author Cary A. Jardin
 */
public class inifile extends Object{

    //Variable declaration
    private Hashtable    IniSections      = new Hashtable(10);
    private String       FileName         = "";    //Create an IO stream from name
    private InputStream  FileIn           = null; //used for Applets


    /**
     * Setting Current_Section makes all references local to that section
     * until otherwise specified.
     */
    public String       Current_Section  = "";

    //Constructors

    /**
     * The passed file name is used to read in the local file.  This file name will
     * be used in subsequent calls to save the files.  A relative or absolute path are
     * accepted. If the file does not exist, the object will not contain any elements.
     *
```

```
   * NOTE: Do not use this constructor if using an Applet.
   *
   * @param filename      The absolute or relative file path.
   */
public inifile(String filename){
      super();
      FileName = filename;
      LoadFromFile();
}


/**
   * The input parameter is used only to initialize the object. Subsequent calls
   * to save the file, will fail.
   *
   * NOTE: Use this constructor if using an Applet.
   *
   * @param fileinput      Input stream of the config file.
   */
public inifile(InputStream fileinput){
    super();
    FileIn = fileinput;
    LoadFromFile();
}


/**
   * Creates a new section with the specified name.
   * <br><br>
   * [SectionName]<br><br>
   *
   *
   * @param SectionName      The section name to be added.
   * @return                 Returns false if the section already exists. Otherwise true.
   */
public boolean NewSection(String SectionName){
      Properties temp = null;

      temp = (Properties)IniSections.put(new String(SectionName),new Properties());

      //it already existed, fail
      if(temp != null){
          IniSections.put(new String(SectionName),temp);
          return false;
      }

      Current_Section = SectionName;
      return true;
```

```
}

/**
 * Copies all the elements from one section, to another
 *<br><br>
 * [From]<br>
 * ~<br>
 * ~<br>
 *<br>
 *<br>
 * [To]<br>
 * ~<br>
 * ~<br>
 *<br><br>
 * @param From      The section to copy.
 * @param To        The section to copy to.
 * @return          Fails if either the "To" section already exists, or the
 *                  "From" section doesn't exist..
 */
public boolean CopySection(String From, String To){

    Properties from = null;
    Properties to   = null;

    from = (Properties)IniSections.get(new String(From));
    //if it doesn't already existed, fail
    if(from == null)
        return false;

    to = (Properties)IniSections.get(new String(To));
    if(to != null)
        return false;

    IniSections.put(To,from);
    Current_Section = To;
    return true;


}

/**
 * Deletes the specified section.
 *
 *
 * @param SectionName     The section name to be deleted.
 * @return                Returns false if the section doesn't already exists.
```

```java
 */
public boolean DeleteSection(String SectionName){
    return (IniSections.remove(new String(SectionName)) != null);
}


/**
 * Adds a property and a value to the specified section. If the section doesn't
 * exist, it will be created.  On success the passed section will become the
 * Current_Section.
 * <br><br>
 * [SectionName]<br>
 * PropertyName=Value<br>
 * <br><br>
 * @param SectionName     The section name into which the property is to be added.
 * @param PropertyName    The property name.
 * @param Value           The passed property's value.
 * @return                Returns false if property already exists.
 */
public boolean AddProperty(String SectionName, String PropertyName, String Value){

    Properties temp = null;

    //check to see if it exists
    if (IniSections.get(new String(SectionName)) == null)
        NewSection(SectionName);

    temp = (Properties)IniSections.get(new String(SectionName));

    //if it already exist, fail
    if(temp.getProperty(PropertyName) != null)
        return false;

    temp.put(PropertyName,Value);
    IniSections.put(new String(SectionName),temp);
    Current_Section = SectionName;
    return true;
}


/**
 * Adds a property and a value to Current_Section.
 * <br><br>
 * [Current_Section]<br>
 * PropertyName=Value<br>
 * <br><br>
```

```
 * @param PropertyName      The property name.
 * @param Value             The passed property's value.
 * @return                  Returns false if either the property already exists
 *                          or if Current_Section is not set.
 */
public boolean AddProperty(String PropertyName, String Value){
    if(Current_Section != "")
        return AddProperty(Current_Section,PropertyName,Value);
    else
        return false;
}


/**
 * Modifies the passed property's value. On success the passed section will become the
 * Current_Section.
 * <br><br>
 * [SectionName]<br>
 * PropertyName=Value<br>
 * <br><br>
 * @param SectionName       The section name in which the property is contained.
 * @param PropertyName      The property name.
 * @param Value             The passed property's value.
 * @return                  Returns false if the property does not exists.
 */
public boolean ModifyProperty(String SectionName, String PropertyName, String Value){
    Properties temp = null;

    //if it doesn't exist fail
    if (IniSections.get(new String(SectionName)) == null)
        return false;

    temp = (Properties)IniSections.get(new String(SectionName));

    temp.put(PropertyName,Value);
    IniSections.put(new String(SectionName),temp);
    Current_Section = SectionName;
    return true;
}


/**
 * Modifies the passed property's value.
 * <br><br>
 * [Current_Section]<br>
 * PropertyName=Value<br>
 * <br><br>
 * @param PropertyName      The property name.
 * @param Value             The passed property's value.
 * @return                  Returns false if either the property does not exists,
```

```
*                            or if Current_Section is not set .
 */
public boolean ModifyProperty(String PropertyName, String Value){
    if(Current_Section != "")
        return ModifyProperty(Current_Section,PropertyName,Value);
    else
        return false;
}


/**
 * Deletes the passed property.  On success the passed section will become the
 * Current_Section.
 * <br><br>
 * [SectionName]<br>
 * XXPropertyNameXX<br>
 * <br><br>
 * @param SectionName     The section name in which the property is contained.
 * @param PropertyName    The property name to delete.
 * @return                Returns false if the property does not exists.
 */
public boolean DeleteProperty(String SectionName, String PropertyName){


    Properties   temp = null;
    boolean      returnvalue = false;

    //if it doesn't exist fail
    if (IniSections.get(new String(SectionName)) == null)
        return false;

    temp = (Properties)IniSections.get(new String(SectionName));

    returnvalue = temp.remove(PropertyName) != null;

    if(returnvalue){
        IniSections.put(new String(SectionName),temp);
        Current_Section = SectionName;
    }

    return returnvalue;
}

/**
 * Deletes the passed property.
 * <br><br>
 * [Current_Section]<br>
```

```
 * XXPropertyNameXX<br>
 * <br><br>
 * @param PropertyName    The property name to delete.
 * @return               Returns false if either the property does not exist,
 *                       or if Current_Section is not set .
 */
public boolean DeleteProperty(String PropertyName){
    if(Current_Section != "")
        return DeleteProperty(Current_Section,PropertyName);
    else
        return false;
}


/**
 * Retrieves the passed property.  On success the passed section will become the
 * Current_Section.
 * <br><br>
 * [SectionName]<br>
 * PropertyName=returned value<br>
 * <br><br>
 * @param SectionName    The section name in which the property is contained.
 * @param PropertyName   The property's value to retrieve.
 * @param DefaultValue   If the property does not exist, this value will be returned.
 * @return               Returns either the property's value, or DefaultValue on error.
 */
public String GetProperty(String SectionName, String PropertyName, String DefaultValue){

    Properties  temp = null;

    //if it doesn't exist fail
    if (IniSections.get(new String(SectionName)) == null)
        return DefaultValue;

    temp = (Properties)IniSections.get(new String(SectionName));
    Current_Section = SectionName;
    return temp.getProperty(PropertyName, DefaultValue);
}


/**
 * Retrieves the passed property.
 * <br><br>
 * [Current_Section]<br>
 * PropertyName=returned value<br>
 * <br><br>
 * @param PropertyName   The property's value to retrieve.
 * @param DefaultValue   If the property does not exist, this value will be returned.
 * @return               Returns either the property's value, or DefaultValue on error.
```

```
    */
public String GetProperty(String PropertyName, String DefaultValue){
    if(Current_Section != "")
        return GetProperty(Current_Section,PropertyName,DefaultValue);
    else
        return DefaultValue;
}


/**
  * Checks the existence of a property.
  * <br><br>
  * [SectionName]<br>
  * ? PropertyName=value<br>
  * <br><br>
  * @param SectionName     The section name in which the property is contained.
  * @param PropertyName     The property to check.
  * @return                 Returns true if the property exists.
  */
public boolean PropertyExits(String SectionName, String PropertyName){
    Properties  temp = null;

    //if it doesn't exist, return false
    if (IniSections.get(new String(SectionName)) == null)
        return false;

    temp = (Properties)IniSections.get(new String(SectionName));
    Current_Section = SectionName;

    return (temp.getProperty(PropertyName) != null);
}


/**
  * Checks the existence of a property.
  * <br><br>
  * [Current_Section]<br>
  * ? PropertyName=value<br>
  * <br><br>
  * @param PropertyName     The property to check.
  * @return                 Returns true if the property exists.
  */
public boolean PropertyExits(String PropertyName){
    if(Current_Section != "")
        return PropertyExits(Current_Section,PropertyName);
    else
        return false;
}
```

```java
/**
 * Checks the existence of a section.
 * <br><br>
 * ?[SectionName]<br>
 * <br><br>
 * @param SectionName     The section to check.
 * @return               Returns true if the property exists.
 */
public boolean SectionExits(String SectionName){
    //if it doesn't exist, return false
    return (IniSections.get(new String(SectionName)) != null);
}


/**
 * Saves the configuration to file name passed on construct. If the file already
 * exists it will be overridden.  This function will fail if the InputStream
 * constructor was used.
 * @return               Returns true if the file is successfully saved.
 */
public boolean SaveToFile(){

    FileOutputStream output = null;
    Enumeration sections = IniSections.keys();
    Properties temp = null;
    String tmpsection;
    byte sectionheading[]=null;

    //make sure the file is valid, and OK to write
    if( (FileName == "") || (FileIn != null))
        return false;

    //re-write the file
    try{
        output = new FileOutputStream(FileName);
    }
    catch(Exception e){
        return false;
    }

    //Output the sections
    for (;sections.hasMoreElements();) {
        tmpsection =(String)sections.nextElement();
        temp = (Properties)IniSections.get(new String(tmpsection));
        if(temp != null)
        {
            String s = "["+tmpsection+"]\n";
            sectionheading = new byte[s.length()];
```

```
            s.getBytes(0, s.length(),sectionheading,0);
            try{
                output.write(sectionheading);
            }
            catch(Exception e){
                return false;
            }

            temp.save(output,null);
        }
    }

    //try to close
    try{
        output.close();
    }
    catch(Exception e)
    {
        return false;
    }
    return true;
}

private boolean LoadFromFile(){
    StreamTokenizer parser    = null;
    FileInputStream input     = null;
    int     tokentype         = 0;
    boolean lastsection       = false;
    boolean lastproperty      = false;
    boolean lastvalue         = false;
    String token              = "";
    String Section            = "";
    String Property           = "";
    String Value              = "";

    //make sure the file is valid, and OK to write
    if((FileName == "") && (FileIn == null))
        return false;

    if(FileIn == null){
        try{
            input = new FileInputStream(FileName);
        }
        catch(Exception e){
            return false;
        }
```

```
        parser = new StreamTokenizer(input);
    }else
        parser = new StreamTokenizer(FileIn);

//setup the parser
parser.resetSyntax();
parser.wordChars(33, 126);
parser.whitespaceChars(0,32);
parser.commentChar('#');
parser.eolIsSignificant(true);
parser.ordinaryChar('=');
try{

    for(;;){

        tokentype = parser.nextToken();
        if(tokentype == parser.TT_WORD){
            token = parser.sval;
            if(IsSection(token)){
                if(parser.nextToken() == parser.TT_EOL){
                    Section    = StripSection(token);
                    Property   = "";
                    Value      = "";
                }
                else
                    parser.pushBack();
            }

            tokentype = parser.nextToken();
            if((tokentype == parser.TT_EOL)||(tokentype == parser.TT_EOF)){
                if((Section != "")&& (Property != "")){
                    Value = token;
                    AddProperty(Section,Property,Value);
                    Property   = "";
                    Value      = "";
                }
            }
            else
                if(parser.ttype == '='){
                    Property   = token;
                    Value      = "";
                }
        }
        if(tokentype == parser.TT_EOF)
          break;
    }
```

```
            }
            catch(Exception e){
                return false;
            }

            //close the stream
            try{
                input.close();
            }
            catch(Exception e){
            }

             return true;
        }

    private boolean IsSection(String in){
        return ((in.indexOf('[') != -1) && (in.indexOf(']') != -1));
    }

    private String StripSection(String in){
        int begin = in.indexOf('[');
        int end   = in.indexOf(']');

        if((begin == -1)||(end == -1))
            return null;

        return in.substring(begin+1,end);
    }


}
```

Configuration File Usage

Use of the configuration file library will vary whether accessing from an applet or from a stand-alone application. Applets do not have the ability to write changes to a file, whereas all other Java applications do. To accommodate these two distinct uses, *inifile* offers two separate constructors, one for applets and one for stand-alone applications.

```
inifile ini = new inifile("delme.ini");
```

This example creates an *inifile* object with the filename of the configuration file. The use of this constructor gives the *inifile* the ability to open, create, and write to the specified file. Below is an example of how an applet would construct objects. Notice how a URL is used to obtain an input stream.

```
inifile ini = new inifile((new URL("http://www.xprime.com/test/test.ini")).openStream());
```

Once the object is initialized, you are free to start loading or retrieving properties at will. Be warned that when loading properties, you must call the *SaveToFile* method to commit your changes to files. The following is an example of loading properties into the file, then issuing the *SaveToFile* method. Notice that the section name is passed on the first "Add" of each section. This does two things: It sets that section as the default section for all subsequent "Add" calls, and if the section does not exist, it is created.

```
inifile ini = new inifile("delme.ini");
ini.AddProperty("FirstSection","Name","Hello");
ini.AddProperty("Address","MyName");
ini.AddProperty("2ndSection","Name","Hello");
if(ini.SaveToFile())
   System.out.println("GOOD");
```

delme.ini would appear as follows.

```
[FirstSection]
#Mon Sep 23 19:26:44  1996
Name=Hello
Address=MyName
[2ndSection]
#Mon Sep 23 19:26:44  1996
Name=Hello
```

Order Storage Device

The ability to feed HTML form information into a waiting program is essentially CGI. However, once the CGI application has that information, it has to do something with it. Commerce CGI applications need to store the customer's order so that it can be processed at a later time. Thus, the need for the order storage device.

As the name implies, the order storage device is designed to store form-based information in a file that can be retrieved at a later time. If you perused the supplied configuration file library, you might think that this device is nothing more than a wrapper around the *inifile*, which is exactly the case. However, this wrapper provides automatic unique filename creation and the ability to add multiple properties with the same name.

Order Storage Device Interface

```
Class CommerceUtils.orderfile
```

```
java.lang.Object
   |
```

```
+----CommerceUtils.orderfile
```

public class orderfile
extends Object
The orderfile provides a generic storage device for orders. The order information is
contained in an ini file format in the specified directory and with the specified extension.
The actual file name is created dynamically.

Constructors

orderfile
public orderfile(String orderpath,
String orderextension)

The constructor initiates the ini file, to include creating a unique file name. The passed
path should contain a trailing \, and the extension is assumed to be proceeded with a "." if
you so desire.

Parameters:
orderpath - The absolute or relative path in which to save the order files. The path is
assumed to have a trailing \.
orderextension - The order extension will be appended onto the generated file name.

Methods

AddProperty
public boolean AddProperty(String Name,
String Value)

AddProperty adds name and value pairs to the order file. You can add multiple values using
the same name. In such a case multiple names will have a number appended onto the end of the
name. That is:

ITEMNUMBER = 2234
ITEMNUMBER1 = 334
ITEMNUMBER2 = 23434
...

Parameters:
Name - The title of the value to store;
Value - The value to store;

Returns:
Returns true if the value was successfully added.

Save
```
public boolean Save()
```

Commits the order to a file at the specified path and with the specified extension.

Returns:
Returns true if the file was successfully saved.

Order Storage Device Code Listing

```java
package CommerceUtils;

import java.io.File;
import java.util.Random;


//orderfile.java

/**
 * The <tt>orderfile</tt> provides a generic storage device for
 * orders.  The order information is contained in an ini file format
 * in the specified directory and with the specified extension.
 * The actual file name is created dynamically.
 *
 * @version 1.0
 * @author Cary A. Jardin
 */
public class orderfile extends Object{

        private inifile          OrderStorage    = null;
        private String           OrderPath       = "";
        private String           OrderExtension  = "";
        private static String    OrderStamp      = "CGIOrder";
        private static int       NameLength      = 8;
        private Random           filegenerator   = new Random();


        //Constructors

        /**
         * The constructor initiates the ini file, to include creating a
         * unique file name.  The passed path should contain a trailing \, and
         * the extension is assumed to be proceeded with a "." if you so desire.
         *
         * @param orderpath        The absolute or relative path in which to save the
         *                         order files.  The path is assumed to have a trailing \.
         * @param orderextension   The order extension will be appended onto the generated file
```

```
name.
    */
    public orderfile(String orderpath,String orderextension){
        super();
        OrderPath        = orderpath;
        OrderExtension   = orderextension;

        //create the new orderfile
        OrderStorage = new inifile(GenFileNewName());
    }

    /**
     * AddProperty adds name and value pairs to the order file.
     * You can add multiple values using the same name.  In such
     * a case multiple names will have a number appended onto the end
     * of the name. That is:
     * <br> <br>
     * ITEMNUMBER  = 2234<br>
     * ITEMNUMBER1 = 334<br>
     * ITEMNUMBER2 = 23434<br>
     * ...<br>
     *
     * @param Name            The title of the value to store;
     *
     * @param Value           The value to store;
     *
     * @return                Returns true if the value was successfully added.
     */
    public boolean AddProperty(String Name, String Value){
        int i;
        //check to see if it already exists.
        if(!OrderStorage.PropertyExits(OrderStamp,Name))
            return OrderStorage.AddProperty(OrderStamp,Name,Value);
        else{
            for(i = 1;;++i)
                if(!OrderStorage.PropertyExits(OrderStamp,Name+i))
                    break;
            return OrderStorage.AddProperty(OrderStamp,Name+i,Value);
        }
    }

    /**
     * Commits the order to a file at the specified path and with the
     * specified extension.
     *
     *
```

```
     * @return                  Returns true if the file was successfully saved.
     */
    public boolean Save(){
        return OrderStorage.SaveToFile();
    }

    private String GenFileNewName(){

        String  temp   = "";
        String  good   = "";
        File    tryme  = null;

        for(;;){
            //generate a random id
            temp = "" + Math.abs(filegenerator.nextInt());

            //see if that id exists
            try{
                if(temp.length() > NameLength)
                    good = OrderPath + temp.substring(0,NameLength-1) + OrderExtension;
                else
                    good = OrderPath + temp + OrderExtension;
                tryme = new File(good);
            }
            catch(Exception e){
            }

            if(!tryme.exists())
                break;
        }

        return good;
    }
}
```

Order Storage Device Usage

Although *orderfile* uses the configuration file class, it does not have the same usage characteristics. In fact, the use of *orderfile* is much cleaner. It contains only one constructor and only a limited number of members. The following example incorporates the usage of the entire library.

```
orderfile ordr = new orderfile(".\\",".ord");
ordr.AddProperty("Name","Cary A. Jardin");
ordr.AddProperty("OrderedItem","00234");
ordr.AddProperty("OrderedItem","002345");
ordr.AddProperty("OrderedItem","04234");
ordr.AddProperty("OrderedItem","040234");
```

```
ordr.AddProperty("OrderedItem","0430234");
ordr.AddProperty("OrderedItem","040234");
ordr.AddProperty("OrderedItem","040234");
ordr.Save();
```

Notice that only two parameters are passed to the constructor, ".\\" which is where to store the file, and ".*ord*" which is the order file extension. The object will randomly generate the file located in the supplied directory and containing the supplied extension. The following is a listing of the file generated by the above code.

```
[CGIOrder]
#Sat Sep 28 12:26:49  1996
Name=Cary A. Jardin
OrderedItem6=040234
OrderedItem5=040234
OrderedItem4=0430234
OrderedItem3=040234
OrderedItem2=04234
OrderedItem1=002345
OrderedItem=00234
```

State Storage Device

If you are creating a CGI application with only one order, or form page, this library will not add any benefit. However, if you are creating a shopping cart CGI application, this library will prove itself as useful and as fundamental as the CGI library. Simply put, in shopping cart CGI applications two pieces of information are crucial, whose cart is whose and what is in the cart. The *usermanager* class provides the following set of functionality:

- Automatic creation of distinct user ids

- Maintenance of user storage files

- Maintenance of user state, or where they have been

- Maintenance of user state-specific information

- Maintenance of user static information

All of the above should be self-evident, except possibly for the last item. The *usermanager* has a concept of two distinct types of information that users can possess. The first set of information is local to the position in the Web site. That is, say they insert something in their shopping cart on one page, then use the back button, on their Web browser, to get to a page that they viewed prior to placing the item into the cart. This type of information is called stateful information, for it changes from user state to state, or in Web terms from page to page.

Static information is information that does not change, regardless of the user's position in the Web site. For example, at some point in the Web site, users enters their address and telephone number. This information is not dependent on any other page in the site, and thus it should remain a constant. Information that is to be retained regardless of state is static information.

The *usermanager* is a very helpful mechanism for the creation of Web shopping cart applications. Chapter 14 will use the *usermanager* extensively to create the provided example CGI shopping cart application. If the concept of static and stateful does not jump out at you as obvious and logical, wait until Chapter 14. The use of the *usermanager* will become apparent at that time.

State Storage Device Interface

```
Class CommerceUtils.usermanager


java.lang.Object
    |
    +----CommerceUtils.usermanager


public class usermanager
extends Object
```

The usermanager provides the ability to keep track of a user as they make their way through a series of connected Web pages. In specific, the usermanager provides the means to facilitate a "Shopping Cart" Commerce interface. The system revolves around to distinct sets of data, static and statefull. The Static set remains constant regardless of state. State information contains information local to the current Web page. If the user decides to "go back" to a previous page, the information will reflect this jump.

Variables

```
NextState
  public int NextState
```

NextState provides the next state identifier

```
User
  public String User
```
The User property contains the unique UserID

Constructors

```
usermanager
  public usermanager(String UserID,
                     String State,
                     String basepath,
```

```
String stateextension,
boolean CpyLast) throws IOException
```

The constructor will load the state specified by "State" for "UserID". On success the state information will be available, and NextState will be incremented to the next state. If the object is unable to be created properly, all methods will return an error. The CpyLast flag can be set to copy the information from the last state the NextState.

Parameters:
UserID - The user ID, if value is null a new User will be initiated.
State - The state's information to load.
basepath - The base path of where the User files are to be stored. Assumed to contain a trailing a "\".
stateextension - The extension to append onto the User files.
CpyLast - Copy all of the information stored in the past state, into the NextState. Used if one state retains a memory of prior state.

Throws: IOException
Will be thrown for two reasons, each of which will contain the following message, "Invalid State", or "Invalid UserId"

usermanager
```
public usermanager(String UserID,
                   String State) throws IOException
```

The constructor will load the state specified by "State" for "UserID". On success the state information will be available, and NextState will be incremented to the next state. This constructor assume that default values for the following will be used, basepath, stateextension, CpyLast.

Parameters:
UserID - The user ID, if value is null a new User will be initiated.

Throws: IOException
Will be thrown for two reasons, each of which will contain the following message, "Invalid State", or "Invalid UserId"

usermanager
```
public usermanager() throws IOException
```

This constructor will init a new User, and load the beginning state. Further default value for the following will be used, basepath, stateextension, CpyLast.

Throws: IOException
Will be thrown for two reasons, each of which will contain the following message, "Invalid State", or "Invalid UserId"

Methods

GetStateProperty
```
public String GetStateProperty(String property,
                              String defaultvalue)
```

Retrieves the passed state property's value.

Parameters:
property - The property's value to retrieve.
DefaultValue - If the property does not exist, this value will be returned.

Returns:
Returns either the property's value, or DefaultValue on error.

AddStateProperty
```
public boolean AddStateProperty(String property,
                                String value)
```

Adds a property and a value to current state.

Parameters:
property - The property's name to add.
Value - The passed property's value.

Returns:
Returns false if the property already exists.

ModifyStateProperty
```
public boolean ModifyStateProperty(String property,
                                   String value)
```

Modifies a property's value in the current state.

Parameters:
property - The property's name to be modified.
Value - The passed property's value.

Returns:

Returns false if the property does not exist.

StatePropertyExists
  public boolean StatePropertyExists(String property)

Checks the existence of a state property.

Parameters:
PropertyName - The property to check.

Returns:
Returns true if the property exists.

DeleteStateProperty
  public boolean DeleteStateProperty(String property)

Deletes the passed state property.

Parameters:
PropertyName - The property name to delete.

Returns:
Returns false if the property does not exist.

GetStaticProperty
  public String GetStaticProperty(String property,
                              String defaultvalue)

Retrieves the passed static property's value.

Parameters:
property - The property's value to retrieve.
DefaultValue - If the property does not exist, this value will be returned.

Returns:
Returns either the property's value, or DefaultValue on error.

AddStaticProperty
  public boolean AddStaticProperty(String property,
                                String value)

Adds a property and a value to the static information.

Parameters:
property - The property's name to add.
Value - The passed property's value.

Returns:
Returns false if the property already exists.

ModifyStaticProperty
   public boolean ModifyStaticProperty(String property,
                                         String value)

Modifies a property's value in the static set.

Parameters:
property - The property's name to be modified.
Value - The passed property's value.

Returns:
Returns false if the property does not exist.

StaticPropertyExists
   public boolean StaticPropertyExists(String property)
Checks the existence of a static property.

Parameters:
PropertyName - The property to check.

Returns:
Returns true if the property exists.

DeleteStaticProperty
   public boolean DeleteStaticProperty(String property)

Deletes the passed static property.

Parameters:
PropertyName - The property name to delete.

Returns:
Returns false if the property does not exist.

SaveState
  public boolean SaveState()

Saves the state information to the user's file.

Returns:
Returns true if the file is successfully saved.

State Storage Device Code Listing

```
package CommerceUtils;

import java.io.IOException;
import java.io.File;
import java.util.Random;


//inifile.java

/**
 * The <tt>usermanager</tt> provides the ability to keep track of a
 * user as they make their way through a series of connected
 * Web pages.  In specific, the <tt>usermanager</tt> provides the
 * means to facilitate a "Shopping Cart" Commerce interface.
 *
 * The system revolves around to distinct sets of data, static and
 * statefull.  The Static set remains constant regardless of state.
 * State information contains information local to the current Web page.
 * If the user decides to "go back" to a previous page, the information will
 * reflect this jump.
 *
 * @version 1.0
 * @author Cary A. Jardin
 */
public class usermanager extends Object{
    private static String Static_Header    =    "STATIC";
    private static String BaseHeader       =    "STATE";
    private static int    BaseState        =    345;
    private static int    NameLength       =    8;

    private String  BasePath               =    ".\\";
    private String  StateExtension         =    ".usr";
    private boolean CopyPrevState          =    true;
```

```
private inifile StateStorage              =   null;
private Random  filegenerator             =   new Random();
private boolean OkState                    =   false;

/**
 * NextState provides the next state identifier
 */
public  int     NextState                  =   0;

/**
 * The User property contains the unique UserID
 */
public  String  User                       =   "";


//Constructors

/**
 * The constructor will load the state specified by "State"
 * for "UserID".  On success the state information will be
 * available, and NextState will be incremented to the next
 * state.
 *
 * If the object is unable to be created properly, all methods
 * will return an error.
 *
 * The CpyLast flag can be set to copy the information from the
 * last state the NextState.
 *
 * @param UserID           The user ID, if value is null a new User will
 *                         be initiated.
 * @param State            The state's information to load.
 * @param basepath         The base path of where the User files are to be stored.
 *                         Assumed to contain a trailing a "\".
 * @param stateextension   The extension to append onto the User files.
 * @param CpyLast          Copy all of the information stored in the past state,
 *                         into the NextState. Used if one state retains a memory
 *                         of prior state.
 * @exception IOException  Will be thrown for two reasons, each of which will
 *                         contain the following message, "Invalid State", or
 *                         "Invalid UserId"
 */
public usermanager(String UserID, String State,
                   String basepath, String stateextension,
                   boolean CpyLast) throws IOException
{
    super();
```

```
        initstate(UserID,State,basepath,stateextension,CpyLast);
}


/**
 * The constructor will load the state specified by "State"
 * for "UserID".  On success the state information will be
 * available, and NextState will be incremented to the next
 * state. This constructor assume that default values for the following
 * will be used, basepath, stateextension, CpyLast.
 *
 *
 * @param UserID          The user ID, if value is null a new User will
 *                        be initiated.
 * @exception IOException Will be thrown for two reasons, each of which will
 *                        contain the following message, "Invalid State", or
 *                        "Invalid UserId"
 */
public usermanager(String UserID, String State) throws IOException{

        super();
        initstate(UserID,State,BasePath,StateExtension,CopyPrevState);
}

/**
 * This constructor will init a new User, and load the beginning state. Further
 * default value for the following will be used, basepath, stateextension,
 * CpyLast.
 *
 * @exception IOException  Will be thrown for two reasons, each of which will
 *                         contain the following message, "Invalid State", or
 *                         "Invalid UserId"
 */
public usermanager() throws IOException{

        super();
        initstate(null,null,BasePath,StateExtension,CopyPrevState);
}

/**
 * Retrieves the passed state property's value.
 *
 * @param property       The property's value to retrieve.
 * @param DefaultValue   If the property does not exist, this value will be returned.
 * @return               Returns either the property's value, or DefaultValue on error.
 */
```

```
public String GetStateProperty(String property, String defaultvalue){
    if(!OkState)
        return defaultvalue;
    else
        return StateStorage.GetProperty(BaseHeader + NextState , property,
defaultvalue);
}

/**
 * Adds a property and a value to current state.
 *
 * @param property        The property's name to add.
 * @param Value           The passed property's value.
 * @return                Returns false if the property already exists.
 */
public boolean AddStateProperty(String property, String value){
    if(!OkState)
        return false;
    else
        return StateStorage.AddProperty(BaseHeader +NextState ,property, value);
}



/**
 * Modifies a property's value in the current state.
 *
 * @param property        The property's name to be modified.
 * @param Value           The passed property's value.
 * @return                Returns false if the property does not exist
 */
public boolean ModifyStateProperty(String property, String value){
    if(!OkState)
        return false;
    else
        return StateStorage.ModifyProperty(BaseHeader +NextState ,property, value);
}

/**
 * Checks the existence of a state property.
 *
 * @param PropertyName    The property to check.
 * @return                Returns true if the property exist.
 */
public boolean StatePropertyExists(String property){
    if(!OkState)
        return false;
    else
```

```
        return StateStorage.PropertyExits(BaseHeader + NextState , property);
}

/**
 * Deletes the passed state property.
 *
 * @param PropertyName    The property name to delete.
 * @return                Returns false if the property does not exist.
 */
public boolean DeleteStateProperty(String property){
    if(!OkState)
        return false;
    else
        return StateStorage.DeleteProperty(BaseHeader +NextState ,property);
}

/**
 * Retrieves the passed static property's value.
 *
 * @param property        The property's value to retrieve.
 * @param DefaultValue    If the property does not exist, this value will be returned.
 * @return                Returns either the property's value, or DefaultValue on error.
 */
public String GetStaticProperty(String property, String defaultvalue){
    if(!OkState)
        return "";
    else
        return StateStorage.GetProperty(Static_Header , property, defaultvalue);
}

/**
 * Adds a property and a value to the static information.
 *
 * @param property        The property's name to add.
 * @param Value           The passed property's value.
 * @return                Returns false if the property already exists.
 */
public boolean AddStaticProperty(String property, String value){
        if(!OkState)
            return false;
        else
            return StateStorage.AddProperty(Static_Header,property, value);
}

/**
 * Modifies a property's value in the static set.
 *
```

```
 * @param property          The property's name to be modified.
 * @param Value             The passed property's value.
 * @return                  Returns false if the property does not exist
 */
public boolean ModifyStaticProperty(String property, String value){
    if(!OkState)
        return false;
    else
        return StateStorage.ModifyProperty(Static_Header ,property, value);
}


/**
  * Checks the existence of a static property.
  *
  * @param PropertyName     The property to check.
  * @return                 Returns true if the property exists.
  */
public boolean StaticPropertyExists(String property){
    if(!OkState)
        return false;
    else
        return StateStorage.PropertyExits(Static_Header , property);
}


/**
  * Deletes the passed static property.
  *
  * @param PropertyName     The property name to delete.
  * @return                 Returns false if the property does not exist.
  */
public boolean DeleteStaticProperty(String property){
    if(!OkState)
        return false;
    else
        return StateStorage.DeleteProperty(Static_Header ,property);
}


/**
  * Saves the state information to the user's file.
  *
  * @return                 Returns true if the file is successfully saved.
  */
public boolean SaveState(){
    if(!OkState)
        return false;
    else
        return StateStorage.SaveToFile();
```

```
    }

private void initstate(String UserID, String State,
                    String basepath, String stateextension,
                    boolean CpyLast) throws IOException
        {

        String Filename = "";

        BasePath        =   basepath;
        StateExtension  =   stateextension;
        CopyPrevState   =   CpyLast;

        //check for the file
        if(UserID == null){
            CopyPrevState   = false;
            NextState       = BaseState;
            Filename        = GenFileNewName();
            StateStorage = new inifile(GenFileNewName());
        }
        else{

            User = UserID;

            if(!FileExists(UserID)){
                throw(new IOException("Invalid UserId"));
            }

            StateStorage = new inifile(BasePath + UserID + StateExtension);

            //load the state;

            if(!StateStorage.SectionExits(State)){
                throw(new IOException("Invalid State"));
            }

            try{
                NextState = new Integer(State).intValue() + 1;
            }
            catch(Exception e){
                throw(new IOException("Invalid State"));
            }

            //delete it if it exists
            StateStorage.DeleteSection(BaseHeader+NextState);

            if(CopyPrevState)
```

```
                        StateStorage.CopySection(BaseHeader + (NextState - 1),BaseHeader +
NextState);
                else
                        StateStorage.NewSection(BaseHeader + NextState);
            }

            OkState = true;
    }

    private boolean FileExists(String tryme){

        File trymefile = null;

        try{
            trymefile = new File(BasePath + tryme + StateExtension);
        }
        catch(Exception e){
            //If their is a problem, don't use that file
            return true;
        }

        return trymefile.exists();
    }

    private String GenFileNewName(){

        String  temp    = "";
        String  good    = "";
        File    tryme   = null;

        for(;;){
            //generate a random id
            temp = "" + Math.abs(filegenerator.nextInt());

            User = temp;
            //see if that id exists
            try{
                if(temp.length() > NameLength)
                    good = BasePath + temp.substring(0,NameLength-1) + StateExtension;
                else
                    good = BasePath + temp + StateExtension;
                tryme = new File(good);
            }
            catch(Exception e){
            }

            if(!tryme.exists())
```

```
            break;
      }

      return good;
   }

}
```

State Storage Device Usage

The use of the state storage device is very similar to the *inifile* library, with some minor adjustments. With the state storage device, you have access to store reference information in only two different regions, the static information and the current state information. The following creates a new storage device and loads some information. To get the essence of how to use this device, refer to Chapter 14, where this device is used extensively to facilitate a CGI shopping cart application.

```
usermanager state = null;
try{
   state = new usermanager();
}
catch(Exception e){
}

state.AddStaticProperty("TIME","Lunch Time");
state.AddStateProperty("HALFTIME","Lunch Time");
state.SaveState();
```

The state storage file contains the following:

```
[STATE345]
#Tue Sep 24 12:04:56  1996
HALFTIME=Lunch Time
[STATIC]
#Tue Sep 24 12:04:56  1996
TIME=Lunch Time
```

File String Replacement Facility

Creating robust and reusable CGI solutions revolves around the CGI's ability to adapt to change. The presentation of Web content changes often to keep the interest of patrons or just to spruce up the site. However the actual content, as it pertains to the CGI, remains fairly static. As you will see in Chapter 13, an effective model for creating CGI applications uses template files to produce CGI output. In this manner, the look and feel of an HTML file can change, without having to change a single line of code. To facilitate the use of template files, the CGI must be able to read in a file, look for a template tag, and replace it with the generated CGI output. For this sole purpose *filereplace* was created to allow CGI applications the ability to do such a replacement.

File Replace Interface
```
Class CommerceUtils.filereplace
```

```
java.lang.Object
   |
   +----CommerceUtils.filereplace
```

```
public class filereplace
extends Object
```

filereplace is a file string replacement facility. All of the strings in the provided properties list are search for and replaced by the propertie's associated value. The string newly created from doing the replacments can be accessed by a call to "GetOutputString".

Constructors
```
filereplace
   public filereplace(String InFile,
                      Properties replace)
```

The constructors for the filereplace class reads in the passed file and does all of the specified replacments. All path entries are required to contain a trailing \.

```
Parameters:
InFile - Provides the path to the input file.
replace - The replacments to be made. The properties name is what is to be replaced, and the
value is what to replace it with.
```

Methods
```
GetOutputString
   public String GetOutputString()
```

GetOutputString retrieves the result replacement string.

```
Returns:
Returns the result replacement string.
```

File Replace Code Listing

```java
package CommerceUtils;

import java.util.Properties;
import java.util.Enumeration;
import java.io.FileInputStream;
import java.io.DataInputStream;


//filereplace.java

/**
 * <tt>filereplace</tt> is a file string replacement facility. All
 * of the strings in the provided properties list are search for and
 * replaced by the propertie's associated value.
 *
 * The string newly created from doing the replacments can be accessed by
 * a call to "GetOutputString".
 *
 * @version 1.23
 * @author Cary A. Jardin
 */

public class filereplace extends Object{

    private String  Output  =   "";


    /**
     * The constructors for the filereplace class reads in the passed
     * file and does all of the specified replacments.
     *
     * All path entries are required to contain a trailing \
     *
     * @param InFile          Provides the path to the input file.
     * @param replace         The replacments to be made.  The properties
     *                        name is what is to be replaced, and the
     *                        value is what to replace it with.
     */
    public filereplace(String InFile, Properties replace){
        super();
        LoadFile(InFile);
        ReplaceTags(replace);
    }

    /**
     * GetOutputString retrieves the result replacement string.
     *
```

```
    * @return   Returns the result replacement string.
    */

public String GetOutputString(){
    return Output;
}

private void LoadFile(String InFile){
    DataInputStream  input  =   null;
    String in   =   "";
    try{
        input = new DataInputStream(new FileInputStream(InFile));
    }
    catch(Exception e){
    }

    try{
        for(;;){
                in = input.readLine();
                if(in == null)
                    break;
                Output += in + "\n";
        }
    }
    catch(Exception e){
    }

    try{
        // close the stream
        input.close();
    }
    catch(Exception e){
    }

    return;
}

private void ReplaceTags(Properties replaceme){

    String NewOut            =   "";
    String Replace           =   "";
    String ReplaceWith       =   "";
    String Tmp               =   "";
    String Tmp2              =   "";
    int    i                 =   0;
    int    lastindex         =   0;
    Enumeration replacelst   =   replaceme.propertyNames();
```

```
for(;replacelst.hasMoreElements();){
    try{
        Replace =    (String)replacelst.nextElement();
    }
    catch(Exception e){
    }

    ReplaceWith = replaceme.getProperty(Replace);
    lastindex = 0;
    for(;;){
        i    =   Output.indexOf(Replace,lastindex);
        if(i == -1)// Not Found;
            break;

        try{
            Tmp = Output.substring(0,i);
            Tmp2 = Output.substring(i+Replace.length(),Output.length());
            lastindex = (Tmp + ReplaceWith).length()-1;
            Output = Tmp + ReplaceWith + Tmp2;
        }
        catch(Exception e){
            break;
        }
    }

}
}
}
```

File Replace Usage

The basic mechanism for *filereplace* revolves around two elements, the file to read in and the replacements. The file to read in is provided to the constructor in the form of a String. The replacements are handled in the form of a Properties object, where the property name is what is to be replaced and the property's value is what to replace it with. The following is an example of a standard use:

```
Properties   p   =   new Properties();

p.put("Thanx","Thank You");
p.put("TITLE","TITLE2");
p.put("FF","AA");
filereplace FR = new filereplace("thankyou.html",p);
System.out.println(FR.GetOutputString());
```

Credit-Card Processing with IC Verify

IC Verify offer applications the ability to integrate credit-card processing functionality via a simple and easy-to-use interface. Chapter 8 discusses the usability issues as well as how to purchase a copy of IC Verify. If you are a commerce developer who can benefit from IC Verify, this set of libraries will aid you in integrating IC Verify into your CGI commerce solution.

The supplied IC Verify support libraries provide a ready-to-use framework for the processing of credit-card transactions, specifically sale transactions. IC Verify offers a complete set of credit-card processing facilitators including pre-authorization, void sale, and return. Taking an online return is not something commonly done, and thus it is not apart of the supplied support libraries.

Request File Support

From the application standpoint, there are three factors in interfacing with IC Verify: the request file, the command line, and the response file. *request* provides a storage device for entries in the request file. Later in the *icverify* class, you will see how this class is used to store and generate the IC Verify request file. For all intents and purposes, this class should be invisible to you if you use the *icverify* class. It is discussed here as background for the *icverify* class.

Request File Interface

```
Class CommerceUtils.request


java.lang.Object
   |
   +----CommerceUtils.request

public class request
extends Object

request is a storage and serialization device for IC Verify request files. Input is assumed
to be in the proper, valid format. Only sale transactions are supported. Not a lot of call
for on-line return desk. NOTE : Expiration date should be stored in YYMM format
```

Constructors

```
request
   public request(String clerk,
                  String comment,
                  String cardnumber,
                  String expiration,
```

```
            String amount,
            String zip,
            String address)
```

The constructor acts as a loading device for the internal request storage.

Parameters:
clerk - Clerk field
comment - Comment field
cardnumber - The Credit Card to process
expiration - The Credit Card's expiration date in YYMM form
amount - The amount of the sale in ##.## form
zip - The zip code of the customer, optional can be ""
address - The address of the customer, optional can be ""

request
```
  public request(String clerk,
            String comment,
            String cardnumber,
            String expiration,
            String amount)
```

The constructor acts as a loading device for the internal request storage.

Parameters:
clerk - Clerk field
comment - Comment field
cardnumber - The Credit Card to process
expiration - The Credit Card's expiration date in YYMM form
amount - The amount of the sale in ##.## form

request
```
  public request(boolean IgnoreME,
            String merchant,
            String comment,
            String cardnumber,
            String expiration,
            String amount,
            String zip,
            String address)
```

The constructor acts as a loading device for the internal request storage. NOTE: This constructor is ONLY used for locations that have a single installation of IC Verify for multiple companies.

Parameters:
IgnoreME - Really! Ignore the var
merchant - The merchant .set file to use
comment - Comment field
cardnumber - The Credit Card to process
expiration - The Credit Card's expiration date in YYMM form
amount - The amount of the sale in ##.## form
zip - The zip code of the customer, optional can be ""
address - The address of the customer, optional can be ""

Methods

Serialize
  public String Serialize()

Serializes the fields into a comma delimited format.

Returns:
  Returns the stored fields in a comma delimited format.

Request File Code Listing

```
package CommerceUtils;
//request.java

/**
 * <tt>request<\tt> is a storage and serialization device
 * for IC Verify request files. Input is assumed to be in
 * the proper, valid format.
 *
 * Only sale transactions are supported.  Not a lot of call
 * for on-line return desk.
 *
 * NOTE : Expiration date should be stored in YYMM format
 *
 * @version 1.0
 * @author Cary A. Jardin
 */
public class request extends Object{

    private static String SaleToken = "C1";

    private String Clerk       =    "";
    private String Comment     =    "";
```

```java
private String CardNumber    =    "";
private String Expiration    =    "";  //in YYMM format
private String Amount        =    "";
private String ZipCode       =    "";  //Optional
private String Address       =    "";  //Optional
private String Merchant      =    "";  //Optional

//Constructors

/**
 * The constructor acts as a loading device for the internal
 * request storage.
 *
 *
 * @param clerk         Clerk field
 * @param comment       Comment field
 * @param cardnumber    The Credit Card to process
 * @param expiration    The Credit Card's expiration date in YYMM form
 * @param amount        The amount of the sale in ##.## form
 * @param zip           The zip code of the customer, optional can be ""
 * @param address       The address of the customer, optional can be ""
 */
public request(String clerk, String comment, String cardnumber,
     String expiration, String amount, String zip, String address){

     super();
     Clerk        =        clerk;
     Comment      =        comment;
     CardNumber   =        cardnumber;
     Expiration   =        expiration;
     Amount       =        amount;
     ZipCode      =        zip;
     Address      =        address;

}

/**
 * The constructor acts as a loading device for the internal
 * request storage.
 *
 *
 * @param clerk         Clerk field
 * @param comment       Comment field
 * @param cardnumber    The Credit Card to process
 * @param expiration    The Credit Card's expiration date in YYMM form
 * @param amount        The amount of the sale in ##.## form
```

```
    */
   public request(String clerk, String comment, String cardnumber,
       String expiration, String amount){

       super();
       Clerk           =           clerk;
       Comment         =           comment;
       CardNumber      =           cardnumber;
       Expiration      =           expiration;
       Amount          =           amount;
       ZipCode         =           "";
       Address         =           "";
   }


   /**
    * The constructor acts as a loading device for the internal
    * request storage.
    *
    * NOTE: This constructor is ONLY used for locations that have
    * a single installation of IC Verify for multiple companies.
    *
    * @param IgnoreME       Really! Ignore the var
    * @param merchant       The merchant .set file to use
    * @param comment        Comment field
    * @param cardnumber     The Credit Card to process
    * @param expiration     The Credit Card's expiration date in YYMM form
    * @param amount         The amount of the sale in ##.## form
    * @param zip            The zip code of the customer, optional can be ""
    * @param address        The address of the customer, optional can be ""
    */
   public request(boolean IgnoreME, String merchant, String comment, String cardnumber,
       String expiration, String amount, String zip, String address){

       super();
       Clerk           =           "";
       Comment         =           comment;
       CardNumber      =           cardnumber;
       Expiration      =           expiration;
       Amount          =           amount;
       ZipCode         =           zip;
       Address         =           address;
       Merchant        =           merchant;

   }

   /**
```

```
     * Serializes the fields into a comma delimited format.
     *
     * @returns     Returns the stored fields in a comma delimited format.
     *
     */
    public String Serialize(){
        String out = "";

        out = "\""+SaleToken+"\",";

        if(Merchant != "")
            out += "\"~"+Merchant+"~\",";
        else
            out += "\""+Clerk+"\",";

        out += "\""+Comment+"\",";
        out += "\""+CardNumber+"\",";
        out += "\""+Expiration+"\",";

        if((ZipCode != "") || (Address != ""))
            out += "\""+Amount+"\",";
        else{
            out += "\""+Amount+"\"";
            return out;
        }

        if(Address != "")
            out += "\""+ZipCode+"\",";
        else{
            out += "\""+ZipCode+"\"";
            return out;
        }

        out += "\""+Address+"\"";
        return out;
    }

}
```

Response File Support

Similar to the *request* class, the *response* class does the inverse operation of the *request* class. The *request* class is used to load the IC Verify transaction request file. The *response* class reads in the output from running IC Verify against the generated requests. Once again, like the *request* class, the *response* class is supplied as background for the *icverify* class. If you use the *icverify* class, you should not have to worry about this class.

Response File Interface

Class CommerceUtils.response

java.lang.Object
    |
    +----CommerceUtils.response

public class response
extends Object
response is a storage and loading device for IC Verify response files. Input is assumed to be
in the proper, valid format. Only sale transactions are supported. Not a lot of call for online return desks. NOTE : Evaluated Response should be set to format type B

Variables

Approved
   public boolean Approved

Approved will be true if the transaction was approved.

ApprovalCode
   public String ApprovalCode

If the transaction was approved ApprovalCode will hold the six digit approval code, else the
value will be "".

ReferenceNumber
   public String ReferenceNumber

If the transaction was approved ReferenceNumber will hold the eight digit Reference code,
else the value will be "".

ErrorCode
   public String ErrorCode

If the transaction was denied ErrorCode will hold the error code. Also if there is a problem
with the constructor's input, ErrorCode will be "BADFRM"

CreditCardNum
   public String CreditCardNum

The CardNumber of the transaction

Constructors

response
```
  public response(String Echo,
                  String Response)
```

The constructor will take the supplied Echo, and strings and parse them into the appropriate public vars.

Parameters:
Echo - Echo of the initial request.
Response - The response line, in comma delimited.

Response Code Listing

```
package CommerceUtils;

import java.util.StringTokenizer;

//response.java

/**
 * <tt>response<\tt> is a storage and loading device
 * for IC Verify response files. Input is assumed to be in
 * the proper, valid format.
 *
 * Only sale transactions are supported.  Not a lot of call
 * for on-line return desks.
 *
 * NOTE : Evaluated Response should be set to format type B
 *
 * @version 1.0
 * @author Cary A. Jardin
 */
public class response extends Object{

        /**
         * Approved will be true if the transaction was approved.
         */
        public boolean Approved          = false;

        /**
         * If the transaction was approved ApprovalCode will hold the
         * six digit approval code, else the value will be "".
         */
        public String  ApprovalCode      = "";
```

```
/**
 * If the transaction was approved ReferenceNumber will hold the
 * eight digit Reference code, else the value will be "".
 */
public String  ReferenceNumber  = "";

/**
 * If the transaction was denied ErrorCode will hold the
 * error code. Also if there is a problem with the constructor's
 * input, ErrorCode will be "BADFRM"
 */
public String  ErrorCode        = "";

/**
 * The CardNumber of the transaction
 *
 */
public String  CreditCardNum    = "";

/**
 * The constructor will take the supplied Echo, and strings and
 * parse them into the appropriate public vars.
 *
 * @param Echo           Echo of the initial request.
 * @param Response       The response line, in comma delimited.
 *
 */
public response(String Echo,String Response){

    super();
    LoadCardNumber(Echo);
    ProcessResponse(Response);
}

private void ProcessResponse(String Authorization){

    //Char 0 is a '"', Char 1 is 'Y' for approved, 'N' for declined
    //String should be in the format "YAAAAAARRRRRRRR", or "YAAAAAA"
    if(Authorization.charAt(1) == 'Y'){// good
        try{
            Approved = true;
            ApprovalCode    = Authorization.substring(2,8);
            if(Authorization.length() > 10) //check to see if the Refnum is appended
                ReferenceNumber = Authorization.substring(8,16);
            else
                ReferenceNumber = "";
```

```
            }
        catch(Exception e){
            Approved = false;
            ErrorCode = "BADFRM";
        }
    }
    else{
        try{
            Approved = false;
            ErrorCode    = Authorization.substring(2,Authorization.length()-1);
        }
        catch(Exception e){
            Approved = false;
            ErrorCode = "BADFRM";
        }
    }

}

private void LoadCardNumber(String Echo_Line){

    StringTokenizer parser = new StringTokenizer(Echo_Line,",",false);

    // Skip Sale Command;
    parser.nextToken();

    //Skip the Clerk
    parser.nextToken();

    //Skip the Comment
    parser.nextToken();

    //Load the Card Number and forget the rest
    CreditCardNum = StripField(parser.nextToken());
}

private String StripField(String StripME){

    String out = "";

    for(int i = 0;i < (StripME.length() - 1);++i)
        if(StripME.charAt(i) != '"')
            out += StripME.charAt(i);

    return out;
}
```

```
}
```

IC Verify Support

The basic operating characteristics of processing credit cards using IC Verifyare these. A request file is created containing the credit cards to process. Once created, the "ICVERIFY" application is executed, which reads in the generated request file, processes the requests, and outputs the results into a response file. When "ICVERIFY" terminates, the calling application must read in the response file to obtain the status of the generated request. All in all, it is not that difficult an interface to work with, but it is always nice if you can leverage the work of another to make your life easier. For this reason, the *icverify* class is provided.

icverify utilizes *response* and *request* classes to store their associated information. A large portion of the *icverify* class revolves around the loading and unloading of this information. Chapters 13 and 14 will incorporate this class into the example CGI applications to provide credit-card authorization facilities.

IC Verify Interface

```
Class CommerceUtils.icverify


java.lang.Object
   |
   +----CommerceUtils.icverify


public class icverify
extends Object
icverify provides a simple interface for the processing of credit card sales using IC Verify.
The operating procedure for this object is the following:

Call "AddRequest" one or more times.
Call "ProcessRequests" to process the previously added requests.
Call the appropriate "get" functions to retrieve the desired information.
```

Constructors

```
icverify
   public icverify(String ICVpath,
                   String ICVDataPath,
                   String ShlCmd,
                   boolean Debug)


The constructors for the icverify class, set the object with its needed operational
characteristics. This constructor provides the highest degree of configuration. All path
entries are required to contain a trailing \
```

Parameters:

ICVpath - Provides the path to the IC Verify executable path.

ICVDataPath - Provides the path to the IC Verify data path.

ShlCmd - This is a machine specific parameter, on NT the string should equal "cmd.exe /C", 95 "command.com /C".

Debug - This flag is used for testing. In debug mode IC Verify will not dial.

icverify
```
public icverify(String ICVpath,
                String ICVDataPath,
                boolean Debug)
```

The constructors for the icverify class, set the object with its needed operational characteristics. This constructor uses the following defaults: Shell command = SHELL_CMD All path entries are required to contain a trailing \

Parameters:

ICVpath - Provides the path to the IC Verify executable path.

ICVDataPath - Provides the path to the IC Verify data path.

ShlCmd - This is a machine specific parameter, on NT the string should equal "cmd.exe /C", 95 "command.com /C".

Debug - This flag is used for testing. In debug mode IC Verify will not dial.

icverify
```
public icverify(String ICVpath,
                boolean Debug)
```

The constructors for the icverify class, set the object with its needed operational characteristics. This constructor uses the following defaults: Shell command = SHELL_CMD Data path = the executable path All path entries are required to contain a trailing \

Parameters:

ICVpath - Provides the path to the IC Verify executable path.

ICVDataPath - Provides the path to the IC Verify data path.

ShlCmd - This is a machine specific parameter, on NT the string should equal "cmd.exe /C", 95 "command.com /C".

Debug - This flag is used for testing. In debug mode IC Verify will not dial.

Methods

AddRequest
```
public void AddRequest(String clerk,
                       String comment,
```

```
            String cardnumber,
            String expiration,
            String amount,
            String zip,
            String address)
```

AddRequest adds a request into the processing pool, to be processed when "ProcessRequests" is called.

Parameters:
clerk - The clerk for the sale
comment - Any comments to a company the sale
cardnumber - The Credit Card to charge the sale to
expiration - The Credit Card's expiration date in YYMM format
amount - The amount of the sale
zip - The customer's zip code
address - The customer's address

AddRequest
```
   public void AddRequest(String clerk,
                   String comment,
                   String cardnumber,
                   String expiration,
                   String amount)
```

AddRequest adds a request into the processing pool, to be processed when "ProcessRequests" is called.

Parameters:
clerk - The clerk for the sale
comment - Any comments to a company the sale
cardnumber - The Credit Card to charge the sale to
expiration - The Credit Card's expiration date in YYMM format
amount - The amount of the sale

AddRequest
```
   public void AddRequest(boolean IgnoreMe,
                   String merchant,
                   String comment,
                   String cardnumber,
                   String expiration,
                   String amount,
                   String zip,
```

                    String address)

AddRequest adds a request into the processing pool, to be processed when "ProcessRequests" is called. NOTE : Use this function IIF there are multiple companies using a single installation of IC Verify.

Parameters:
IgnoreMe - Really! Ignore this parameter
merchant - The merchant ID in ### format.
comment - Any comments to a company the sale
cardnumber - The Credit Card to charge the sale to
expiration - The Credit Card's expiration date in YYMM format
amount - The amount of the sale
zip - The customer's zip code
address - The customer's address

ProcessRequests
   public boolean ProcessRequests()

ProcessRequests processes all the requests in the request pool. NOTE: All prior responses will be lost.

Returns:
Retruns false upon failure.

IsApproved
   public boolean IsApproved(String CardNumber)

IsApproved Checks to see if the passed card number was approved or not.

Parameters:
CardNumber - The card number to check.

Returns:
Retruns true if the card was approved.

GetApprovalCode
   public String GetApprovalCode(String CardNumber)

GetApprovalCode Returns the approval code for the passed credit card number.

Parameters:
CardNumber - The card number.

Returns:
Returns the approval code if the card was approved, otherwise "" will be returned.

GetReferenceNumber
```
public String GetReferenceNumber(String CardNumber)
```

GetReferenceNumber Returns the reference code for the passed credit card number.

Parameters:
CardNumber - The card number.

Returns:
Returns the reference code if the card was approved and a reference code was supplied, otherwise "" will be returned.

ErrorCode
```
public String ErrorCode(String CardNumber)
```

ErrorCode Returns the error code for the passed credit card number.

Parameters:
CardNumber - The card number.

Returns:
Returns the error code if the card was not approved, otherwise "" will be returned.

GetProcCardNumbers
```
public Enumeration GetProcCardNumbers()
```

GetProcCardNumbers Returns all of the card numbers currently in the response pool.

Returns:
Returns an enumeration of the credit card numbers currently in the response pool.

IC Verify Code Listing

```
package CommerceUtils;

import java.util.Stack;
```

```java
import java.util.Hashtable;
import java.util.Enumeration;
import CommerceUtils.request;
import CommerceUtils.response;
import java.io.FileOutputStream;
import java.io.FileInputStream;
import java.io.DataInputStream;
import java.io.File;


//icverify.java

/**
 * <tt>icverify</tt> provides a simple interface for the processing of credit
 * card sales using IC Verify. The operating procedure for this object is the following:
 * <br><br>
 * Call "AddRequest" one or more times.<br>
 * Call "ProcessRequests" to process the previously added requests.<br>
 * Call the appropriate "get" functions to retrieve the desired information.
 * <br><br>
 * IC Verify can be purchased from www.icverify.com
 *
 * @version 1.20
 * @author Cary A. Jardin
 */
public class icverify extends Object{

    //Variable declaration
    private static String ICVerify_String        = "ICVERIFY /B ";
    private static String ICVerify_Debug_String  = "ICVERIFY /D /B ";
    private static String Req_File_Name          = "req.dat";
    private static String Response_File_Name     = "res.dat";

    private Stack   ProcessMe                 = new Stack();

    private String ICVerify_Path              = ".\\";
    private String ICVerify_DataPath          = ".\\";
    private String SHELL_CMD                  = "cmd.exe /C ";
    private Hashtable Processed               = new Hashtable(10);
    private boolean Debug_On                  = false;



    //Constructors

    /**
     * The constructors for the icverify class, set the object with its
```

```
 * needed operational characteristics.  This constructor provides the
 * highest degree of configuration.
 *
 * All path entries are required to contain a trailing \
 *
 * @param ICVpath          Provides the path to the IC Verify executable path.
 * @param ICVDataPath      Provides the path to the IC Verify data path.
 * @param ShlCmd           This is a machine specific parameter, on NT the string
 *                         should equal "cmd.exe /C", 95 "command.com /C".
 * @param Debug            This flag is used for testing. In debug mode IC Verify
 *                         will not dial.
 */
public icverify(String ICVpath, String ICVDataPath, String ShlCmd,boolean Debug){
     ICVerify_Path       =        ICVpath;
     ICVerify_DataPath   =        ICVDataPath;
     SHELL_CMD           =        ShlCmd;
     Debug_On            =        Debug;
}


/**
 * The constructors for the icverify class, set the object with its
 * needed operational characteristics.  This constructor uses the following
 * defaults:
 * Shell command = SHELL_CMD
 *
 * All path entries are required to contain a trailing \
 *
 * @param ICVpath          Provides the path to the IC Verify executable path.
 * @param ICVDataPath      Provides the path to the IC Verify data path.
 * @param ShlCmd           This is a machine specific parameter, on NT the string
 *                         should equal "cmd.exe /C", 95 "command.com /C".
 * @param Debug            This flag is used for testing. In debug mode IC Verify
 *                         will not dial.
 */
public icverify(String ICVpath, String ICVDataPath,boolean Debug){
     ICVerify_Path       =        ICVpath;
     ICVerify_DataPath   =        ICVDataPath;
     SHELL_CMD           =        SHELL_CMD;
     Debug_On            =        Debug;
}


/**
 * The constructors for the icverify class, set the object with its
 * needed operational characteristics.  This constructor uses the following
 * defaults:
 * Shell command = SHELL_CMD
 * Data path = the executable path
 *
```

```
   * All path entries are required to contain a trailing \
   *
   * @param ICVpath          Provides the path to the IC Verify executable path.
   * @param ICVDataPath      Provides the path to the IC Verify data path.
   * @param ShlCmd           This is a machine specific parameter, on NT the string
   *                         should equal "cmd.exe /C", 95 "command.com /C".
   * @param Debug            This flag is used for testing. In debug mode IC Verify
   *                         will not dial.
   */
  public icverify(String ICVpath,boolean Debug){
      ICVerify_Path      =      ICVpath;
      ICVerify_DataPath  =      ICVpath;
      SHELL_CMD          =      SHELL_CMD;
      Debug_On           =      Debug;
  }


  /**
   * <tt>AddRequest<\tt> adds a request into the processing pool, to be processed when
   * "ProcessRequests" is called.
   *
   * @param clerk          The clerk for the sale
   * @param comment        Any comments to a company the sale
   * @param cardnumber     The Credit Card to charge the sale to
   * @param expiration     The Credit Card's expiration date in YYMM format
   * @param amount         The amount of the sale
   * @param zip            The customer's zip code
   * @param address        The customer's address
   *
   */
  public void AddRequest(String clerk, String comment, String cardnumber,
      String expiration, String amount, String zip, String address){

      ProcessMe.push(new request(clerk,comment,cardnumber,expiration,amount,zip,address));
  }


  /**
   * <tt>AddRequest<\tt> adds a request into the processing pool, to be processed when
   * "ProcessRequests" is called.
   *
   * @param clerk          The clerk for the sale
   * @param comment        Any comments to a company the sale
   * @param cardnumber     The Credit Card to charge the sale to
   * @param expiration     The Credit Card's expiration date in YYMM format
   * @param amount         The amount of the sale
   *
   */
  public void AddRequest(String clerk, String comment, String cardnumber,
```

```
              String expiration, String amount){

              ProcessMe.push(new request(clerk,comment,cardnumber,expiration,amount));
      }

      /**
       * <tt>AddRequest<\tt> adds a request into the processing pool, to be processed when
       * "ProcessRequests" is called.
       *
       * NOTE : Use this function IIF their are multiple companies using a single
       * installation of IC Verify.
       *
       * @param IgnoreMe          Really! Ignore this parameter
       * @param merchant          The merchant ID in ### format.
       * @param comment           Any comments to a company the sale
       * @param cardnumber        The Credit Card to charge the sale to
       * @param expiration        The Credit Card's expiration date in YYMM format
       * @param amount            The amount of the sale
       * @param zip               The customer's zip code
       * @param address           The customer's address
       *
       */
      public void AddRequest(boolean IgnoreMe, String merchant, String comment, String
cardnumber,
              String expiration, String amount, String zip, String address){

              ProcessMe.push(new
request(IgnoreMe,merchant,comment,cardnumber,expiration,amount,zip,address));
      }

      /**
       * <tt>ProcessRequests<\tt> processes all the requests in the request pool.
       *
       * NOTE: All prior responses will be lost.
       *
       * @return                  Retruns false upon failure.
       *
       */
      public boolean ProcessRequests(){
          Process P = null;

          //delete the request file
          try{
              File f = new File(ICVerify_Path + Response_File_Name);
              f.delete();
          }
          catch(Exception e){
```

```
        }

        if(!LoadRequests())
            return false;

        try{
            Runtime r = Runtime.getRuntime();
            if(Debug_On)
                P = r.exec(SHELL_CMD + ICVerify_Path + ICVerify_Debug_String +
                            Req_File_Name + " " + Response_File_Name);
            else
                P = r.exec(SHELL_CMD + ICVerify_Path + ICVerify_String +
                            Req_File_Name + " " + Response_File_Name);
            P.waitFor();
        }
        catch(Exception e){
            return false;
        }

        return LoadResponses();
    }

/**
 * <tt>IsApproved<\tt> Checks to see if the passed card number
 * was approved or not.
 *
 * @param   CardNumber          The card number to check.
 * @return                      Retruns true if the card was approved.
 *
 */
public boolean IsApproved(String CardNumber){
    response r = (response)Processed.get(new String(CardNumber));

    if(r == null)
        return false;
    return r.Approved;
}


/**
 * <tt>GetApprovalCode<\tt> Returns the approval code for the
 * passed credit card number.
 *
 * @param   CardNumber          The card number.
 * @return                      Returns the approval code if the card was approved,
 *                              otherwise "" will be returned.
 *
 */
```

```
    */
    public String GetApprovalCode(String CardNumber){
        response r = (response)Processed.get(new String(CardNumber));

        if((r == null)||(!r.Approved))
            return "";

        return r.ApprovalCode;
    }


    /**
     * <tt>GetReferenceNumber<\tt> Returns the reference code for the
     * passed credit card number.
     *
     * @param     CardNumber          The card number.
     * @return                        Returns the reference code if the card was approved and
a
     *                                reference code was supplied, otherwise "" will be
returned.
     *
     */
    public String GetReferenceNumber(String CardNumber){
        response r = (response)Processed.get(new String(CardNumber));

        if((r == null)||(!r.Approved))
            return "";

        return r.ReferenceNumber;
    }


    /**
     * <tt>ErrorCode<\tt> Returns the error code for the
     * passed credit card number.
     *
     * @param     CardNumber          The card number.
     * @return                        Returns the error code if the card was not approved,
     *                                otherwise "" will be returned.
     *
     */
    public String ErrorCode(String CardNumber){
        response r = (response)Processed.get(new String(CardNumber));

        if((r == null)||(r.Approved))
            return "";

        return r.ErrorCode;
```

```
    }

    /**
     * <tt>GetProcCardNumbers<\tt> Returns all of the card numbers
     * currently in the response pool.
     *
     * @return                          Returns an enumeration of the credit card
     *                                  numbers currently in the response pool.
     *
     */
    public Enumeration GetProcCardNumbers(){
        return Processed.keys();
    }

    private boolean LoadResponses(){
        DataInputStream  input  =   null;
        response r = null;
        try{
            input = new DataInputStream(new FileInputStream(ICVerify_Path +
Response_File_Name));
        }
        catch(Exception e){
            System.out.println("IO ERROR");
            return false;
        }
        // Clear the old responses
        Processed.clear();
        try{
            for(;;){
             r = new response(input.readLine(),input.readLine());
             if(r != null)
                 Processed.put(new String(r.CreditCardNum), r);
            }
        }
        catch(Exception e){
        }

        // close the stream

        try{
            input.close();
        }
        catch(Exception e){
            return false;
        }

        return true;
```

```
    }


private boolean LoadRequests(){

        FileOutputStream RespFile = null;
        String output = "";
        boolean AllGood = true;

        if(ProcessMe.empty())
            return false;

        for(;!ProcessMe.empty();){
            request r = (request) ProcessMe.pop();
            output += r.Serialize()+"\n";
        }

        //Create the file
        try{
            RespFile = new FileOutputStream(ICVerify_DataPath+Req_File_Name);
        }
        catch(Exception e)
        {
            return false;
        }

        byte brequests[] = new byte[output.length()];
        output.getBytes(0 , output.length() - 1,brequests,0);

        //write the file and close
        try{
            RespFile.write(brequests);
        }
        catch(Exception e)
        {
            AllGood = false;
        }

        try{
            RespFile.close();
        }
        catch(Exception e)
        {
            AllGood = false;
        }

        // If error return
```

```
        return AllGood;
    }

}
```

IC Verify Usage

The standard use of the *icverify* class can be broken into three key events the creation of the object, loading the request, and retrieving the responses. Most applications will process a single application at a time. However, the class supports the processing of multiple requests. The following is a generic usage of the *icverify* class.

```
icverify proc = new icverify("c:\\icverify\\","c:\\icverify\\demo19\\",true);

    proc.AddRequest("Cary","CGI","5419840000000003","9710","25.00");

    proc.ProcessRequests();

    if(!proc.IsApproved("5419840000000003"))
        System.out.println(proc.ErrorCode("5419840000000003"));
    else{

        System.out.println("Aproval Code = " +
                proc.GetApprovalCode("5419840000000003"));
        System.out.println("Ref Code = " +
                proc.GetReferenceNumber("5419840000000003"));

    }
```

Notice that all response information is referenced by the credit card of the request. Remember this class supports multiple requests; thus, it must support multiple responses. Chapters 13 and 14 utilize this class to facilitate real-time credit-card processing.

Summary

The tools in this chapter provide a ready-to-use toolbox for Web commerce development, specifically Java-based CGI and applet development. Chapters 12, 13, and 14 will use this set of tools to develop a series of complete commerce solutions. At this point, it is not necessary to fully understand each of the tools, and in what context to use them. Rather, this chapter provides a reference for further development. All of the examples that are to be developed in the subsequent chapters will rely on the functionality of these tools, and like most good development tools, as long as they work, great. In many cases, it is easier to understand what a tool does when it is viewed in action. This chapter makes you aware of what to watch for. The accompanying CD-ROM contains all source code and a JavaDoc API reference for your use. If you run into a problem with any of the supplied tools, http://www.xprime.com provides the latest and greatest versions.

Chapter 11

Using the CardShield API

For nonprogrammers, CardShield offers an off-the-shelf solution ready to be plugged into an awaiting Web site. For programmers, CardShield offers an API for the secure transport and processing of credit-card sale transactions. Even though the off-the-shelf applet provides a turnkey solution that lacks uniqueness, the API does give the developer full creative freedom. This chapter is written for a fairly technical reader, one who understands fundamental object-oriented programming concepts and some Internet application issues. The CardShield API, along with the HTML help pages, can be found on the CD-ROM. The goal of this chapter is to provide an entry point for further exploration and development.

The CardShield API

The CardShield API does one thing and one thing only: It securely process a credit-card sale transaction. The entire API consists of a single constructor and a method called "SecureSale." The simplicity of the API cannot be overstated—it does the job and does it well. However, some things are not entirely obvious from the supplied documentation; for example, a CardShield Merchant account is required, and the API facilities retain all the processing features of the CardShield applet.

CardShield is essentially a service, a credit-card processing service. The applet and the API are both agents for using the service, and so the same process must be followed in setting up the service. In Chapter 7, the CardShield merchant setup process was discussed for the CardShield applet. The very same process must be completed to use the CardShield API. The only difference is that API users have no need to fill in the applet setup facility. CardShield is a service, regardless of what the service is accessed with or how the service is used; all of the fees and all associated processes apply.

The CardShield applet boasts that orders can be either e-mailed or faxed to the merchant on completion of the sale. Further, the applet produces a daily transaction file that can be downloaded from a secure FTP site. Although the applet advertises these features, commerce applications that utilize the CardShield API do not necessarily have access to the same processing features. The fact is, e-mailing, faxing, and daily settlement files are all part of the CardShield service. All applications written with the CardShield API have access to the full benefit of the CardShield service, including e-mail, fax, and settlement files. From the standpoint of the CardShield service, both the applet and custom API applications are the same. Both have access to the same feature set that makes up the CardShield name.

CardShield API

```
Class CardShield.CardShieldAPI


CardShield.CardShieldAPI
public class CardShieldAPI


Copyright (c) 1996 Shielded Technologies, Inc. All Rights Reserved. Permission to use, copy,
modify, and distribute this software and its documentation for NON-COMMERCIAL purposes and
without fee is hereby granted provided that this copyright notice appears in all copies.
SHIELDED TECHNOLOGIES MAKES NO REPRESENTATIONS OR WARRANTIES ABOUT THE SUITABILITY OF THE
SOFTWARE, EITHER EXPRESS OR IMPLIED, INCLUDING BUT NOT LIMITED TO THE IMPLIED WARRANTIES OF
MERCHANTABILITY, FITNESS FOR A PARTICULAR PURPOSE, OR NON-INFRINGEMENT. SHIELDED SHALL NOT BE
LIABLE FOR ANY DAMAGES SUFFERED BY LICENSEE AS A RESULT OF USING, MODIFYING OR DISTRIBUTING
THIS SOFTWARE OR ITS DERIVATIVES. The CardShield API is provided to facilitate real-time
credit card sale processing. In its current version, the API consists of a single
constructor, and two methods for secure sale transactions. The security of the all sales are
facilitated by RCS(c), Shielded's patented security mechanism.

In order to use the supplied functionality of the CardShield API, the proper merchant setup
information must be completed at Shielded's Web page. There you will find complete
instruction of how to setup a CardShield merchant account.
```

NOTE: Sales that utilize the CardShield API are treated in the same manner as all other CardShield Applet sale transaction. Thus being so, the order delivery mechanism, email or fax, selected during the merchant setup will hold for all CardShield API transactions.

To receive more information, or setup a CardShield account, or to get the latest API goto http://www.shielded.com.

Variables

Approved
   public static String Approved

On a successful SecureSale, the return will be the value of "Approved"

NetError
   public static String NetError

Returned from SecureSale if a Network error occurred

CardFormatError
   public static String CardFormatError

Returned from SecureSale if the passed card's format is invalid. The proper format should ONLY include numeric characters.

ExpireFormatError
   public static String ExpireFormatError

Returned from SecureSale if the passed expiration date format is invalid. The proper format should be YYMM format.

Constructors

CardShieldAPI
   **public CardShieldAPI(String CSMID,
                        boolean isApplet)**

The constructor for the CardShield API take two parameters. The fist is the CardShield Merchant ID, that is supplied once the CardShield merchant setup has been completed. The second parameter is a flag to be set if the calling application is an Applet. Due to Applet security, if used from inside an Applet the CardShield Passive Agent must be present and running on the associated Web server. A free copy of the CardShield Passive Agent can be obtained from the Shielded home page.

Parameters:
CSMID - CardShield Merchant ID, which is provided by once the merchant setup has been completed.
isApplet - Flag to be set to true if the calling application is an Applet.

Methods

SecureSale

```
public String SecureSale(String clerk,
                         String comment,
                         String cardnumber,
                         String expiration,
                         String amount,
                         String zip,
                         String address,
                         Properties AdditionalInfo)
```

The Secure sale methods provide a secure mechanism for the processing of a credit card sale transactions protected by RCS. The response will either be "Approved" or a detailed error message.

Parameters:
clerk - The required clerk name for the transaction.
comment - The required comments for the transaction.
cardnumber - The required credit card number for the transaction.
expiration - The required credit card expiration date for the transaction.
amount - The required amount of the transaction.
zip - The required customer's zip code for the transaction.
address - The required customer's address for the transaction.
AdditionalInfo - The optional additional information. The additional information should include any additional information that is needed to complete the order. This information will accompany either the email or fax order confirmation, as well as the day end settlement file. If the parameter is set to null, only the above "required information will accompany the email or fax, and the settlement file.

SecureSale

```
public String SecureSale(String clerk,
                         String comment,
                         String cardnumber,
                         String expiration,
                         String amount,
                         String zip,
                         String address)
```

The Secure sale methods provide a secure mechanism for the processing of a credit card sale transactions protected by RCS. The response will either be "Approved" or a detailed error message.

```
Parameters:
clerk - The required clerk name for the transaction.
comment - The required comments for the transaction.
cardnumber - The required credit card number for the transaction.
expiration - The required credit card expiration date for the transaction.
amount - The required amount of the transaction.
zip - The required customer's zip code for the transaction.
address - The required customer's address for the transaction.
```

A Word on Applet Security

Take a look at the above CardShield API. Notice the constructor's parameter "isApplet". This parameter serves a very useful role. If you are familiar with the security restrictions placed on applets, the need for such a parameter should be clear. If you are not familiar with the inherent security restrictions placed on applets, here is your chance to be enlightened. Without getting into a lengthy discussion of applet restrictions, the following are the two key hindrances to Java-based, specifically applet-based, commerce:

- Inability to write to a disk

- Ability to communicate only with their origin server

Applets' inability to write to disk prohibits the storing of order information. This is not to say that applets are unable to act as network data collection devices. Rather, applets, by themselves, are unable to act as network data collection devices. The difference in these two statements parallels the difference between stand-alone and client/server applications. In a stand-alone application, the application must rely solely on its ability. Client/server technology allows the client to utilize the abilities of another application to facilitate what it cannot. In terms of applets, applets by themselves might not be able to store information, but applets can rely on a server to do so. Besides just offering secure credit-card sales processing, the CardShield API also offers applets access to a collection device, the CardShield service. Applets can use the API to store pertinent order information for retrieval at a later time.

That applets can communicate only with their origin server might not be as obvious a problem as not being able to write to a disk unless you have a background in client/server development. Think of the computer that is running a Web server, which is responsible for feeding hungry browsers content stored on that machine.

One such piece of content is a Web page containing your applet storefront. In this scenario, the computer, which is running the Web server, is the applet's origin server—so far, no problem. Now add the twist that your storefront applet uses the CardShield API, which relies on the CardShield service, which definitely is not on the same computer as your Web server—herein lies the problem. The CardShield API has to communicate with the CardShield service server, which is running somewhere out on the Internet. However, the applet, which came from the Web server machine, cannot talk to the CardShield service. In short, you can't get there from here. To overcome this obstacle, Shielded Technologies provides a Java application called the CardShield Passive Agent.

CardShield Passive Agent

The CardShield Passive Agent, which is provided on the accompanying CD-ROM, is a freely distributed tool from Shielded Technologies. Simply put, the Passive Agent acts as a "go-between" from the client's applet to the CardShield service. It functions by running on the applet's origin server, usually a Web server, and routing information from the applet to the CardShield service. If you will be running your custom applet storefront from your own dedicated server, using the Passive Agent means installing and executing the .class files. If your applet will be hosted on an ISP's server, the process is the same for the installation and execution, with the added task of talking the ISP into doing it for you. Either on your own machine or on an ISP's, the Passive Agent must be running for your storefront applet to function. Detailed platform-specific instructions are provided by Shielded Technologies and can be found on the CD-ROM as well.

Using the CardShield API

How you use the CardShield API depends on whether the calling application is an applet or a stand-alone application. The following sections provide a basic, nonrobust example of each of these usages. More complete and full-featured examples can be found in Chapters 12, 13, and 14.

Applet Usage

The following is an example applet using the CardShield API to process a credit-card order. Unfortunately, an applet really isn't the best way to show the use of the API because of the GUI overhead associated with the construction of an applet. The CGI example better illustrates the ease of use, but, as for the example, the actual API call takes place in the private method "AuthSale". Notice that the CardShield object is created with the "isApplet" flag set to true, corresponding with the fact that this is an applet. A more complete, and some what more useful, set of examples can be found in Chapter 14. The following is an illustration of a storefront applet.

```
import java.applet;
import java.awt.*;
import java.util.Properties;
import CardShield.*;

public class CSAGENT extends Applet {
    //support functions
    private Properties LoadProperties(){
        Properties p = new Properties();

        //load up all the widgets
        p.put("CUSTNAME",CustName.getText());
        p.put("CCNUM",CustNum.getText());
        p.put("ITEM",Products.getSelectedItem());
        p.put("ADDRESS",Address.getText());
        p.put("CITY",City.getText());
        p.put("STATE",State.getText());
        p.put("ZIP",Zip.getText());

        if(UPS.getState())
            p.put("SHIPPING","UPS");

        if(TwoDay.getState())
            p.put("SHIPPING","TwoDay");

        if(FedEx.getState())
            p.put("SHIPPING","FedEx");

        p.put("COMMENTS",textArea1.getText());

        return p;
    }

    private String AuthSale(){
        Properties P = LoadProperties();
        CardShieldAPI CS    = new CardShieldAPI("1234567A", true);

        return CS.SecureSale("TEST CGI",
                             "Java CGI",
                             P.getProperty("CCNUM"),
                             "99/01",
                             "10.00",
                             P.getProperty("ZIP"),
                             P.getProperty("ADDRESS"),
                             P);
```

```
}


//generated functions.
  void OkBtn_Clicked(Event event) {
        (new QuitDialog(this,AuthSale(), false)).show();
  }

  void Open_Action(Event event) {
        OpenFileDialog.show();
  }

  void About_Action(Event event) {
        (new AboutDialog(this, "About...", false)).show();
  }

  void Exit_Action(Event event) {
        (new QuitDialog(this, "Quit the Application?", false)).show();
  }

  public JDBCAGENT() {

        //{{INIT_CONTROLS
        setLayout(null);
        addNotify();
        resize(insets().left + insets().right + 615,insets().top + insets().bottom + 396);
        setBackground(new Color(12632256));
        OpenFileDialog = new java.awt.FileDialog(this, "Open",FileDialog.LOAD);
        label1 = new java.awt.Label("Customer Name :");
        label1.reshape(insets().left + 21,insets().top + 25,141,17);
        label1.setFont(new Font("TimesRoman", Font.BOLD, 14));
        add(label1);
        CustName = new java.awt.TextField();
        CustName.reshape(insets().left + 183,insets().top + 25,219,24);
        CustName.setFont(new Font("TimesRoman", Font.PLAIN, 14));
        add(CustName);
        label2 = new java.awt.Label("Credit Card Number :");
        label2.reshape(insets().left + 21,insets().top + 67,141,17);
        label2.setFont(new Font("TimesRoman", Font.BOLD, 14));
        add(label2);
        CustNum = new java.awt.TextField();
        CustNum.reshape(insets().left + 183,insets().top + 67,219,24);
        CustNum.setFont(new Font("TimesRoman", Font.PLAIN, 14));
        add(CustNum);
        Products = new java.awt.Choice();
```

```
Products.addItem("Brownies");
Products.addItem("G -Boards");
Products.addItem("More Stuff ...");
add(Products);
Products.reshape(insets().left + 431,insets().top + 34,165,70);
Products.setFont(new Font("TimesRoman", Font.BOLD, 14));
textArea1 = new java.awt.TextArea();
textArea1.reshape(insets().left + 423,insets().top + 130,171,199);
add(textArea1);
label3 = new java.awt.Label("Comments :");
label3.reshape(insets().left + 411,insets().top + 102,93,21);
label3.setFont(new Font("TimesRoman", Font.BOLD, 14));
label3.setForeground(new Color(0));
add(label3);
panel1 = new java.awt.Panel();
panel1.setLayout(null);
panel1.reshape(insets().left + 15,insets().top + 123,396,164);
panel1.setBackground(new Color(8421504));
add(panel1);
label4 = new java.awt.Label("Address :");
label4.reshape(6,21,141,17);
label4.setFont(new Font("TimesRoman", Font.BOLD, 14));
panel1.add(label4);
Address = new java.awt.TextField();
Address.reshape(168,21,219,24);
Address.setFont(new Font("TimesRoman", Font.PLAIN, 14));
panel1.add(Address);
label5 = new java.awt.Label("City :");
label5.reshape(6,56,141,17);
label5.setFont(new Font("TimesRoman", Font.BOLD, 14));
panel1.add(label5);
City = new java.awt.TextField();
City.reshape(168,56,219,24);
City.setFont(new Font("TimesRoman", Font.PLAIN, 14));
panel1.add(City);
label6 = new java.awt.Label("State :");
label6.reshape(6,91,141,17);
label6.setFont(new Font("TimesRoman", Font.BOLD, 14));
panel1.add(label6);
State = new java.awt.TextField();
State.reshape(168,91,219,24);
State.setFont(new Font("TimesRoman", Font.PLAIN, 14));
panel1.add(State);
label7 = new java.awt.Label("Zip :");
label7.reshape(6,126,141,17);
```

```java
label7.setFont(new Font("TimesRoman", Font.BOLD, 14));
panel1.add(label7);
Zip = new java.awt.TextField();
Zip.reshape(168,126,219,24);
Zip.setFont(new Font("TimesRoman", Font.PLAIN, 14));
panel1.add(Zip);
Group1 = new CheckboxGroup();
UPS = new java.awt.Checkbox("UPS", Group1, false);
UPS.reshape(insets().left + 19,insets().top + 311,100,40);
UPS.setFont(new Font("TimesRoman", Font.BOLD, 14));
add(UPS);
TwoDay = new java.awt.Checkbox("UPS - 2nd Day", Group1, false);
TwoDay.reshape(insets().left + 135,insets().top + 312,117,40);
TwoDay.setFont(new Font("TimesRoman", Font.BOLD, 14));
add(TwoDay);
FedEx = new java.awt.Checkbox("Fed-Ex", Group1, false);
FedEx.reshape(insets().left + 303,insets().top + 312,100,40);
FedEx.setFont(new Font("TimesRoman", Font.BOLD, 14));
add(FedEx);
OkBtn = new java.awt.Button("&OK");
OkBtn.reshape(insets().left + 465,insets().top + 340,75,26);
OkBtn.setFont(new Font("TimesRoman", Font.BOLD, 14));
add(OkBtn);
OUTPUT = new java.awt.Label("");
OUTPUT.reshape(insets().left + 81,insets().top + 347,351,31);
add(OUTPUT);
label8 = new java.awt.Label("Product :");
label8.reshape(insets().left + 431,insets().top + 11,70,15);
add(label8);
setTitle("A Basic Application");
//}}

//{{INIT_MENUS
mainMenuBar = new java.awt.MenuBar();

menu1 = new java.awt.Menu("File");
menu1.add("Open...");
menu1.add("Save");
menu1.add("Save As...");
menu1.addSeparator();
menu1.add("Exit");
mainMenuBar.add(menu1);

menu2 = new java.awt.Menu("Edit");
menu2.add("Cut");
```

```
        menu2.add("Copy");
        menu2.add("Paste");
        mainMenuBar.add(menu2);

        menu3 = new java.awt.Menu("Help");
        menu3.add("About");
        mainMenuBar.add(menu3);
        setMenuBar(mainMenuBar);
        //}}
    }

    public JDBCAGENT(String title) {
        this();
        setTitle(title);
    }

public synchronized void show() {
    move(50, 50);
    super.show();
}

    public boolean handleEvent(Event event) {
    if (event.id == Event.WINDOW_DESTROY) {
     hide();            // hide the Frame
        dispose();
        System.exit(0);
        return true;
    }
        if (event.target == OkBtn && event.id == Event.ACTION_EVENT) {
            OkBtn_Clicked(event);
        }
        return super.handleEvent(event);
    }

    public boolean action(Event event, Object arg) {
        if (event.target instanceof MenuItem) {
            String label = (String) arg;
            if (label.equalsIgnoreCase("Open...")) {
                Open_Action(event);
                return true;
            } else
            if (label.equalsIgnoreCase("About")) {
                About_Action(event);
                return true;
            } else
```

```
        if (label.equalsIgnoreCase("Exit")) {
            Exit_Action(event);
            return true;
        }
    }
    return super.action(event, arg);
}

static public void main(String args[]) {
    (new JDBCAGENT()).show();
}

//{{DECLARE_CONTROLS
java.awt.FileDialog OpenFileDialog;
java.awt.Label label1;
java.awt.TextField CustName;
java.awt.Label label2;
java.awt.TextField CustNum;
java.awt.Choice Products;
java.awt.TextArea textArea1;
java.awt.Label label3;
java.awt.Panel panel1;
java.awt.Label label4;
java.awt.TextField Address;
java.awt.Label label5;
java.awt.TextField City;
java.awt.Label label6;
java.awt.TextField State;
java.awt.Label label7;
java.awt.TextField Zip;
java.awt.Checkbox UPS;
CheckboxGroup Group1;
java.awt.Checkbox TwoDay;
java.awt.Checkbox FedEx;
java.awt.Button OkBtn;
java.awt.Label OUTPUT;
java.awt.Label label8;
//}}

//{{DECLARE_MENUS
java.awt.MenuBar mainMenuBar;
java.awt.Menu menu1;
java.awt.Menu menu2;
java.awt.Menu menu3;
//}}
}
```

CGI Usage

The following example falls short of providing a complete CGI commerce solution, but it does show the relative ease of the CardShield API usage. Notice that the CardShield API takes up only two lines of this code. The first is for the construction of the object, and the second is to process the sale. By CGI's very nature—it is not an applet—the second parameter of the CardShieldAPI constructor is false, effectively allowing the application to access the CardShield service without relying on the CardShield Passive Agent. The following is an example that exemplifies the API's ease of use. Refer to Chapter 12 for a fully functional example.

```
import CommerceUtils.*;
import CardShield.*;

public class cgi {
    public static void main(String args[]) {
        cgilib CGIinfo       = new cgilib();
        CardShieldAPI CS     = new CardShieldAPI("1234567A", false);
        String Good          = "";

        Good = CS.SecureSale(CGIinfo.FormVars.getProperty("CLERK","TEST CGI"),
                        CGIinfo.FormVars.getProperty("COMMENT","Java CGI"),
                        CGIinfo.FormVars.getProperty("CCNUM"),
                        CGIinfo.FormVars.getProperty("CCEXPIRE"),
                        CGIinfo.FormVars.getProperty("AMOUNT"),
                        CGIinfo.FormVars.getProperty("ZIP"),
                        CGIinfo.FormVars.getProperty("ADDRESS"),
                        CGIinfo.FormVars);
        if(Good == CS.Approved)
            CGIinfo.Redirect("http://www.xprime.com/allgood.html");
        else
            CGIinfo.Redirect("http://www.xprime.com/OutOLuck.html");


        }

}
```

Summary

The CardShield API lets Java commerce developers quickly integrate the ability to process credit-card sales without requiring a dedicated connection. Along with the API's apparent use of secure credit-card sale processing comes the set of features associated with the CardShield service, such as e-mail, fax, and daily transaction settlement files. Applets rely on the CardShield Passive Agent to communicate to the CardShield service. Chapters 12, 13, and 14 provide real-world usable examples of solutions utilizing the CardShield API. Also included in those chapters are instructions for facilitating the CardShield functionality using IC Verify for processing the sale, which does require a dedicated connection. Use this chapter as a reference for the API, and later chapters will provide a useful set of examples.

12

Single-Page CGI

This chapter provides a single-page CGI commerce application. "Single-page" refers to the fact that the CGI processes only a single-page order, as opposed to the contents of Chapter 13, which explores a multipage shopping cart application. The key focus of this chapter is to provide a ready-to-use commerce solution, with four slight variations. The first is a single-page CGI that stores orders to an order file and does not process the credit-card sale. The second and third variations provide the same functionality as the first, plus they add CardShield and IC Verify, respectively, for credit-card sale processing. The last CGI utilizes JDBC to obtain order information and store entered orders, as well as provides IC Verify sale processing. For the nonprogrammer, this chapter furnishes a legend for the provided CGI resources. Programmers will find this chapter to contain helpful examples of the tools introduced in Chapter 10. All code listings can be found on the accompanying CD-ROM.

The Clients

Typically, the client for a CGI application is an HTML form. However, the advent of applets brought about a new, semi-intelligent CGI application called a "Feeder" applet. Both the HTML and the "Feeder" applet achieve the same task: feeding information to an awaiting CGI. The following supplied CGI clients provide examples of both the HTML- and applet-based clients. These examples do not have any inherent security. All CGI-based commerce applications must rely on the security mechanisms of the Web server, as discussed in Chapter 2.

HTML Form

The provided form is given as a base template. If you choose to use this CGI form combo you will want to modify the appearance of the form. HTML offers the ability to take the same content in multiple ways. For the purpose of modifying the HTML form to fit your needs, the content is the form information. Graphics and/or text can be added or modified in this from, but be careful not to modify the field names. It is vital to the proper execution of the CGI that the field name information match what the CGI is expecting; this match is case-sensitive.

Code Listing

```
<HTML>
<HEAD>
<TITLE>Stuff For Sale</TITLE>
</HEAD>
<BODY BGCOLOR="FFFFFF">
<BLOCKQUOTE>
<H1>Your Name Here: My Shop</H1>
<HR>
<H2>Please Enter Your Order</H2>

<FORM Method="Get" Action="/cgi-bin/testme.bat" >

<TABLE>
<tr><td>First Name</td><td><input name="FirstName" type="TEXT"  size="36"></td></tr>
<tr><td>Last Name</td><td><input name="LastName" type="TEXT"  size="36"></td></tr>
<tr><td>Address</td><td> <input name="Address1" type="TEXT"  size="53"></td></tr>
<tr><td></td><td> <input name="Address2" type="TEXT"  size="53"></td></tr>
<tr><td>City</td><td><input name="City" type="TEXT"  size="20">
        State <input name="State" type="TEXT"  size="2"></td></tr>
<tr><td>Zip Code</td><td><input name="Zip" type="TEXT"  size="20">
<tr><td>Phone Number</td><td><input name="PhoneNumber" type="TEXT" size="36"> </td></tr>
<tr><td>Fax Number</td><td><input name="FaxNumber" type="TEXT" size="36"></td></tr>
<tr><td>Email Address</td><td><input name="Email" type="TEXT" size="36"></td></tr>
</TABLE>
<HR>

<TABLE>
```

```
<tr><td>Item Code</td><td><input name="I1" type="TEXT"  size="6">
        Quantity <input name="Q1" type="TEXT"  size="2"></td>
        Price <input name="P1" type="TEXT"  size="10"></tr>
<tr><td>Item Code</td><td><input name="I2" type="TEXT"  size="6">
        Quantity <input name="Q2" type="TEXT"  size="2"></td>
        Price <input name="P2" type="TEXT"  size="10"></tr>
<tr><td>Item Code</td><td><input name="I3" type="TEXT"  size="6">
        Quantity <input name="Q3" type="TEXT"  size="2"></td>
        Price <input name="P3" type="TEXT"  size="10"></tr>
<tr><td>Item Code</td><td><input name="I4" type="TEXT"  size="6">
        Quantity <input name="Q4" type="TEXT"  size="2"></td>
        Price <input name="P4" type="TEXT"  size="10"></tr>
<tr><td>Total</td><td><input name="Total" type="TEXT"  size="10"></td></tr>
</TABLE>
<br>
<HR>
<TABLE>
<tr><td>Credit Card Number</td><td><input name="CCNUM" type="TEXT"  size="20">
        Expires in the format YYMM (Y = Year, M = Month)<input name="CCEXP" type="TEXT"
size="10"></td></tr>
</TABLE>
<br><br>
<P>
All orders are shipped UPS ground at no additional charge.
<br><br>
<input  type="SUBMIT" value="Order">
<input  type="RESET" value="Clear Form">
<input  type="HIDDEN" name="FormNum" value="2">
</FORM>
</BODY>
</HTML>
```

"Feeder" Applet

A relatively new, and possibly obscure, use of applets is what is called a "Feeder" applet. A Feeder looks identical to a normal applet order-entry device; the difference comes when the applet sends the information back to the server. Normal applets would use a mechanism such as JDBC or some other client/server method to save the collected information. A Feeder applet uses the same user interface as a normal applet, but when the time comes to load the information to the server something different happens. Feeder applets encode all of the collected information into a URL, to which the browser then jumps. This is identical to HTML forms; however, in this case the applet handles the URL packing that normally the browser takes care of. Essentially, Feeder applets are directly equivalent to HTML form, except that they offer a client-side interface.

Unlike a Feeder's HTML counterpart, modifying the appearance of the content takes a decent amount of programming. The use of Feeder applets is focused on the demand to provide a Java substitute for an HTML facility. In all practicality, the HTML approach is usually much cleaner. However, if you find yourself in need of a Feeder applet, included on the accompanying CD-ROM is a ground-zero template for such an applet in a Visual Café project.

Plain Vanilla

Development always begins with a base set of functionality. In the case of a single-page CGI order application, this is it. Simply put, this CGI tries to validate the form information, stores the order to disk, and generates a receipt HTML page. All entered item information is stored in a CGI-accessible configuration file. If you choose to use this example, the following is a list of things to modify. All source and referenced configuration files can be found on the accompanying CD-ROM.

If you wish to use this solution on your own site, the following is a check list modification required to fit your specific needs:

- Load the configuration file with the items you wish to sell.

- Generate all referenced error HTML pages, or change the associated URL string.

- Change the path of the stored order files if needed.

- Change the header and the footer HTML for the generated receipt.

- Modify either the Feeder applet or the HTML form to suit your needs.

Caveats

The error handling and field validation of this and the following examples leave a lot to be desired. Basic-level validation is performed on the fields, by checking the length of the entered information. If a validation fails, or if a problem arises, the error is caught to the extent of giving the user a general idea of what is wrong. However, the CGI does not provide a specific and detailed account of what went wrong.

Code Listing

```
import CommerceUtils.*;
import CardShield.*;
import java.util.Date;
```

```java
import java.util.Enumeration;
import java.util.StringTokenizer;


/**
 * CGIPRocessor is a generic handler for single page order forms.
 * It provides a preliminary frame work for further develop. A
 * potential weak spot is the lack of accurate field verification.
 *
 *
 * Usage: The object should be created by passing in the path of
 * where to store the order files, as well as the extension to be placed
 * on the newly created order files.
 *
 *
 * Note: Page redirection on errors is used in lue of generating error
 * pages. These provides more flexibility of appearance.
 *
 */

public class CGIProcessor{

    /**
     * ItemFile is the name of the configuration file containing the
     * stores items
     */
    public static String ItemFile            =    "items.ini";

    /**
     * BadInputURL points to the page which the user will be directed to
     * if a form input error occurs. This error will occur if any of the
     * input fields does not pass the verification function.
     */
    public static String BadInputURL         =    "/badinput.html";

    /**
     * BadItemURL points to the page which the user will be directed to
     * if a form item input error occurs. This error will occur if any of the
     * items are invalid or missing.
     */
    public static String BadItemURL          =    "/baditem.html";

    /**
     * BadTotalURL points to the page which the user will be directed to
     * if a form total error occurs. This error will occur if the user enters
```

```
 * a total that does not match the calculated total.
 */
public static String BadTotalURL          =    "/badtotal.html";

/**
 * BadExpirelURL points to the page which the user will be directed to
 * if credit card's expiration date is invalid. This error will occur if the user enters
 * a data fails verification.
 */
public static String BadExpirelURL        =    "/badexpire.html";

/**
 * BadCardURL points to the page which the user will be directed to
 * if credit card number is invalid. This error will occur if the user enters
 * a card number that fails verification.
 */
public static String BadCardURL           =    "/badcard.html";

/**
 * ReceiptHeader holds the top portion of the HTML page that is
 * generated if all is validated.
 */
public static String ReceiptHeader        =    "<html>\n<head>\n<title>"+
                                               "Thank You</title>\n</head>\n<body>\n"+
                                               "<H1>Your Order Has Been Processed</H1>";
/**
 * ReceiptFooter holds the bottom portion of the HTML page that is
 * generated if all is validated.
 */
public static String ReceiptFooter        =    "<br><br>Thank-You\n</body></html>";


//The calculated total of the entered items.
private float  Total            =    0.00f;

//Holds the HTML coded sale receipt.
private String GeneratedReceipt =    "";


/**
 * CGIinfo is the cgilib containing all CGI information.
 */
public cgilib   CGIinfo      =    null;

/**
 * ItemInfo is the inifile holding all item information.
```

```
 */
public inifile  ItemInfo   =   null;

/**
 * OrderPath is the path to store the generated order in.
 */
public String   OrderPath  =   ".\\";

/**
 * OrderPath is the extension to be placed on the generated order.
 */
public String   OrderExt   =   ".ord";


/**
 * The constructor initializes the all needed objets and variables, including
 * the cgilib, the item inifile.
 *
 * @param orderpath         The path to store the generated orders in.
 * @param ordertext         The extension to be placed on the generated orders.
 *
 */
public CGIProcessor(String orderpath, String ordertext){

    CGIinfo      = new cgilib(); //create the cgi library
    ItemInfo     = new inifile(ItemFile); //create the ini holding the item info.
    OrderPath    = orderpath;
    OrderExt     = ordertext;
}


/**
 * ProcesForm is the entry point for the processing of the form. After construct
 * this member should be called.  The member : verifies the input, credit card, and
items,
 * and generates all resulting HTML.
 *
 */
public void ProcesForm(){

    //Verify that all customer input is ok.
    if(!VerifyInput()){
        CGIinfo.Redirect(BadInputURL);
        return;
    }
```

```
        //Verify that all items are valid and generate the receipt
        if(!VerifyItems()){
            CGIinfo.Redirect(BadItemURL);
            return;
        }

        //Verify that the total the user enter   maches the calculated total.
        if(!VerifyTotal()){
            CGIinfo.Redirect(BadTotalURL);
            return;
        }

         //Verify Expiration Date
        if(CGIinfo.FormVars.getProperty("CCEXP").length() != 4){
            CGIinfo.Redirect(BadExpirelURL);
            return;
        }

        //Verify credit card Number
        if(FormatCCNum(CGIinfo.FormVars.getProperty("CCNUM")) == ""){
            CGIinfo.Redirect(BadCardURL);
            return;
        }

        //store the order to the order file.
        StoreOrder();

        //Print the standard CGI response
        CGIinfo.PrintHeader();

        System.out.println(ReceiptHeader); //top of HTML page
        System.out.println(GeneratedReceipt); //the receipt
        System.out.println(ReceiptFooter); //the bottom
        return;
    }


/*Check each of the required fields return false if any fail.
  Only size is checked, to assure better response additional
  verification logic should be added.
 */
private boolean VerifyInput(){

    //Verify Customer Name
    if((CGIinfo.FormVars.getProperty("FirstName") == null) ||
```

```
(CGIinfo.FormVars.getProperty("FirstName").length() < 2))
        return false;
    if((CGIinfo.FormVars.getProperty("LastName") == null) ||
(CGIinfo.FormVars.getProperty("LastName").length() < 2))
        return false;


    //Verify Address
    if((CGIinfo.FormVars.getProperty("Address1") == null) ||
(CGIinfo.FormVars.getProperty("Address1").length() < 5))
        return false;


    //Verify City
    if((CGIinfo.FormVars.getProperty("City") == null) ||
(CGIinfo.FormVars.getProperty("City").length() < 4))
        return false;


    //Verify State
    if((CGIinfo.FormVars.getProperty("State") == null) ||
(CGIinfo.FormVars.getProperty("State").length() < 1))
        return false;


    //Verify Zip
    if((CGIinfo.FormVars.getProperty("Zip") == null) ||
(CGIinfo.FormVars.getProperty("Zip").length() < 5))
        return false;


    //Verify Phone
    if((CGIinfo.FormVars.getProperty("PhoneNumber") == null) ||
(CGIinfo.FormVars.getProperty("PhoneNumber").length() < 10))
        return false;


    return true;
}


/* This function verifies the validity of the inputted item codes, as well
   as generating a sale receipt.  The item information comes out of the items.ini
   file.  If any item is entered incorrectly false will be returned.
*/
private boolean VerifyItems(){

    GeneratedReceipt = "";
    float price = 0.00f;
    int qty   = 0;
```

```
        //Verifies if the item 1 exists. If it does, then the item is added to the receipt.
        if((CGIinfo.FormVars.getProperty("I1") != null) &&
(ItemInfo.SectionExits(CGIinfo.FormVars.getProperty("I1")))){
                GeneratedReceipt += CGIinfo.FormVars.getProperty("I1") + "------>";
                GeneratedReceipt += ItemInfo.GetProperty(CGIinfo.FormVars.getProperty("I1"),
                             "Description","Description Missing") + "------>";

                try{
                    price = new Float(ItemInfo.GetProperty("Price","0.00")).floatValue();
                    qty = new Integer(CGIinfo.FormVars.getProperty("Q1")).intValue();
                }
                catch(Exception e){
                }

                GeneratedReceipt += "$" + price + " x " + qty + " = $" + (qty * price) +
"<BR>\n";

                Total += (qty * price);
        }

        //Verifies if the item 2 exists. If it does, then the item is added to the receipt.
        if((CGIinfo.FormVars.getProperty("I2") != null) &&
(ItemInfo.SectionExits(CGIinfo.FormVars.getProperty("I2")))){
                GeneratedReceipt += CGIinfo.FormVars.getProperty("I2") + "------>";
                GeneratedReceipt += ItemInfo.GetProperty(CGIinfo.FormVars.getProperty("I2"),
                             "Description","Description Missing") + "------>";

                try{
                    price = new Float(ItemInfo.GetProperty("Price","0.00")).floatValue();
                    qty = new Integer(CGIinfo.FormVars.getProperty("Q2")).intValue();
                }
                catch(Exception e){
                }

                GeneratedReceipt += "$" + price + " x " + qty + " = $" + (qty * price) +
"<BR>\n";

                Total += (qty * price);
        }

        //Verifies if the item 3 exists. If it does, then the item is added to the receipt.
        if((CGIinfo.FormVars.getProperty("I3") != null) &&
(ItemInfo.SectionExits(CGIinfo.FormVars.getProperty("I3")))){
                GeneratedReceipt += CGIinfo.FormVars.getProperty("I3") + "------>";
                GeneratedReceipt += ItemInfo.GetProperty(CGIinfo.FormVars.getProperty("I3"),
```

```
                             "Description","Description Missing") + "------>";

                try{
                    price = new Float(ItemInfo.GetProperty("Price","0.00")).floatValue();
                    qty = new Integer(CGIinfo.FormVars.getProperty("Q3")).intValue();
                }
                catch(Exception e){
                }

                GeneratedReceipt += "$" + price + " x " + qty + " = $" + (qty * price) +
"<BR>\n";

                Total += (qty * price);
        }

        //Verifies if the item 4 exists. If it does, then the item is added to the receipt.
        if((CGIinfo.FormVars.getProperty("I4") != null) &&
(ItemInfo.SectionExits(CGIinfo.FormVars.getProperty("I4")))){
                GeneratedReceipt += CGIinfo.FormVars.getProperty("I4") + "------>";
                GeneratedReceipt += ItemInfo.GetProperty(CGIinfo.FormVars.getProperty("I4"),
                             "Description","Description Missing") + "------>";

                try{
                    price = new Float(ItemInfo.GetProperty("Price","0.00")).floatValue();
                    qty = new Integer(CGIinfo.FormVars.getProperty("Q4")).intValue();
                }
                catch(Exception e){
                }

                GeneratedReceipt += "$" + price + " x " + qty + " = $" + (qty * price) +
"<BR>\n";

                Total += (qty * price);
        }

        if(GeneratedReceipt == "")
            return false;
        else
            return true;
    }


    /* Part of the verification of the items was to generate a sale receipt,
       to include the calculated total.  This function compares the calculated
```

```
       total with the user entered total.
*/
private boolean VerifyTotal(){

    float Tmp_Total = 0.00f;

    try{
        Tmp_Total = new Float(CGIinfo.FormVars.getProperty("Total")).floatValue();
    }
    catch(Exception e){
        return false;
    }

    if(Tmp_Total != Total)
        return false;
    else
        return true;
}


/*
 Besides checking for Alpha characters in the credit card number,
 this function will take out spaces and '-' characters.
*/
private String FormatCCNum(String in){

    if(in == null)
        return "";

    String out  =   "";
    Character C  =   new Character('c');


    for(int i = 0 ; i < in.length();++i)
        if((in.charAt(i) != '-')&&(in.charAt(i) != ' ')){
            if(C.isDigit(in.charAt(i)))
                out += "" + in.charAt(i);
            else
                return "";
        }

    CGIinfo.FormVars.put("CCNUM",new String(out));
    return out;
}

/*
```

```
    Commits all of the form's information to a file using
    the orderfile utility.
    */
    private void StoreOrder(){

        orderfile order = new orderfile(OrderPath,OrderExt);
        Enumeration E = CGIinfo.FormVars.keys();
        String tmp_val = "";
        String tmp_key = "";

        for(;E.hasMoreElements ();){
            tmp_key = (String) E.nextElement();
            tmp_val = CGIinfo.FormVars.getProperty (tmp_key);
            order.AddProperty(tmp_key,tmp_val);
        }

        order.Save();
    }
}
```

Sale Processing with CardShield API

If the last example was plain vanilla, it could be said that this example is CardShield flavored. One of the short comings of the prior example is its inability to process the credit-card sales; instead, it would simply store the orders to disk, without processing the credit-card sale. Processing the credit-card transaction has its advantages; however, having a dedicated Internet connection has its disadvantages. To gain the best of both worlds this example fits the prior plain vanilla example with CardShield sale-processing functionality.

Because a Java-based CGI does not have the same security restrictions as an applet, a CGI can communicate freely with CardShield. In many instances, ISPs provide users with access to their own Java-enabled cgi-bin. In such a setup, the CGI that follows is ready and willing for deployment.

All entered item information is stored in a CGI-accessible configuration file. All source and referenced configuration files can be found on the accompanying CD-ROM. If you choose to use this example, the following is a list of things to modify

- Load the configuration file with the items you wish to sell.

- Generate all referenced error HTML pages, or change the associated URL string.

- Change the path of the stored order files if needed.

- Change the header and the footer HTML for the generated receipt.

- Modify the entered CSMID to match your CardShield account.

- Modify either the Feeder or the HTML form to suit your needs.

Caveats

Like the previous example, the error handling and field validation is not very good. Another shortcoming of this example is its inability to handle CardShield-provided error codes. Embedded in the string that is returned by CardShield's SercureSale function is some useful information that should be propagated to the user. The current implementation checks only to see if it was approved, and all error codes are ignored.

Code Listing

```java
import CommerceUtils.*;
import CardShield.*;
import java.util.Date;
import java.util.Enumeration;
import java.util.StringTokenizer;


/**
 * CGIPRocessor is a generic handler for single page order forms.
 * It provides an a preliminary frame work for further develop. Some
 * potential weak spots is the lack of accurate field verification.
 *
 *
 * Usage: The object should be created by passing in the path of
 * where to store the order files, as well as the extension to be placed
 * on the newly created order files.
 *
 *
 * Note: Page redirection on errors is used in lue of generating error
 * pages. These provides more flexibility of appearance.
 *
 */

public class CGIProcessor{

    /**
     * ItemFile is the name of the configuration file containing the
     * stores items
     */
    public static String ItemFile          =    "items.ini";
```

```
/**
 * BadInputURL points to the page which the user will be directed to
 * if a form input error occurs. This error will occur if any of the
 * input fields does not pass the verification function.
 */
public static String BadInputURL        =   "/badinput.html";

/**
 * BadItemURL points to the page which the user will be directed to
 * if a form item input error occurs. This error will occur if any of the
 * items are invalid or missing.
 */
public static String BadItemURL         =   "/baditem.html";

/**
 * BadTotalURL points to the page which the user will be directed to
 * if a form total error occurs. This error will occur if the user enters
 * a total that does not match the calculated total.
 */
public static String BadTotalURL        =   "/badtotal.html";

/**
 * BadExpirelURL points to the page which the user will be directed to
 * if credit card's expiration date is invalid. This error will occur if the user enters
 * a data fails verification.
 */
public static String BadExpirelURL      =   "/badexpire.html";

/**
 * BadCardURL points to the page which the user will be directed to
 * if credit card number is invalid. This error will occur if the user enters
 * a card number that fails verification.
 */
public static String BadCardURL         =   "/badcard.html";

/**
 * NotApprovedURL points to the page which the user will be directed to
 * if credit card fails to be approved for the sale. This error will occur
 * if the user enters either and invalid card number, invalid expiration date,
 * or the card was refused.
 */
public static String NotApprovedURL         =   "/notapproved.html";


/**
```

```
 * ReceiptHeader holds the top portion of the HTML page that is
 * generated if all is validated.
 */
public static String ReceiptHeader       =    "<html>\n<head>\n<title>"+
                                              "Thank You</title>\n</head>\n<body>\n"+
                                              "<H1>Your Order Has Been Processed</H1>";

/**
 * ReceiptFooter holds the bottom portion of the HTML page that is
 * generated if all is validated.
 */
public static String ReceiptFooter       =    "<br><br>Thank-You\n</body></html>";


//The calculated total of the entered items.
private float  Total            =    0.00f;

//Holds the HTML coded sale receipt.
private String GeneratedReceipt =    "";


/**
 * CGIinfo is the cgilib containing all CGI information.
 */
public cgilib   CGIinfo       =    null;

/**
 * ItemInfo is the inifile holding all item information.
 */
public inifile  ItemInfo      =    null;

/**
 * OrderPath is the path to store the generated order in.
 */
public String   OrderPath     =    ".\\";

/**
 * OrderPath is the extension to be placed on the generated order.
 */
public String   OrderExt      =    ".ord";


/**
 * The constructor initializes the all needed objets and variables, including
 * the cgilib, the item inifile.
 *
 * @param orderpath          The path to store the generated orders in.
```

```
 * @param ordertext          The extension to be placed on the generated orders.
 *
 */
public CGIProcessor(String orderpath, String ordertext){

    CGIinfo     = new cgilib(); //create the cgi library
    ItemInfo    = new inifile(ItemFile); //create the ini holding the item info.
    OrderPath   = orderpath;
    OrderExt    = ordertext;
}



/**
 * ProcesForm is the entry point for the processing of the form. After construct
 * this member should be called.  The member : verifies the input, credit card, and items,
 * and generates all resulting HTML.
 *
 */
public void ProcesForm(){

    //Verify that all customer input is ok.
    if(!VerifyInput()){
        CGIinfo.Redirect(BadInputURL);
        return;
    }

    //Verify that all items are valid and generate the receipt
    if(!VerifyItems()){
        CGIinfo.Redirect(BadItemURL);
        return;
    }

    //Verify that the total the user enter maches the calculated total.
    if(!VerifyTotal()){
        CGIinfo.Redirect(BadTotalURL);
        return;
    }

     //Verify Expiration Date
    if(CGIinfo.FormVars.getProperty("CCEXP").length() != 4){
        CGIinfo.Redirect(BadExpirelURL);
        return;
    }

    //Verify credit card Number
    if(FormatCCNum(CGIinfo.FormVars.getProperty("CCNUM")) == ""){
```

```
            CGIinfo.Redirect(BadCardURL);
            return;
    }

    //Try and process the sale. The call will return false
    //if the card, expiration is not valid , or it is not
    //Approved.
    if(!ProcessSale()){
        CGIinfo.Redirect(NotApprovedURL);
        return;
    }

    //store the order to the order file.
    StoreOrder();

    //Print the standard CGI response
    CGIinfo.PrintHeader();

    System.out.println(ReceiptHeader); //top of HTML page
    System.out.println(GeneratedReceipt); //the receipt
    System.out.println(ReceiptFooter); //the bottom
    return;
}


/*
    This function process the credit card sale using CardShield.
    SecureSale produces a string error code, for more robust
    error handling this string should be propagated to the user.
    This function will fail if the card or expiration is invalid,
    or the card is not approved.
*/

private boolean ProcessSale(){

  //Init the CardShield object. The first param is the CSMID
  //second is false reflecting the fact that this is not an Applet
  CardShieldAPI CS = new CardShieldAPI("123456A",false);


  return (CS.SecureSale("MYCGI","TESTCGI",CGIinfo.FormVars.getProperty("CCNUM"),
          CGIinfo.FormVars.getProperty("CCEXP"),"" + Total,
          CGIinfo.FormVars.getProperty("Zip"),
          CGIinfo.FormVars.getProperty("Address1")) == CS.Approved);
```

```
        }


    /*Check each of the required fields return false if any fail.
      Only size is checked, to assure better response additional
      verification logic should be added.
     */
    private boolean VerifyInput(){

        //Verify Customer Name
        if((CGIinfo.FormVars.getProperty("FirstName") == null) ||
(CGIinfo.FormVars.getProperty("FirstName").length() < 2))
            return false;
        if((CGIinfo.FormVars.getProperty("LastName") == null) ||
(CGIinfo.FormVars.getProperty("LastName").length() < 2))
            return false;


        //Verify Address
        if((CGIinfo.FormVars.getProperty("Address1") == null) ||
(CGIinfo.FormVars.getProperty("Address1").length() < 5))
            return false;


        //Verify City
        if((CGIinfo.FormVars.getProperty("City") == null) ||
(CGIinfo.FormVars.getProperty("City").length() < 4))
            return false;


        //Verify State
        if((CGIinfo.FormVars.getProperty("State") == null) ||
(CGIinfo.FormVars.getProperty("State").length() < 1))
            return false;


        //Verify Zip
        if((CGIinfo.FormVars.getProperty("Zip") == null) ||
(CGIinfo.FormVars.getProperty("Zip").length() < 5))
            return false;


        //Verify Phone
        if((CGIinfo.FormVars.getProperty("PhoneNumber") == null) ||
(CGIinfo.FormVars.getProperty("PhoneNumber").length() < 10))
            return false;


        return true;
    }
```

```
/* This function verifies the validity of the inputted item codes, as well
   as generating a sale receipt.  The item information comes out of the items.ini
   file.  If any item is entered incorrectly false will be returned.
*/
private boolean VerifyItems(){

    GeneratedReceipt = "";
    float price = 0.00f;
    int qty   = 0;

    //Verifies if the item 1 exists. If it does, then the item is added to the receipt.
    if((CGIinfo.FormVars.getProperty("I1") != null) &&
(ItemInfo.SectionExits(CGIinfo.FormVars.getProperty("I1")))){
            GeneratedReceipt += CGIinfo.FormVars.getProperty("I1") + "------>";
            GeneratedReceipt += ItemInfo.GetProperty(CGIinfo.FormVars.getProperty("I1"),
                            "Description","Description Missing") + "------>";

            try{
                price = new Float(ItemInfo.GetProperty("Price","0.00")).floatValue();
                qty = new Integer(CGIinfo.FormVars.getProperty("Q1")).intValue();
            }
            catch(Exception e){
            }

            GeneratedReceipt += "$" + price + " x " + qty + " = $" + (qty * price) +
"<BR>\n";

            Total += (qty * price);
    }

    //Verifies if the item 2 exists. If it does, then the item is added to the receipt.
    if((CGIinfo.FormVars.getProperty("I2") != null) &&
(ItemInfo.SectionExits(CGIinfo.FormVars.getProperty("I2")))){
            GeneratedReceipt += CGIinfo.FormVars.getProperty("I2") + "------>";
            GeneratedReceipt += ItemInfo.GetProperty(CGIinfo.FormVars.getProperty("I2"),
                            "Description","Description Missing") + "------>";

            try{
                price = new Float(ItemInfo.GetProperty("Price","0.00")).floatValue();
                qty = new Integer(CGIinfo.FormVars.getProperty("Q2")).intValue();
            }
            catch(Exception e){
            }

            GeneratedReceipt += "$" + price + " x " + qty + " = $" + (qty * price) +
```

```
"<BR>\n";

                Total += (qty * price);
        }

        //Verifies if the item 3 exists. If it does, then the item is added to the receipt.
        if((CGIinfo.FormVars.getProperty("I3") != null) &&
(ItemInfo.SectionExits(CGIinfo.FormVars.getProperty("I3")))){
                GeneratedReceipt += CGIinfo.FormVars.getProperty("I3") + "------>";
                GeneratedReceipt += ItemInfo.GetProperty(CGIinfo.FormVars.getProperty("I3"),
                                "Description","Description Missing") + "------>";

                try{
                    price = new Float(ItemInfo.GetProperty("Price","0.00")).floatValue();
                    qty = new Integer(CGIinfo.FormVars.getProperty("Q3")).intValue();
                }
                catch(Exception e){
                }

                GeneratedReceipt += "$" + price + " x " + qty + " = $" + (qty * price) +
"<BR>\n";

                Total += (qty * price);
        }

        //Verifies if the item 4 exists. If it does, then the item is added to the receipt.
        if((CGIinfo.FormVars.getProperty("I4") != null) &&
(ItemInfo.SectionExits(CGIinfo.FormVars.getProperty("I4")))){
                GeneratedReceipt += CGIinfo.FormVars.getProperty("I4") + "------>";
                GeneratedReceipt += ItemInfo.GetProperty(CGIinfo.FormVars.getProperty("I4"),
                                "Description","Description Missing") + "------>";

                try{
                    price = new Float(ItemInfo.GetProperty("Price","0.00")).floatValue();
                    qty = new Integer(CGIinfo.FormVars.getProperty("Q4")).intValue();
                }
                catch(Exception e){
                }

                GeneratedReceipt += "$" + price + " x " + qty + " = $" + (qty * price) +
"<BR>\n";

                Total += (qty * price);
        }
```

```
        if(GeneratedReceipt == "")
            return false;
        else
            return true;
    }


    /* Part of the verification of the items was to generate a sale receipt,
       to include the calculated total.  This function compares the calculated
       total with the user entered total.
    */
    private boolean VerifyTotal(){

        float Tmp_Total = 0.00f;

        try{
            Tmp_Total = new Float(CGIinfo.FormVars.getProperty("Total")).floatValue();
        }
        catch(Exception e){
            return false;
        }

        if(Tmp_Total != Total)
            return false;
        else
            return true;
    }


    /*
     Besides checking for Alpha characters in the credit card number,
     this function will take out spaces and '-' characters.
    */
    private String FormatCCNum(String in){

        if(in == null)
            return "";

        String out  =    "";
        Character C  =    new Character('c');


        for(int i = 0 ; i < in.length();++i)
            if((in.charAt(i) != '-')&&(in.charAt(i) != ' ')){
                if(C.isDigit(in.charAt(i)))
                    out += "" + in.charAt(i);
```

```
            else
                return "";
        }

    CGIinfo.FormVars.put("CCNUM",new String(out));
    return out;
    }

    /*
     Commits all of the form's information to a file using
     the orderfile utility.
    */
    private void StoreOrder(){

        orderfile order = new orderfile(OrderPath,OrderExt);
        Enumeration E = CGIinfo.FormVars.keys();
        String tmp_val = "";
        String tmp_key = "";

        for(;E.hasMoreElements ();){
            tmp_key = (String) E.nextElement();
            tmp_val = CGIinfo.FormVars.getProperty (tmp_key);
            order.AddProperty(tmp_key,tmp_val);
        }

        order.Save();
    }
}
```

Sale Processing with IC Verify

If you already have a dedicated connection at your disposal, you might opt to use IC Verify instead of CardShield. What this example provides is the same functionality as the "CardShield flavored vanilla" example.

All entered item information is stored in a CGI-accessible configuration file. All source and referenced configuration files can be found on the accompanying CD-ROM. If you choose to use this example, the following things must be modified:

- Load the configuration file with the items you wish to sell.

- Generate all referenced error HTML pages, or change the associated URL string.

- Change the path of the stored order files if needed.

- Change the header and the footer HTML for the generated receipt.

- Modify the IC Verify paths to match the IC Verify setup configurations.

- For production, change the debug flag of IC Verify to off.

- Modify either the Feeder or the HTML form to suit your needs.

Caveats

The major shortcoming of this example is its inability to handle the IC Verify-provided error codes. Accompanying each transaction response is an error string containing useful information that should be propagated to the user. The current implementation checks to see only if the sale was approved, and the error code field is ignored.

Code Listing

```
import CommerceUtils.*;
import CardShield.*;
import java.util.Date;
import java.util.Enumeration;
import java.util.StringTokenizer;


/**
 * CGIPRocessor is a generic handler for single page order forms.
 * It provides an a preliminary frame work for further develop. Some
 * potential weak spots is the lack of accurate field verification.
 *
 *
 * Usage: The object should be created by passing in the path of
 * where to store the order files, as well as the extension to be placed
 * on the newly created order files.
 *
 *
 * Note: Page redirection on errors is used in lue of generating error
 * pages. These provides more flexibility of appearance.
 *
 */

public class CGIProcessor{

    /**
     * ItemFile is the name of the configuration file containing the
     * stores items
     */
```

```java
public static String ItemFile          =    "items.ini";

/**
 * BadInputURL points to the page which the user will be directed to
 * if a form input error occurs. This error will occur if any of the
 * input fields does not pass the verification function.
 */
public static String BadInputURL       =    "/badinput.html";

/**
 * BadItemURL points to the page which the user will be directed to
 * if a form item input error occurs. This error will occur if any of the
 * items are invalid or missing.
 */
public static String BadItemURL        =    "/baditem.html";

/**
 * BadTotalURL points to the page which the user will be directed to
 * if a form total error occurs. This error will occur if the user enters
 * a total that does not match the calculated total.
 */
public static String BadTotalURL       =    "/badtotal.html";

/**
 * BadExpirelURL points to the page which the user will be directed to
 * if credit card's expiration date is invalid. This error will occur if the user enters
 * a data fails verification.
 */
public static String BadExpirelURL     =    "/badexpire.html";

/**
 * BadCardURL points to the page which the user will be directed to
 * if credit card number is invalid. This error will occur if the user enters
 * a card number that fails verification.
 */
public static String BadCardURL        =    "/badcard.html";

/**
 * NotApprovedURL points to the page which the user will be directed to
 * if credit card fails to be approved for the sale. This error will occur
 * if the user enters either and invalid card number, invalid expiration date,
 * or the card was refused.
 */
public static String NotApprovedURL       =    "/notapproved.html";
```

```
/**
 * ReceiptHeader holds the top portion of the HTML page that is
 * generated if all is validated.
 */
public static String ReceiptHeader      =    "<html>\n<head>\n<title>"+
                                             "Thank You</title>\n</head>\n<body>\n"+
                                             "<H1>Your Order Has Been Processed</H1>";

/**
 * ReceiptFooter holds the bottom portion of the HTML page that is
 * generated if all is validated.
 */
public static String ReceiptFooter      =    "<br><br>Thank-You\n</body></html>";


//The calculated total of the entered items.
private float  Total              =    0.00f;

//Holds the HTML coded sale receipt.
private String GeneratedReceipt =     "";


/**
 * CGIinfo is the cgilib containing all CGI information.
 */
public cgilib    CGIinfo      =    null;

/**
 * ItemInfo is the inifile holding all item information.
 */
public inifile   ItemInfo     =    null;

/**
 * OrderPath is the path to store the generated order in.
 */
public String    OrderPath    =    ".\\";

/**
 * OrderPath is the extension to be placed on the generated order.
 */
public String    OrderExt     =    ".ord";


/**
 * The constructor initializes the all needed objets and variables, including
 * the cgilib, the item inifile.
 *
```

```
     * @param orderpath          The path to store the generated orders in.
     * @param ordertext          The extension to be placed on the generated orders.
     *
     */
    public CGIProcessor(String orderpath, String ordertext){

        CGIinfo        = new cgilib(); //create the cgi library
        ItemInfo       = new inifile(ItemFile); //create the ini holding the item info.
        OrderPath      = orderpath;
        OrderExt       = ordertext;
    }



    /**
     * ProcesForm is the entry point for the processing of the form. After construct
     * this member should be called.  The member : verifies the input, credit card, and
items,
     * and generates all resulting HTML.
     *
     */
    public void ProcesForm(){

        //Verify that all customer input is ok.
        if(!VerifyInput()){
            CGIinfo.Redirect(BadInputURL);
            return;
        }

        //Verify that all items are valid and generate the receipt
        if(!VerifyItems()){
            CGIinfo.Redirect(BadItemURL);
            return;
        }

        //Verify that the total the user enter maches the calculated total.
        if(!VerifyTotal()){
            CGIinfo.Redirect(BadTotalURL);
            return;
        }

         //Verify Expiration Date
        if(CGIinfo.FormVars.getProperty("CCEXP").length() != 4){
            CGIinfo.Redirect(BadExpirelURL);
            return;
        }
```

```
    //Verify credit card Number
    if(FormatCCNum(CGIinfo.FormVars.getProperty("CCNUM")) == ""){
        CGIinfo.Redirect(BadCardURL);
        return;
    }

    //Try and process the sale. The call will return false
    //if the card, expiration is not valid , or it is not
    //Approved.
    if(!ProcessSale()){
        CGIinfo.Redirect(NotApprovedURL);
        return;
    }

    //store the order to the order file.
    StoreOrder();

    //Print the standard CGI response
    CGIinfo.PrintHeader();

    System.out.println(ReceiptHeader); //top of HTML page
    System.out.println(GeneratedReceipt); //the receipt
    System.out.println(ReceiptFooter); //the bottom
    return;
}


/*
    This function process the credit card sale using CardShield.
    The icverify util provides ErrorCode function for returning
    the appropriate error code, for more robust
    error handling this string should be propagated to the user.
    This function will fail if the card or expiration is invalid,
    or the card is not approved.
*/

private boolean ProcessSale(){

  //Init the CardShield object. The first param is the CSMID
  //second is false reflecting the fact that this is not an Applet

    icverify IC    =   new icverify ("c:\\icverify\\","c:\\icverify\\demo19\\",true);

    //Add the order to the process request pool

    IC.AddRequest("MYCGI","TESTCGI",CGIinfo.FormVars.getProperty("CCNUM"),
```

```
            CGIinfo.FormVars.getProperty("CCEXP"),"" + Total,
            CGIinfo.FormVars.getProperty("Zip"),
            CGIinfo.FormVars.getProperty("Address1"));

    //Process the request
    IC.ProcessRequests();

    return IC.IsApproved(CGIinfo.FormVars.getProperty("CCNUM"));

}


/*Check each of the required fields return false if any fail.
  Only size is checked, to assure better response additional
  verification logic should be added.
 */
private boolean VerifyInput(){

    //Verify Customer Name
    if((CGIinfo.FormVars.getProperty("FirstName") == null) ||
(CGIinfo.FormVars.getProperty("FirstName").length() < 2))
        return false;
    if((CGIinfo.FormVars.getProperty("LastName") == null) ||
(CGIinfo.FormVars.getProperty("LastName").length() < 2))
        return false;

    //Verify Address
    if((CGIinfo.FormVars.getProperty("Address1") == null) ||
(CGIinfo.FormVars.getProperty("Address1").length() < 5))
        return false;

    //Verify City
    if((CGIinfo.FormVars.getProperty("City") == null) ||
(CGIinfo.FormVars.getProperty("City").length() < 4))
        return false;

    //Verify State
    if((CGIinfo.FormVars.getProperty("State") == null) ||
(CGIinfo.FormVars.getProperty("State").length() < 1))
        return false;

    //Verify Zip
    if((CGIinfo.FormVars.getProperty("Zip") == null) ||
(CGIinfo.FormVars.getProperty("Zip").length() < 5))
        return false;
```

```
        //Verify Phone
        if((CGIinfo.FormVars.getProperty("PhoneNumber") == null) ||
(CGIinfo.FormVars.getProperty("PhoneNumber").length() < 10))
            return false;

        return true;
    }


    /* This function verifies the validity of the inputted item codes, as well
       as generating a sale receipt.  The item information comes out of the items.ini
       file.  If any item is entered incorrectly false will be returned.
    */
    private boolean VerifyItems(){

        GeneratedReceipt = "";
        float price = 0.00f;
        int qty   = 0;

        //Verifies if the item 1 exists. If it does, then the item is added to the receipt.
        if((CGIinfo.FormVars.getProperty("I1") != null) &&
(ItemInfo.SectionExits(CGIinfo.FormVars.getProperty("I1")))){
                GeneratedReceipt += CGIinfo.FormVars.getProperty("I1") + "------>";
                GeneratedReceipt += ItemInfo.GetProperty(CGIinfo.FormVars.getProperty("I1"),
                            "Description","Description Missing") + "------>";

                try{
                    price = new Float(ItemInfo.GetProperty("Price","0.00")).floatValue();
                    qty = new Integer(CGIinfo.FormVars.getProperty("Q1")).intValue();
                }
                catch(Exception e){
                }

                GeneratedReceipt += "$" + price + " x " + qty + " = $" + (qty * price) +
"<BR>\n";

                Total += (qty * price);
        }

        //Verifies if the item 2 exists. If it does, then the item is added to the receipt.
        if((CGIinfo.FormVars.getProperty("I2") != null) &&
(ItemInfo.SectionExits(CGIinfo.FormVars.getProperty("I2")))){
                GeneratedReceipt += CGIinfo.FormVars.getProperty("I2") + "------>";
                GeneratedReceipt += ItemInfo.GetProperty(CGIinfo.FormVars.getProperty("I2"),
                            "Description","Description Missing") + "------>";
```

```
                    try{
                        price = new Float(ItemInfo.GetProperty("Price","0.00")).floatValue();
                        qty = new Integer(CGIinfo.FormVars.getProperty("Q2")).intValue();
                    }
                    catch(Exception e){
                    }

                    GeneratedReceipt += "$" + price + " x " + qty + " = $" + (qty * price) +
"<BR>\n";

                    Total += (qty * price);
            }

        //Verifies if the item 3 exists. If it does, then the item is added to the receipt.
        if((CGIinfo.FormVars.getProperty("I3") != null) &&
(ItemInfo.SectionExits(CGIinfo.FormVars.getProperty("I3")))){
                GeneratedReceipt += CGIinfo.FormVars.getProperty("I3") + "------>";
                GeneratedReceipt += ItemInfo.GetProperty(CGIinfo.FormVars.getProperty("I3"),
                                "Description","Description Missing") + "------>";

                    try{
                        price = new Float(ItemInfo.GetProperty("Price","0.00")).floatValue();
                        qty = new Integer(CGIinfo.FormVars.getProperty("Q3")).intValue();
                    }
                    catch(Exception e){
                    }

                    GeneratedReceipt += "$" + price + " x " + qty + " = $" + (qty * price) +
"<BR>\n";

                    Total += (qty * price);
            }

        //Verifies if the item 4 exists. If it does, then the item is added to the receipt.
        if((CGIinfo.FormVars.getProperty("I4") != null) &&
(ItemInfo.SectionExits(CGIinfo.FormVars.getProperty("I4")))){
                GeneratedReceipt += CGIinfo.FormVars.getProperty("I4") + "------>";
                GeneratedReceipt += ItemInfo.GetProperty(CGIinfo.FormVars.getProperty("I4"),
                                "Description","Description Missing") + "------>";

                    try{
                        price = new Float(ItemInfo.GetProperty("Price","0.00")).floatValue();
                        qty = new Integer(CGIinfo.FormVars.getProperty("Q4")).intValue();
                    }
                    catch(Exception e){
                    }
```

```
                GeneratedReceipt += "$" + price + " x " + qty + " = $" + (qty * price) +
"<BR>\n";

                Total += (qty * price);
        }


        if(GeneratedReceipt == "")
            return false;
        else
            return true;
    }


    /* Part of the verification of the items was to generate a sale receipt,
       to include the calculated total.  This function compares the calculated
       total with the user entered total.
    */
    private boolean VerifyTotal(){

        float Tmp_Total = 0.00f;

        try{
            Tmp_Total = new Float(CGIinfo.FormVars.getProperty("Total")).floatValue();
        }
        catch(Exception e){
            return false;
        }

        if(Tmp_Total != Total)
            return false;
        else
            return true;
    }


    /*
     Besides checking for Alpha characters in the credit card number,
     this function will take out spaces and '-' characters.
    */
    private String FormatCCNum(String in){

        if(in == null)
            return "";

        String out  =   "";
```

```
    Character C  =   new Character('c');


    for(int i = 0 ; i < in.length();++i)
        if((in.charAt(i) != '-')&&(in.charAt(i) != ' ')){
            if(C.isDigit(in.charAt(i)))
                out += "" + in.charAt(i);
            else
                return "";
        }

    CGIinfo.FormVars.put("CCNUM",new String(out));
    return out;
}

/*
 Commits all of the form's information to a file using
 the orderfile utility.
*/
private void StoreOrder(){

    orderfile order = new orderfile(OrderPath,OrderExt);
    Enumeration E = CGIinfo.FormVars.keys();
    String tmp_val = "";
    String tmp_key = "";

    for(;E.hasMoreElements ();){
        tmp_key = (String) E.nextElement();
        tmp_val = CGIinfo.FormVars.getProperty (tmp_key);
        order.AddProperty(tmp_key,tmp_val);
    }

    order.Save();
}
}
```

JDBC and IC Verify-Enabled CGI

Just as processing the credit-card transaction in real-time saves an extra processing step, so does storing the information directly into a database. Up until now, all the examples packed the entered order information into individual files on the disk. Nine times out of 10, eventually the information in those individual files will need to be extrapolated and stored in a database. The logical alternative is to store the information directly to the database, which is exactly what this example does. Using JDBC, this CGI inserts a record into a database for each order entered.

All entered item information is stored in a CGI-accessible configuration file. All source and referenced configuration files can be found on the accompanying CD. If you choose to use this example, the following is a list of things to modify:

- Load the configuration file with the items you wish to sell.

- Generate all referenced error HTML pages, or change the associated URL string.

- Change the path of the stored order files if needed.

- Change the header and the footer HTML for the generated receipt.

- Modify the IC Verify paths to match the IC Verify setup configurations.

- For production, change the debug flag of IC Verify to off.

- Modify the SQL "Insert" statement to correspond with your order database.

- Modify either the Feeder or the HTML form to suit your needs.

Caveats

This example is unable to handle the IC Verify-provided error codes properly. Accompanying each transaction response is an error string containing useful information that should be propagated to the user. The current implementation checks to see only if the sale was approved, and the error code field is ignored.

Last, the specific JDBC errors are not propagated; in fact, no error is trapped. In fixing this, you will need to consider the scenario of a credit-card transaction being authorized and the order not being saved. The solution to this is fairly complex, dealing with a commit and a rollback. If the database insert fails, you need to be able to "rollback" the sale transaction. This will entail issuing a void command to IC Verify, which the icverify tool does not support. In many cases, you may write a complicated recovery routine just to never have it be used. However, if you are feeling lucky, which isn't really like rolling the dice, you will opt to leave it be.

Code Listing

```
import CommerceUtils.*;
import CardShield.*;
import java.util.Date;
import java.util.Enumeration;
import java.util.StringTokenizer;
```

```java
import java.sql.*;
import weblogic.db.jdbc.*;
import java.util.Properties;


/**
 * CGIPRocessor is a generic handler for single page order forms.
 * It provides an a preliminary frame work for further develop. Some
 * potential weak spots is the lack of accurate field verification.
 *
 *
 * Usage: The object should be created by passing in the path of
 * where to store the order files, as well as the extension to be placed
 * on the newly created order files.
 *
 *
 * Note: Page redirection on errors is used in lue of generating error
 * pages. These provides more flexibility of appearance.
 *
 */

public class CGIProcessor{

    /**
     * ItemFile is the name of the configuration file containing the
     * stores items
     */
    public static String ItemFile          =   "items.ini";

    /**
     * BadInputURL points to the page which the user will be directed to
     * if a form input error occurs. This error will occur if any of the
     * input fields does not pass the verification function.
     */
    public static String BadInputURL       =   "/badinput.html";

    /**
     * BadItemURL points to the page which the user will be directed to
     * if a form item input error occurs. This error will occur if any of the
     * items are invalid or missing.
     */
    public static String BadItemURL        =   "/baditem.html";

    /**
     * BadTotalURL points to the page which the user will be directed to
     * if a form total error occurs. This error will occur if the user enters
```

```
 * a total that does not match the calculated total.
 */
public static String BadTotalURL        =    "/badtotal.html";


/**
 * BadExpirelURL points to the page which the user will be directed to
 * if credit card's expiration date is invalid. This error will occur if the user enters
 * a data fails verification.
 */
public static String BadExpirelURL      =    "/badexpire.html";


/**
 * BadCardURL points to the page which the user will be directed to
 * if credit card number is invalid. This error will occur if the user enters
 * a card number that fails verification.
 */
public static String BadCardURL         =    "/badcard.html";


/**
 * NotApprovedURL points to the page which the user will be directed to
 * if credit card fails to be approved for the sale. This error will occur
 * if the user enters either and invalid card number, invalid expiration date,
 * or the card was refused.
 */
public static String NotApprovedURL        =    "/notapproved.html";



/**
 * ReceiptHeader holds the top portion of the HTML page that is
 * generated if all is validated.
 */
public static String ReceiptHeader      =    "<html>\n<head>\n<title>"+
                                             "Thank You</title>\n</head>\n<body>\n"+
                                             "<H1>Your Order Has Been Processed</H1>";
/**
 * ReceiptFooter holds the bottom portion of the HTML page that is
 * generated if all is validated.
 */
public static String ReceiptFooter      =    "<br><br>Thank-You\n</body></html>";



//The calculated total of the entered items.
private float  Total              =    0.00f;

//Holds the HTML coded sale receipt.
private String GeneratedReceipt =    "";
```

```java
/**
 * CGIinfo is the cgilib containing all CGI information.
 */
public cgilib   CGIinfo    =   null;

/**
 * ItemInfo is the inifile holding all item information.
 */
public inifile  ItemInfo   =   null;

/**
 * OrderPath is the path to store the generated order in.
 */
public String   OrderPath  =   ".\\";

/**
 * OrderPath is the extension to be placed on the generated order.
 */
public String   OrderExt   =   ".ord";


/**
 * The constructor initializes the all needed objets and variables, including
 * the cgilib, the item inifile.
 *
 * @param orderpath         The path to store the generated orders in.
 * @param ordertext         The extension to be placed on the generated orders.
 *
 */
public CGIProcessor(String orderpath, String ordertext){

    CGIinfo     = new cgilib(); //create the cgi library
    ItemInfo    = new inifile(ItemFile); //create the ini holding the item info.
    OrderPath   = orderpath;
    OrderExt    = ordertext;
}


/**
 * ProcesForm is the entry point for the processing of the form. After construct
 * this member should be called.  The member : verifies the input, credit card, and items,
 * and generates all resulting HTML.
 *
 */
public void ProcesForm(){
```

```
//Verify that all customer input is ok.
if(!VerifyInput()){
    CGIinfo.Redirect(BadInputURL);
    return;
}

//Verify that all items are valid and generate the receipt
if(!VerifyItems()){
    CGIinfo.Redirect(BadItemURL);
    return;
}

//Verify that the total the user enter maches the calculated total.
if(!VerifyTotal()){
    CGIinfo.Redirect(BadTotalURL);
    return;
}

 //Verify Expiration Date
if(CGIinfo.FormVars.getProperty("CCEXP").length() != 4){
    CGIinfo.Redirect(BadExpirelURL);
    return;
}

//Verify credit card Number
if(FormatCCNum(CGIinfo.FormVars.getProperty("CCNUM")) == ""){
    CGIinfo.Redirect(BadCardURL);
    return;
}

//Try and process the sale. The call will return false
//if the card, expiration is not valid , or it is not
//Approved.
if(!ProcessSale()){
    CGIinfo.Redirect(NotApprovedURL);
    return;
}

//store the order to the order file.
StoreOrder();

//Print the standard CGI response
CGIinfo.PrintHeader();

System.out.println(ReceiptHeader); //top of HTML page
System.out.println(GeneratedReceipt); //the receipt
```

```
        System.out.println(ReceiptFooter); //the bottom
        return;
    }



    /*
        This function process the credit card sale using CardShield.
        The icverify util provides ErrorCode function for returning
        the appropriate error code, for more robust
        error handling this string should be propagated to the user.
        This function will fail if the card or expiration is invalid,
        or the card is not approved.
    */

    private boolean ProcessSale(){

       //Init the CardShield object. The first param is the CSMID
       //second is false reflecting the fact that this is not an Applet

        icverify IC     =    new icverify ("c:\\icverify\\","c:\\icverify\\demo19\\",true);

        //Add the order to the process request pool

        IC.AddRequest("MYCGI","TESTCGI",CGIinfo.FormVars.getProperty("CCNUM"),
                CGIinfo.FormVars.getProperty("CCEXP"),"" + Total,
                CGIinfo.FormVars.getProperty("Zip"),
                CGIinfo.FormVars.getProperty("Address1"));

        //Process the request
        IC.ProcessRequests();

        return IC.IsApproved(CGIinfo.FormVars.getProperty("CCNUM"));

    }


    /*Check each of the required fields return false if any fail.
      Only size is checked, to assure better response additional
      verification logic should be added.
     */
    private boolean VerifyInput(){

        //Verify Customer Name
        if((CGIinfo.FormVars.getProperty("FirstName") == null) ||
(CGIinfo.FormVars.getProperty("FirstName").length() < 2))
            return false;
```

```
        if((CGIinfo.FormVars.getProperty("LastName") == null) ||
(CGIinfo.FormVars.getProperty("LastName").length() < 2))
            return false;

        //Verify Address
        if((CGIinfo.FormVars.getProperty("Address1") == null) ||
(CGIinfo.FormVars.getProperty("Address1").length() < 5))
            return false;

        //Verify City
        if((CGIinfo.FormVars.getProperty("City") == null) ||
(CGIinfo.FormVars.getProperty("City").length() < 4))
            return false;

        //Verify State
        if((CGIinfo.FormVars.getProperty("State") == null) ||
(CGIinfo.FormVars.getProperty("State").length() < 1))
            return false;

        //Verify Zip
        if((CGIinfo.FormVars.getProperty("Zip") == null) ||
(CGIinfo.FormVars.getProperty("Zip").length() < 5))
            return false;

        //Verify Phone
        if((CGIinfo.FormVars.getProperty("PhoneNumber") == null) ||
(CGIinfo.FormVars.getProperty("PhoneNumber").length() < 10))
            return false;

        return true;
    }


    /* This function verifies the validity of the inputted item codes, as well
       as generating a sale receipt.  The item information comes out of the items.ini
       file.  If any item is entered incorrectly false will be returned.
    */
    private boolean VerifyItems(){

        GeneratedReceipt = "";
        float price = 0.00f;
        int qty   = 0;

        //Verifies if the item 1 exists. If it does, then the item is added to the receipt.
        if((CGIinfo.FormVars.getProperty("I1") != null) &&
(ItemInfo.SectionExits(CGIinfo.FormVars.getProperty("I1")))){
```

```
        GeneratedReceipt += CGIinfo.FormVars.getProperty("I1") + "------>";
        GeneratedReceipt += ItemInfo.GetProperty(CGIinfo.FormVars.getProperty("I1"),
                            "Description","Description Missing") + "------>";

        try{
            price = new Float(ItemInfo.GetProperty("Price","0.00")).floatValue();
            qty = new Integer(CGIinfo.FormVars.getProperty("Q1")).intValue();
        }
        catch(Exception e){
        }

        GeneratedReceipt += "$" + price + " x " + qty + " = $" + (qty * price) +
"<BR>\n";

        Total += (qty * price);
    }

    //Verifies if the item 2 exists. If it does, then the item is added to the receipt.
    if((CGIinfo.FormVars.getProperty("I2") != null) &&
(ItemInfo.SectionExits(CGIinfo.FormVars.getProperty("I2")))){
        GeneratedReceipt += CGIinfo.FormVars.getProperty("I2") + "------>";
        GeneratedReceipt += ItemInfo.GetProperty(CGIinfo.FormVars.getProperty("I2"),
                            "Description","Description Missing") + "------>";

        try{
            price = new Float(ItemInfo.GetProperty("Price","0.00")).floatValue();
            qty = new Integer(CGIinfo.FormVars.getProperty("Q2")).intValue();
        }
        catch(Exception e){
        }

        GeneratedReceipt += "$" + price + " x " + qty + " = $" + (qty * price) +
"<BR>\n";

        Total += (qty * price);
    }

    //Verifies if the item 3 exists. If it does, then the item is added to the receipt.
    if((CGIinfo.FormVars.getProperty("I3") != null) &&
(ItemInfo.SectionExits(CGIinfo.FormVars.getProperty("I3")))){
        GeneratedReceipt += CGIinfo.FormVars.getProperty("I3") + "------>";
        GeneratedReceipt += ItemInfo.GetProperty(CGIinfo.FormVars.getProperty("I3"),
                            "Description","Description Missing") + "------>";

        try{
            price = new Float(ItemInfo.GetProperty("Price","0.00")).floatValue();
```

```
                    qty = new Integer(CGIinfo.FormVars.getProperty("Q3")).intValue();
                }
                catch(Exception e){
                }

                GeneratedReceipt += "$" + price + " x " + qty + " = $" + (qty * price) +
"<BR>\n";

                Total += (qty * price);
        }

        //Verifies if the item 4 exists. If it does, then the item is added to the receipt.
        if((CGIinfo.FormVars.getProperty("I4") != null) &&
(ItemInfo.SectionExits(CGIinfo.FormVars.getProperty("I4")))){
                GeneratedReceipt += CGIinfo.FormVars.getProperty("I4") + "------>";
                GeneratedReceipt += ItemInfo.GetProperty(CGIinfo.FormVars.getProperty("I4"),
                            "Description","Description Missing") + "------>";

                try{
                    price = new Float(ItemInfo.GetProperty("Price","0.00")).floatValue();
                    qty = new Integer(CGIinfo.FormVars.getProperty("Q4")).intValue();
                }
                catch(Exception e){
                }

                GeneratedReceipt += "$" + price + " x " + qty + " = $" + (qty * price) +
"<BR>\n";

                Total += (qty * price);
        }


        if(GeneratedReceipt == "")
            return false;
        else
            return true;
    }


    /* Part of the verification of the items was to generate a sale receipt,
       to include the calculated total.  This function compares the calculated
       total with the user entered total.
    */
    private boolean VerifyTotal(){

        float Tmp_Total = 0.00f;
```

```
    try{
        Tmp_Total = new Float(CGIinfo.FormVars.getProperty("Total")).floatValue();
    }
    catch(Exception e){
        return false;
    }

    if(Tmp_Total != Total)
        return false;
    else
        return true;
}


/*
 Besides checking for Alpha characters in the credit card number,
 this function will take out spaces and '-' characters.
*/
private String FormatCCNum(String in){

    if(in == null)
        return "";

    String out  =    "";
    Character C  =    new Character('c');


    for(int i = 0 ; i < in.length();++i)
        if((in.charAt(i) != '-')&&(in.charAt(i) != ' ')){
            if(C.isDigit(in.charAt(i)))
                out += "" + in.charAt(i);
            else
                return "";
        }

    CGIinfo.FormVars.put("CCNUM",new String(out));
    return out;
}

/*
 Commits all of the form's information to a file using
 the orderfile utility.
*/
private void StoreOrder(){

    try{
```

```
            //Setup the database login properties
            Properties props = new java.util.Properties();
            props.put("user",      "JDBCAGENT");
            props.put("password",  "BLAHBLAH");
            props.put("server",    "DUALBEAST");

            //Get the JDBC class, and initialize the driver with the login properties.
            Class.forName("weblogic.jdbc.dblib.Driver");
            java.sql.Connection conn =
java.sql.DriverManager.getConnection("jdbc:weblogic:mssqlserver", props);

            //Create the SQL insert statement

            Enumeration E = CGIinfo.FormVars.keys();
            String tmp_val = "";
            String tmp_key = "";
            String Fields = "";
            String Values = "";

            for(;E.hasMoreElements ();){
                tmp_key = (String) E.nextElement();
                tmp_val = CGIinfo.FormVars.getProperty (tmp_key);
                Fields += tmp_key + ",";
                Values += "'" + tmp_val + "',";
            }

            //delete the trailing ','

            Fields = Fields.substring(0, Fields.length() - 1 );
            Values = Values.substring(0, Values.length() - 1 );

             String insert = "insert into NEWORDER(" + Fields + ")"+
             " values (" + Values + ")" ;

            //Open a  statement constext
            Statement stmt1 = conn.createStatement();
            //execute the insert
            stmt1.execute(insert);
            //Close the statement and the connection
            stmt1.close();
            conn.close();

        }catch(Exception e){//Generic handler
        }

    }
}
```

Summary

This chapter has been identified as the provider of ready-to-use solutions. In actuality, this chapter is a *single* solution with a number of variations, of which one might find a place in your new virtual storefront. For the client side, two CGI browser agents were discussed as well as HTML forms and Feeder applets. The next chapter will focus on multiple-page, shopping cart, CGI applications. It might appear as if single-page order forms would be less difficult than a shopping cart application, when in fact they are about equal. Single-page applications have far less ability to handle specific errors, and they have more to do at any one time. Shopping cart applications have to keep track of more, but the bulk of their user interface is expanded out for a number of pages, giving more freedom and more usability. Use this chapter as a possible tool in creating your Web storefront, but make sure to examine all the provided examples before making your selection.

13

Shopping Cart CGI

This chapter supplies a multipage CGI shopping cart style commerce application. Shopping cart applications give users the ability to select an item and place it in their own personal shopping cart, for later check out. Chapter 12 provided a solution that revolved around the user's completing a single HTML order form, in which the user was responsible for accurately filling in item information. Shopping cart applications provide a logical progression from such single-page applications.

The key focus of this chapter is to furnish a ready-to-use commerce solution, with four slight variations. The first is a shopping cart CGI that stores orders to an order file and does not process the credit-card sale. The second and third variations provide the same functionality as the first, plus they add CardShield and IC Verify, respectively, for credit-card sale processing. The last CGI utilizes JDBC to obtain order information and store entered orders; it also provides IC Verify sale processing. For the nonprogrammer, this chapter furnishes a legend for the provided CGI resources. Programmers will find this chapter to contain helpful examples of the tools introduced in Chapter 10. All code listings can be found on the accompanying CD-ROM.

Support Files

Making a CGI application as flexible as possible is crucial to its usefulness. If the CGI's code must be changed every time a slight modification is needed, it will not only cause extreme heartache but will limit the life span of the application considerably. The more flexible the CGI, the easier it can be changed and the more people are available to modify it. For this reason, all of the CGI applications in this chapter revolve around the use of a series of external support files. The following is a list of these files:

- Item configuration file, which contains all the items and information about those items that will be sold in the application

- items.html, which is the template file from which the main product listing is generated

- checkoutform.html, which is the template file of the final checkout form

- thankyou.html, which is the file that will thank the user upon the completion of the order

- Item template files, which provide individual control of what each item's description page looks like

Item Configuration

The CGI's item configuration file is specified on construction of the CGI object. This file has detailed information about each item in the store, including individual item template files. The following is a sample CGI object construction where the file name "items.ini" is specified as the configuration filename, a listing of the items.ini file. Use and knowledge of this file are crucial to the successful deployment of the CGIs in this chapter.

```
CGIProcessor CGI  = new CGIProcessor(".\\",".ord","items.ini",".\\",".usr");


[AB123]
#Comment 2
TemplatePage=123.html
ItemPictURL=/123.gif
Description=Log From BlamO
ShortDescription=Log From BlamO
Price=12.00
Shipping=0.00

[AB125]
#Comment 2
TemplatePage=123.html
```

```
ItemPictURL = /125.gif
Description = Round Ball
ShortDescription = Round Ball
Price=2.00
Shipping=0.00
```

items.html

The use of template files permeates the examples in this chapter. The basic premise behind them is to provide a means for HTML to be modified around the use of certain keywords. At the time the CGI is executed, these keywords will be replaced with CGI information. An example of the use of such a template file is items.html. items.html is the main entry screen to the storefront, and you are free to change it as long as you retain the appropriate use of keywords (words that begin with ##!!##). The following is an example usage of items.html.

```
<HTML>
<HEAD>
<TITLE>WELCOME</TITLE>
</HEAD>
<BODY BGCOLOR="FFFFFF">
<BLOCKQUOTE>
<H1>Please Make Your Selection</H1>
<HR>
##!!##ITEMS
<HR>
<A href="##!!##CheckOUT">Check Out</A>
</BODY>
</HTML>
```

checkoutform.html

Just as items.html provides a template file for the creation of the storefront catalog page, checkoutform.html gives a template for the store's checkout facility. The following is an example of its usage. You are free to add your own fields into this form; the CGI will handle them appropriately.

```
<HTML>
<HEAD>
<TITLE>Stuff For Sale</TITLE>
</HEAD>
<BODY BGCOLOR="FFFFFF">
<BLOCKQUOTE>
<H1>Your Name Here: My Shop</H1>
<HR>
<H2>Your Order:<BR>
```

Figure 13.1 Entry screen.

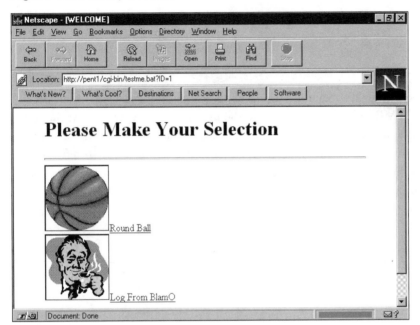

```
##!!##Receipt
<BR>
Total  = ##!!##Total
</H2>


<FORM Method="Get" Action="##!!##ACTION" >

<TABLE>
<tr><td>First Name</td><td><input name="FirstName" type="TEXT"  size="36"></td></tr>
<tr><td>Last Name</td><td><input name="LastName" type="TEXT"  size="36"></td></tr>
<tr><td>Address</td><td> <input name="Address1" type="TEXT"  size="53"></td></tr>
<tr><td></td><td> <input name="Address2" type="TEXT"  size="53"></td></tr>
<tr><td>City</td><td><input name="City" type="TEXT"  size="20">
        State <input name="State" type="TEXT"  size="2"></td></tr>
<tr><td>Zip Code</td><td><input name="Zip" type="TEXT"  size="20">
<tr><td>Phone Number</td><td><input name="PhoneNumber" type="TEXT" size="36"> </td></tr>
<tr><td>Fax Number</td><td><input name="FaxNumber" type="TEXT" size="36"></td></tr>
<tr><td>Email Address</td><td><input name="Email" type="TEXT" size="36"></td></tr>
</TABLE>
<HR>
```

```
<br>
<HR>
<TABLE>
<tr><td>Credit Card Number</td><td><input name="CCNUM" type="TEXT"  size="20">
        Expires in the format YYMM (Y = Year, M = Month)<input name="CCEXP" type="TEXT"
size="10"></td></tr>
</TABLE>
<br><br>
<P>
All orders are shipped UPS ground at no additional charge.
<br><br>
<input   type="SUBMIT" value="Order">
<input   type="RESET" value="Clear Form">
<input   type="HIDDEN" name="NEXTFORM" value="3">
<input   type="HIDDEN" name="USERID" value="##!!##USERID">
<input   type="HIDDEN" name="STATE" value="##!!##STATE">
<input   type="HIDDEN" name="TOTAL" value="##!!##TOTALFIELD">
</FORM>
</BODY>
</HTML>
```

Figure 13.2 Checkout screen.

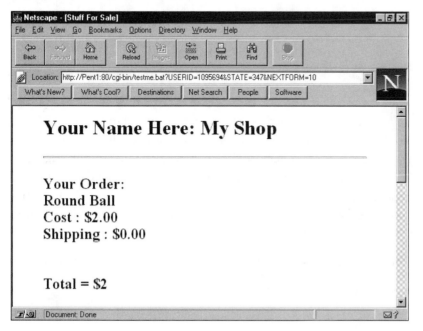

thankyou.html

Unlike a template file, thankyou.html is simply a page to which the user is directed when the checkout form has been completed. You have complete control over this file; it simply must reside in the location specified in the CGI's code. By default, this location is the server's Web root.

Item template files

If you take a look at the item configuration format, each item specifies its own template file. This allows for each file to have its own separate Web page describing itself. The CGI will utilize the information in the configuration file to obtain the name of the item's template file. When a user clicks on the item for the main catalog page, he or she will be directed to the completed item's template file. The following is a sample item configuration file.

```
<HTML>
<HEAD>
<TITLE>##!!##ShortDesc</TITLE>
</HEAD>
<BODY BGCOLOR="FFFFFF">
<BLOCKQUOTE>
<H1>Buy Me!</H1>
<HR>
##!!##ITEM
<HR>
<A href=##!!##ReturnReturn</A>
</BODY>
</HTML>
```

Base Model

Development always begins with a base set of functionality. In the case of a shopping cart CGI application, this is it. This application bestows the base-level functionality for the subsequent examples. The shopping cart CGI consists of an item catalog interface, item description pages, and a main checkout page. Once the order has been completed, the application will store the entire contents of the checkout form, including, the ordered items, to an order file. All source and referenced configuration files can be found on the accompanying CD-ROM. If you choose to use this example, the following is a list of things to modify:

- Load the configuration file with the items you wish to sell and all associated information.

- Generate all needed template files with the proper CGI tags.

Figure 13.3 Item description screen.

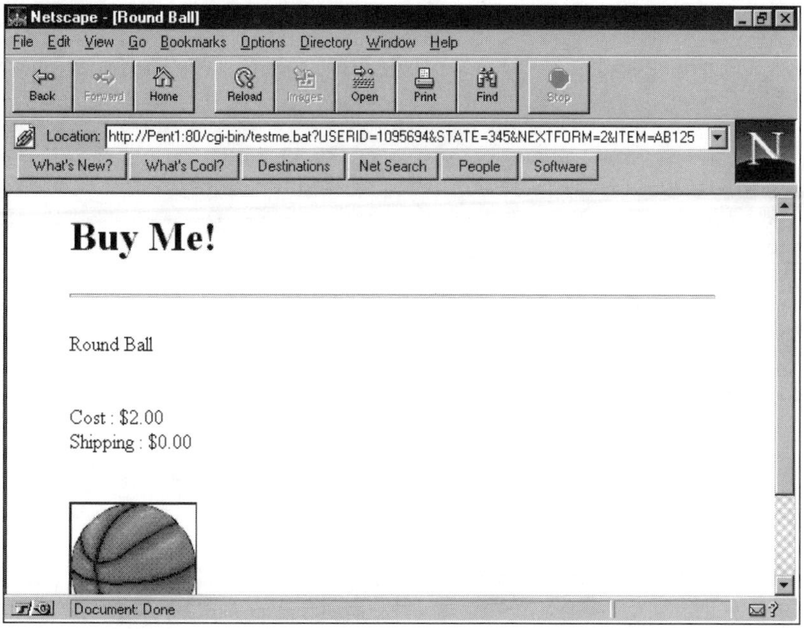

- Generate the thankyou.html file.

- Change the path of the stored order files if needed.

Caveats

Due to the limited user interaction of a shopping cart CGI, most of the points of failure associated with the single-page example are eliminated. However, this application still ails from detailed checkout form data validation. The application makes the assumption that all template files are in place and contain the proper keyword tags.

Code Listing

```
import CommerceUtils.*;
import java.util.Enumeration;
import java.util.Properties;

//CGIProcessor.java

/**
 * CGIPRocessor is a generic handler for a shopping cart style solutions
```

```
 * It provides a preliminary frame work for further develop. A
 * potential weak spot is the lack of accurate field verification.
 *
 * @version 2.0
 * @author Cary A. Jardin
 */

public class CGIProcessor{

        //The initial state on startup.
        private int     NextState    =   -1;
        //Global user ID
        private String UserID        =    "";
        //The path to store the orders into
        private String OrderPath     =    "";
        //The path to extension to be placed on the order files
        private String OrderExt      =    "";
        //The configuration file that holds the item information
        private String ItemFile      =    "";
        //The path to store the user files into
        private String UserPath      =    "";
        //The Extension to be place on the user files
        private String UserExt       =    "";
        //The main item catalog template HTML
        private String ItemTmpltFile=   "items.html";
        //The checkout form HTML template
        private String CheckOutForm =    "checkoutform.html";
        //Final screen URL
        private String ThankYou      =    "/thankyou.html";
        //The maximum items the sysytem can hold per user
        private int     MaxItems     =   300;

        //The CGI library
        private cgilib CGIinfo;

        //The ITEM configuration file
        private inifile ItemInfo;
        //The user manger, to store the CGI users.
        private usermanager UM;

        /**
         * The constructor initializes the all needed objets and variables, including
         * the cgilib, the item inifile.
         *
         * @param orderpath          The path to store the generated orders in.
         * @param ordertext          The extension to be placed on the generated orders.
```

```
    * @param itemfile          The configuration file holding the item information.
    * @param usrpath           The path to store the generated user files in.
    * @param usrtext           The extension to be placed on the user files.
    *
    */
   public CGIProcessor(String orderpath, String orderext,
                    String itemfile , String userpath,
                    String userext){

       CGIinfo         = new cgilib();
       ItemInfo        = new inifile(itemfile);
       OrderPath       = orderpath;
       OrderExt        = orderext;
       ItemFile        = itemfile;
       UserPath        = userpath;
       UserExt         = userext;
   }


   /**
    * ProcesForm is the entry point for the processing of the form. After construct
    * this member should be called.  The member : verifies the input, credit card, and
items,
    * and generates all resulting HTML.
    *
    */
   public void ProcesForm(){

       //NextForm is used to tell the CGI what page to go to.
       String Test =  CGIinfo.FormVars.getProperty("NEXTFORM");

       //Initial entry point.
       if(Test == null)
           init_new_state();
       else //At the catalog - goto the item page
       if(Test.compareTo("2") == 0)
           gen_item();
       else//At the item page going pack to the catalog page
       if(Test.compareTo("1") == 0){
           pre_item();
       }
       else//At the catalog page going to the checkout page
       if(Test.compareTo("10") == 0)
           gen_check_out();
       else//At the checkout page, verify input and end.
       if(Test.compareTo("3") == 0){
           if(!VerifyInput())
```

```
                return;
            //store the order to the order file.
            StoreOrder();
            //generate thank you.
            CGIinfo.Redirect(ThankYou);
        }

        return;

    }

    /*Check each of the required fields return false if any fail.
      Only size is checked, to assume better response additional
      verification logic should be added.
     */
    private boolean VerifyInput(){

        //Verify Customer Name
        if((CGIinfo.FormVars.getProperty("FirstName") == null) ||
(CGIinfo.FormVars.getProperty("FirstName").length() < 2)){
            CGIinfo.CgiError("Input Error","Please Enter Your First Name");
            return false;
        }
        if((CGIinfo.FormVars.getProperty("LastName") == null) ||
(CGIinfo.FormVars.getProperty("LastName").length() < 2)){
            CGIinfo.CgiError("Input Error","Please Enter Your Last Name");
            return false;
        }

        //Verify Address
        if((CGIinfo.FormVars.getProperty("Address1") == null) ||
(CGIinfo.FormVars.getProperty("Address1").length() < 5)){
            CGIinfo.CgiError("Input Error","Please Enter Correct Address");
            return false;
        }

        //Verify City
        if((CGIinfo.FormVars.getProperty("City") == null) ||
(CGIinfo.FormVars.getProperty("City").length() < 4)){
            CGIinfo.CgiError("Input Error","Please Enter Correct City");
            return false;
        }

        //Verify State
        if((CGIinfo.FormVars.getProperty("State") == null) ||
(CGIinfo.FormVars.getProperty("State").length() < 1)){
```

```
                CGIinfo.CgiError("Input Error","Please Enter Correct State");
                return false;
        }

        //Verify Zip
        if((CGIinfo.FormVars.getProperty("Zip") == null) ||
(CGIinfo.FormVars.getProperty("Zip").length() < 5)){
                CGIinfo.CgiError("Input Error","Please Enter Correct Zip");
                return false;
        }

        //Verify Phone
        if((CGIinfo.FormVars.getProperty("PhoneNumber") == null) ||
(CGIinfo.FormVars.getProperty("PhoneNumber").length() < 10)){
                CGIinfo.CgiError("Input Error","Please Enter Correct Phone Number");
                return false;
        }

        //Verify Expiration Date
        if(CGIinfo.FormVars.getProperty("CCEXP").length() != 4){
            CGIinfo.CgiError("Input Error","Please Enter Correct Credit Card Expiration Date
"+
                        "In the Form: <BR>" + "YYMM (Y = Year, M = Month)");
            return false;
        }

        //Verify credit card Number
        if(FormatCCNum(CGIinfo.FormVars.getProperty("CCNUM")) == ""){
            CGIinfo.CgiError("Input Error","Please Enter Correct Credit Card Number");
            return false;
        }

        return true;
    }

    /*
        Handle the state where the user is returning to the catalog from an item page.
        The basic order of events is, load the user manage, check for items to add,
        then generate the catalog page.
    */
    private void pre_item(){


        //begin of user manager init
        String NextItem = "";
            try{
```

```
                NextState   = new Integer(CGIinfo.FormVars.getProperty("STATE")).intValue();
            }
            catch(Exception e){
            }

            UserID      =  ToAllDigits(CGIinfo.FormVars.getProperty("USERID"));

            try{
                UM = new usermanager(UserID,"" + NextState,UserPath,UserExt,true);
            }
            catch(Exception e){
                CGIinfo.CgiError("ERROR",e.getMessage() + " - UserManager failed to init -
*"+UserID+"*");
                return;
            }

            NextState   =   UM.NextState;

        //end of user manager init

            //If User wants to ADD an Item
            if(CGIinfo.FormVars.getProperty("ADDITEM") != null){
                NextItem = "ITEM";
                for(int i = 0 ; i < MaxItems ; ++i)
                    if(!UM.StatePropertyExists(NextItem+i)){
                        NextItem += i;
                            break;
                    }
                UM.AddStateProperty(NextItem, CGIinfo.FormVars.getProperty("ADDITEM"));
            }
            if(!UM.SaveState()){
                CGIinfo.CgiError("ERROR : UserManager","Failed to Create New User");
                return;
            }

            //generate the catalog page
            gen_item_list();
    }

    /*
        This member is called to itialize a new user, then generate the catalog page.
    */
    private void init_new_state(){
        //begin of user manager init
        try{
            UM = new usermanager(null,null,UserPath,UserExt,true);
```

```
    }
    catch(Exception e){
        CGIinfo.CgiError("ERROR : UserManager","UserManager failed to init");
        return;
    }

    NextState   =   UM.NextState;
    UserID      =   UM.User;

    UM.AddStateProperty("PLACEHOLD", "NEWSTATE");

    if(!UM.SaveState()){
        CGIinfo.CgiError("ERROR : UserManager","Failed to Create New User");
        return;
    }
    //begin of user manager init

    gen_item_list();
}

//generate the catalog page.  It is assumed that the user manager is initialized.
private void gen_item_list(){
    String      ItemList =   "";
    String      Checkout  =   "";
    String      Item      =   "";
    Properties  P         =   new Properties();


    //Generate an HTML listing of all the items in the config ini.

    Enumeration E    =   ItemInfo.IniSections.keys();
    for(;E.hasMoreElements();){
        ItemList += "<a href=\"" + CGIinfo.MyBaseUrl() +"?USERID="+ UserID;
        ItemList += "&STATE=" + NextState + "&NEXTFORM=2&";
        Item = (String)E.nextElement();
        ItemList += "ITEM=" + Item + "\">";
        //Use the config file defined graphic file.
        ItemList += "<img src=\"" + ItemInfo.GetProperty(Item,"ItemPictURL","") + "\">";
        ItemList += ItemInfo.GetProperty(Item,"ShortDescription","")+"</a><BR>\n";
    }

    //generate the Checkout link
    Checkout += CGIinfo.MyBaseUrl() +"?USERID="+ UserID;
    Checkout += "&STATE=" + NextState + "&NEXTFORM=10";

    //do a search and replace on the catalog page template
```

```
        P.put("##!!##ITEMS",ItemList);
        P.put("##!!##CheckOUT",Checkout);
        filereplace tmplt = new filereplace(ItemTmpltFile, P);
        CGIinfo.PrintHeader();
        System.out.println(tmplt.GetOutputString());


        return;
    }


    //Generates the specific item, using the config file
    //defined HTML template.
    private void gen_item(){

        String Output              =   "";
        String NotBuying           =   "";
        String Item                =   CGIinfo.FormVars.getProperty("ITEM")   ;
        Properties  P              =   new Properties();

        //begin of user manager init
        try{
            NextState   = new Integer(CGIinfo.FormVars.getProperty("STATE")).intValue();
        }
        catch(Exception e){
            return;
        }

        UserID      =   ToAllDigits(CGIinfo.FormVars.getProperty("USERID"));


        try{
            UM = new usermanager(UserID,"" + NextState,UserPath,UserExt,true);
        }
        catch(Exception e){
            CGIinfo.CgiError("ERROR",e.getMessage() + " - UserManager failed to init -
*"+UserID+"*");
            return;
        }

        NextState   =   UM.NextState;
        //end of user manager init

        //Create a little HTML description of the item
        Output = "<P>" + ItemInfo.GetProperty(Item,"Description","") + "</P><BR>";
        Output += "Cost : $" + ItemInfo.GetProperty(Item,"Price","") + "<BR>";
        Output += "Shipping : $" + ItemInfo.GetProperty(Item,"Shipping","") + "<BR><BR><BR>";
        Output += "<A href=\"" + CGIinfo.MyBaseUrl() +"?USERID="+ UserID;
```

```
        Output += "&STATE=" + NextState + "&NEXTFORM=1&";
        Output += "ADDITEM=" + Item + "\">";
        Output += "<img src=\"" + ItemInfo.GetProperty(Item,"ItemPictURL","") + "\">";
        Output += "Add To Shopping Cart</A><BR>\n";

        //Create the link if the don't want to add the item
        NotBuying += "\"" + CGIinfo.MyBaseUrl() +"?USERID="+ UserID;
        NotBuying += "&STATE=" + NextState + "&NEXTFORM=1\">";

        //do a search and replace of the specified item template file
        P.put("##!!##ShortDesc",ItemInfo.GetProperty(Item,"ShortDescription",""));
        P.put("##!!##ITEM",Output);
        P.put("##!!##Return",NotBuying);
        filereplace tmplt = new filereplace(ItemInfo.GetProperty(Item,"TemplatePage",""), P);

        //make sure to save the state
        if(!UM.SaveState()){
            CGIinfo.CgiError("ERROR : UserManager","Failed to Create New User");
            return;
        }

        CGIinfo.PrintHeader();
        System.out.println(tmplt.GetOutputString());
        return;
    }

//Generate the checkout form from the HTML template
private void gen_check_out(){
    String Output          =    "";
    String Temp            =    "";
    String NextItem        =    "";
    String tmpitem         =    "";
    float   Total          =    0.00f;
    float   tmpval         =    0.00f;
    Properties  P          =    new Properties();


    //begin of user manager init
    try{
        NextState   = new Integer(CGIinfo.FormVars.getProperty("STATE")).intValue();
    }
    catch(Exception e){
        return;
    }

    UserID      = ToAllDigits(CGIinfo.FormVars.getProperty("USERID"));
```

```
        try{
             UM = new usermanager(UserID,"" + NextState,UserPath,UserExt,true);
        }
        catch(Exception e){
             CGIinfo.CgiError("ERROR",e.getMessage() + " - UserManager failed to init -
*"+UserID+"*");
             return;
        }

        NextState    =    UM.NextState;

        //end of user manager init

        //generate the Receipt from the user manager info
          NextItem = "ITEM";
          for(int i = 0 ; i < MaxItems ; ++i){
            if(!UM.StatePropertyExists(NextItem+i))
               break;

            tmpitem = UM.GetStateProperty(NextItem+i,"");

            Output   += ItemInfo.GetProperty(tmpitem,"ShortDescription","") + "<BR>";
            Output   += "Cost : $" + ItemInfo.GetProperty(tmpitem,"Price","") + "<BR>";
            Output   += "Shipping : $" + ItemInfo.GetProperty(tmpitem,"Shipping","") +
"<BR>";
            Output   += "<BR>\n";
            //upadte the total
            try{
                 tmpval = new Float(ItemInfo.GetProperty(tmpitem,"Price","")).floatValue();
                 Total += tmpval;

                 tmpval = new
Float(ItemInfo.GetProperty(tmpitem,"Shipping","")).floatValue();
            }
            catch(Exception e){
            }
          }
        //do a search and replace of the specified check out template file
        P.put("##!!##Receipt",Output);
        P.put("##!!##Total","$" + Total);
        P.put("##!!##ACTION",CGIinfo.MyBaseUrl());
        P.put("##!!##USERID",UserID);
        P.put("##!!##STATE","" +  NextState);
        P.put("##!!##TOTALFIELD","" +  Total);
        filereplace tmplt = new filereplace(CheckOutForm, P);
```

```java
    //save the sate
    if(!UM.SaveState()){
        CGIinfo.CgiError("ERROR : UserManager","Failed to Create New User");
        return;
    }

    CGIinfo.PrintHeader();
    System.out.println(tmplt.GetOutputString());

    return;
}

/*
 Besides checking for Alpha characters in the credit card number,
 this function will take out spaces and '-' charcters.
*/
private String FormatCCNum(String in){

    if(in == null)
        return "";

    String out   =    "";
    Character C   =    new Character('c');


    for(int i = 0 ; i < in.length();++i)
        if((in.charAt(i) != '-')&&(in.charAt(i) != ' ')){
            if(C.isDigit(in.charAt(i)))
                out += "" + in.charAt(i);
            else
                return "";
        }

    CGIinfo.FormVars.put("CCNUM",new String(out));
    return out;
}

//Removes any non-numeric values
private String ToAllDigits(String in){
    String out    =        "";
    Character C   =        new Character('C');

    for(int i = 0 ; i < in.length() ; ++i)
        if(C.isDigit(in.charAt(i)))
            out += in.charAt(i);
```

```
        return out;
    }

    /*
     Commits all of the form's information to a file using
     the orderfile utility.
    */
    private void StoreOrder(){

        if(UM == null){
            try{
                NextState    = new Integer(CGIinfo.FormVars.getProperty("STATE")).intValue();
            }
            catch(Exception e){
                return;
            }

            UserID       =  ToAllDigits(CGIinfo.FormVars.getProperty("USERID"));

            try{
                UM = new usermanager(UserID,"" + NextState,UserPath,UserExt,true);
            }
            catch(Exception e){
                CGIinfo.CgiError("ERROR",e.getMessage() + " - UserManager failed to init -
*"+UserID+"*");
                return;
            }

            NextState    =   UM.NextState;
        }


        orderfile order = new orderfile(OrderPath,OrderExt);
        Enumeration E = CGIinfo.FormVars.keys();
        String tmp_val = "";
        String tmp_key = "";

        String NextItem = "ITEM";
        for(int i = 0 ; i < MaxItems ; ++i){
            if(!UM.StatePropertyExists(NextItem+i))
                break;
            order.AddProperty(NextItem + i,UM.GetStateProperty(NextItem+i,""));
        }

        for(;E.hasMoreElements ();){
```

```
            tmp_key = (String) E.nextElement();
            tmp_val = CGIinfo.FormVars.getProperty (tmp_key);
            order.AddProperty(tmp_key,tmp_val);
        }

        order.Save();
    }

}
```

Usage

The main body of the CGI application will contain only the construction of the CGIProcessor, and a call to ProcesForm(). The following is an example CGI execution.

```
import CommerceUtils.*;

public class cgi {


    public static void main(String args[]) {
        CGIProcessor CGI  = new CGIProcessor(".\\",".ord","items.ini",".\\",".usr");
        CGI.ProcesForm();
    }

}
```

To launch the CGI from an existing HTML page you would add a URL to the CGI specifying only a single parameter. The following is an example HTML link.

```
<A href="/cgi-bin/shoppingcart.bat?ID=1">Go Shopping</A>
```

CardShield-Enabled Shopping Cart

As an added feature of the prior example, this example provides credit-card processing through the use of the CardShield API. The prior example would simply store the orders to disk, without processing the credit-card sale. Processing the credit-card transaction has its advantages; however, having a dedicated Internet connection has its disadvantages. To gain the best of both worlds, this example fits the prior "plain vanilla" example with CardShield sale processing functionality.

Because a Java-based CGI does not have the same security restrictions as an applet, a CGI can communicate freely with CardShield. In many instances, ISPs provide users with access to their own Java-enabled cgi-bin. In such a setup, the CGI that follows is ready and willing for deployment.

All entered item information is stored in a CGI-accessible configuration file. All source and referenced configuration files can be found on the accompanying CD-ROM. If you choose to use this example, the following is a list of things to modify:

- Load the configuration file with the items you wish to sell and all associated information.

- Generate all needed template files with the proper CGI tags.

- Generate the thankyou.html file.

- Change the path of the stored order files if needed.

- Modify the entered CSMID to match your CardShield account.

Caveats

An important shortcoming of this example is its inability to handle CardShield-provided error codes. Embedded in the string that is returned by CardShield's SecureSale function is some useful information that should be propagated to the user. The current implementation checks to see only if it was approved, and all error codes are ignored.

Code Listing

```java
import CommerceUtils.*;
import CardShield.*;
import java.util.Enumeration;
import java.util.Properties;

//CGIProcessor.java

/**
 * CGIPRocessor is a generic handler for a shopping cart style solutions
 * It provides a preliminary frame work for further develop. A
 * potential weak spot is the lack of accurate field verification.
 *
 * @version 2.0
 * @author Cary A. Jardin
 */

public class CGIProcessor{

    //The initial state on startup.
```

```
private int     NextState    =    -1;
//Global user ID
private String UserID        =     "";
//The path to store the orders into
private String OrderPath     =     "";
//The path to extension to be placed on the order files
private String OrderExt      =     "";
//The configuration file that holds the item information
private String ItemFile      =     "";
//The path to store the user files into
private String UserPath      =     "";
//The Extension to be place on the user files
private String UserExt       =     "";
//The main item catalog template HTML
private String ItemTmpltFile=    "items.html";
//The checkout form HTML template
private String CheckOutForm =    "checkoutform.html";
//Final screen URL
private String ThankYou      =     "/thankyou.html";
//The maximum items the sysytem can hold per user
private int     MaxItems     =    300;


//The CGI library
private cgilib CGIinfo;


//The ITEM configuration file
private inifile ItemInfo;
//The user manger, to store the CGI users.
private usermanager UM;

/**
 * The constructor initializes the all needed objets and variables, including
 * the cgilib, the item inifile.
 *
 * @param orderpath         The path to store the generated orders in.
 * @param ordertext         The extension to be placed on the generated orders.
 * @param itemfile          The configuration file holding the item information.
 * @param usrpath           The path to store the generated user files in.
 * @param usrtext           The extension to be placed on the user files.
 *
 */
public CGIProcessor(String orderpath, String orderext,
                    String itemfile , String userpath,
                    String userext){

    CGIinfo         = new cgilib();
```

```
        ItemInfo        = new inifile(itemfile);
        OrderPath       = orderpath;
        OrderExt        = orderext;
        ItemFile        = itemfile;
        UserPath        = userpath;
        UserExt         = userext;
    }


    /**
     * ProcesForm is the entry point for the processing of the form. After construct
     * this member should be called.  The member : verifies the input, credit card, and
items,
     * and generates all resulting HTML.
     *
     */
    public void ProcesForm(){

        //NextForm is used to tell the CGI what page to go to.
        String Test =  CGIinfo.FormVars.getProperty("NEXTFORM");

        //Initial entry point.
        if(Test == null)
            init_new_state();
        else //At the catalog - goto the item page
        if(Test.compareTo("2") == 0)
            gen_item();
        else//At the item page going pack to the catalog page
        if(Test.compareTo("1") == 0){
            pre_item();
        }
        else//At the catalog page going to the checkout page
        if(Test.compareTo("10") == 0)
            gen_check_out();
        else//At the checkout page, verify input and end.
        if(Test.compareTo("3") == 0){
            if(!VerifyInput())
                return;
            //store the order to the order file.
            StoreOrder();
            //verify the credit card
            if(!ProcessSale()){
                CGIinfo.CgiError("Credit Card Error","Please verify your credit card
information,"+
                        "or try another card");
                return;
            }
```

```
                        //generate thank you.
                        CGIinfo.Redirect(ThankYou);
                    }

                return;

            }

        /*Check each of the required fields return false if any fail.
          Only size is checked, to assume better response additional
          verification logic should be added.
         */
        private boolean VerifyInput(){

                //Verify Customer Name
                if((CGIinfo.FormVars.getProperty("FirstName") == null) ||
(CGIinfo.FormVars.getProperty("FirstName").length() < 2)){
                        CGIinfo.CgiError("Input Error","Please Enter Your First Name");
                        return false;
                }
                if((CGIinfo.FormVars.getProperty("LastName") == null) ||
(CGIinfo.FormVars.getProperty("LastName").length() < 2)){
                        CGIinfo.CgiError("Input Error","Please Enter Your Last Name");
                        return false;
                }

                //Verify Address
                if((CGIinfo.FormVars.getProperty("Address1") == null) ||
(CGIinfo.FormVars.getProperty("Address1").length() < 5)){
                        CGIinfo.CgiError("Input Error","Please a Correct Address");
                        return false;
                }

                //Verify City
                if((CGIinfo.FormVars.getProperty("City") == null) ||
(CGIinfo.FormVars.getProperty("City").length() < 4)){
                        CGIinfo.CgiError("Input Error","Please Enter Correct City");
                        return false;
                }

                //Verify State
                if((CGIinfo.FormVars.getProperty("State") == null) ||
(CGIinfo.FormVars.getProperty("State").length() < 1)){
                        CGIinfo.CgiError("Input Error","Please Enter Correct State");
                        return false;
                }
```

```
        //Verify Zip
        if((CGIinfo.FormVars.getProperty("Zip") == null) ||
(CGIinfo.FormVars.getProperty("Zip").length() < 5)){
            CGIinfo.CgiError("Input Error","Please Enter Correct Zip");
            return false;
        }

        //Verify Phone
        if((CGIinfo.FormVars.getProperty("PhoneNumber") == null) ||
(CGIinfo.FormVars.getProperty("PhoneNumber").length() < 10)){
            CGIinfo.CgiError("Input Error","Please Enter Correct Phone Number");
            return false;
        }

        //Verify Expiration Date
        if(CGIinfo.FormVars.getProperty("CCEXP").length() != 4){
            CGIinfo.CgiError("Input Error","Please Enter Correct Credit Card Expiration Date
"+
                        "In the Form: <BR>" + "YYMM (Y = Year, M = Month)");
            return false;
        }

        //Verify credit card Number
        if(FormatCCNum(CGIinfo.FormVars.getProperty("CCNUM")) == ""){
            CGIinfo.CgiError("Input Error","Please Enter Correct Credit Card Number");
            return false;
        }

        return true;
    }

    /*
        Handle the state where the user is returning to the catalog from an item page.
        The basic order of events is, load the user manage, check for items to add,
        then generate the catalog page.
    */
    private void pre_item(){


        //begin of user manager init
        String NextItem = "";
            try{
                NextState    = new Integer(CGIinfo.FormVars.getProperty("STATE")).intValue();
            }
            catch(Exception e){
            }
```

```
            UserID      =  ToAllDigits(CGIinfo.FormVars.getProperty("USERID"));

            try{
                UM = new usermanager(UserID,"" + NextState,UserPath,UserExt,true);
            }
            catch(Exception e){
                CGIinfo.CgiError("ERROR",e.getMessage() + " - UserManager failed to init -
*"+UserID+"*");
                return;
            }

            NextState   =  UM.NextState;

        //end of user manager init

            //If User wants to ADD an Item
            if(CGIinfo.FormVars.getProperty("ADDITEM") != null){
                NextItem = "ITEM";
                for(int i = 0 ; i < MaxItems ; ++i)
                    if(!UM.StatePropertyExists(NextItem+i)){
                        NextItem += i;
                            break;
                    }
                UM.AddStateProperty(NextItem, CGIinfo.FormVars.getProperty("ADDITEM"));
            }
            if(!UM.SaveState()){
                CGIinfo.CgiError("ERROR : UserManager","Failed to Create New User");
                return;
            }

            //generate the catalog page
            gen_item_list();
    }


    /*
        This member is called to itialize a new user, then generate the catalog page.
    */
    private void init_new_state(){
        //begin of user manager init
        try{
            UM = new usermanager(null,null,UserPath,UserExt,true);
        }
        catch(Exception e){
            CGIinfo.CgiError("ERROR : UserManager","UserManager failed to init");
            return;
        }
```

```
        NextState    =    UM.NextState;
        UserID       =    UM.User;

        UM.AddStateProperty("PLACEHOLD", "NEWSTATE");

        if(!UM.SaveState()){
            CGIinfo.CgiError("ERROR : UserManager","Failed to Create New User");
            return;
        }
        //begin of user manager init

        gen_item_list();
    }


    //generate the catalog page.  It is assumed that the user manager is initialized.
    private void gen_item_list(){
        String       ItemList =    "";
        String       Checkout =    "";
        String       Item     =    "";
        Properties   P        =    new Properties();


        //Generate an HTML listing of all the items in the config ini.

        Enumeration E    =    ItemInfo.IniSections.keys();
        for(;E.hasMoreElements();){
            ItemList += "<a href=\"" + CGIinfo.MyBaseUrl() +"?USERID="+ UserID;
            ItemList += "&STATE=" + NextState + "&NEXTFORM=2&";
            Item = (String)E.nextElement();
            ItemList += "ITEM=" + Item + "\">";
            //Use the config file defined graphic file.
            ItemList += "<img src=\"" + ItemInfo.GetProperty(Item,"ItemPictURL","") + "\">";
            ItemList += ItemInfo.GetProperty(Item,"ShortDescription","")+"</a><BR>\n";
        }

        //generate the Checkout link
        Checkout += CGIinfo.MyBaseUrl() +"?USERID="+ UserID;
        Checkout += "&STATE=" + NextState + "&NEXTFORM=10";

        //do a search and replace on the catalog page template
        P.put("##!!##ITEMS",ItemList);
        P.put("##!!##CheckOUT",Checkout);
        filereplace tmplt = new filereplace(ItemTmpltFile, P);
        CGIinfo.PrintHeader();
        System.out.println(tmplt.GetOutputString());
```

```
            return;
      }

      //Generates the specific item, using the config file
      //defined HTML template.
      private void gen_item(){

            String Output           =     "";
            String NotBuying        =     "";
            String Item             =     CGIinfo.FormVars.getProperty("ITEM")    ;
            Properties  P           =    new Properties();

            //begin of user manager init
            try{
                NextState   = new Integer(CGIinfo.FormVars.getProperty("STATE")).intValue();
            }
            catch(Exception e){
                return;
            }

            UserID       =  ToAllDigits(CGIinfo.FormVars.getProperty("USERID"));


            try{
                UM = new usermanager(UserID,"" + NextState,UserPath,UserExt,true);
            }
            catch(Exception e){
                CGIinfo.CgiError("ERROR",e.getMessage() + " - UserManager failed to init -
*"+UserID+"*");
                return;
            }

            NextState   =   UM.NextState;
            //end of user manager init

            //Create a little HTML description of the item
            Output = "<P>" + ItemInfo.GetProperty(Item,"Description","") + "</P><BR>";
            Output += "Cost : $" + ItemInfo.GetProperty(Item,"Price","") + "<BR>";
            Output += "Shipping : $" + ItemInfo.GetProperty(Item,"Shipping","") + "<BR><BR><BR>";
            Output += "<A href=\"" + CGIinfo.MyBaseUrl() +"?USERID="+ UserID;
            Output += "&STATE=" + NextState + "&NEXTFORM=1&";
            Output += "ADDITEM=" + Item + "\">";
            Output += "<img src=\"" + ItemInfo.GetProperty(Item,"ItemPictURL","") + "\">";
            Output += "Add To Shopping Cart</A><BR>\n";

            //Create the link if the don't want to add the item
```

```
        NotBuying += "\"" + CGIinfo.MyBaseUrl() +"?USERID="+ UserID;
        NotBuying += "&STATE=" + NextState + "&NEXTFORM=1\">";

        //do a search and replace of the specified item template file
        P.put("##!!##ShortDesc",ItemInfo.GetProperty(Item,"ShortDescription",""));
        P.put("##!!##ITEM",Output);
        P.put("##!!##Return",NotBuying);
        filereplace tmplt = new filereplace(ItemInfo.GetProperty(Item,"TemplatePage",""), P);

        //make sure to save the state
        if(!UM.SaveState()){
            CGIinfo.CgiError("ERROR : UserManager","Failed to Create New User");
            return;
        }

        CGIinfo.PrintHeader();
        System.out.println(tmplt.GetOutputString());
        return;
    }

//Generate the checkout form from the HTML template
private void gen_check_out(){
    String Output       =   "";
    String Temp         =   "";
    String NextItem     =   "";
    String tmpitem      =   "";
    float  Total        =   0.00f;
    float  tmpval       =   0.00f;
    Properties  P       =   new Properties();


    //begin of user manager init
    try{
        NextState   = new Integer(CGIinfo.FormVars.getProperty("STATE")).intValue();
    }
    catch(Exception e){
        return;
    }

    UserID      = ToAllDigits(CGIinfo.FormVars.getProperty("USERID"));


    try{
        UM = new usermanager(UserID,"" + NextState,UserPath,UserExt,true);
    }
    catch(Exception e){
```

```
            CGIinfo.CgiError("ERROR",e.getMessage() + " - UserManager failed to init -
*"+UserID+"*");
            return;
        }

        NextState    =    UM.NextState;

        //end of user manager init

        //generate the Receipt from the user manager info
          NextItem = "ITEM";
          for(int i = 0 ; i < MaxItems ; ++i){
            if(!UM.StatePropertyExists(NextItem+i))
              break;

            tmpitem = UM.GetStateProperty(NextItem+i,"");

            Output   += ItemInfo.GetProperty(tmpitem,"ShortDescription","") + "<BR>";
            Output   += "Cost : $" + ItemInfo.GetProperty(tmpitem,"Price","") + "<BR>";
            Output   += "Shipping : $" + ItemInfo.GetProperty(tmpitem,"Shipping","") +
"<BR>";
            Output   += "<BR>\n";
            //upadte the total
            try{
                tmpval = new Float(ItemInfo.GetProperty(tmpitem,"Price","")).floatValue();
                Total += tmpval;

                tmpval = new
Float(ItemInfo.GetProperty(tmpitem,"Shipping","")).floatValue();
            }
            catch(Exception e){
            }
          }
        //do a search and replace of the specified check out template file
        P.put("##!!##Receipt",Output);
        P.put("##!!##Total","$" + Total);
        P.put("##!!##ACTION",CGIinfo.MyBaseUrl());
        P.put("##!!##USERID",UserID);
        P.put("##!!##STATE","" + NextState);
        P.put("##!!##TOTALFIELD","" + Total);
        filereplace tmplt = new filereplace(CheckOutForm, P);


        //save the sate
        if(!UM.SaveState()){
            CGIinfo.CgiError("ERROR : UserManager","Failed to Create New User");
```

```
            return;
    }

    CGIinfo.PrintHeader();
    System.out.println(tmplt.GetOutputString());

    return;
}

/*
 Besides checking for Alpha characters in the credit card number,
 this function will take out spaces and '-' charcters.
*/
private String FormatCCNum(String in){

    if(in == null)
        return "";

    String out  =    "";
    Character C  =    new Character('c');


    for(int i = 0 ; i < in.length();++i)
        if((in.charAt(i) != '-')&&(in.charAt(i) != ' ')){
            if(C.isDigit(in.charAt(i)))
                out += "" + in.charAt(i);
            else
                return "";
        }

    CGIinfo.FormVars.put("CCNUM",new String(out));
    return out;
}


    /*
    This function process the credit card sale using CardShield.
    SecureSale produces a string error code, for more robust
    error handling this string should be propagated to the user.
    This function will fail if the card or expiration is invalid,
    or the card is not approved.
    */

private boolean ProcessSale(){

    //Init the CardShield object. The first param is the CSMID
    //second is false reflecting the fact that this is not an Applet
```

```
        CardShieldAPI CS = new CardShieldAPI("123456A",false);


        return (CS.SecureSale("MYCGI","TESTCGI",CGIinfo.FormVars.getProperty("CCNUM"),
                CGIinfo.FormVars.getProperty("CCEXP"),"" +
CGIinfo.FormVars.getProperty("TOTAL"),
                CGIinfo.FormVars.getProperty("Zip"),
                CGIinfo.FormVars.getProperty("Address1")) == CS.Approved);

    }


    //Removes any non-numeric values
    private String ToAllDigits(String in){
        String out  =       "";
        Character C =       new Character('C');

        for(int i = 0 ; i < in.length() ; ++i)
            if(C.isDigit(in.charAt(i)))
                out += in.charAt(i);

        return out;
    }

    /*
     Commits all of the form's information to a file using
     the orderfile utility.
    */
    private void StoreOrder(){

        if(UM == null){
            try{
                NextState   = new Integer(CGIinfo.FormVars.getProperty("STATE")).intValue();
            }
            catch(Exception e){
                return;
            }

            UserID      = ToAllDigits(CGIinfo.FormVars.getProperty("USERID"));

            try{
                UM = new usermanager(UserID,"" + NextState,UserPath,UserExt,true);
            }
            catch(Exception e){
                CGIinfo.CgiError("ERROR",e.getMessage() + " - UserManager failed to init -
*"+UserID+"*");
```

```
            return;
        }

        NextState    =    UM.NextState;
    }


    orderfile order = new orderfile(OrderPath,OrderExt);
    Enumeration E = CGIinfo.FormVars.keys();
    String tmp_val = "";
    String tmp_key = "";

    String NextItem = "ITEM";
    for(int i = 0 ; i < MaxItems ; ++i){
        if(!UM.StatePropertyExists(NextItem+i))
            break;
        order.AddProperty(NextItem + i,UM.GetStateProperty(NextItem+i,""));
    }

    for(;E.hasMoreElements ();){
        tmp_key = (String) E.nextElement();
        tmp_val = CGIinfo.FormVars.getProperty (tmp_key);
        order.AddProperty(tmp_key,tmp_val);
    }

    order.Save();
    }

}
```

Usage

The main body of the CGI application has only the construction of the CGIProcessor and a call to ProcesForm(). An example CGI execution follows.

```
import CommerceUtils.*;

public class cgi {


    public static void main(String args[]) {
        CGIProcessor CGI  = new CGIProcessor(".\\",".ord","items.ini",".\\",".usr");
        CGI.ProcesForm();
    }


}
```

To launch the CGI from an existing HTML page you would add a URL to the CGI specifying only a single parameter. The following is an example HTML link.

```
<A href="/cgi-bin/shoppingcart.bat?ID=1">Go Shopping</A>
```

IC Verify Enabled Shopping Cart

If you already have a dedicated connection at your disposal, you might opt to use IC Verify instead of CardShield. This example provides the identical functionality as the "CardShield flavored vanilla" example.

All entered item information is stored in a CGI-accessible configuration file. All source and referenced configuration files can be found on the accompanying CD-ROM. If you choose to use this example, the following is a list of things to modify:

- Load the configuration file with the items you wish to sell and all associated information.

- Generate all needed template files with the proper CGI tags.

- Generate the thankyou.html file.

- Change the path of the stored order files if needed.

- Modify the IC Verify paths to match the IC Verify setup configurations.

- For production, change the debug flag of IC Verify to off.

Caveats

This example is unable to handle the IC Verify-provided error codes. Accompanying each transaction response is an error string containing useful information that should be generated to the user. The current implementation checks to see only if the sale was approved, and the error code field is ignored.

Code Listing

```
import CommerceUtils.*;
import java.util.Enumeration;
import java.util.Properties;

//CGIProcessor.java

/**
```

```
* CGIPRocessor is a generic handler for a shopping cart style solutions
* It provides a preliminary frame work for further develop. A
* potential weak spot is the lack of accurate field verification.
*
* @version 2.0
* @author Cary A. Jardin
*/

public class CGIProcessor{

    //The initial state on startup.
    private int     NextState    =    -1;
    //Global user ID
    private String UserID        =    "";
    //The path to store the orders into
    private String OrderPath      =    "";
    //The path to extension to be placed on the order files
    private String OrderExt       =    "";
    //The configuration file that holds the item information
    private String ItemFile       =    "";
    //The path to store the user files into
    private String UserPath       =    "";
    //The Extension to be place on the user files
    private String UserExt        =    "";
    //The main item catalog template HTML
    private String ItemTmpltFile=    "items.html";
    //The checkout form HTML template
    private String CheckOutForm =    "checkoutform.html";
    //Final screen URL
    private String ThankYou       =    "/thankyou.html";
    //The maximum items the sysytem can hold per user
    private int     MaxItems     =    300;

    //The CGI library
    private cgilib CGIinfo;

    //The ITEM configuration file
    private inifile ItemInfo;
    //The user manger, to store the CGI users.
    private usermanager UM;

    /**
     * The constructor initializes the all needed objets and variables, including
     * the cgilib, the item inifile.
     *
     * @param orderpath          The path to store the generated orders in.
```

```
     * @param ordertext        The extension to be placed on the generated orders.
     * @param itemfile         The configuration file holding the item information.
     * @param usrpath          The path to store the generated user files in.
     * @param usrtext          The extension to be placed on the user files.
     *
     */
    public CGIProcessor(String orderpath, String orderext,
                        String itemfile , String userpath,
                        String userext){

        CGIinfo         = new cgilib();
        ItemInfo        = new inifile(itemfile);
        OrderPath       = orderpath;
        OrderExt        = orderext;
        ItemFile        = itemfile;
        UserPath        = userpath;
        UserExt         = userext;
    }


    /**
     * ProcesForm is the entry point for the processing of the form. After construct
     * this member should be called.  The member : verifies the input, credit card, and
items,
     * and generates all resulting HTML.
     *
     */
    public void ProcesForm(){

        //NextForm is used to tell the CGI what page to go to.
        String Test =  CGIinfo.FormVars.getProperty("NEXTFORM");

        //Initial entry point.
        if(Test == null)
            init_new_state();
        else //At the catalog - goto the item page
        if(Test.compareTo("2") == 0)
            gen_item();
        else//At the item page going pack to the catalog page
        if(Test.compareTo("1") == 0){
            pre_item();
        }
        else//At the catalog page going to the checkout page
        if(Test.compareTo("10") == 0)
            gen_check_out();
        else//At the checkout page, verify input and end.
        if(Test.compareTo("3") == 0){
```

```
            if(!VerifyInput())
                 return;
            //store the order to the order file.
            StoreOrder();
            //generate thank you.
            CGIinfo.Redirect(ThankYou);
        }

    return;

    }

    /*Check each of the required fields return false if any fail.
      Only size is checked, to assume better response additional
      verification logic should be added.
     */
    private boolean VerifyInput(){

        //Verify Customer Name
        if((CGIinfo.FormVars.getProperty("FirstName") == null) ||
(CGIinfo.FormVars.getProperty("FirstName").length() < 2)){
             CGIinfo.CgiError("Input Error","Please Enter Your First Name");
             return false;
        }
        if((CGIinfo.FormVars.getProperty("LastName") == null) ||
(CGIinfo.FormVars.getProperty("LastName").length() < 2)){
             CGIinfo.CgiError("Input Error","Please Enter Your Last Name");
             return false;
        }

        //Verify Address
        if((CGIinfo.FormVars.getProperty("Address1") == null) ||
(CGIinfo.FormVars.getProperty("Address1").length() < 5)){
             CGIinfo.CgiError("Input Error","Please a Correct Address");
             return false;
        }

        //Verify City
        if((CGIinfo.FormVars.getProperty("City") == null) ||
(CGIinfo.FormVars.getProperty("City").length() < 4)){
             CGIinfo.CgiError("Input Error","Please Enter Correct City");
             return false;
        }

        //Verify State
        if((CGIinfo.FormVars.getProperty("State") == null) ||
```

```
(CGIinfo.FormVars.getProperty("State").length() < 1)){
        CGIinfo.CgiError("Input Error","Please Enter Correct State");
        return false;
    }

    //Verify Zip
    if((CGIinfo.FormVars.getProperty("Zip") == null) ||
(CGIinfo.FormVars.getProperty("Zip").length() < 5)){
        CGIinfo.CgiError("Input Error","Please Enter Correct Zip");
        return false;
    }

    //Verify Phone
    if((CGIinfo.FormVars.getProperty("PhoneNumber") == null) ||
(CGIinfo.FormVars.getProperty("PhoneNumber").length() < 10)){
        CGIinfo.CgiError("Input Error","Please Enter Correct Phone Number");
        return false;
    }

    //Verify Expiration Date
    if(CGIinfo.FormVars.getProperty("CCEXP").length() != 4){
        CGIinfo.CgiError("Input Error","Please Enter Correct Credit Card Expiration Date "+
                    "In the Form: <BR>" + "YYMM (Y = Year, M = Month)");
        return false;
    }

    //Verify credit card Number
    if(FormatCCNum(CGIinfo.FormVars.getProperty("CCNUM")) == ""){
        CGIinfo.CgiError("Input Error","Please Enter Correct Credit Card Number");
        return false;
    }

    return true;
}

/*
    Handle the state where the user is returning to the catalog from an item page.
    The basic order of events is, load the user manage, check for items to add,
    then generate the catalog page.
*/
private void pre_item(){


    //begin of user manager init
    String NextItem = "";
        try{
```

```
                NextState    = new Integer(CGIinfo.FormVars.getProperty("STATE")).intValue();
            }
            catch(Exception e){
            }

            UserID      =  ToAllDigits(CGIinfo.FormVars.getProperty("USERID"));

            try{
                UM = new usermanager(UserID,"" + NextState,UserPath,UserExt,true);
            }
            catch(Exception e){
                CGIinfo.CgiError("ERROR",e.getMessage() + " - UserManager failed to init -
*"+UserID+"*");
                return;
            }

            NextState   =   UM.NextState;

        //end of user manager init

            //If User wants to ADD an Item
            if(CGIinfo.FormVars.getProperty("ADDITEM") != null){
                NextItem = "ITEM";
                for(int i = 0 ; i < MaxItems ; ++i)
                    if(!UM.StatePropertyExists(NextItem+i)){
                        NextItem += i;
                            break;
                    }
                UM.AddStateProperty(NextItem, CGIinfo.FormVars.getProperty("ADDITEM"));
            }
            if(!UM.SaveState()){
                CGIinfo.CgiError("ERROR : UserManager","Failed to Create New User");
                return;
            }

            //generate the catalog page
            gen_item_list();
    }

    /*
        This member is called to itialize a new user, then generate the catalog page.
    */
    private void init_new_state(){
        //begin of user manager init
        try{
            UM = new usermanager(null,null,UserPath,UserExt,true);
```

```
        }
        catch(Exception e){
            CGIinfo.CgiError("ERROR : UserManager","UserManager failed to init");
            return;
        }

        NextState   =   UM.NextState;
        UserID      =   UM.User;

        UM.AddStateProperty("PLACEHOLD", "NEWSTATE");

        if(!UM.SaveState()){
            CGIinfo.CgiError("ERROR : UserManager","Failed to Create New User");
            return;
        }
        //begin of user manager init

        gen_item_list();
    }

//generate the catalog page.  It is assumed that the user manager is initialized.
private void gen_item_list(){
        String      ItemList    =   "";
        String      Checkout    =   "";
        String      Item        =   "";
        Properties  P           =   new Properties();


        //Generate an HTML listing of all the items in the config ini.

        Enumeration E   =   ItemInfo.IniSections.keys();
        for(;E.hasMoreElements();){
            ItemList += "<a href=\"" + CGIinfo.MyBaseUrl() +"?USERID="+ UserID;
            ItemList += "&STATE=" + NextState + "&NEXTFORM=2&";
            Item = (String)E.nextElement();
            ItemList += "ITEM=" + Item + "\">";
            //Use the config file defined graphic file.
            ItemList += "<img src=\"" + ItemInfo.GetProperty(Item,"ItemPictURL","") + "\">";
            ItemList += ItemInfo.GetProperty(Item,"ShortDescription","")+"</a><BR>\n";
        }

        //generate the Checkout link
        Checkout += CGIinfo.MyBaseUrl() +"?USERID="+ UserID;
        Checkout += "&STATE=" + NextState + "&NEXTFORM=10";

        //do a search and replace on the catalog page template
```

```
        P.put("##!!##ITEMS",ItemList);
        P.put("##!!##CheckOUT",Checkout);
        filereplace tmplt = new filereplace(ItemTmpltFile, P);
        CGIinfo.PrintHeader();
        System.out.println(tmplt.GetOutputString());


        return;
    }

    //Generates the specific item, using the config file
    //defined HTML template.
    private void gen_item(){

        String Output          =    "";
        String NotBuying        =    "";
        String Item             =    CGIinfo.FormVars.getProperty("ITEM")    ;
        Properties  P           =    new Properties();

        //begin of user manager init
        try{
            NextState    = new Integer(CGIinfo.FormVars.getProperty("STATE")).intValue();
        }
        catch(Exception e){
            return;
        }

        UserID       =  ToAllDigits(CGIinfo.FormVars.getProperty("USERID"));


        try{
            UM = new usermanager(UserID,"" + NextState,UserPath,UserExt,true);
        }
        catch(Exception e){
            CGIinfo.CgiError("ERROR",e.getMessage() + " - UserManager failed to init -
*"+UserID+"*");
            return;
        }

        NextState    =   UM.NextState;
        //end of user manager init

        //Create a little HTML description of the item
        Output = "<P>" + ItemInfo.GetProperty(Item,"Description","") + "</P><BR>";
        Output += "Cost : $" + ItemInfo.GetProperty(Item,"Price","") + "<BR>";
        Output += "Shipping : $" + ItemInfo.GetProperty(Item,"Shipping","") + "<BR><BR><BR>";
        Output += "<A href=\"" + CGIinfo.MyBaseUrl() +"?USERID="+ UserID;
```

```
        Output += "&STATE=" + NextState + "&NEXTFORM=1&";
        Output += "ADDITEM=" + Item + "\">";
        Output += "<img src=\"" + ItemInfo.GetProperty(Item,"ItemPictURL","") + "\">";
        Output += "Add To Shopping Cart</A><BR>\n";

        //Create the link if the don't want to add the item
        NotBuying += "\"" + CGIinfo.MyBaseUrl() +"?USERID="+ UserID;
        NotBuying += "&STATE=" + NextState + "&NEXTFORM=1\">";

        //do a search and replace of the specified item template file
        P.put("##!!##ShortDesc",ItemInfo.GetProperty(Item,"ShortDescription",""));
        P.put("##!!##ITEM",Output);
        P.put("##!!##Return",NotBuying);
        filereplace tmplt = new filereplace(ItemInfo.GetProperty(Item,"TemplatePage",""), P);

        //make sure to save the state
        if(!UM.SaveState()){
            CGIinfo.CgiError("ERROR : UserManager","Failed to Create New User");
            return;
        }

        CGIinfo.PrintHeader();
        System.out.println(tmplt.GetOutputString());
        return;
}


//Generate the checkout form from the HTML template
private void gen_check_out(){
        String Output          =     "";
        String Temp            =     "";
        String NextItem        =     "";
        String tmpitem         =     "";
        float  Total           =     0.00f;
        float  tmpval          =     0.00f;
        Properties  P          =     new Properties();


        //begin of user manager init
        try{
            NextState   = new Integer(CGIinfo.FormVars.getProperty("STATE")).intValue();
        }
        catch(Exception e){
            return;
        }

        UserID      = ToAllDigits(CGIinfo.FormVars.getProperty("USERID"));
```

```
        try{
            UM = new usermanager(UserID,"" + NextState,UserPath,UserExt,true);
        }
        catch(Exception e){
            CGIinfo.CgiError("ERROR",e.getMessage() + " - UserManager failed to init -
*"+UserID+"*");
            return;
        }

        NextState    =    UM.NextState;

        //end of user manager init

        //generate the Receipt from the user manager info
          NextItem = "ITEM";
          for(int i = 0 ; i < MaxItems ; ++i){
            if(!UM.StatePropertyExists(NextItem+i))
              break;

            tmpitem = UM.GetStateProperty(NextItem+i,"");

            Output  += ItemInfo.GetProperty(tmpitem,"ShortDescription","") + "<BR>";
            Output  += "Cost : $" + ItemInfo.GetProperty(tmpitem,"Price","") + "<BR>";
            Output  += "Shipping : $" + ItemInfo.GetProperty(tmpitem,"Shipping","") +
"<BR>";
            Output  += "<BR>\n";
            //upadte the total
            try{
                tmpval = new Float(ItemInfo.GetProperty(tmpitem,"Price","")).floatValue();
                Total += tmpval;

                tmpval = new
Float(ItemInfo.GetProperty(tmpitem,"Shipping","")).floatValue();
            }
            catch(Exception e){
            }
          }
        //do a search and replace of the specified check out template file
        P.put("##!!##Receipt",Output);
        P.put("##!!##Total","$" + Total);
        P.put("##!!##ACTION",CGIinfo.MyBaseUrl());
        P.put("##!!##USERID",UserID);
        P.put("##!!##STATE","" +  NextState);
        P.put("##!!##TOTALFIELD","" +  Total);
        filereplace tmplt = new filereplace(CheckOutForm, P);
```

```
        //save the sate
        if(!UM.SaveState()){
            CGIinfo.CgiError("ERROR : UserManager","Failed to Create New User");
            return;
        }

        CGIinfo.PrintHeader();
        System.out.println(tmplt.GetOutputString());

        return;
    }

    /*
     Besides checking for Alpha characters in the credit card number,
     this function will take out spaces and '-' charcters.
    */
    private String FormatCCNum(String in){

        if(in == null)
            return "";

        String out  =   "";
        Character C =   new Character('c');


        for(int i = 0 ; i < in.length();++i)
            if((in.charAt(i) != '-')&&(in.charAt(i) != ' ')){
                if(C.isDigit(in.charAt(i)))
                    out += "" + in.charAt(i);
                else
                    return "";
            }

        CGIinfo.FormVars.put("CCNUM",new String(out));
        return out;
    }

//Removes any non-numeric values
    private String ToAllDigits(String in){
        String out  =       "";
        Character C =       new Character('C');

        for(int i = 0 ; i < in.length() ; ++i)
            if(C.isDigit(in.charAt(i)))
                out += in.charAt(i);
```

```
        return out;
    }

    /*
        This function process the credit card sale using CardShield.
        The icverify util provides ErrorCode function for returning
        the appropriate error code, for more robust
        error handling this string should be propagated to the user.
        This function will fail if the card or expiration is invalid,
        or the card is not approved.
    */

    private boolean ProcessSale(){

        //Init the CardShield object. The first param is the CSMID
        //second is false reflecting the fact that this is not an Applet

        icverify IC    =   new icverify ("c:\\icverify\\","c:\\icverify\\demo19\\",true);

        //Add the order to the process request pool

        IC.AddRequest("MYCGI","TESTCGI",CGIinfo.FormVars.getProperty("CCNUM"),
                CGIinfo.FormVars.getProperty("CCEXP"),"" +
CGIinfo.FormVars.getProperty("TOTAL"),
                CGIinfo.FormVars.getProperty("Zip"),
                CGIinfo.FormVars.getProperty("Address1"));

        //Process the request
        IC.ProcessRequests();

        return IC.IsApproved(CGIinfo.FormVars.getProperty("CCNUM"));

    }


    /*
     Commits all of the form's information to a file using
     the orderfile utility.
    */
    private void StoreOrder(){

        if(UM == null){
            try{
                NextState    = new Integer(CGIinfo.FormVars.getProperty("STATE")).intValue();
            }
            catch(Exception e){
```

```
                return;
            }

            UserID    = ToAllDigits(CGIinfo.FormVars.getProperty("USERID"));

            try{
                UM = new usermanager(UserID,"" + NextState,UserPath,UserExt,true);
            }
            catch(Exception e){
                CGIinfo.CgiError("ERROR",e.getMessage() + " - UserManager failed to init -
*"+UserID+"*");
                return;
            }

            NextState   =   UM.NextState;
        }


        orderfile order = new orderfile(OrderPath,OrderExt);
        Enumeration E = CGIinfo.FormVars.keys();
        String tmp_val = "";
        String tmp_key = "";

        String NextItem = "ITEM";
        for(int i = 0 ; i < MaxItems ; ++i){
            if(!UM.StatePropertyExists(NextItem+i))
                break;
            order.AddProperty(NextItem + i,UM.GetStateProperty(NextItem+i,""));
        }

        for(;E.hasMoreElements ();){
            tmp_key = (String) E.nextElement();
            tmp_val = CGIinfo.FormVars.getProperty (tmp_key);
            order.AddProperty(tmp_key,tmp_val);
        }

        order.Save();
    }

}
```

Usage

The main body of the CGI application will contain only the construction of the CGIProcessor, and a call to ProcesForm(). The following is an example CGI execution.

```
import CommerceUtils.*;

public class cgi {


    public static void main(String args[]) {
        CGIProcessor CGI  = new CGIProcessor(".\\",".ord","items.ini",".\\",".usr");
        CGI.ProcesForm();
    }


}
```

To launch the CGI from an existing HTML page you would add a URL to the CGI specifying only a single parameter. The following is an example HTML link.

```
<A href="/cgi-bin/shoppingcart.bat?ID=1">Go Shopping</A>
```

JDBC and IC Verify-Enabled Shopping Cart

Just as processing the credit-card transaction in real-time saves an extra processing step, so does storing the information directly into a database. Up until now, all the examples packed the entered order information into individual files on the disk. Nine times out of 10, eventually the information in those individual files will need to be extrapolated and stored into a database. The logical alternative is to store the information directly to the database, which is exactly what this example does. Using JDBC, this CGI inserts a record into a database for each order entered.

All entered item information is stored in a CGI-accessible configuration file. All source and referenced configuration files can be found on the accompanying CD-ROM. If you choose to use this example, the following is a list of things to modify:

- Load the configuration file with the items you wish to sell, and all associated information.

- Generate all needed template files with the proper CGI tags.

- Generate the thankyou.html file.

- Change the path of the stored order files if needed.

- Modify the IC Verify paths to match the IC Verify setup configurations.

- For production, change the debug flag of IC Verify to off.

- Modify the SQL Server Connection properties to correspond with your database server.

- Modify the SQL "Insert" statement to correspond with your order database.

Caveats

As in the previous example, the IC Verify-provided error codes in this example are not handled properly. Along with each transaction response is an error string holding useful information that should be propagated to the user. The current implementation checks to see only if the sale was approved, and the error code field is ignored.

Last, the specific JDBC errors are not propagated; in fact, no error is trapped. In fixing this, you will need to consider the scenario of a credit-card transaction being authorized and the order not being saved. The solution to this is fairly complex, dealing with a commit and a rollback. If the database insert fails, you need to be able to "roll back" the sale transaction. This will entail issuing a void command to IC Verify, which the icverify tool does not support. In many cases, you may write a complicated recovery routine just to never have it be used. However, if you are feeling lucky, which isn't really like rolling the dice, you will opt to leave it be.

Code Listing

```java
import CommerceUtils.*;
import java.util.Enumeration;
import java.util.Properties;
import java.sql.*;
import weblogic.db.jdbc.*;


//CGIProcessor.java

/**
 * CGIPRocessor is a generic handler for a shopping cart style solutions
 * It provides a preliminary frame work for further develop. A
 * potential weak spot is the lack of accurate field verification.
 *
 * @version 2.0
 * @author Cary A. Jardin
 */

public class CGIProcessor{

    //The initial state on startup.
    private int    NextState    =    -1;
    //Global user ID
```

```
private String UserID        =    "";
//The path to store the orders into
private String OrderPath      =    "";
//The path to extension to be placed on the order files
private String OrderExt       =    "";
//The configuration file that holds the item information
private String ItemFile       =    "";
//The path to store the user files into
private String UserPath       =    "";
//The Extension to be place on the user files
private String UserExt        =    "";
//The main item catalog template HTML
private String ItemTmpltFile=    "items.html";
//The checkout form HTML template
private String CheckOutForm =    "checkoutform.html";
//Final screen URL
private String ThankYou       =    "/thankyou.html";
//The maximum items the sysytem can hold per user
private int    MaxItems       =    300;

//The CGI library
private cgilib CGIinfo;

//The ITEM configuration file
private inifile ItemInfo;
//The user manger, to store the CGI users.
private usermanager UM;

/**
 * The constructor initializes the all needed objets and variables, including
 * the cgilib, the item inifile.
 *
 * @param orderpath        The path to store the generated orders in.
 * @param ordertext        The extension to be placed on the generated orders.
 * @param itemfile         The configuration file holding the item information.
 * @param usrpath          The path to store the generated user files in.
 * @param usrtext          The extension to be placed on the user files.
 *
 */
public CGIProcessor(String orderpath, String orderext,
                    String itemfile , String userpath,
                    String userext){

    CGIinfo        = new cgilib();
    ItemInfo       = new inifile(itemfile);
    OrderPath      = orderpath;
```

```
        OrderExt        = orderext;
        ItemFile        = itemfile;
        UserPath        = userpath;
        UserExt         = userext;
    }


    /**
     * ProcesForm is the entry point for the processing of the form. After construct
     * this member should be called.  The member : verifies the input, credit card, and
items,
     * and generates all resulting HTML.
     *
     */
    public void ProcesForm(){

        //NextForm is used to tell the CGI what page to go to.
        String Test =  CGIinfo.FormVars.getProperty("NEXTFORM");

        //Initial entry point.
        if(Test == null)
            init_new_state();
        else //At the catalog - goto the item page
        if(Test.compareTo("2") == 0)
            gen_item();
        else//At the item page going pack to the catalog page
        if(Test.compareTo("1") == 0){
            pre_item();
        }
        else//At the catalog page going to the checkout page
        if(Test.compareTo("10") == 0)
            gen_check_out();
        else//At the checkout page, verify input and end.
        if(Test.compareTo("3") == 0){
            if(!VerifyInput())
                return;
            //store the order to the order file.
            StoreOrder();
            //generate thank you.
            CGIinfo.Redirect(ThankYou);
        }

        return;

    }


    /*Check each of the required fields return false if any fail.
```

```
    Only size is checked, to assume better response additional
    verification logic should be added.
  */
private boolean VerifyInput(){

    //Verify Customer Name
    if((CGIinfo.FormVars.getProperty("FirstName") == null) ||
(CGIinfo.FormVars.getProperty("FirstName").length() < 2)){
        CGIinfo.CgiError("Input Error","Please Enter Your First Name");
        return false;
    }
    if((CGIinfo.FormVars.getProperty("LastName") == null) ||
(CGIinfo.FormVars.getProperty("LastName").length() < 2)){
        CGIinfo.CgiError("Input Error","Please Enter Your Last Name");
        return false;
    }

    //Verify Address
    if((CGIinfo.FormVars.getProperty("Address1") == null) ||
(CGIinfo.FormVars.getProperty("Address1").length() < 5)){
        CGIinfo.CgiError("Input Error","Please a Correct Address");
        return false;
    }

    //Verify City
    if((CGIinfo.FormVars.getProperty("City") == null) ||
(CGIinfo.FormVars.getProperty("City").length() < 4)){
        CGIinfo.CgiError("Input Error","Please Enter Correct City");
        return false;
    }

    //Verify State
    if((CGIinfo.FormVars.getProperty("State") == null) ||
(CGIinfo.FormVars.getProperty("State").length() < 1)){
        CGIinfo.CgiError("Input Error","Please Enter Correct State");
        return false;
    }

    //Verify Zip
    if((CGIinfo.FormVars.getProperty("Zip") == null) ||
(CGIinfo.FormVars.getProperty("Zip").length() < 5)){
        CGIinfo.CgiError("Input Error","Please Enter Correct Zip");
        return false;
    }
```

```
        //Verify Phone
        if((CGIinfo.FormVars.getProperty("PhoneNumber") == null) ||
(CGIinfo.FormVars.getProperty("PhoneNumber").length() < 10)){
            CGIinfo.CgiError("Input Error","Please Enter Correct Phone Number");
            return false;
        }

        //Verify Expiration Date
        if(CGIinfo.FormVars.getProperty("CCEXP").length() != 4){
            CGIinfo.CgiError("Input Error","Please Enter Correct Credit Card Expiration Date
"+
                        "In the Form: <BR>" + "YYMM (Y = Year, M = Month)");
            return false;
        }

        //Verify credit card Number
        if(FormatCCNum(CGIinfo.FormVars.getProperty("CCNUM")) == ""){
            CGIinfo.CgiError("Input Error","Please Enter Correct Credit Card Number");
            return false;
        }

        return true;
    }

    /*
        Handle the state where the user is returning to the catalog from an item page.
        The basic order of events is, load the user manage, check for items to add,
        then generate the catalog page.
    */
    private void pre_item(){

        //begin of user manager init
        String NextItem = "";
            try{
                NextState   = new Integer(CGIinfo.FormVars.getProperty("STATE")).intValue();
            }
            catch(Exception e){
            }

            UserID      = ToAllDigits(CGIinfo.FormVars.getProperty("USERID"));

            try{
                UM = new usermanager(UserID,"" + NextState,UserPath,UserExt,true);
            }
```

```
                catch(Exception e){
                    CGIinfo.CgiError("ERROR",e.getMessage() + " - UserManager failed to init -
*"+UserID+"*");
                    return;
                }

                NextState    =    UM.NextState;

        //end of user manager init

                //If User wants to ADD an Item
                if(CGIinfo.FormVars.getProperty("ADDITEM") != null){
                    NextItem = "ITEM";
                    for(int i = 0 ; i < MaxItems ; ++i)
                        if(!UM.StatePropertyExists(NextItem+i)){
                            NextItem += i;
                                break;
                        }
                    UM.AddStateProperty(NextItem, CGIinfo.FormVars.getProperty("ADDITEM"));
                }
                if(!UM.SaveState()){
                    CGIinfo.CgiError("ERROR : UserManager","Failed to Create New User");
                    return;
                }

                //generate the catalog page
                gen_item_list();
        }

    /*
        This member is called to itialize a new user, then generate the catalog page.
    */
    private void init_new_state(){
        //begin of user manager init
        try{
            UM = new usermanager(null,null,UserPath,UserExt,true);
        }
        catch(Exception e){
            CGIinfo.CgiError("ERROR : UserManager","UserManager failed to init");
            return;
        }

        NextState    =    UM.NextState;
        UserID       =    UM.User;
```

```
        UM.AddStateProperty("PLACEHOLD", "NEWSTATE");

        if(!UM.SaveState()){
            CGIinfo.CgiError("ERROR : UserManager","Failed to Create New User");
            return;
        }
        //begin of user manager init

        gen_item_list();
}


//generate the catalog page.   It is assumed that the user manager is initialized.
private void gen_item_list(){
        String      ItemList  =    "";
        String      Checkout  =    "";
        String      Item      =    "";
        Properties  P         =    new Properties();


        //Generate an HTML listing of all the items in the config ini.

        Enumeration E   =   ItemInfo.IniSections.keys();
        for(;E.hasMoreElements();){
            ItemList += "<a href=\"" + CGIinfo.MyBaseUrl() +"?USERID="+ UserID;
            ItemList += "&STATE=" + NextState + "&NEXTFORM=2&";
            Item = (String)E.nextElement();
            ItemList += "ITEM=" + Item + "\">";
            //Use the config file defined graphic file.
            ItemList += "<img src=\"" + ItemInfo.GetProperty(Item,"ItemPictURL","") + "\">";
            ItemList += ItemInfo.GetProperty(Item,"ShortDescription","")+"</a><BR>\n";
        }

        //generate the Checkout link
        Checkout += CGIinfo.MyBaseUrl() +"?USERID="+ UserID;
        Checkout += "&STATE=" + NextState + "&NEXTFORM=10";

        //do a search and replace on the catalog page template
        P.put("##!!##ITEMS",ItemList);
        P.put("##!!##CheckOUT",Checkout);
        filereplace tmplt = new filereplace(ItemTmpltFile, P);
        CGIinfo.PrintHeader();
        System.out.println(tmplt.GetOutputString());

        return;
}
```

```java
//Generates the specific item, using the config file
//defined HTML template.
private void gen_item(){

    String Output           =    "";
    String NotBuying        =    "";
    String Item             =    CGIinfo.FormVars.getProperty("ITEM")    ;
    Properties  P           =    new Properties();

    //begin of user manager init
    try{
        NextState   = new Integer(CGIinfo.FormVars.getProperty("STATE")).intValue();
    }
    catch(Exception e){
        return;
    }

    UserID      =    ToAllDigits(CGIinfo.FormVars.getProperty("USERID"));


    try{
        UM = new usermanager(UserID,"" + NextState,UserPath,UserExt,true);
    }
    catch(Exception e){
        CGIinfo.CgiError("ERROR",e.getMessage() + " - UserManager failed to init -
*"+UserID+"*");
        return;
    }

    NextState   =    UM.NextState;
    //end of user manager init

    //Create a little HTML description of the item
    Output = "<P>" + ItemInfo.GetProperty(Item,"Description","") + "</P><BR>";
    Output += "Cost : $" + ItemInfo.GetProperty(Item,"Price","") + "<BR>";
    Output += "Shipping : $" + ItemInfo.GetProperty(Item,"Shipping","") + "<BR><BR><BR>";
    Output += "<A href=\"" + CGIinfo.MyBaseUrl() +"?USERID="+ UserID;
    Output += "&STATE=" + NextState + "&NEXTFORM=1&";
    Output += "ADDITEM=" + Item + "\">";
    Output += "<img src=\"" + ItemInfo.GetProperty(Item,"ItemPictURL","") + "\">";
    Output += "Add To Shopping Cart</A><BR>\n";

    //Create the link if the don't want to add the item
    NotBuying += "\"" + CGIinfo.MyBaseUrl() +"?USERID="+ UserID;
    NotBuying += "&STATE=" + NextState + "&NEXTFORM=1\">";
```

```
        //do a search and replace of the specified item template file
        P.put("##!!##ShortDesc",ItemInfo.GetProperty(Item,"ShortDescription",""));
        P.put("##!!##ITEM",Output);
        P.put("##!!##Return",NotBuying);
        filereplace tmplt = new filereplace(ItemInfo.GetProperty(Item,"TemplatePage",""), P);

        //make sure to save the state
        if(!UM.SaveState()){
            CGIinfo.CgiError("ERROR : UserManager","Failed to Create New User");
            return;
        }

        CGIinfo.PrintHeader();
        System.out.println(tmplt.GetOutputString());
        return;
    }

    //Generate the checkout form from the HTML template
    private void gen_check_out(){
        String Output          =    "";
        String Temp            =    "";
        String NextItem        =    "";
        String tmpitem         =    "";
        float  Total           =    0.00f;
        float  tmpval          =    0.00f;
        Properties  P          =    new Properties();


        //begin of user manager init
        try{
            NextState   = new Integer(CGIinfo.FormVars.getProperty("STATE")).intValue();
        }
        catch(Exception e){
            return;
        }

        UserID      = ToAllDigits(CGIinfo.FormVars.getProperty("USERID"));


        try{
            UM = new usermanager(UserID,"" + NextState,UserPath,UserExt,true);
        }
        catch(Exception e){
            CGIinfo.CgiError("ERROR",e.getMessage() + " - UserManager failed to init -
*"+UserID+"*");
```

```
              return;
          }

      NextState    =    UM.NextState;

      //end of user manager init

      //generate the Receipt from the user manager info
        NextItem = "ITEM";
        for(int i = 0 ; i < MaxItems ; ++i){
           if(!UM.StatePropertyExists(NextItem+i))
             break;

           tmpitem = UM.GetStateProperty(NextItem+i,"");

           Output  += ItemInfo.GetProperty(tmpitem,"ShortDescription","") + "<BR>";
           Output  += "Cost : $" + ItemInfo.GetProperty(tmpitem,"Price","") + "<BR>";
           Output  += "Shipping : $" + ItemInfo.GetProperty(tmpitem,"Shipping","") +
"<BR>";
           Output  += "<BR>\n";
           //upadte the total
           try{
               tmpval = new Float(ItemInfo.GetProperty(tmpitem,"Price","")).floatValue();
               Total += tmpval;

               tmpval = new
Float(ItemInfo.GetProperty(tmpitem,"Shipping","")).floatValue();
           }
           catch(Exception e){
           }
         }
      //do a search and replace of the specified check out template file
      P.put("##!!##Receipt",Output);
      P.put("##!!##Total","$" + Total);
      P.put("##!!##ACTION",CGIinfo.MyBaseUrl());
      P.put("##!!##USERID",UserID);
      P.put("##!!##STATE","" + NextState);
      P.put("##!!##TOTALFIELD","" + Total);
      filereplace tmplt = new filereplace(CheckOutForm, P);


      //save the sate
      if(!UM.SaveState()){
          CGIinfo.CgiError("ERROR : UserManager","Failed to Create New User");
          return;
```

```
        }

        CGIinfo.PrintHeader();
        System.out.println(tmplt.GetOutputString());

        return;
    }

    /*
     Besides checking for Alpha characters in the credit card number,
     this function will take out spaces and '-' charcters.
    */
    private String FormatCCNum(String in){

        if(in == null)
            return "";

        String out  =   "";
        Character C  =   new Character('c');


        for(int i = 0 ; i < in.length();++i)
            if((in.charAt(i) != '-')&&(in.charAt(i) != ' ')){
                if(C.isDigit(in.charAt(i)))
                    out += "" + in.charAt(i);
                else
                    return "";
            }

        CGIinfo.FormVars.put("CCNUM",new String(out));
        return out;
    }

    //Removes any non-numeric values
    private String ToAllDigits(String in){
        String out   =      "";
        Character C  =      new Character('C');

        for(int i = 0 ; i < in.length() ; ++i)
            if(C.isDigit(in.charAt(i)))
                out += in.charAt(i);

        return out;
    }
```

```
        for(;E.hasMoreElements ();){
            tmp_key = (String) E.nextElement();
            tmp_val = CGIinfo.FormVars.getProperty (tmp_key);
            Fields += tmp_key + ",";
            Values += "'" + tmp_val + "',";
        }

        //Add the ordered items

        Fields += "ITEMSORDERS";
        Values += "'" + items + "',";

         String insert = "insert into NEWORDER(" + Fields + ")"+
         " values (" + Values + ")" ;

        //Open a stament constext
        Statement stmt1 = conn.createStatement();
        //execute the insert
        stmt1.execute(insert);
        //Close the statement and the connection
        stmt1.close();
        conn.close();

    }catch(Exception e){//Generic handeler
    }

  }


}
```

Usage

The CGI application's main body will contain only the construction of the CGIProcessor and a call to ProcesForm(). An example CGI execution follows.

```
import CommerceUtils.*;

public class cgi {


    public static void main(String args[]) {
        CGIProcessor CGI  = new CGIProcessor(".\\",".ord","items.ini",".\\",".usr");
        CGI.ProcesForm();
    }


}
```

To launch the CGI from an existing HTML page you would add a URL to the CGI specifying only a single parameter. The following is an example HTML link.

```
<A href="/cgi-bin/shoppingcart.bat?ID=1">Go Shopping</A>
```

Summary

Shopping cart CGI commerce solutions have become the industry standard. Their ease of use and ability to captivate the user make the shopping cart application a welcome addition to any Web commerce site. This chapter presented a shopping cart CGI application with three variations. One example utilizes CardShield for credit-card sale processing, another uses IC Verify, and a third offers a JDBC and IC Verify solution. Through the use of the template and configuration files, any of the provided solutions can be molded to fit a wide variety of Web commerce needs. By far, the examples in this chapter display the highest level of usability and functionality of all of the supplied commerce solutions. They do lack the ability to interact with the user quickly and intelligently. To solve this problem, Chapter 14 will provide a set of commerce applets that represents the cutting edge in the realm of Web commerce solutions. As for this chapter, use, play with, and coerce one of these examples to work for you. Just keep in mind, "It will work if you let it."

Applet Commerce
Solutions

The use of Applets as commerce devices is in its infancy. Applet security restrictions, the nonexistence of secure data transport facilities, and the relative newness of JDBC technology have brought applet commerce production to a standstill. However, many of these hindrances are now emerging onto the technology field, and they may light the fire for further technology advances. For now, the scope of commerce applet creation revolves around the use of the CardShield API.

What the CardShield API provided is the ability to process credit-card sales securely, e-mail or fax an order back for processing, and create daily database update files. The use of CardShield greatly simplifies applet commerce creation by providing all needed commerce functionality. This chapter focuses on the creation of custom CardShield applications, which are custom-built commerce applets that rely on the CardShield functionality to facilitate the secure data storage and credit-card sale. This chapter presents two such applets, one that uses only the Java supplied facilities, and one that describes and utilizes third-party widget tool kits. The technical level of this chapter is geared toward Java programmers, but nonprogrammers can still gain some valuable information, including knowledge of how to use the examples in their own storefront.

Slide Show Store Applet

Providing customers a means to view and purchase items for sale is essential. Creating a solution that is flexible enough to accommodate changes in products is also crucial, not for the customer, but for the merchant. The example that follows is a "Slide Show" style commerce applet. The general feel is that users can flip through items and select which one they choose to purchase. When they have found an item to purchase, they click the "purchase" button to place the item into their shopping cart, for later checkout. In many ways this approach can be viewed as a direct translation of Chapter 13's CGI-based solution ported into an applet. As the CGI relied on an "items.in" for item information, so does this applet. The following is an example of an applet item file. Through the modification of this file, the items and all of the item's associated information can be modified.

```
[AB123]
#Comment 2
ItemPictURL=123.gif
Description=Log From BlamO
ShortDescription=Log From BlamO
Price=12.00
Shipping=0.00

[AB125]
#Comment 2
ItemPictURL = 125.gif
Description = Round Ball
ShortDescription = Round Ball
Price=2.00
Shipping=0.00
```

The relatively simple appearance of this example should not imply that the underlying code is also simple. For many reasons not mentioned here, working with the Java AWT (Abstract Windows Toolkit) is, at best, a trying experience. This applet does not use any third-party libraries; all code directly calls AWT classes. The other example in this chapter displays the use of third-party libraries for the creation of a more advanced user interface.

Support Classes

The slide show store applet utilizes two primary support classes. The first is the checkout form, which, appropriately enough, handles the customer's purchasing of the selected items. The second is a dialog class used to display error messages that occur during the checkout process.

Figure 14.1 Slide show selection screen.

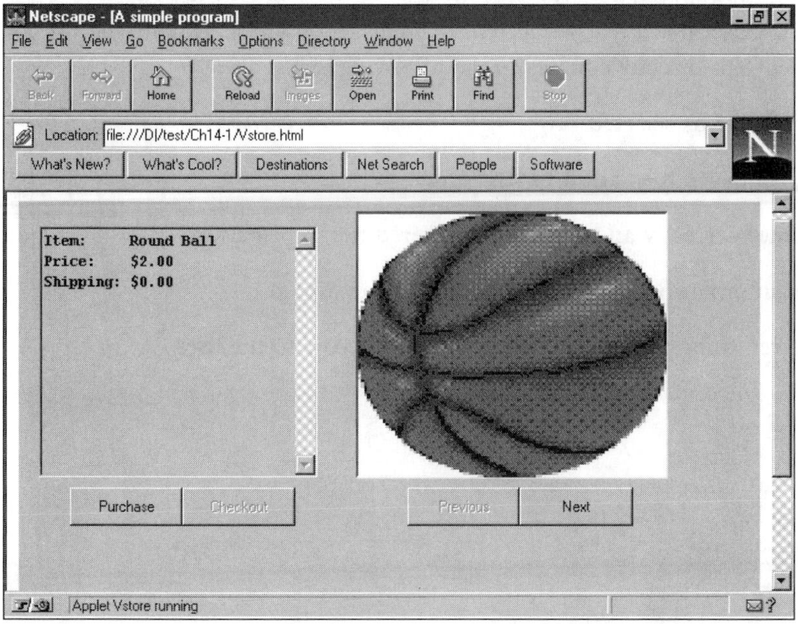

Figure 14.2 Checkout screen.

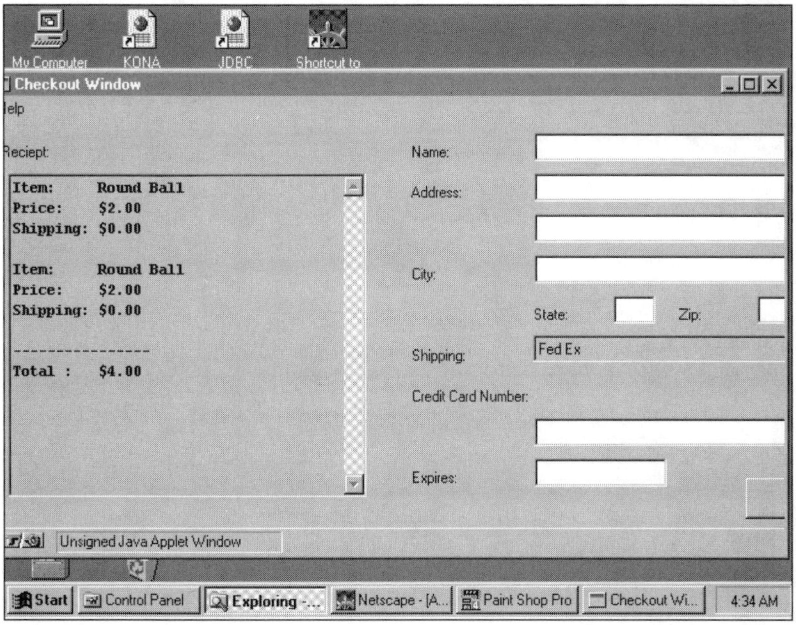

The message dialog class is relatively simple, containing only a text box and an OK button. The real meat and potatoes of this application come in the checkout form. At the point that the checkout form is launched, the user has already selected the items to purchase, leaving the check-out form to process the order. This directly equates to the following tasks:

1. Displaying a receipt for the items selected

2. Gathering the needed customer information for the order

3. Verifying that the customer correctly and completely entered the information

4. Loading all of the order information to send to CardShield for storage

5. Processing the sale, and returning any credit-card processing errors to the user

CheckOutFrm Code Listing

```
/*
    This class is a basic extension of the Frame class.  It can be used
    by an Applet or application.  To use it, create a reference to the
    class, then instantiate an object of the class, and call the show() method.


    example:

    CheckOutFrm theCheckOutFrm;
    theCheckOutFrm = new CheckOutFrm();
    theCheckOutFrm.show();

    You can add controls or menus to CheckOutFrm with Cafe Studio.
 */

import java.awt.*;
import java.util.Properties;
import CardShield.*;

/**
 * CheckOutFrm provides the orderenty ability of the example Applet.
 * CardShield API is used to verify credit card information, as well as transmit
 * the collected information.
 */
public class CheckOutFrm extends Frame {

    // CSMID is the CardShield Merchant ID for your CardShield Account
    private static String CSMID    =    "1235A";
```

```
/* OutPut hold all the orders information, including the selected items.
   Any needed information can be added to the property list, it will
   accompany the Standard CardShield information.
*/
public Properties  OutPut  =   new Properties();

//VStore will load this value with the order's total
public float    TotalCost   =   0.00f;

//Used to set the Receipt box
public void LoadStatment(String receipt){
    stmnt.setText(receipt);
}

//The gathered information is loaded into the OutPut property list
public void StoreProperties(){

    OutPut.put("Name",Name.getText());
    OutPut.put("Address1",Address1.getText());
    OutPut.put("Address2",Address2.getText());
    OutPut.put("City",City.getText());
    OutPut.put("State",State.getText());
    OutPut.put("Zip",Zaip.getText());
    OutPut.put("Shipping",Shipping.getSelectedItem());
    OutPut.put("CCNUM",CCNum.getText());
    OutPut.put("CCEXPIR",CCExpir.getText());
}

/* Verifies the entered information, as will as process the sale.
   False will be returned on failure, and a descriptive message will
   be displayed in a dialog box.
*/
public boolean VerifyInput(){
    CardShieldAPI CS = new CardShieldAPI(CSMID,true);

    String ErrorString =   "";

    if(Name.getText().length() < 3)
        ErrorString = "Name Must be Specified";
    else
    if(Address1.getText().length() < 4)
        ErrorString = "An Address Must Be Provided";
    else
    if(City.getText().length() < 3)
        ErrorString = "City Must Be Provided";
```

```
        else
        if(State.getText().length() < 2)
            ErrorString = "State Must Be Provided";
        else
        if(Zaip.getText().length() < 5)
            ErrorString = "Zip Code Must Be Provided";
        else
        if(CCNum.getText().length() < 10)
            ErrorString = "A Credit Card Number Must be Specified";
        else
        if(CCExpir.getText().length() != 4)
            ErrorString = "Expiration Date Must be in YYMM Format";

        //If there is an error, display it and return
        if(ErrorString != ""){
            dlg   =   new MsgOk(this,"Input Error");
            dlg.textbox.setText(ErrorString);
            dlg.show();
            return false;
        }

        //Load the properties to be submitted to CardShield
        StoreProperties();
        //Process the Sale
        ErrorString = CS.SecureSale("TEST","Applet Agent",CCNum.getText(),CCExpir.getText(),
            "" + TotalCost, Zaip.getText(), Address1.getText(), OutPut);

        //If the Card wasn't approved tell the user
        if(ErrorString != CS.Approved){
            dlg   =   new MsgOk(this,"Credit Card Error");
            dlg.textbox.setText("CardShield Returned :"+ ErrorString);
            dlg.show();
            return false;
        }
        return true;
    }

/*All but one line of this code was generated by Symantec resource
  editor.
*/
public CheckOutFrm() {

    super("Checkout Window");

    //Set the Applet Background Color
    setBackground(Color.lightGray);
```

```
//{{INIT_CONTROLS
setLayout(null);
addNotify();
resize(insets().left + insets().right + 747, insets().top + insets().bottom + 338);
stmnt=new TextArea(12,28);
stmnt.setFont(new Font("Courier",Font.BOLD,12));
add(stmnt);
stmnt.reshape(insets().left + 14,insets().top + 40,292,256);
label1=new Label("Receipt:");
add(label1);
label1.reshape(insets().left + 9,insets().top + 16,90,16);
Name=new TextField(28);
add(Name);
Name.reshape(insets().left + 441,insets().top + 8,288,24);
label2=new Label("Name:");
add(label2);
label2.reshape(insets().left + 342,insets().top + 16,90,16);
Address1=new TextField(28);
add(Address1);
Address1.reshape(insets().left + 441,insets().top + 40,288,24);
label3=new Label("Address:");
add(label3);
label3.reshape(insets().left + 342,insets().top + 48,90,16);
Address2=new TextField(28);
add(Address2);
Address2.reshape(insets().left + 441,insets().top + 72,288,24);
City=new TextField(28);
add(City);
City.reshape(insets().left + 441,insets().top + 104,288,24);
label4=new Label("City:");
add(label4);
label4.reshape(insets().left + 342,insets().top + 112,90,16);
State=new TextField(3);
add(State);
State.reshape(insets().left + 504,insets().top + 136,36,24);
label5=new Label("State:");
add(label5);
label5.reshape(insets().left + 441,insets().top + 144,54,16);
Zaip=new TextField(10);
add(Zaip);
Zaip.reshape(insets().left + 621,insets().top + 136,108,24);
label6=new Label("Zip:");
add(label6);
label6.reshape(insets().left + 558,insets().top + 144,54,16);
Shipping= new Choice();
add(Shipping);
```

```
        Shipping.reshape(insets().left + 441,insets().top + 168,234,80);
        Shipping.addItem("Fed Ex");
        Shipping.addItem("UPS Ground");
        Shipping.addItem("Express Mail");
        Buy=new Button("Purchase");
        add(Buy);
        Buy.reshape(insets().left + 612,insets().top + 280,117,32);
        CCNum=new TextField(28);
        add(CCNum);
        CCNum.reshape(insets().left + 441,insets().top + 232,288,24);
        label7=new Label("Credit Card Number:");
        add(label7);
        label7.reshape(insets().left + 342,insets().top + 208,180,16);
        CCExpir=new TextField(10);
        add(CCExpir);
        CCExpir.reshape(insets().left + 441,insets().top + 264,108,24);
        label8=new Label("Expires:");
        add(label8);
        label8.reshape(insets().left + 342,insets().top + 272,81,16);
        label9=new Label("Shipping:");
        add(label9);
        label9.reshape(insets().left + 342,insets().top + 176,90,16);
        //}}

        //{{INIT_MENUS
        MenuBar mb = new MenuBar();
        Hlp = new Menu("Help");
        Hlp.add(hlpitem = new MenuItem("Help"));
        Hlp.add(aboutitem = new MenuItem("About"));
        mb.add(Hlp);
        setMenuBar(mb);
        //}}

        //*** This line was added to dis-allow user modification of the receipt
      stmnt.setEditable(false);
}

//**********Generated Code - Begin
public synchronized void show() {
  move(50, 50);
  super.show();
}

public boolean handleEvent(Event event) {
    if (event.id == Event.ACTION_EVENT && event.target == Shipping) {
        selectedShipping();
```

```
            return true;
        }
        else
        if (event.id == Event.ACTION_EVENT && event.target == Buy) {
            clickedBuy();
            return true;
        }
        else

        if (event.id == Event.WINDOW_DESTROY) {
            hide();
            return true;
        }
        return super.handleEvent(event);
}

//{{DECLARE_MENUS
Menu Hlp;
MenuItem hlpitem;
MenuItem aboutitem;
//}}

//{{DECLARE_CONTROLS
TextArea stmnt;
Label label1;
TextField Name;
Label label2;
TextField Address1;
Label label3;
TextField Address2;
TextField City;
Label label4;
TextField State;
Label label5;
TextField Zaip;
Label label6;
Choice Shipping;
Button Buy;
TextField CCNum;
Label label7;
TextField CCExpir;
Label label8;
Label label9;
//}}
//**********Generated Code - End
```

```
    //MsgOk is a simple OK dialog, with a textbox property for displaying a message
    private MsgOk dlg    = null;
    public void clickedBuy() {
        // Verify, and process the order. If ok all done.
        if(VerifyInput())
            dispose();
    }
    public void selectedShipping() {
        // to do: put event handler code here.
    }
}
```

MsgOk Code Listing

The Message OK dialog is almost entirely generated by the Symantec resource editor. Its intended purpose is to provide a mechanism to display a message dialog to the user. The beginning portion of the code has a brief description of how to use this dialog.

```
/*
    This class is a basic extension of the Dialog class.  It can be used
    by subclasses of Frame.  To use it, create a reference to the class,
    then instantiate an object of the class (pass 'this' in the constructor),
    and call the show() method.

    example:

    MsgOk theMsgOk;
    theMsgOk = new MsgOk(this,"Hello");
    theMsgOk.show();

    You can add controls to AboutBox with Cafe Studio.
    (Menus can be added only to subclasses of Frame.)
 */

import java.awt.*;

//99.9% of this code was generated by Symantec Resource Editor
public class MsgOk extends Dialog {

    // The Title parmeter was added to for naming the dialog window
    public MsgOk(Frame parent, String Title) {

        super(parent, Title, true);

        //{{INIT_CONTROLS
        setLayout(null);
```

```
        addNotify();
        resize(insets().left + insets().right + 474, insets().top + insets().bottom + 225);
        textbox=new TextArea(5,35);
        textbox.setFont(new Font("Courier",Font.PLAIN,12));
        add(textbox);
        textbox.reshape(insets().left + 56,insets().top + 32,357,111);
        OKbtn=new Button("OK");
        add(OKbtn);
        OKbtn.reshape(insets().left + 189,insets().top + 158,91,30);
        //}}
        textbox.setEditable(false);
        setResizable(false);
    }

public synchronized void show() {
    Rectangle bounds = getParent().bounds();
    Rectangle abounds = bounds();

    move(bounds.x + (bounds.width - abounds.width)/ 2,
            bounds.y + (bounds.height - abounds.height)/2);

    super.show();
}

public synchronized void wakeUp() {
    notify();
}

public boolean handleEvent(Event event) {
    if (event.id == Event.ACTION_EVENT && event.target == OKbtn) {
            clickedOKbtn();
            return true;
    }
    else
    if (event.id == Event.WINDOW_DESTROY) {
        hide();
        return true;
    }
    return super.handleEvent(event);
}

//{{DECLARE_CONTROLS
TextArea textbox;
Button OKbtn;
//}}
//Dismiss when OK is pressed
```

```
    public void clickedOKbtn() {
        dispose();
    }
}
```

The Applet

The applet is the primary entry point for this example. This is not to say that it contains all of the application's logic; rather, it is merely the entry point. The scope of the applet's responsibilities are to do the following:

- Load the items from the item's configuration file

- Display the slide show style interface for users to select items

- Keep track of the selected items in the user's shopping cart

- When the user presses the checkout button, generate the receipt, and call the checkout form

To successfully employ this application, you will need to modify the item configuration file to contain the items you wish to sell. Also, the use of CardShield in this application requires that the computer containing the Web server must have the CardShield Passive Agent loaded and running. This example is a fairly robust and highly adaptive application that can be used for a wide variety of virtual storefronts. The following is the line to be entered into an HTML page that allows the applet to be viewed.

```
<APPLET CODE="Vstore.class" WIDTH=600 HEIGHT=400></APPLET>
```

Applet Code Listing

```
import java.awt.*;
import java.applet.*;
import java.util.Hashtable;
import java.util.Stack;
import java.util.Enumeration;
import java.net.URLConnection;
import java.net.URL;
import java.io.InputStream;
import CheckOutFrm;
import CommerceUtils.*;

/*
    ItemEntry is a storage class for items.
    This class is used to store item information, as
    well as ordered item information.
```

```
*/
class ItemEntry extends Object{

    //Item Code
    public String    Item              =    "";

    //Long Item Description
    public String    Desc              =    "";

    //Short Item Description
    public String    ShortDesc         =    "";

    /*The item's mage URL. NOTE: ONLY the image file name is needed if
      image is in the Applets directory.
    */
    public String    ImgURL            =    "";

    //Cost of the Item
    public float     Cost              =    0.00f;

    //Shipping Cost of the Item
    public float     ShippingCost      =    0.00f;

    //The constructor will load all members
    public ItemEntry(String item,String desc, String shortdesc, String imgurl,
            float cost, float shippingcost){
        Desc            =        desc;
        ShortDesc       =        shortdesc;
        ImgURL          =        imgurl;
        Cost            =        cost;
        ShippingCost    =        shippingcost;
        Item            =        item;
    }


}

/* ImagePanel Provide two distinct services. The first, it will
   paint a 3D looking rectangle around the panel's parameter. Second,
   it provides ready access to display images in the panel.
*/
class ImagePanel extends Panel {

    //The current image
    private Image    Img =    null;
```

```
/*Each time paint is call, the current image will be repainted
  and the 3D border will be redrawn.
*/
public void paint(Graphics g) {
    super.paint(g);
    Dimension dim = size();

    g.setColor(new Color(75, 75, 75));
    g.drawLine(0,0, dim.width-1, 0);
    g.drawLine(1,1, dim.width-2, 1);

    g.drawLine(0,0, 0, dim.height-1);
    g.drawLine(1,1, 1, dim.height-2);

    g.setColor(new Color(240, 240, 240));


    g.drawLine(dim.width-1,0, dim.width-1, dim.height-1);
    g.drawLine(dim.width-2,1, dim.width-2, dim.height-2);

    g.drawLine(0,dim.height-1, dim.width-1, dim.height-1);
    g.drawLine(1,dim.height-2, dim.width-2, dim.height-2);

    if(Img != null)
        g.drawImage(Img,2,2, dim.width-3, dim.height-3, this);
}

/*Draws the passed image. If success full, the image will become
  the new current image.  The member will fail if the image was
  unable to be loaded, or painted.
*/
public boolean drawimage(Image img){
    Graphics g     =   getGraphics();
    Dimension dim  =   size();

    Img = img;

    if(Img == null)
        return false;
    else
        return g.drawImage(Img,2,2, dim.width-3, dim.height-3, this);
}
}


/*
    This is the primary Applet and the solutions entry point.  The basic
```

premise of the solution is as follows:

1. Item information is read in from "items.ini".
2. User gets to flip through pictures of items.
3. When the desired item is found the "purchase button is hit.
4. Once all the items have been selected the user will checkout.

```
*/
public class Vstore extends Applet {

    /*The URL of the item configuration file.  The base path is
      the Applets residing directory.
    */
    private static String iniURL        =    "items.ini";

    //The Items retrieved from items.ini contained in ItemEntry objects
    private Hashtable Items              =    new Hashtable(10);

    //The User's selected items.
    private Stack ShoppingCart           =    new Stack();

    //The current showwing item.
    private int CurrentItem              =    0;

    //Total number of items.  Will Be loaded from the item file info.
    private int NumberOfItems            =    0;

    /*The Following set of finctions turn the associated button
      on or off.
    */
    //BEGIN
    private void PurchBTnOff(){
        PurchBTn.disable();
    }

    private void PurchBTnOn(){
        PurchBTn.enable();
    }

    private void CheckoutBtnOff(){
        CheckoutBtn.disable();
    }

    private void CheckoutBtnOn(){
        CheckoutBtn.enable();
    }
```

Rather, this section provides an example use of third-party Java libraries. The example in this chapter does utilize the MicroLine Component Toolkit to aid in development.

Third-Party Libraries

If you are sitting in a room of Java developers, probably the safest conversation you can make would be discussing problems with the Java AWT (Abstract Windows Toolkit). The AWT has problems, and its use goes beyond the scope of this book. However, what should be mentioned is the fact that leveraging the work of others is always a good thing. For example, there are a number of third-party AWT widgets libraries available. You could implement all the widgets in these libraries yourself, but why? The AWT has enough little quirks that if someone else got it to work, you should jump up and down and thank Gates that you don't have to implement it yourself. Further, if you decided to buy a library, the manufacturer guarantees that the library functions correctly; if it doesn't they will find and correct the problem for you.

The example in this section utilizes the MicroLine Component Toolkit, for which a trail kit can be found on the accompanying CD-ROM. In particular, the example uses the tab notebook and the hierarchy tree. The tool kit sells for $399 and can be purchased on MicroLine's Web site (http://www.microline.com). Also, the CD-ROM provides another freeware library for you to play with.

Support Classes

The support classes for this example are identical to the classes of the previous example. Refer to the prior example for full code listings. The following is a listing of the two configuration files needed to operate this example. The first is the "items.ini", which is used as a storage device for the items that wish to be sold in the application. The second file is the "vstore.ini", which contains the name of the welcome graphic. Both of these files must be present in the same directory as the applet.

```
[AB123]
#Comment 2
ItemPictURL=123.gif
Description=Log From BlamO
ShortDescription=Log From BlamO
Price=12.00
Shipping=0.00

[AB125]
#Comment 2
ItemPictURL = 125.gif
Description = Round Ball
```

```
ShortDescription = Round Ball
Price=2.00
Shipping=0.00


[MAIN]
#Comment 2
HelloURL=hello.jpg
```

The Applet

Using the MicroLine Toolkit, this example shows the use of a tabbed notebook and a hierarchy tree. Using third-party libraries simplifies development. However, comparing the complexity of the prior example to this example is an apple-to-orange comparison. The prior example had fewer moving parts to contend with, whereas this example is a more complicated interface. All attempts were made to document the example to provide a firm understanding of the workings. The following is the basic flow of the application:

1. The applet creates an application specific wrapper for the tab notebook widget.

2. The wrapper creates a panel for the welcome screen and the selection screen.

3. The welcome screen is loaded with the welcome image and added to the widget.

4. The selection screen is created, entailing the items being loaded and populated into the selection tree.

5. The selection screen panel monitors the user's activity and stores the selected items.

6. The selection screen panel launches the checkout form on request.

Applet Code Listing

```
/*
    This class is a basic extension of the Applet class.  It would generally be
    used as the main class with a Java browser or the AppletViewer.  But an instance
    can be added to a subclass of Container.  To use this applet with a browser or
    the AppletViewer, create an html file with the following code:

    <HTML>
    <HEAD>
    <TITLE> A simple program </TITLE>
    </HEAD>
    <BODY>

    <APPLET CODE="Vstore.class" WIDTH=332 HEIGHT=169></APPLET>
```

Figure 14.3 Welcome screen.

Figure 14.4 Tree selection screen.

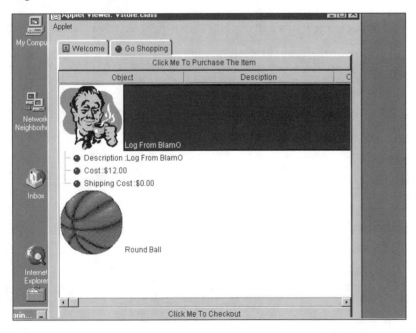

Figure 14.5 Checkout screen.

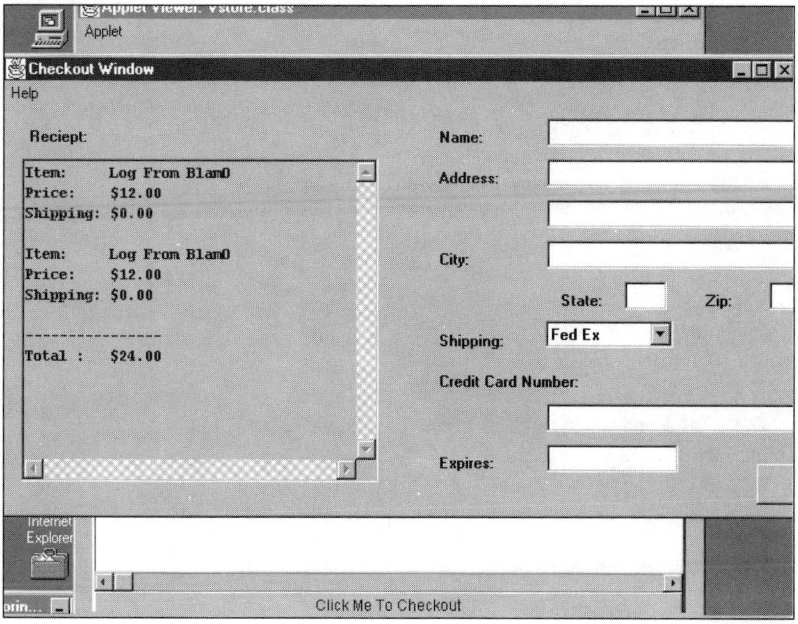

```
</BODY>

    </HTML>

    You can add controls to Vstore with Cafe Studio.
    (Menus can be added only to subclasses of Frame.)
 */

import java.awt.*;
import java.applet.*;
import java.net.URL;
import java.io.InputStream;
import java.util.Hashtable;
import java.util.Enumeration;
import java.util.Stack;
import mlsoft.mct.*;
import CommerceUtils.*;
import CheckOutFrm;
```

```
/*
    ItemEntry is a storage class for items.
    This class is used to store item information, as
    well as ordered item information.
*/
class ItemEntry extends Object{

    //Item Code
    public String    Item             =    "";

    //Long Item Description
    public String    Desc             =    "";

    //Short Item Description
    public String    ShortDesc        =    "";

    /*The item's mage URL. NOTE: ONLY the image file name is needed if
      image is in the Applets directory.
    */
    public Image    ImgURL           =    null;

    //Cost of the Item
    public float    Cost             =    0.00f;

    //Shipping Cost of the Item
    public float    ShippingCost     =    0.00f;

    //The constructor will load all members
    public ItemEntry(String item,String desc, String shortdesc, Image imgurl,
            float cost, float shippingcost){
        Desc            =        desc;
        ShortDesc       =        shortdesc;
        ImgURL          =        imgurl;
        Cost            =        cost;
        ShippingCost    =        shippingcost;
        Item            =        item;
    }

    //Formats a float into a Dollar string
    public static String FormatDollar(float f){
        String out  =    "" + f;

        if(out.indexOf('.') != -1){
            if((out.indexOf('.')+2) > (out.length() -1))
                out = "$" + out + "0";
            else
```

```
                out += "$";
        }
        else
            out = "$" + out + ".00";
        return out;
    }


}

//New Class ------------------------------------------------------------

/*
    The Selection page provides an encapilation for the items selection tab.
    From the point of view of the tab notebook widget, this panel is a single
    entity.  It is up the the panel to display, and handle any associated
    events. The following are performed tasks.

    1. Generate the GUI, including the selection tree.
    2. Place items into the shopping cart
    3. Processing the order for checkout

    The checkout process is handled by the CheckOutFrm

*/
class SelectionPage extends Panel {

    //The Tree Widget
    private MlTree Tree;

    //The Button for purchasing and Item
    private Button BuyME;

    //The Button to checkout
    private Button CheckOut;

    //The generated item dot image
    private Image dotImage;

    //The selected items
    private Stack CheckoutItems =   new Stack();

    /*
    The Currently selected Item, this will be set each time a
    new items is selected.
    */
```

```
private ItemEntry SelectedItem = null;


//The constructor adds the widgets and loads the tree.
public SelectionPage(Hashtable Items){
    super();
    setLayout(new BorderLayout());

    //load the tree
    Tree = new MlTree();
    add("Center",Tree);

    BuyME = new Button("Click Me To Purchase The Item");
    add("North",BuyME);

    CheckOut = new Button("Click Me To Checkout");
    add("South",CheckOut);

    makeIcons();
    loaditems(Items);
}

/*
    Given the passed Hashtable of items, the tree is populated.
    Also, each item element is added to all corisponding items.
*/
public void loaditems(Hashtable Items){

    MlResources res = new MlResources();
    Enumeration EnumItems = Items.keys();
    ItemEntry CrntItem;
    Integer tmp;
    int j = 0;

    //Setup the heading Row
    res.add("headingRows", 1);
    res.add("columns", 3);
    res.add("simpleHeadings", "Object|Desciption|Cost");
    res.add("simpleWidths", "10c 40c 10c");
    res.add("allowColumnResize", true);
    Tree.setValues(res);

    //Set the Colors
    res.add("rowType", "HEADING");
    res.add("cellBackground", "#c0c0c0");
    res.add("cellLeftBorderType", "BORDER_LINE");
```

```
res.add("cellRightBorderType", "BORDER_LINE");
res.add("cellTopBorderType", "BORDER_LINE");
res.add("cellBottomBorderType", "BORDER_LINE");
Tree.setValues(res);

//Set the Column alignment
res.clear();
res.add("cellDefaults", true);
res.add("column", 2);
res.add("cellAlignment", "ALIGNMENT_RIGHT");
Tree.setValues(res);

//Generate the tree from the hashtable
for(int i = 0; EnumItems.hasMoreElements() ;){
    tmp = (Integer)EnumItems.nextElement();
    CrntItem = (ItemEntry) Items.get(tmp);

    //Add the parent node
    Tree.addRow(0, true, false, -1, CrntItem.ImgURL , CrntItem.Desc);
    //Add the associate item information
    res.clear();
    res.add("row", i++);
    res.add("rowUserObject", CrntItem);
    Tree.setValues(res);

    //Add the child nodes
    Tree.addRow(1, false, false, -1, dotImage,"Description :" + CrntItem.ShortDesc);
    res.clear();
    res.add("row", i++);
    res.add("rowUserObject", CrntItem);
    Tree.setValues(res);

    Tree.addRow(1, false, false, -1, dotImage,"Cost :"+
        CrntItem.FormatDollar(CrntItem.Cost));
    res.clear();
    res.add("row", i++);
    res.add("rowUserObject", CrntItem);
    Tree.setValues(res);

     Tree.addRow(1, false, false, -1, dotImage,"Shipping Cost :" +
        CrntItem.FormatDollar(CrntItem.ShippingCost));
    res.clear();
    res.add("row", i++);
    res.add("rowUserObject", CrntItem);
    Tree.setValues(res);
}
```

```
}

/*
    Very simply put this function make the dot icon. The Microline
    library has facilities for creating icons in code, the following
    is an example.
*/
public void makeIcons(){

    MlIconMaker im;

    im = new MlIconMaker();
    im.setDimensions(16, 16);
    im.setColor('B', 0xff000080);
    im.setColor('K', 0xff000000);
    im.setColor('G', 0xff808080);

    im.setPixels("                ");
    im.setPixels("                ");
    im.setPixels("                ");
    im.setPixels("                ");
    im.setPixels("     BBBBB      ");
    im.setPixels("     BBBBBB     ");
    im.setPixels("    BBBBBBBB    ");
    im.setPixels("   BBB BBBBBB   ");
    im.setPixels("   BBB BBBBBB   ");
    im.setPixels("   BBBBBBBBBB   ");
    im.setPixels("   BBBBBBBBBB   ");
    im.setPixels("   BBBBBBBBBB   ");
    im.setPixels("    BBBBBBBB    ");
    im.setPixels("     BBBBBB     ");
    im.setPixels("      BBBBB     ");
    im.setPixels("                ");
    dotImage = im.createImage(this);
}

//Generic Event handeler
public boolean handleEvent(Event event) {

    MlTreeEvent treeEvent;

    if (event.id == Event.ACTION_EVENT && event.target == BuyME) {
            clickedBuyMe();
            return true;
    }
    else
```

```java
    if (event.id == Event.ACTION_EVENT && event.target == CheckOut) {
            clickedCheckoutBtn();
            return true;
    }
    else
    //when an item is selected, set that item to the current item
    if (event.target == Tree && event.id == MlGridEvent.SELECT_ROW){
        treeEvent = (MlTreeEvent)event;
        SelectedItem = (ItemEntry) Tree.getRowValue(treeEvent.row,"rowUserObject");
        return true;
    }
    return super.handleEvent(event);
}

//The purchase button pressed, thus add it to the shopping cart.
private void clickedBuyMe(){

    if(SelectedItem == null)
        return;

    CheckoutItems.push(SelectedItem);
}

/* If the Check out button was clicked generate the
   order's receipt and lanch the CheckOutFrm.
*/
public void clickedCheckoutBtn() {

    String Receipt  =    "";
    float total = 0;
    CheckOutFrm theCheckOutFrm;
    theCheckOutFrm = new CheckOutFrm();
    ItemEntry CrntItem;

    //load the Receipt
    for(int i = 0;!CheckoutItems.isEmpty();++i){
        CrntItem = (ItemEntry) CheckoutItems.pop();
        theCheckOutFrm.OutPut.put("ITEM" + i, CrntItem.Item);
        Receipt += "Item:      " + CrntItem.ShortDesc + "\n";
        total   += CrntItem.Cost;
        Receipt += "Price:     " + CrntItem.FormatDollar(CrntItem.Cost) + "\n";
        Receipt += "Shipping: " + CrntItem.FormatDollar(CrntItem.ShippingCost) + "\n";
        total   += CrntItem.ShippingCost;
        Receipt += "\n";
    }
    Receipt += "---------------\n";
```

```
          Receipt += "Total :    " + ItemEntry.FormatDollar(total);
          theCheckOutFrm.LoadStatment(Receipt);
          theCheckOutFrm.TotalCost = total;
          theCheckOutFrm.show();
     }


}

//New Class --------------------------------------------------------

/* ImagePanel Provide two distinct services. The first, it will
   paint a 3D looking rectangle around the panel's parameter. Second,
   it provides ready access to display images in the panel.
*/
class ImagePanel extends Panel {

    //The current image
    private Image   Img =   null;

    /*Each time paint is call, the current image will be repainted
      and the 3D border will be redrawn.
    */


    public void paint(Graphics g) {
        super.paint(g);
        Dimension dim = size();

        g.setColor(new Color(75, 75, 75));
        g.drawLine(0,0, dim.width-1, 0);
        g.drawLine(1,1, dim.width-2, 1);

        g.drawLine(0,0, 0, dim.height-1);
        g.drawLine(1,1, 1, dim.height-2);

        g.setColor(new Color(240, 240, 240));


        g.drawLine(dim.width-1,0, dim.width-1, dim.height-1);
        g.drawLine(dim.width-2,1, dim.width-2, dim.height-2);

        g.drawLine(0,dim.height-1, dim.width-1, dim.height-1);
        g.drawLine(1,dim.height-2, dim.width-2, dim.height-2);

        if(Img != null)
```

```
            g.drawImage(Img,2,2, dim.width-3, dim.height-3, this);
    }

    public ImagePanel(Image img){
        super();
        Img = img;
    }

    /*Draws the passed image. If success full, the image will become
      the new current image.  The member will fail if the image was
      unable to be loaded, or painted.
    */
    public boolean drawimage(Image img){
        Graphics g       =   getGraphics();
        Dimension dim    =   size();

        Img = img;

        if(Img == null)
            return false;
        else
            return g.drawImage(Img,2,2, dim.width-3, dim.height-3, this);
    }
}


//New Class ------------------------------------------------------------
/*
    MainTabPanel is the embodyment of the tab note book.
    This class is responsible for loading the notebook
    tabs.
*/
class MainTabPanel extends MlTabPanel{

    private Image HelloImage;
    private Image ShoppingImage;

    //the welcome tab
    private ImagePanel Welcome;
    //the selection tab
    private SelectionPage SelectItems;

    //Add the tabs
    public MainTabPanel(Image Hello, Hashtable Items){
        super();
        makeIcons();
```

```
        setValue("marginWidth", 3);
        setValue("spacing", 1);

        MakeWelcomePage(Hello);
        add("Welcome",HelloImage, Welcome);
        SelectItems = new SelectionPage(Items);
        add("Go Shopping",ShoppingImage, SelectItems);
    }

    //Creates the Welcome tab by creating a ImagePanel with the Welcome image

    public void MakeWelcomePage(Image Hello){

        Dimension D = preferredSize();

        Welcome = new ImagePanel(Hello);
        Welcome.reshape(2,2,D.width -2,D.height -2);
    }

    //Creates the used icons
    public void makeIcons(){

        MlIconMaker im;

        im = new MlIconMaker();

        im.setDimensions(16, 16);
        im.setColor('B', 0xff000080);
        im.setColor('K', 0xff000000);
        im.setColor('G', 0xff808080);


        im.setPixels("                  ");
        im.setPixels("                  ");
        im.setPixels("    KKKKKKKKKKK    ");
        im.setPixels("    KGGGGGGGGGGK   ");
        im.setPixels("    KG       GK    ");
        im.setPixels("    KG  GBG  GK    ");
        im.setPixels("    KG GBBBG GK    ");
        im.setPixels("    KG GBBBG GK    ");
        im.setPixels("    KG  GBG  GK    ");
        im.setPixels("    KGGGGBGGGGK    ");
        im.setPixels("    KGGGBBBGGGK    ");
        im.setPixels("    KGGB   BGGK    ");
        im.setPixels("    KGGBB BBGGK    ");
        im.setPixels("    KKKKKKKKKKK    ");
        im.setPixels("                  ");
        im.setPixels("                  ");
```

```
        HelloImage = im.createImage(this);


        im.clear();
        im.setPixels("                        ");
        im.setPixels("                        ");
        im.setPixels("                        ");
        im.setPixels("                        ");
        im.setPixels("        BBBBB           ");
        im.setPixels("       BBBBBBB          ");
        im.setPixels("      BBBBBBBBB         ");
        im.setPixels("      BBB  BBBBBB       ");
        im.setPixels("      BBB BBBBBBB       ");
        im.setPixels("      BBBBBBBBBBB       ");
        im.setPixels("      BBBBBBBBBBB       ");
        im.setPixels("      BBBBBBBBBBB       ");
        im.setPixels("       BBBBBBBBB        ");
        im.setPixels("        BBBBBBB         ");
        im.setPixels("         BBBBB          ");
        im.setPixels("                        ");
        ShoppingImage = im.createImage(this);
    }


}


//New Class ------------------------------------------------------------

/*
    The primary Applet class is entry point for the Application.
    Its primary role is to load the information needed to create
    the MainTabPanel which is the only component of the Applet.
*/
public class Vstore extends Applet {

    private static String ITEMiniURL        =   "items.ini";
    private static String APPiniURL         =   "vstore.ini";
    private Hashtable Items                  =   new Hashtable(10);

    public void init() {
        Image Hello;
        inifile ini;
        super.init();

      //try and get a input stream to create the inifile
        try{
```

```
            URL tmp = new URL(getDocumentBase(),APPiniURL);
            InputStream in = tmp.openStream();
            ini = new inifile(in);
        }
        catch(Exception e){
            return;
        }

        //get the intro picture
        Hello = getImage(getDocumentBase() ,ini.GetProperty("MAIN","HelloURL",""));

        setBackground(Color.lightGray);
        setLayout(new BorderLayout());
        //{{INIT_CONTROLS
        setLayout(null);
        resize(505,468);

        //load the items
        LoadItems();
        //crete the main tab panel with the Hello graphic
        panel1 = new MainTabPanel(Hello,Items);
        add(panel1);
        panel1.reshape(12,11,481,444);
        //}}
    }

/*Load the items from the item config file and place them into
  Items Hashtable.
*/
public void LoadItems(){

    inifile ini;
    Enumeration itemlist;
    String Item;
    int i;
    //try and get a input stream to create the inifile
    try{
        URL tmp = new URL(getDocumentBase(),ITEMiniURL);
        InputStream in = tmp.openStream();
        ini = new inifile(in);
    }
    catch(Exception e){
        return;
    }

    itemlist = ini.IniSections.keys();
```

```
        for(i = 0 ; itemlist.hasMoreElements() ; ++i){
            Item = (String) itemlist.nextElement();
            //The try is for the Float conversions
            try{
                Items.put(new Integer(i), new
ItemEntry(Item,ini.GetProperty(Item,"Description","No Description"),
                    ini.GetProperty(Item,"ShortDescription","No Description"),
                    getImage(getDocumentBase() ,ini.GetProperty(Item,"ItemPictURL","")),
                    new Float(ini.GetProperty(Item,"Price","")).floatValue(),
                    new Float(ini.GetProperty(Item,"Shipping","")).floatValue()));
            }
            catch(Exception e){
                break;
            }

        }
    }


    public boolean handleEvent(Event event) {
        return super.handleEvent(event);
    }

    //{{DECLARE_CONTROLS
    MainTabPanel panel1;
    //}}

}
```

Summary

The use of applets as Web commerce devices is still very much in its infancy. In fact, without CardShield, there would be no off-the-shelf way for applets to transmit credit-card information securely. The next year may bring a number of changes to this technology, including the Sun-provided Security API. When the security API is available, the applets provided in this chapter can either remain as is or be used with IC Verify to provide alternatives to CardShield. This chapter began by creating an applet solution that was 80 percent generated from the Symantec resource editor and ended by displaying the use of a third-party Toolkit. The examples in this chapter provide some good, stable solutions that can be either ready-to-use solutions, or almost-ready-to-use solutions. As I said earlier, "Leveraging the work of others is always a good thing."

15

Emerging Technologies

Every day something changes on the Net. If you devoted all day to just keeping up on Internet technology, you wouldn't be able to keep up on it all. It has been said that the Web lives in dog years. That is, Web technologies tend to move at least seven times faster than other fields. With a pace like that, the best strategy to keeping up to date is examining a selected group of reference points to provide the general trend. This chapter explores future Java technologies as well as some electronic commerce vendors. Keeping up to date isn't easy. When life moves this fast, its easy to let things pass you by.

The New Way to Shop Using Java

It has been estimated that current Web commerce constitutes $40 million a year in the U.S. alone. Even the most conservative estimates of Web commerce put the same figure into the $400 billion range by the year 2000. That kind of jump is more than just an increase of people on the Web, its an entirely new way of shopping.

Recently, the next generation of home Web solutions began appearing on the U.S. market. Companies like Philips, Magnavox, and Sun introduced computing devices for viewing the Internet on existing TVs. Network Computers, as they are called, are the catalyst agent that will drive the Web commerce market into the $400 billion range. In this section, you will be exposed to the latest rage in "Set-Top Boxes," and learn how these new device are redefining "Websavvy."

Set-Top Boxes

Getting connected needs to be easier for the mass market to embrace the Internet. To most people, programming a VCR to record a favorite show is still considered a marvel. If the mass market is to embrace the Internet, retrieving an e-mail message must become easier than checking an answering machine. Steps to achieve this goal are beginning to come of age. In particular, Internet-ready cable boxes are the mechanism to deliver the Internet to the mass market.

The idea behind set-top boxes is simple: create an economical, standard, and easy-to-use Internet access device, an "Agent." The goal and standard framework for such a device is specified in Sun's "Network Computer Reference Profile." This profile specifies a standard device that can then be produced for the mass market by different companies, all of whom are achieving the same goal, a cost-effective Internet Agent. Oracle best termed these Internet agents as "under $500 Internet-ready computers that plug into a TV."

More than 70 companies have signed on to create these "Network Computer Reference" devices, with the first expected to hit the market second quarter of 1997. Undoubtedly, these devices are aimed to bring the mass market onto the Internet, and eventually will push the Internet into the mass market. It is going to happen; the question is just when. Figure 15.1 shows how Mitsubishi is leading the way for electronics manufacturers to bring the Internet to the mass market.

TV interface

With the advent of the set-top boxes, the line between TV and the Web will cease to exist. At present, computers and TVs offer distinct functionality, contained in two totally different pieces of equipment. TVs are used strictly for entertainment, while computers are used for a number of different things. Set-top boxes will appear to the user as a computer inside the cable box; in a sense, the TV and the computer will merge to form a single entity.

The Web and TV will not exactly be synonymous, but to the end user, the difference will be analogous to one channel offering sports, one channel offering movies, and another offering Web content. The TV will become the delivery mechanism for the Web, and Web content will migrate to provide the television appeal appropriate for the new media. Web commerce will migrate with trends to provide interactive commercials, giving viewers the ability to make impulse, as well as educated, purchases using only a TV, remote control, and a Lazy-Boy (see Figure 15.2).

Figure 15.1 An online press release from Mitsubishi detailing the link between the Internet and television.

```
Netscape - [AH-5000]                                              _ ฿ ×
File  Edit  View  Go  Bookmarks  Options  Directory  Window  Help

 Back  Forward  Home    Reload  Images  Open   Print   Find   Stop

 Netsite: http://www.mitsubishi.com/whatsnew/DiamondWeb.htm          ▾    N

 What's New?  What's Cool?  Destinations  Net Search  People  Software
```

MITSUBISHI CONSUMER ELECTRONICS TO INTRODUCE
DIAMONDWEB[a] INTERNET TELEVISION

All-In-One, Consumer Friendly, Network-Centric Televisions

NORCROSS, Ga., August 28, 1996 -- In a decision that positions Mitsubishi Consumer
Electronics America, Inc. (MCEA) as a major player in the digital revolution, the company today
announced plans to bring DiamondWeb[a] television, an all-in-one, consumer-friendly,
network-centric television, to market as early as next summer. The initial introduction will focus on
large screens up to 40 inches in size.

"MCEA is committed to an all-in-one solution to adding Internet capabilities to the television," said
Andy Tasaki, vice president and general manager, Mitsubishi Consumer Electronics Engineering
Center, Costa Mesa, Calif. "By clicking one button, consumers will have access to the World Wide
Web and Internet services."

Additional benefits of the all-in-one design include a single remote, no input switching or

```
 📄   Document: Done                                                  ✉
```

Figure 15.2 The future of "at home shopping."

http://www.elmaestro.com

Electronic Commerce Vendors

Web commerce is in a state of flux. A number of different vendors are struggling for market share, with no apparent leader. It would be foolhardy to predict a clear winner of the commerce battle at this time. Thus, this section introduces you to the major electronic commerce solution vendors. Included for each company is the product name, URL, platforms, price, features, company's description, and Web site screen capture. For further information check out the vendor's Web site.

Datamax Research

Company: Datamax Research

Product: PageCommerce

URL: www.iwinpak.com

Platform: Windows 3.1, 95, and NT

Price: $99

Features: PGP. No dedicated connection required. Encrypted forms managing.

Company's Description: "Provides PGP clients for transporting credit-card information via e-mail. Does not require a dedicated connection, only a server-side CGI processor and a client-side reader." (See Figure 15.3.)

iCat

Company: iCat

Product: iCat Electronic Commerce Suite

URL: www.icat.com

Platform: Macintosh, UNIX, Windows 95, and NT

Price: $4,995

Features: Exchange - Order processing, and Publisher - CD-ROM/Web catalog builder

Company's Description: "The iCat Electronic Commerce Suite is the only complete software for instant electronic commerce. For Internet catalogs, it includes the iCat Commerce Publisher and the iCat Commerce Exchange (see Figure 15.4). For CD-ROM catalogs, just add the iCat Commerce Player. The iCat Electronic Commerce Suite is available in both single-user and multiuser client/server versions and supports Internet servers running on Macintosh, Windows, Sun, and SGI platforms."

Microsoft

Company: Microsoft

Product: Microsoft Merchant System

URL: www.microsoft.com

Platform: Windows NT

Figure 15.3 Sample PGP credit card applications are available from Datamax Research.

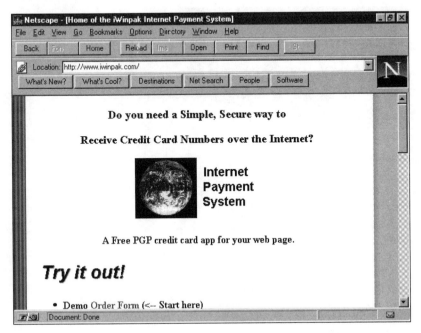

Price: Not Currently Available

Features: Verifone credit-card processing.

Company's Description: The Microsoft Merchant System is a secure, comprehensive Internet retailing software product that empowers companies that want to sell on the Internet with the ability to create a compelling consumer experience with limited custom development (see Figure 15.5).

The Microsoft Merchant System can be used to run a single storefront or to host multiple storefronts, for example, in an Internet mall environment. Incorporating many of the technologies obtained in the June 1996 acquisition of eShop, the technology provides numerous benefits to companies that set up Internet commerce sites, including the ability to do the following:

- Create a compelling and secure shopping experience

- Conduct dynamic, promotion-based merchandising by combining detailed user and order tracking with targeted discount promotions

Figure 15.4 The iCat Corporation's Web site.

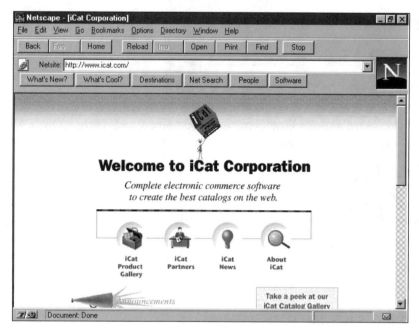

Figure 15.5 The Microsoft Electronic Commerce Web site.

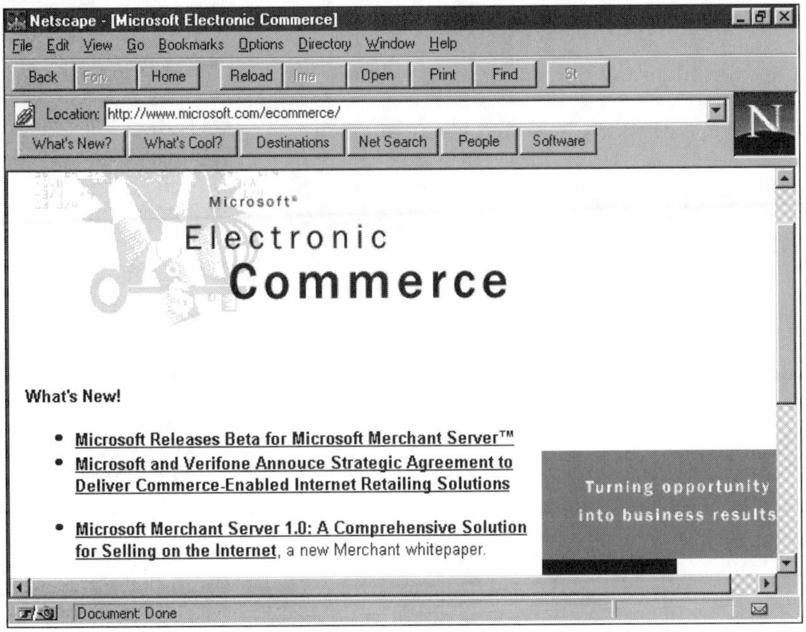

- Integrate Internet storefronts with existing systems

- Conduct secure Internet payment as supported by Verifone's vPOS technology

Mind the Store

Company: Mind the Store

Product: Mind the Store V7

URL: www.mindthestore.com

Platform: Windows NT

Price: $9,995

Features: Real-time payment and inventory management with a secure server

Company's Description: "Mind The Virtual Store"

Everything You Need To Set Up Shop On The Internet

The product does the following:

- Provides all the functionality of high-end custom designed systems at a fraction of the cost

- Provides a complete interactive, real-time integrated electronic commerce Web site

- Offers real-time ultra-secure credit-card authorization and draft-capturing of payment while customer is still online

- Provides an end-to-end Merchant Management System that directly interacts with a live database

- Manages the order fulfillment process, inventory, customers, payment procedures, and financial reporting

- Cost effectively gives small to midsized merchant operations the same functionality that large companies typically spend millions to develop

- Provides maximum transaction security, using two layers of encryption

- Eliminates e-mail-based transactions, making mailbox theft impossible

- Deposits payment funds directly into your company's bank account in a true draft-capture system

- Establishes compelling Web site graphics for your business that can be easily modified on an ongoing basis

- Allows you to quickly and easily change text and product information on your Web site, for example, for daily specials, and provides all back-office functions

- Automatically checks product availability when a customer places an order

- Automatically creates invoices, manifests, shipping labels, and much more

- Ensures excellent customer relations by allowing customers to track their orders and view their buying history (customers have access to billing information, delivery dates, and last 10 purchases made)

Figure 15.6 Mind the Store provides a comprehensive program for "setting up shop" on the Internet.

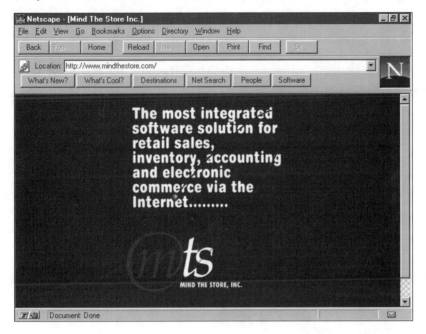

- Allows for supplier drop shipping, sending orders directly to your suppliers via EDI (Electronic Data Interchange) and having your suppliers ship directly to your customers

- Provides a search function for your online catalog, permitting customers to search for products by category, description, or price range

NCR

Company: NCR

Product: TOP END

URL: www.ncr.com/products/topend

Platform: UNIX and Windows 3.1, 95, NT

Price: Contact NCR for pricing

Features: Robust transaction processing capabilities and Java clients

Company's Description: Robust middleware for business-critical computing

One of the key challenges facing business-critical computing today is how to integrate all the disparate computing components of the information system into a single, cohesive environment. Businesses need to be able to access mission-critical data from any component in the system at any time in order to best serve their customers' needs. TOP END is robust client/server middleware that pulls the critical pieces of the enterprise together (see Figure 15.7). Some key features include the following:

- Scalable message passing with real-time and queuing options

- GUI-based global administration of the entire distributed enterprise

- Location and network transparency for distributed services

- Portability, scalability, and interoperability across multiple vendor platforms

- Dynamic load balancing of distributed workload

- Full support for legacy systems coexistence

- Open systems standards support

- Single system image for users, administrators, and programmers throughout enterprise

- High availability

- Distributed nature that inherently supports multitiered application architecture

- Support for heterogeneous databases

- Full security services

- Tools support for rapid development and deployment of new applications and services

- Support for large, high-volume, distributed enterprise systems

- Robust Middleware, which simplifies development of distributed applications by freeing the applications developer from worrying about the underlying networking, communications, security, or distributed computing services

Figure 15.7 TOP END is a middleware that joins various computing components into a single, cohesive environment.

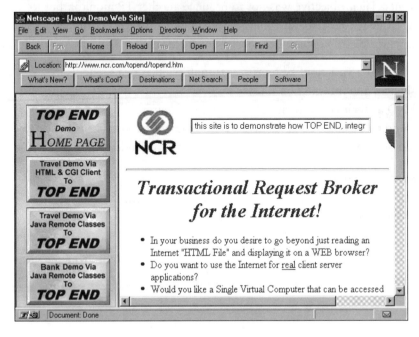

- Client/Server Computing, which eases the task of integrating and managing distributed applications. TOP END allows a single administrator to manage thousands of clients and servers while maximizing system availability and optimizing the use of computing resources.

- Legacy Coexistence, which facilitates interoperability with existing mainframe environments, connection of existing terminal networks, and the addition of new services without impact to the current environment

- Business Critical Computing, providing real-time online transaction processing in a distributed, heterogeneous, highly available environment with Data Warehouse Value-Add, providing features like transactional-oriented deferred queuing to capture direct online updates and route them on to the data warehouse for later analysis

- Global Information Processing, providing seamless access to any piece of information or computing resource anywhere in the global enterprise

For today's global information solutions, TOP END combines a rich set of services for database assurance, application-transparent security, failure management, and service synchronization.

TOP END was designed by architects and developers who leveraged decades of experience in distributed transaction processing technology, including commercial experience and knowledge of large distributed environments. Their objective was not to produce another TP monitor, but to develop a middleware to seamlessly join disparate computing components together to meet today's business requirements for distributed applications.

Because TOP END works with a variety of systems across multiple platforms, end users have reliable, secure access to services and information located anywhere in the enterprise. Many businesses have chosen TOP END as their strategic middleware to help their enterprise compete more successfully in today's demanding business climate. TOP END is the most comprehensive scalable software platform for distributed, business-critical computing systems available today.

NetConsult Communications

Company: NetConsult Communications

Product: Intershop Online

URL: www.intershop.net

Platform: UNIX and Windows NT

Price: $4,999

Features: Real-time payment and inventory management using Sybase SQL database

Company's Description: "Intershop Online software provides a ready-made, professional-looking virtual store for businesses that want to sell on the Web. With Intershop Online, a merchant gets a complete store 'shell,' entirely customizable, which is ready to be stocked with products, as well as an integrated administrative 'back office.' Intershop Online incorporates all business processes necessary to sell online and provides a breakthrough solution for retailers, catalogers, and Web developers who want to set up an online shop easily, affordably, and professionally."

Open Market

Company: Open Market

Product: Merchant Solution

URL: www.openmarket.com

Figure 15.8 Intershop Online.

Platform: UNIX and Windows 3.1 (only for store builder)

Price: $19,995

Features: Store builder, order processing, and site analysis with a secure server

Company's Description: The benefits of using Open Market technology to commerce-enable your business include the following:

- Peace of mind with the Internet's toughest security

- A scalable Internet commerce solution that grows with your business

- Leading-edge partners at every stage in the Internet commerce process

- Worry-free back-office operations with OM-Transact

- Order management

- Transaction processing (sales tax, fax, EDI)

- Record keeping

- Customer service

- Authentication

- Subscription

Summary

The Internet is a big place, and it's going to get much bigger. The good part of the Net's accelerated growth is there is more opportunity to make a potential sale. Just as the gold miners saw the West as the land of endless possibilities, current Web content and commerce providers see the Web as an equally intriguing opportunity. Technology like "Set-top Boxes" and new, more fluid Web content are the cobblestones that will lay the road to the $400 billion and higher mark for Web commerce. The road to Web growth is and will be a bumpy one filled with infinite

Figure 15.9 Open Market's Merchant Solution provides services for conducting secure commerce on the Internet.

cracks and holes. The commerce solutions provided in this chapter are merely the stones that make up that road. What fills the holes are the hopes, dreams, and hard work of those creating and developing new and exciting technologies. How much of a role you play in creating the Web of the future is up to you; this book simply gave you the tools to state your claim in the Wild Wild Web (WWW).

What's on the CD-ROM?

What's on the CD-ROM?

The following is a complete listing of all materials provided on the enclosed CD-ROM. In addition to these items, you will find a "ReadMe.html" file that provides more detailed information about each item as well as installation instructions. You'll also find a link to the Sun Microsystems Web page that houses the Java Developer Kit (JDK), a complete Java programming toolkit.

Hardware Requirements

The contents of the CD-ROM require either Windows 95 or NT. The minimum hardware requirements are as follows:

Pentium 66 - or equivalent

Windows 95/NT

16 MB Ram

20 MB free hard drive space

Installing the Software

Contained on the CD is an HTML file provided to aid in the installation and use of the CD-ROM material. To access this file perform the following steps.

1. Start Windows on your computer.

2. Place the CD-ROM into your CD-ROM drive.

3. Launch your favorite Web browser software, like Netscape.

4. Select the "Open File In Browser" item from the File menu and specify the following path: X:\ReadMe.html (where **X** is the correct letter of your CD-ROM drive)

5. Follow the directions in html file to complete the installation.

Using the Software

The materials provided on the CD-ROM are discussed throughout the course of the book. For detailed information on how to get the most out of the CD-ROM materials, refer to the following section to obtain the chapter in which the material is discussed.

Commerce Tools

Name: CardShield API & Passive Agent
Developer: Shielded Technologies, Inc.
Location: CardShield

Shielded Technologies provides a series of commerce facilities, including the CardShield API & Passive Agent. Through the use of the CardShield API & Passive Agent secure credit-card authorization and tracking are just a few key strokes away. Chapter 7 explains the entire CardShield commerce solution in depth, providing a step by step guide to reregistering your merchant information with Shielded. Chapters 11, 12, 13, and 14 contain complete ready-to-use CardShield API & Passive Agent examples, which are also included on the CD.

Name: Kona product family

Developer: Web Logic

Location: Web Logic

The Web Logic Kona family of products provides a robust, flexible, and inexpensive facility for connecting Java applications with existing databases. The package on the CD contains everything necessary to connect to an existing Sybase, Oracle, or MSQL database server. Chapters 12, 13, and 14 utilize the Kona products to store gathered customer and credit-card information into a database.

Name: Java Commerce Utilities

Developer: Cary A. Jardin

Location: CommerceUtils

Throughout the book, a number of Java class libraries are developed to aid commerce application development. CommerceUtils is a Java package that contains numerous helpful libraries like a CGI library and a local credit-card authorization class using IC Verify. Chapters 12, 13, and 14 utilize these libraries intensively in the development of the provided commerce solutions.

Name: Java Commerce Utilities HTML documentation

Developer: Cary A. Jardin

Location: Tool_Docs

Accompanying the provided commerce utility library is a full set of HTML documentation pages. Through the use of a handy Web browser you can point and click your way through the entire commerce utility library. These pages are provided as a reference for further development utilizing the tools found in this book.

Examples and Solutions

All code and solutions developed in this book are available on the CD. The examples range from getting comfortable with Java Applets and applications, to complete CGI and Applet commerce solutions. Each directory correlates with the specific chapter in which it was discussed.

Chapter 9

Location: CH9-1

This example is an introduction to Applet development using Symantec's Café. In the classic tradition of "hello" programs, this Hello World Java Applet provides a first step in Java development.

Location: CH9-2

This example is an introduction to Java console application development using Symantec's Café. This Hello World console application provides an important first step in Java development.

Location: CH9-4

Its not an Java Applet, it just looks like one. This example is an introduction to Java standalone application development using Symantec's Café.

Chapter 10

Location: CH10-1

Part of the use of a commerce application is to collect and store the customer and order information. This example provides a customer order entry screen which stores the collected information into a database using the supplied Web Logic facilities.

Chapter 12

Location: CH12-1

This example provides a complete Java commerce solution, ready for your use. By using a single page HTML form and this CGI application, you will have the ability to collect customer orders. In this example practically nothing is done with the order. It is simply stored into a file without any sort of processing.

Location: CH12-2

This example provides a complete Java commerce solution, ready for your use. By using a single page HTML form and this CGI application, you will have the ability to collect customer orders. Using the CardShield API, the CGI will feed the information into the API for credit-card processing and storage.

Location: CH12-3

This example provides a complete Java commerce solution, ready for your use. By using a single page HTML form and this CGI application, you will have the ability to collect customer orders. Using the provided commerce tools, this example will locally process the credit-card information and store it to file.

Location: CH12-4

This example provides a complete Java commerce solution, ready for your use. By using a single page HTML form and this CGI application, you will have the ability to collect customer orders. Using the provided commerce tools, this example will locally process the credit-card information and store it to an existing database using the Web Logic kona tools.

Chapter 13

Location: CH13-1

This example provides a complete Java commerce solution, ready for your use. By using a multi-page HTML form and this CGI application, you will have the ability to collect customer orders. In this example practically nothing is done with the order. It is simply stored into a file without any sort of processing.

Location: CH13-2

This example provides a complete Java commerce solution, ready for your use. By using a multi-page HTML form and this CGI application, you will have the ability to collect customer orders. Using the CardShield API, the CGI will feed the information into the API for credit-card processing and storage.

Location: CH13-3

This example provides a complete Java commerce solution, ready for your use. By using a multi-page HTML form and this CGI application, you will have the ability to collect customer orders. Using the provided commerce tools, this example will locally process the credit-card information and store it to file.

Location: CH13-4

This example provides a complete Java commerce solution, ready for your use. By using a multi-page HTML form and this CGI application, you will have the ability to collect customer orders. Using the provided commerce tools, this example will locally process the credit-card information and store it to an existing database using the Web Logic kona tools.

Chapter 14

Location: CH14-1
Using a Java Applet and the CardShield API, this example provides a catalog type of commerce solution. Once the user has selected the desired item, a customer information screen appears which closes, saves, and processes the credit-card sale.

Location: CH14-2
Using a Java Applet and the CardShield API, this example provides a tree type of commerce solution. The user selects the desired items by search through a hierarchical tree of items and options. Once the User has selected the desired item, a customer information screen appears which closes, saves, and processes the credit-card sale.

Utilities

Name: Acrobat Reader v3.0
Developer: Adobe
Location: Utilities
Many companies, including Sun, are using Adobe Acrobat's file format to store useful documentation. This Acrobat reader application will allow you to view the Java DataBase Connectivity (JDBC) documentation without hassling with a Web download.

Name: WinZip v6.2 evaluation version
Developer: Niko Mak Computing, Inc.
Location: Utilities
Some of the CD's contents are compressed in a "zip" file. This wonderful utility neatly fits into your Window 95/NT desktop to provide compression and decompression of zip file formats. This tool must be used to properly decompress the provided material.

User Assistance and Information

If you have any questions, comments, complaints, or just want to chat the following is my email address. Feel free to use it at will.

cjardin@xprime.com

The software accompanying this book is being provided as is without warranty or support of any kind. Should you require basic installation assistance, or if your media is defective, please call our product support number at (212) 850-6194 weekdays between 9 am and 4 pm Eastern Standard Time. Or, we can be reached via e-mail at: **wprtusw@wiley.com.**

To place additional orders or to request information about other Wiley products, please call (800) 879-4539.

Index

About the CD-ROM

The following is a complete listing of all materials provided on the CD. In addition to these items, you will find a "ReadMe.html" file that provides more detailed information about each item, installation instructions, and any last minute additions to the CD. You'll also find a link to the Sun Microsystems Web page that houses the Java Developer Kit (Java JDK), a complete Java programming toolkit.

Commerce Tools

CardShield API & Passive Agent
Developer: Shielded Technologies, Inc.
Java API's for electronic commerce

Kona product family
Developer: Web Logic
JDBC drivers for a Microsoft mSQL server

Name: Java Commerce Utilities

Developer: Cary A. Jardin

Assorted Java commerce utilities

Name: Java Commerce Utilities HTML documentation

Developer: Cary A. Jardin

Pages of HTML documentation for electronic commerce

Chapter related examples

Chapter 9 examples

- An introduction to Applet development using Symantec's Café.

- An introduction to Java console application development using Symantec's Café.

- An introduction to Java standalone application development using Symantec's Café.

Chapter 10 example

- A customer order entry screen which stores the collected information into a database using the supplied Web Logic facilities.

Chapter 12 examples

- Four examples of complete Java Commerce solutions, ready for your use, using a single page HTML form, and various commerce tools.

Chapter 13 examples

- Four examples of complete Java Commerce solutions, ready for your use, using multi-page HTML forms and various commerce tools.

Chapter 14 examples

- Using a Java Applet and the CardShield API, this example provides a catalog type of commerce solution.

- Using a Java Applet and the CardShield API, this example provides a tree type of commerce solution.

Utilities

Acrobat Reader v3.0
Developer: Adobe

This Acrobat reader application will allow you to view the Java DataBase Connectivity (JDBC) documentation with hassling with a Web download.

WinZip v6.2 evaluation version
Developer: Niko Mak Computing, Inc.

This wonderful utility neatly fits into your Window 95/NT desktop to provide compression and decompression of zip file formats.

Using the Software

This software contains files to help you utilize the models described in the accompanying book. By opening the package, you are agreeing to be bound by the following agreement: